The Official Guide to Jane's Longbow AH-64D

Jennifer Spohrer • Tuesday Frase

in association with Incan Monkey God Productions

CREDITS

MARKETING

Editors	David "I'll read this tonight" Ladyman Melissa "Crunch Monkey" Tyler
Lead Authors	Jennifer "Insane Again Jane" Spohrer Tuesday "Strained-Brain Jane" Frase
Additional Writing	Melissa "Squishy-Brain" Tyler Chris "Primary Extraction Specialist" McCubbin
Front Cover Art	McDonnell Douglas, Sam Yeates
Cover Design	Wendi "Bullets" Dunn
Interior Graphic Design	Wendi "Version Guru" Dunn Lisa "Can I Bring my Dog?" Goodrich
Screen Captures	Chris "Tang Cloud" Plummer Craig "Chickenboy" Miller
Articles	Jane's Information Group Limited
Photos	Courtesy of Jane's Information Group Limited, Lt. Troy Evanovich, McDonnell Douglas Aerospace, and thanks to John "Scan Man" Bowie
Jane's AH-64D Longbow Producer	Andy "Head Skunk" Hollis
Project Leader	Will "Donut" McBurnett

SPECTACULARLY HELPFUL PEOPLE

(In alphabetical order)

Steven Bonds (QA Tester)
Anthony Castoro (QA Tester)
Mike Francis (Designer)
Leonard Hjalmarson (Outside Beta Tester)
Andy Hollis (Producer)
Tsuyoshi Kawahito (Programmer)
Kevin Kushner (Designer)
Steve Muchow (Programmer)
Paul Stankiewicz (Art Director)
Lance Stites (QA Tester)
Reece Thornton (QA Project Leader)
Rod White (Outside Beta Tester)
Wendy White (Programmer)
Rob Windisman (QA Tester)
Graham Wood (Asst. QA Project Leader)

Special Thanks	McDonnell Douglas Aerospace, Jane's Information Group, Allison Vollmer, Lt. Troy Evanovich

CAV POCKET TACSOP
ANNEX G (AH-64 CONSIDERATIONS)

REVISED AUGUST 1994

2. PRE-MOVEMENT PHASE: PRIOR TO MOVEMENT OF PERSONNEL, GROUND SUPPORT EQUIPMENT, AIRCRAFT, OR VEHICLES, THE FOLLOWING CHECKS WILL BE MADE:

A. INDIVIDUALS:

(1) UNIFORM WORN:

NON-AIRCREW:
BDUs
ID TAGS
ID CARD
BLACK BOOTS
FIELD JACKET
BLACK LEATHER GLOVES W/ INSERTS
KEVLAR HELMET WITH COVER & RANK
CAMOUFLAGE BAND WITH NAME
LBE = 2 AMMO POUCHES
FIRST AID PACK
CANTEEN WITH COVER & RANK
FLASHLIGHT
PROTECTIVE MASK
INDIVIDUAL WEAPON
MEAL CARD
POCKET TSOP

AIRCREW MEMBERS:
FLIGHT SUIT
ID TAGS
ID CARD
BLACK BOOTS
FLIGHT JACKET
BLACK LEATHER GLOVES WITH INSERTS
KEVLAR HELMET WITH COVER AND RANK
CAMOUFLAGE BAND WITH NAME
LBE = 2 AMMO POUCHES
FIRST AID PACK
CANTEEN WITH COVER AND RANK
FLASHLIGHT
PROTECTIVE MASK
INDIVIDUAL WEAPON
SRU-21P WITH PRC-90
FLIGHT HELMET AND GLOVES
POCKET TSOP

ISBN: 0-929373-34-0

Manufactured in the United States of America.

Incan Monkey God Productions
c/o ORIGIN Systems, Inc.
5918 West Courtyard Drive
Austin, Texas 78730

TABLE OF CONTENTS

Pre-Movement Phase....3

How to Use This Book....6

STRATEGIES & TACTICS

Basic Cockpit Setup....8
- IHADDS Mode....8
- MFD Modes....9
- Other Modes....9

Flight Tips....10
- Flight Controls....11

Tactical Situation Display MFD....11

Cameras and PNVS....12

Co-Pilot/Gunner....12

Autopilot Functions....13

Priority Fire Zones....13

Time Compression....13

Your Weapons....14
- Guns....14
- Target Types....14
- Hellfires....15

Wingmen....16

Terrain....17

Waypoint Manipulation....18

Scoring Hints....19

Campaign Tips....20

Historical Tips....21
- Flying the AH-64A Apache....21

Beating Helicopter Bandits....22

Beating Jet Bandits....23

When You're Damaged....23

Beating Ground Threats....24

Radar & IR Jamming....25
- Relative Jamming Strengths....25

Avoiding Detection....26
- Hiding From Radar....26
  - Low and Slow....27
- Detection Tables....28
  - Radar Detection Statistics....28
  - Visual Detection Statistics....28

Disabling SAM & AAA Sites....30
- Radio-Command SAM Systems....30
- Semi-Active Radar-Guided SAM Systems....31
- IR-Guided SAM Systems....32
- Cannon....33

Fire Methods/Helicopter Gunnery....34

GAME MECHANICS

Helicopter Stats....36

Object Stats & Loadouts....38

Cannon & Machine Gun Stats....40

Missile, Rocket & Bomb Stats....42

Taking Hits....46
- How much damage can a system take?....46
  - How Damage Affects Performance....47

Scoring....48
- Mission Score....48
  - Kill Points....49
  - Realism Modifier....50
  - Flight Model Modifier....51
  - Enemy Modifier....51
  - Landing Modifier....52

Success Modifier 52
Bonus Points 52
Number of FARP Landings 52
Example Equation 53
Promotions 53
Game Commendations 54
Medals 55
Campaign Awards 57
Rules of Engagement 58
Sensor Radius 59

CAMPAIGN MISSIONS

Mission Analyses 60
Maps 60
Notes 61
Campaign Flowchart Notes 61
Baltic Campaign Flowchart 62
Baltic Missions Chart 63
Baltic Campaign Design 64
Baltic Campaign Winning Path 66
Baltic Campaign Losing Path 122
Baltic Campaign Intermediate Path 136
Desert Storm Missions 144
Just Cause Missions 158
Downed Aircraft 170
Helicopter Views 171

INTERVIEWS

Lt. Troy Evanovich, CP/G 172
Andy Hollis, Producer 180
Will McBurnett, Director 187
Paul Stankiewicz, Art Director 190
FARP Procedures 192

JANE'S ARTICLES

Soviet Military Doctrine Implications of the Gulf War 193
AH-64 Blade Gets Modification 195
AH-64A Apache 195
Apache a True Multi-Role Helicopter 196
Apache Reliability in Gulf Questioned 199
Advanced INS for Longbow Apache 199
The Invisible Art of Camouflage 200
Growth Prospects for Thermal Imaging Systems 206
Longbow Links Up 214
Guided Longbow Hellfire Trials 214
Sales Interest Grows in Longbow Apache 214
A New View on the World 215
Longbow Variant Proceeds Towards Production 216
New Helicopters for Old — Too Often an Afterthought? 217
AH-64A Apache Comes to Egypt 218
Longbow Apache Makes its Digital Comms Debut 218
Longbow Apache in Operational Testing 219
Longbow Apache Sails Through Testing 219
Aerial "Pit Bulls": Attack Helicopters Become a Battlefield Necessity 220
Tentative Go-Ahead for Apache and Hellfire 222
Russian Forces are in a 'State of Deep Crisis' 222
SURVEY 224

HOW TO USE THIS BOOK

You've got the guide, and now you want to win the war. Here's a list of all of the sections in this book and what each contains to help you find the information you need:

Strategies & Tactics (pp. 8-33) is the section to turn to if you're looking for general strategies and tips that will improve your game, no matter what mission you fly. The tips are categorized for easy reference:

Basic Cockpit Setup, p. 8

Flight Tips, p. 10

Tactical Situation Display MFD, p. 11

Cameras and PNVS, p. 12

Co-Pilot/Gunner, p. 12

Autopilot Functions, p. 13

Priority Fire Zones, p. 13

Time Compression, p. 13

Your Weapons, p. 14

Wingmen, p. 16

Terrain, p. 17

Waypoint Manipulation, p. 18

Scoring Hints, p. 19

Campaign Tips, p. 20

Historical Tips, p. 21

Beating Helicopter Bandits, p. 22

Beating Jet Bandits, p. 23

When You're Damaged, p. 23

Beating Ground Threats, p. 24

Radar & IR Jamming, p. 25

Avoiding Detection, p. 26

Disabling SAM & AAA sites, p. 30

Helicopter Stats (pp. 36-37) are comparative charts of the maximum speeds, maximum rates of climb, and other performance statistics for all helicopters in the game.

Object Stats & Loadouts (pp. 38-39) lists structural points, armor ratings, kill points, loadouts and maximum velocities for all objects in the game.

Cannon & Machine Gun Stats (pp. 40-41) and **Missile, Rocket & Bomb Stats** (pp. 42-45) list damage points, percent chance of direct hit, accuracy percentages and other statistics for weapons in the game.

Taking Hits (pp. 46-47) explains how your helicopter takes damage and how this damage affects its performance.

Scoring (pp. 48-57) reveals the mechanics of the scoring system, offers tips on maximizing your score, and lists what medals and promotions you receive when.

Mission Analyses (pp. 60-61) explains the icons and symbology used in all of the mission maps in this book.

Campaign Flowchart (pp. 62) is a schematic drawing of possible ways to progress through the campaign (descriptions of the symbols used in this flowchart are on p. 61).

Baltic Missions Chart (pp. 63) lists the objectives, environment and criteria for success and failure for all of the missions in the campaign.

Baltic Campaign Design (pp. 64-65) — Designer Mike Francis talks a bit about the creative thought behind the campaign.

Baltic Campaign Missions (pp. 66-143) offers analyses of the individual missions, including maps showing the location of key friendly and enemy units, suggestions for moving and adding waypoints and tips for using terrain features to your advantage. Analyses for Missions 1-29 are on pp. 66-121, Missions 30-38 are on pp. 122-135, and Missions 50-80 are on pp. 136-143.

Desert Storm Missions (pp. 144-157) offers Designer Kevin Kushner's notes on the Gulf War missions on which the game missions were modeled (pp. 144-145), a thumbnail chart of the objectives and rating criteria for all of the missions (p. 144) and individual mission analyses (pp. 146-157).

Just Cause Missions (pp. 158-169) offers Designer Mike Francis's notes on Operation Just Cause (pp. 158-159), a thumbnail chart of the objectives and rating criteria for all of the missions (p. 158) and individual mission analyses (pp. 160-169).

Interviews (pp. 172-191) — we talked to Lt. Troy Evanovich about his experience as an Apache Co-Pilot/Gunner and to members of the design team — Producer Andy Hollis, Director Will McBurnett and Art Director Paul Stankiewicz — about the creation process.

Jane's Articles (pp. 193-222) includes 21 articles from Jane's Information Group publications (*Jane's Defense Weekly*, *Jane's Intelligence Review* and others) on the AH-64D Longbow Apache and related topics.

Ad and Survey Sheet (pp. 223-224) gives our WWW address and info on how you can order *Official Guides* for other Electronic Arts games. We've included a survey sheet for you to send us feedback on this book and the documentation (install guide, manual, reference card) you received with *AH-46D Longbow*. To entice you further — *one lucky respondent each month receives a free game (of his or her choice)*. So does anyone who sends us a really cool idea that we haven't thought of yet ("really cool" being subject to our editor's judgement ...).

STRATEGIES & TACTICS

Common practice is to identify each strategy and tactics tip with a "bullet," but this book uses a missile (✓) instead. Advanced tips are labeled with two missiles (✓✓). "Cheats" (suggestions of things to do that aren't possible in reality) have green missiles and text.

Basic Cockpit Setup

If you've read the manual and the *Reference Card*, you might have been intimidated by all the different modes and screens in the game. The bad news is that it's going to take some time to learn everything. The good news is that you don't need to know half of the modes to play and win the game. Most of the playtesters — and even some actual pilots — prefer to fly with a certain set of screens active all of the time. In certain cases, you'll need to display something else, but a base set of modes will get you through most situations.

You can adjust all the modes at once by pressing [M]. This cycles through master modes and changes the missile launch, IHADSS and MFD modes simultaneously. If you do this, Indirect is the best mode to fly in. If you don't like this (and most of our playtesters don't), try adjusting the modes individually.

✓ While you're learning, try this cockpit configuration when you take off. It's a favorite among our playtesters.

[R]	Engage rotor.
[U]	Display enemy target IDs on Upfront display.
[Ins]	Switch to LOAL (lock on after launch) missile launch mode.
[,]	Cycle through to ASE MFD page.
[Del]	Change ASE range to 10km.
[End]	Switch to Cruise IHADSS mode.
[Home]	Activate FCR target acquisition mode.
[Pg Dn]	Change FCR range to 10km.
[P]	(Night missions) Activate PNVS.

IHADSS MODE

Unless you want to know every detail of the Longbow's instrumentation, leave your IHADSS in Cruise or Transition mode. Press [End] until one of these appears in the upper left corner of the IHADSS. Either mode is good to fly in — it's a matter of preference. Cruise gives you a pitch ladder, and both Cruise and Transition modes give you an altimeter.

✓ Use the Cruise or Transition IHADSS mode whenever you're flying nap-of-the-earth.

✓✓ Use the Bob-Up mode when you're hovering and want to make sure you don't stray too far away from your original position when you pop up and then descend.

✓✓ Use Hover IHADSS mode whenever you're hovering but don't really care whether you drift or not.

MFD MODES

Press [,] to change the left MFD; [.] to change the right MFD. The Tactical Situation Display (TSD) and Aircraft Survival Equipment (ASE) pages are the most important ones. You'll need the other pages for other things (radar, TADS camera view, system damage, etc.), but these two are the most important ones.

- Keep your ASE open at a longer range than any other pages you have open. You want to see SAMs from as far away as possible.
- It's best to fly with your ASE and TSD pages active in the left/right MFDs. You'll use these more often than the rest of the pages, especially if you're using FCR target acquisition. (When TADS is active, however, you'll probably want to bring up your TADS page instead of the ASE one.)
- The TSD shows you the battle line and what enemies are within FCR range. Try zooming to 10km in this page. The biggest use you'll find for this page is target acquisition. You can acquire a target simply by left-clicking the mouse on a target icon in this page. By right-clicking-and-dragging, you can create a Priority Fire Zone (a designated target area). These are thoroughly explained in pp. 2-25 of the manual.
- The ASE is primarily applicable to SAM avoidance. Keep it zoomed out to 25km (or 10km, at least). This gives you a bigger picture of the battlefield than you can see on the TSD. Most of the time, you'll look at the SAM circles in the ASE to find out how close you are to a SAM's threat radius. The other thing it tells you is whether you're being tracked by enemy radar (a solid line appears) or missiles (a solid diamond appears). If you see either, drop down immediately to break the radar or missile lock.

OTHER MODES

- **LOAL Missile Launch Mode.** If you're using Hellfire missiles, you need this mode 99% of the time. (Some would argue 100%, but we had to leave a little margin for those special cases.) What LOAL effectively means is that you can fire a Hellfire missile even if you don't have a valid lock. Why would you want to do this? Two reasons: first, you can pop up from a hover just before impact and get a valid line of sight to the target. Second, you can move within range by the time the missile impacts.
- **FCR Target Acquisition Mode.** Assuming you're in the D-Model and not the A-Model, you should always stay in FCR. There's only one exception to this, and that's if you're searching for something that can't be detected with a radar. CIS soldiers, for instance, appear on the TSD only if you're in TADS mode. They're too small to be seen by the FCR.
- **Upfront Display Mode.** Keep your Upfront display in target identification mode (press [U]). Otherwise, you may accidentally toast a friendly because you have no other way to ID friendlies.

Flight Tips

- Un-learn all you know about flying jet fighters — the helicopter is a totally different beast.
- Never turn right at low speed. Your wingman always flies on your right flank, and you'll collide with him if you're not extremely careful.
- First-time flyers, do yourself a favor and jump directly into the Advanced or Expert flight models. Once you get used to them, you'll be glad you never bothered with the others. The other flight models keep you from doing steep banks and other maneuvers that can help you become a better AH-64 pilot.
- To make a really tight turn: pitch up, lose collective and apply rudder simultaneously, then nose down.
- In the Advanced and Expert flight models, your primary method of adjusting altitude is the collective control. Keep a consistent watch on the arrow indicator on the left side of your altimeter (on the right side of your IHADSS). The long bar with the scrolling arrow is what you're looking for. When the arrow is in the middle of the bar, you are neither gaining or losing altitude. If the arrow drops, you're losing altitude. Similarly, a rising arrow indicates a gain in altitude.
- If you're flying along and need to lose altitude without gaining any more speed, drop your collective a bit and watch the arrow indicator drop. Once you find an altitude you're happy with, gently restore collective until the arrow is once again centered on the bar.
- How fast you want to descend should be reflected in how quickly you drop collective. Remember that if you drop collective quickly when flying low, *you need to increase collective quickly as well, or you'll crash.* (You can also lose altitude by pitching the nose downward with the cyclic, but this approach increases airspeed.)
- It's a good idea to stay below 50 feet when cruising to your waypoints. Although this keeps you concealed, it also prevents you from seeing what's around you. Try climbing to 200 feet every once in a while to update your FCR and TSD display.
- On realistic flight model, it's hard to stay low and keep a constant speed at the same time. To deal with this, set your collective to about 75% and use the cyclic to change your altitude. You can use collective too, but making large collective adjustments can put you down in a pile of debris before you know it.
- Slowing the Apache down can be quite a task. The easiest way to do this is to drop collective to about 30%, pitch up your chopper's nose, and watch your airspeed drop. This causes you to gain some altitude, but it's the fastest way to bleed off airspeed.

  Once your airspeed drops to 15 knots or lower, level out the helicopter and restore collective to 70 or 80 percent. Next, press [H] to autohover (or transition into a hover).
- When flying with the advanced flight model, make sure you don't have too much forward speed while approaching a waypoint. If you do, you'll find yourself coming in too quickly, then fumbling to slow down as you fly past the targets. Not only does this loft you up, it also makes your chopper a sitting duck for all nearby threats, and they'll lock you up. About 1km before you want to hover, drop collective to zero and glide in. Add slight collective at the end of the glide to avoid crashing.

FLIGHT CONTROLS

- You won't use the tail rotor much at high speeds, but you'll need it all the time at speeds under 60 knots. Your tail rotor is just as important as the collective or cyclic. The more adept you are at controlling all three simultaneously, the better pilot you'll be.
- A good set of external rudder pedals certainly help control the tail rotor and seriously add to the simulation experience. Another useful option is to program the tail rotor controls to a 2-way or 4-way hat switch on a programmable stick or throttle.
- A good programmable joystick is also highly recommended for this simulation. That is, one with at least four buttons, a hat switch and an analog throttle wheel. Controlling the collective precisely is a must in this sim. A separate throttle control is actually your best choice, followed by an analog throttle control.

  The more buttons on your stick, the better. Having more switches and hats to program keystrokes into not only makes this sim more interactive and realistic — it also keeps your hands on the stick and collective instead of the keyboard. You'll find this an indispensable aid during *Longbow*.
- If you don't have a throttle stick or wheel, try assigning the collective [+] and [-] keys to the up/down positions on your hat switch. Then, place the rudder on the left\right positions. This gives you all of your major flight controls on a single control, leaving your other hand free to control the mouse or keyboard.
- Autohover is a good button for your joystick if you've got one with a lot of buttons. Or, you can define the full forward position of your throttle device as the [6] collective setting on the keyboard. This way, if you need to come to a hover, all you have to do is push the throttle all the way forward and let go of the cyclic stick. The only drawback is that you now need to use the keyboard to get 100% collective (or assign it to a joystick button).
- If your joystick has a lot of buttons, assign the wingman "Attack My Target" command ([Ctrl][3]) to one of them. In the heat of battle, you'll be able to send him after something without having to take your hand off the joystick.

Tactical Situation Display MFD

- You can't use the mouse to lock onto TSD targets if TADS targeting is active.
- You must be in FCR target acquisition mode to update the targets that appear in your TSD. If TADS appears in the MFD display, press [Home] to switch to FCR.
- If all the targets on your TSD appear to be little boxes, you're zoomed out too far. Press [Pg Dn] to cycle through its ranges — the boxes will take on individual icon shapes.
- Circles with "tails" represent helicopters, and solid triangles denote enemy aircraft. You must switch to air radar mode to get them to appear on the TSD. Once you pick them up with FCR, they'll stay on the TSD display even if you switch to ground mode.
- Extending the TSD range can sometimes help you ID more targets. Try going to an extended TSD range as you're about to enter enemy territory.

Cameras and PNVS

- A great way to identify your threats visually is to use an exterior camera view. From a hover, press F7 until you find the threat you want to eliminate. Then, jump back to your previous view and unleash your firepower. Always make sure you're at a safe hover altitude before doing this, however.
- Use external cams for target identification, to follow your missiles, and to verify target destruction. Many of the cameras — such as missile view and death view — can be set to pop up on an as-needed basis. See the *Reference Card* for the keystrokes.
- Sometimes you can see an enemy, but it's just under the edge of a hill. You can shoot all day and never hit him. If your system says you can see him but you keep missing, hit F11 to bring up your Inverse Tactical View. It gives you a view from the enemy's perspective. If you (from the enemy view) can't see your chopper, your machine gun won't hit them. You need to climb or otherwise change position.
- Throughout *Longbow*, you'll face many nighttime, dusk and dawn missions. This is a great time to use your Pilot's Night Vision System (PNVS). Press P to toggle it on/off. At first, you may find it a bit eerie, but this enhanced visual system will guide any good pilot through a mission. So, in a nutshell, if a mission grows a bit too dark for you, and you've done all the gamma correction that you can, it's time for PNVS.
- If you're having trouble seeing things in external camera views at night, use gamma correction (use the **IN-FLIGHT OPTION** menu), or adjust your monitor's brightness.
- If you find one threat, use your F11 external view to get it in sight, then pan around to see if there are others in the area.
- If you play in invisible cockpit view a lot, use the Cruise IHADSS mode when flying. The pitch ladder gives you a good, concrete reference to where the ground is in relation to your flight path.
- To get a really good look at what's going on, get rid of your cockpit and use the cockpit-free view (Shift F1). (This is especially useful when you're strafing with your guns and have forward velocity.)

Co-Pilot/Gunner

- You can control both the pilot and CP/G functions in *Longbow*, or assign spotting and/or countermeasure duties to the CP/G in the **IN-FLIGHT OPTION** menu.
- Just because you can't see anything when your CP/G says "Threat Front" doesn't mean that he's rambling random warnings. His vision is just better than yours (and your ASE or TSD range is probably set too low).
- If your CP/G calls out something by name — "Helicopter, 3 o'clock" — it means it's a formidable threat. This is very useful info if you don't like to fly with your ASE up — if you listen to your CP/G, he'll give you a lot of the warnings that the ASE would. You can also keep the ASE autopage feature on, so that the ASE page will automatically pop up in one of your MFDs when you're threatened. (On is the default setting; use Shift A to toggle.)

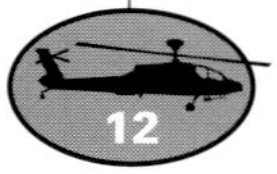

Autopilot Functions

- If you're playing through *Windows* (with no custom shortcut or boot disk), the auto-hover and autopilot functions don't work as well.
- If your helo is damaged and hard to fly, try autopilot. It can sometimes get you home.
- If it's a long stretch between waypoints, you can autopilot (A). In enemy territory, decrease the autopilot speed (Ctrl ←) to reduce your chances of being spotted.
- Remember, you can't hide *and* use autopilot. Autopilot keeps your altitude around 100 feet, so make sure that no one nearby can attack you before you activate it.
- If you get lazy and don't want to spin to bring the waypoint carat into view, hit autopilot briefly. This gets you oriented in the right direction. This is useful if you've got autopilot set up as a joystick or throttle stick button — you don't have to touch the keyboard at all to reorient the helicopter.
- If you insist on using autopilot with enemies around, activate time compression to 8x. This reduces the likelihood of a missile hit.
- You can usually autopilot home to the last waypoint. It will take you home and drop you into a hover over your landing FARP, so all you need to do is drop collective to land.

Priority Fire Zones

- When you carry RF Hellfires, make it a habit to use PFZs. If you don't know what they are, see p. 2.25 of the *Reference Manual*. They make targeting and firing a lot simpler, and you can use them to assign target areas to your wingman.
- If there are two or three sets of targets you want to attack, go ahead and set up your PFZs, then choose the first one you want to use. Q will cycle through them, so when you get close enough, just press Q instead of taking the time to set up a new PFZ.
- Once a PFZ is empty, delete it by clicking on the PFZ label with both mouse buttons simultaneously. Old PFZs will just confuse you, especially if you're trying to cycle through them in the heat of combat.
- Some targets move into a PFZ after it's created. They will *not* be added to the target list, however. To add something (such as a mobile SAM site) to the currently selected PFZ, press and hold Shift and left-click on the target's TSD icon.
- PFZs can cycle through up to 16 targets apiece. Try to avoid creating large zones — keep them small and accurate (i.e., target only a few specific items at a time).

Time Compression

- One small time-saving trick is to turn on your helicopter's rotors, then turn on Time Compression to shorten the time it takes for them to achieve full speed.
- Time compression makes you harder to hit. This is because the game checks every few seconds (in real time) to see where the weapon is in relation to your position. When the game time gets speeded up, the frequency of checks is reduced.

  For the same reason, don't fire *your* weapons while time-compression is active. They're less accurate this way because there are fewer game checks.

Your Weapons

- *Longbow* is not an arcade game in which you can constantly hold down the trigger. When shooting threats with your chain gun, use short, five-second bursts and leave one-second intervals between bursts. If you stick to this guideline, you'll minimize the downtime caused by an overheated gun.
- Don't point your nose down when using Stingers and Hellfires. Always pull your nose up a little bit. This keeps them from slamming into the ground if you're low.
- Reserve ammo until you've reached primary objectives. Then, let loose, but concentrate on "high-point" targets.
- If you're using rockets, you must stay under 100 knots for the pylons to self-articulate (rotate down as much as 30 degrees to aim at the current target).
- Use LOAL for pop-up attacks with Hellfires. LOBL is good for firing at targets in your line of sight when you're not worrying about being shot at.
- Don't forget about FARPs if you run out of fuel or ordnance. They affect your score, but use them when you're more concerned with survival than medals.

GUNS

- Use guns against small artillery pieces and soldiers.
- Strafing is best at speeds under 60 knots an hour. Any faster than that, and you'll have a lack of maneuverability when you need it the most.
- If you're taking out a line of targets with guns, approach from one end and strafe them in a linear path instead of attacking them at a random angle.
- Anything you can kill with rockets, you can kill with guns. You can carry a *lot* more bullets than rockets, and rockets take up space that could be carrying Hellfire missiles.
- Rockets are good for half-load if you're facing a lot of helos. (Campaign Mission 25, the POW rescue mission, is a good one for rockets.)

TARGET TYPES

- Use Stingers only against air targets.
- Deploy only a single Stinger at each air threat, then follow up with guns.
- You can launch Hellfires at air threats if you're at least 2km away from them. However, they're not extremely accurate. Only do this if you're out of Stingers and your gun is inoperative.
- Grounded helicopters are just like ground threats — target them with Hellfires. (Your wingman, however, will launch Stingers at them.)
- Hardened bunkers and tanks are hard to destroy with bullets if REALISTIC WEAPON DAMAGE is active. Use missiles or rockets instead — otherwise, you waste time and rounds.
- Artillery is soft. Don't use rockets or missiles against them, use machine gun fire. They won't really put up a fight. The closer you are, the less ammo you'll need.

HELLFIRES

- Most campaign missions can be flown effectively if you and your wingman carry a double load of Hellfire missiles. In most missions, you'll be thankful that you have 16 Hellfires, instead of the default rack of 8. In the real world, Hellfires would cost too much to load this many. Hooray for simulations!
- Of the three pieces of ordnance you can carry, the Hellfire takes the cake. Tinker around with the different modes of delivery — LOAL and LOBL. You can toggle between them (press Insert).
- Most targets worth destroying take a Hellfire missile apiece to kill. Others, such as hardened bunkers, take two.
- Take radar Hellfires whenever possible. Their range is 7.9km, and you don't have to keep the same target locked until impact. (Laser Hellfires, however, require that you keep it locked. This is because you're using the laser designator in the TADS/PNVS turret to "light up" the target with a laser beam.)
- With laser Hellfires, you can't change targets after launching a missile. This is because you must maintain the laser designator.
- LOBL doesn't have a lot of applications, unless you want to be certain you don't fire off a Hellfire without a valid lock, or if you're extremely picky about target types. In LOBL, you can't fire unless the missile box is solid; in LOAL, you can fire without a lock.

Firing Hellfires in LOAL Mode

- If you plan to mask your position behind terrain and use a bob-up attack method, one of the first things you want to do when you go into hiding is activate LOAL and check the valid LOS altitude (the minimum altitude you need to get VALID LOCK for Hellfires).

  To do so, climb until your LOAL box turns solid. Once you drop back down, you'll know how high you need to go to get the LOS after you fire. Count the number of seconds it takes for you to descend back to your hover position. This lets you know how much time to allot for ascension after you've fired a missile.
- When using Hellfires in LOAL mode, you need to pop up when your missile timer (marked TOF in the IHADSS display) reaches 8 or 10 seconds. This allows you to get a valid LOS (line of sight) before it counts down to zero.
- If you're in a hurry, go in low and fast with LOAL mode active. You can fire while out of line of sight, then pop up as you near missile impact. Your speed gives you altitude, and you can drop down quickly with your cyclic.
- There's a Hellfire trick you can use (which you may have discovered by now). In LOAL mode, you can fire your Hellfires even if you're out of range or don't have a valid missile lock in the IHADSS display. If you move within range or get a good LOS before the missile timer counts down to 1, then 0 seconds, you'll get the hit.
- Fire a Hellfire, then cycle through targets to get the next one you want. This keeps you from wasting missiles in the PFZ on things you can easily destroy with guns later.

Wingmen

- Time compression can leave your wingman behind. Watch out for this when you're about to go into heavy combat.
- He picks his weapons according to his targets. He'll use cannon for lightly armored targets at close range, rockets for medium-armored targets at close range, and Hellfires against heavily armored targets and any long-range threats. He'll use Stingers against air targets.
- He will follow you around relentlessly, unless you are attacked by enemy air threats. He will then break formation to defend you, but you can use Ctrl 5 to call him back.
- He can dogfight. He'll try stand-off attacks first, using Hellfires and Stingers. He can hit targets — even other helicopters — with rockets. He doesn't use textbook maneuvers but will respond to his opponent's moves and try to position himself for a good shot.
- In some situations, you simply need more ordnance than one AH-64 can carry. To ensure you have enough ordnance to complete the mission at hand, always use your wingman's weapons first. A good leader always brings his wingman home with him, but sometimes it's just not possible. Don't feel too guilty about it ... after all, this is war.
- Arm him with Stingers. This greatly increases his chance of survival.
- Your wingman needs you to have a valid line of sight (LOS) before he can fire at a target (it's your targeting system that identifies targets for him). His weapons, however, use his LOS to the target. Hovering can help his accuracy (when you hover, he does too).
- Next to Hellfires, your wingman is your most valuable tool. If you've seen the opening sequence to *Longbow*, you've seen a prime example of how a wingman and wingleader work together. The two AH-64Ds were hidden behind a hillside. Once the lead found the threats, both pilots proceeded to engage them as a team. You should take the same approach.
- Use your wingman as your second set of ordnance. The "Attack My Target" command (Ctrl 3) should become second nature to you. Once you've locked onto a target, hit that command, and your wingman will fire on whatever target you give him. Keep firing on other targets in the area, and alternate until all threats are eliminated.
- Use your wingman against tanks, immobile objects, and other items you don't want to waste your Hellfires on. Your wingman only uses LOBL missile launch mode.
- Don't send your wingman after grounded helicopters. He'll get shot down by surrounding threats.
- If you're waiting around for your wingman to finish up some targets, go to TADS MFD and select the same current target as your wingman. By zooming in as far as possible, you can verify what targets he's destroyed ... they'll appear courtesy of the FLIR/DTV/DVO camera.
- You get points for whatever your wingman takes out. That's why it's important to use up all ammo — even his — if you're at all concerned about scoring. (Scoring is how you earn medals and promotions).

- You may not want to bother with certain mundane targets (like tanks or small artillery sites). Instead, send your wingmen after them.
- You can easily keep track of the number of remaining Hellfires on your wingman's aircraft if you have more than 8 megabytes of RAM. Activate the DETAILED HELICOPTERS option in the **IN-FLIGHT OPTION** menu, then pan the F6 external camera view to see how many Hellfires are still mounted on his wing pylons.

Terrain

- Your cardinal rule as a pilot should be to fly as low as you can whenever you can. Fifty feet is a good bet for cruise altitude, and although it isn't easy to remain that low, you need to master it to survive. Building up the skill to constantly fly nap-of-the-earth is something our playtesters recommend to every aspiring AH-64 pilot.

  Practice as much as you can at that level, and then try to master flying under 30 ft. or less. You'll be thankful later, when your Commanding Officer pins yet another medal to your chest because you completed your objectives and made it back with your chopper intact.
- You can't hide behind buildings.
- If you know something is waiting over a hill for you, go around the hill if possible. That way, you won't have to be so high to get a valid LOS.
- The direction (north, south, west, east) from which you attack a waypoint can be very important. Before you get too close to the primary area, check for hills, valleys and ridges that will let you move within 8km of the area and still conceal your position. If your current direction exposes you too much, manipulate an extra waypoint to make an approach from a different direction. It's okay if waypoint-waypoint lines cross each other.
- If the primary targets lie on flat ground, but are positioned behind a mountain range, search for a canyon passage that will let you slip in unnoticed. This is a prime strategy in some missions, and adding an extra waypoint in a pass often preserves your element of surprise.

Waypoint Manipulation

The further you progress in the game, the more you'll realize that the programmed waypoints sometimes lead you directly into the heart of trouble. This isn't true in all cases — about half of the missions use the best route as the default waypoint progression. You can add, delete or adjust custom waypoints before a mission by using the computer in the Mission Planning Area. During flight, you can do the same thing by opening up the navigation map with the Alt N command.

Some traditional sims require that you visit each and every waypoint. In *Longbow*, however, you aren't required to go anywhere specific. The game doesn't care how you approach the primary targets, as long as you accomplish the mission. You can use this to your advantage in many missions.

The best indication that you should alter waypoints is when you're flying correctly (low and slow), but keep getting shot down by SAMs. Campaign Mission 10 is a prime example, as is Mission 50. Both are littered with SAMs that block the path you're supposed to take. And 90% of the time, what's going to kill you is a missile from a 2S6. By concealing your position behind ridges and traveling through valleys, you can often avoid SAMs, especially 2S6s.

Examine your map carefully before each mission, and follow these few general strategies.

- A good soldier is a well informed one. Before each mission, be sure to absorb information from your navigational map and briefing in the mission planner. They contain intelligence information on just where AAA, SAMs and enemy aircraft have been spotted recently. Don't fly blind!
- If you ever get lost, bring up the your navigational map by pressing Alt N. As long as you keep your waypoint indicator basically visible on your heading tape, you shouldn't get lost. But if you do, this map can help you out.
- Look for conspicuous ridges close to the primary waypoint. The game designers love to position SAM sites just over a ridge, where you won't see them until you bob up or pass over the crest. The same altitude you need to top the hill also gives your presence away — and until a SAM sees you, he won't fire. (This was modeled after actual military strategy.)
- Waypoints that are far apart (15+km) almost always have SAMs or enemy FARPs in between them. Cruise low and bob up to 300 or 400 feet every so often to ID SAMs. When you find them, you can sometimes adjust your waypoints so that you weave around their arcs.
- If a lot of 2S6s appear on one side of your flight path, you'll be tempted to add waypoints that steer you away from them. That's fine, as long as you don't drag the waypoints too far off in the other direction. Almost without exception, you'll place yourself in view of SAMs and helicopters at enemy FARPs. Just stay low, and stay slow.
- You can create waypoints to simply mark places you want to be aware of (for instance, if you want to stop midway through a pass or valley). You can see this type of info while in the nav map, but it's useful to have some quick way to get a point of reference or know when you're about to reach a terrain change.

- You don't have to create a new waypoint every time you need to add one in a mission. If you've already used a custom waypoint, drag it to a new location. Sequencing doesn't matter — the same custom waypoint can serve multiple purposes in a single mission. (For instance, you can mark an entrance to a valley with an custom waypoint, then later drag that waypoint elsewhere to adjust your flight path to avoid SAM sites on the way home.)
- Programmed waypoints are yellow with blue numbers, yours are orange with white numbers. You can right-click-and-drag the orange ones, but not the yellow ones.
- You can manually change your current waypoint by pressing W or Shift W. The number of the current one appears as "WO#" to the left of the High Action Display (the large rectangle at the bottom of the IHADSS display).
- A good way to survive a mission, especially if you're damaged, is to backtrack — instead of heading directly to the last waypoint, go back the way you came. The given path has fresh enemies and can be really dangerous.

  The sneakiest way is to go back to your starting point (which is usually in friendly territory) and then slide on over to the landing point (also in enemy territory). That way you make the last leg of the journey without hostile forces shooting at you. Feel free to modify the nav points.
- After you receive the "Mission Successful" message, you can land at any FARP to end the mission. You don't have to move to the landing FARP waypoint. If you land anywhere else besides a friendly FARP and aren't captured, your score is affected by one of the numbers in the equation (see **Scoring,** p. 48).
- If you die, any waypoints you added/moved reappear when you re-fly the mission.

Scoring Hints

- The default realism and flight model options are set to SIMPLE. A quick way to up your score is to bump these up to ADVANCED or EXPERT. (SIMPLE options reduce your score.)
- You lose 5000 points if you shoot down your wingman. He can't crash on his own ... so there's no proving that it wasn't your fault!
- You don't get points for kills for air/artillery strikes you call in. Reserve these for when you're in trouble and need some help.
- Your score is divided by the number of times you use FARPs to rearm and refuel.
- If you're having trouble finishing a mission because you've run out of missiles, you can temporarily deactivate REALISTIC WEAPON DAMAGE in the **IN-FLIGHT OPTION** menu. It will affect your score *only for that target*, not the entire mission. This allows you to kill anything with a single hit.
- Don't use INVULNERABLE or UNLIMITED AMMO unless you're flying for fun and don't care about score. If you activate either of them, you may score high on the mission, but you'll get zero added to your pilot's score.
- Backtracking to your starting FARP is often a good way to get through a mission. It doesn't affect your score, and you've presumably cleared out a safe flight path by that point. (By contrast, the normal path home is usually a dangerous path.)

Campaign Tips

- The hardest campaign missions are 5-18, according to our expert Quality Assurance department. Mission 25, though difficult, is one of their favorites.
- Many of the campaign missions can and should be completed at a distance. You don't have to necessarily see what you're firing at.
- In early campaign missions, sometimes soldiers will have hand-held weapons or shoulder SAMs if they're protecting a primary target. You need to switch to TADS because the TSD won't track them. They show up as CIS SOLDIER on the TADS MFD.
- You can fly either the A-Model or D-Model Apache in the campaign. It's significantly harder to win, however, in the AH-64A. You've got fewer MFDs and avionics systems, and can only load laser Hellfires.
- In the first four missions, enemy helicopters will ignore you as long as you stay on your side of the border. As soon as you violate their airspace, they will follow you and take warning shots if you stick around too long. If you head back into your own airspace, they will "escort" you to the border and then ignore you. *However, if you fire on them at any point, they will engage you.*
- To avoid losing a campaign mission, you always have the choice to re-fly any mission you fail, as long as you don't ACCEPT the mission by clicking on the door. If you fail too many missions, you're in for a BIG surprise. Let's just say it's going to get pretty hot wherever you are in the campaign. (You should lose at least once just to see the cool flick, if nothing else.)
- You don't actually have to win the last two missions to win the campaign. Theoretically, your side has already established such mastery that you can't lose. This is just sweep-up duty.
- Although normally you shouldn't hover at higher altitudes, there are really not enough threats left by the end of the campaign to worry about. Hover at whatever height you'd like.
- Check out the flowchart on page 62. If you're willing to examine it carefully, you'll figure out all kinds of alternate routes through the campaign and be able to play every mission that was designed.
- To ready yourself for the Baltic campaign, try flying all of the historical missions first. They'll give you an idea of what kind of situations to expect during the campaign and help familiarize you with the default chopper, the AH-64A Apache.
- If you can't get past a mission, try reducing to CAT III enemy skill. This reduces your score, but you still win. Or, try increasing your weapon damage by deselecting REALISTIC WEAPON DAMAGE in the **IN-FLIGHT OPTION** menu.
- You see movies at certain points during the campaign. If you miss part of one, or just want to view it again, use the News Scrapbook. You can find it in the Film Room back on the Base.

Historical Tips

- Even though the AH-64D Longbow wasn't available in the actual Gulf and Panama campaigns, you can give it a test drive in the historical missions.
- In Panama, areas near the coast sometimes look like ground, but act like water. They're swamps, essentially. To determine what kind of terrain it is, shoot it. If the bullets kick up gray dust, it's ground. If you see blue splashes, it's water.
- If you want to get some practice in either Apache model without dying, go to the historical missions and turn on UNLIMITED AMMO, INVULNERABILITY and NO CRASHES. Now try to make it through the mission with the least amount of ammo possible, and without getting hit. You'll be protected against hits, but you should still try to get through the offensive part of mission as if you weren't.
- Desert missions tend to be of the straight "fly to the designated waypoints, kill your primary targets, fly home" variety. Although these desert missions are not particularly challenging, they are a good way to learn the ropes about flying missions with a wingman against multiple threats.

  Remember, these missions are modeled on real-world intelligence, so the briefing map isn't go to show you every danger you face. Just as the pilots in Desert Storm didn't have access to 100% correct information, neither do you.
- In Desert Storm, you can fly a little higher and a little faster, because the terrain is so flat you can see everything coming.
- In Desert Storm, you can pretty much rely on the threats (SAMs, AAA, etc.) being four in a group. They are usually arranged in a diamond layout.
- For historical missions, you'll probably want to keep your wingman on "weapons free" (Ctrl 6) most of the time. If you want to assign him specific targets, however, first put him on "weapons hold" (Ctrl 5). Free him up again after that encounter is over.
- In Desert Storm, you will never face air-to-air threats. The Allies had complete air supremacy the entire time.

FLYING THE AH-64A APACHE

- If you like to keep the realism high, fly the Apache throughout these missions. To compensate for the lack of a TSD, you'll need to cycle through your master modes almost constantly. More importantly, frequently cycle through your available targets as you move over new terrain.
- Fly with TADS as your main MFD. Use U as your Upfront view.
- If you're used to flying a Longbow, use T and Alt T to find targets and best targets. It compensates for not having the TFD showing you where all the targets are on the field. Unless you're constantly cycling through your targets, you have no idea what's out there. Something will come into range while you're still concentrating on the last target you saw.

Beating Helicopter Bandits

- ✓ In helicopter vs. helicopter warfare, make sure you target the Hokums first. They're the only enemy helos that can fire air-to-air missiles at you.
- ✓ You can tempt helicopters away from a SAM-infested FARP by ascending. They'll acquire you and move away from the FARP. This way, you can eliminate them and stay out of the airfield's SAM and artillery range (unless 2S6s are present).
- ✓ Helicopters continually analyze the tactical situation to decide where to go and what to do. If the situation is right, they may perform something that looks like a textbook maneuver. However, this is merely a reaction to their opponent's maneuvers — no "Stern Conversion" string is called up in the AI code. So, as in real life, using a textbook counter-maneuver may not always work.
- ✓ Enemy helicopters will drop chaff and take evasive maneuvers, so it is possible to miss them with a perfect shot.
- ✓ If there's only one enemy chopper, tail him and he won't shoot at you. Avoidance is his first routine.
- ✓ Enemy helicopters can't see behind them. This means it's possible to sneak up on them, if you're careful.
- ✓ If you saw a helicopter a few moments ago, and it no longer appears when you make a 360-degree sweep of the area, chances are he's right on top of you. This is an avoidance routine of sorts ... he won't fire on you, but he will hide directly above you. If this happens, yank back the cyclic stick and apply additional collective. You'll slice backward with your nose up, a perfect position to fire at your opponent with the chain gun.
- ✓ In the AI structure, the preferred position for an enemy helicopter is behind its target, and it will continually maneuver to get there. Use air radar often to "check six."
- ✓ Helicopters paired as wingmen will attempt to support each other (i.e., one will attack from the left and the other will attack from the right).
- ✓ Mi-42 Hind and Mi-28 Havoc enemy choppers are built like flying tanks and have tons of chaff dispensers. Therefore, most of the time it takes two Stingers to bring one of them down. At the same time, Stingers are precious and you won't want to waste two of them on a single chopper. If the first one doesn't take down the helo, wait until you can maneuver within chain gun range.
- ✓ Enemy pilots pick their weapons carefully. They'll use cannon for lightly armored targets at close range, rockets for medium-armored targets at close range, and anti-tanks against heavily armored targets and any long-range threats. They'll use ATA missiles against air targets (and sometimes guns and rockets).

Beating Jet Bandits

- ✓ Not many game missions have planes. In the ones that do, make sure you stay hovering. Although it makes you more vulnerable, it also lets you fire more accurately. Hovering near a FARP is especially preferable. If you get into trouble with fuel or weapons, you'll be able to land and restock your tank and pylons. You'll also have the added support of Avenger SAMs and Patriot missile sites.
- ✓ Su-25 Frogfoots often look like they're running away after they make an attack pass at you. Sometimes they are (especially if they're damaged or out of missiles), but sometimes they're just bugging out far enough to make a second pass.
- ✓ Frogfoots are difficult planes to hit because they're fast. They're good for points, however (at 500, they have the highest point value). If you ever get caught in a moving fight with them, don't fire in a turn ... they are extremely quick. Facing them head-on with Stingers is your best bet.
- ✓ In air target missions, activate ground radar occasionally to check for SAMs. Then, go back to air mode to deal with airborne threats. You don't want to get surprised by a SAM missile.
- ✓ Once they're out of ammo (see **Object Stats & Loadouts**, p. 38, for loadouts) planes will return to where they started. If they start to bug out, you know they've expended most of their stores.
- ✓ You don't have to take out every air threat you encounter. First, determine if you are going to fly through their attack zone. If not, don't worry about them. A good way to determine if they are going to attack you is to go to the F10 or F11 views and see if they're even trying to track you. These views align the camera with the current target. If they aren't, you're fine.

When You're Damaged ...

- ✓ If your tail rotor gets damaged and you haven't gotten an important target yet, try landing and ordering your wingman to attack targets. This sometimes helps, and you'll still be able to autopilot home safely in some cases.
- ✓ If your engines go out or your rotor starts making a strange thumping sound, reduce your forward speed, gain altitude, and try to autorotate (glide without engine power) into the nearest FARP. See the *Auto-Rotational Descent Chart* on p. E.2 of the *Reference Manual* for safe autorotational speeds.
- ✓ If you're really, really damaged, use autopilot to return to base. It's probably more adept at flying an injured aircraft than you are. As long as you have one engine running out of the two, you can usually get home.
- ✓ If you land when damaged and need to take off again, you may need to re-engage your rotor (press R). With one engine out, this can take a long, long time. Time compression helps with this.
- ✓ If at any point in a mission your screen goes black, it probably means you got a dead hit to the center of your cockpit.

Beating Ground Threats

- Always stop and bob up pretty high right before you cross the border. Since SAMs won't usually fire at you while you're in friendly territory, you can get a good read on what awaits you before crossing enemy lines.
- Whenever you approach your primary targets, take out the surrounding AAA and SAM sites first. This removes the deadliest threat to your survival, and lets you move in closer. Close is good; it means you can use guns instead of precious Hellfires.
- All of the SA-series SAMs except the 2S6 have one drawback. If you can sneak up on them and move into weapon range without being detected, you can use guns against them. Why? Because once you're within their minimum missile-firing range (1-3km for radar SAMs), you're too close for their missiles to track you accurately. Hills are your best friend for this tactic — hover behind a hill, pop up and toast him.
- If a SAM locks you up and fires, you can often break the radar and/or missile lock by dropping to a very low altitude. This works even if a missile is already on the way.
- One in every 4 soldiers is carrying some type of shoulder-launched SAM.
- 2S6 and SA-11s tend to cluster together.
- For 2S6s, you'll see a second, smaller circle that indicates their gun range. The gun uses a separate radar to acquire and track you, and is almost as deadly as a missile.
- Don't call air strikes in on 2S6s. They'll probably bring down the A-10s.
- SAMs can only carry three to eight missiles apiece. (Loadouts for SAM sites appear in **Object Stats & Loadouts**, p. 38.) If you've got a lone SAM firing at you, keep track of how many missiles he's launched.
- Against 2S6s, it's vital to remain undetected. They have a long maximum range, and you need to be far inside their threat radius to attack. To take them out, mask yourself with terrain and stay low when you approach. When in Hellfire range, bob-up. It will take them a good 20 seconds to lock you up and fire, so you shouldn't have a problem surprising them. If you get detected first, however, say your prayers.
- 2S6s, SA-8s and ZSU-23s are the most dangerous threats out there. Of them, 2S6s are the most hazardous — they boast both long-range missiles and short-range guns.
- If you're attacking a SAM site, it's okay if he launches a missile as long as you get him first. Even if he has one in the air, it will lose its lock when yours hits.
- Take out radar sites first. Some missiles are radar controlled. Once the radar is gone, they aren't anywhere near the deadly threats they are when they can track you.
- If something that gets its targets from an external radar hasn't detected you yet, all you have to do is destroy its accompanying radar (such as the Snow Drift). If it's seen you, you need to destroy it *and* its radar.
- Your helicopter's radar signature is smaller when you're hovering, and it's harder for radar-guided SAM missiles to track you.
- The signature of dug-in vehicles is reduced by 75%, making them much harder to hit.
- Tanks never fire at you (T80-Us and T-72s). Armored personnel carriers (BRDMs) and fighting vehicles (BMP series), however, will.

Radar & IR Jamming

- Jamming reduces the chance of a guided missile hitting you. But don't forget that your enemies can jam as well. If your missile doesn't kill something, it's probably been deterred.
- You'll want to make sure that your radar and IR jamming devices are active whenever you're in a battle area. [R] activates radar jamming, [I] initiates infrared jamming.
- Most ground threats use radar-guided weapons. The SA-7 and SA-14 (shoulder-held SAMs carried by CIS soldiers), along with the SA-9 and SA-13 SAMs, however, use IR weapons. Don't forget to activate IR jamming.

RELATIVE JAMMING STRENGTHS

The table below provides an idea of the relative strengths of radar and IR jamming devices for each helicopter and aircraft in the game.

Helicopters

Unit	IR Jam	Radar Jam
AH-64A/D	47	30
UH-60	47	0
OH-58	47	0
CH-47	0	0
MH-53	63	78
Mi-28	30	0
Mi-24	30	0
Ka-50	30	0

Airplanes

Unit	IR Jam	Radar Jam
A-10A	0	35
C-130	0	35
Su-25	0	0

Note: *The actual numbers are percentage modifiers for the missile's accuracy and can be counteracted by the missile's ECCM (Electronic Counter-Countermeasure) rating. For example, if a missile has 86% accuracy for the part of the target helicopter it is aiming for, and the target helicopter has a 47% jammer strength, but the missile has a 31% ECCM rating, then the missile actually has a 70% of hitting its target. (Of course, the target could still get lost in ground clutter, etc., but this is the missile's base chance of hitting its target.) See **Missile, Rocket & Bomb Stats**, p. 42, for more details on weapon accuracy and ECCM strengths.*

Avoiding Detection

Much of your success in *AH-64D Longbow* will depend on how well you use terrain and strategy to remain undetected. Staying hidden usually means staying low and among ground cover — decreasing the chance that radar systems can pick you up and pinpoint your location. You want to get a lock on them before they get a lock on you. Understanding how radar systems track and at what altitudes and ranges they can pick you up is invaluable.

Note: *This section includes tables and charts of radar max. and min. ranges, etc. For a quick reference table of all detection statistics, see p. 28.*

Hiding From Radar

If you want to avoid being detected, the best thing you can do is avoid radar. Two general principles hold here.

- Radar systems cannot detect things beyond their maximum range, and the farther away a target within range is, the harder it is to pick up accurately.

When possible, use the nav map before and during your mission to alter your course so that you avoid all known radar systems — the radar ranges for SAM sites show up as red circles. The chart of maximum ranges below will give you an idea of the strength of the radar systems in this game.

All radar systems also have minimum ranges. However, most of these are well within the attached SAM launchers' missile ranges, so getting to this minimum range might be a bit hairy.

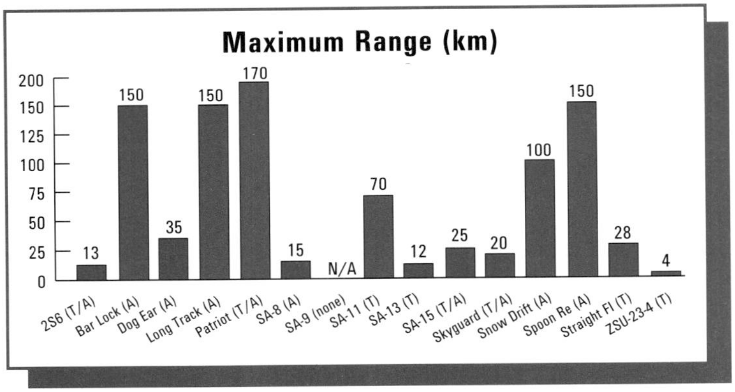

- Radar systems can't see through the earth.

The second best tactic is to put a mountain or hill between you and the radar. Again, you can use the nav map to plot a course that hides you from known radar. Use valleys (dark green areas on the nav map) and pick an attack position near the target where you can stay hidden from nearby radar systems.

See **Waypoint Manipulation**, p. 18, for tips on moving waypoints. Some of the mission notes (p. 66-135) suggest alternative courses for specific missions where appropriate.

In situations where you have to fly through radar ranges and there are no convenient valleys to take cover in, your best course is to stay low and fly slowly. The following tips explain why.

LOW AND SLOW

You've heard it many times before — to avoid being detected, stay low. Well, just how low is low? The minimum altitude at which a radar can pick you up depends on several factors — the strength (and skill level) of the radar, your distance from it, your aspect toward it and your speed.

- The closer you are to a radar system, the lower the altitude at which it can pick you up.

This chart shows the altitudes at which different radar systems can pick you up when you are 10km away from them.

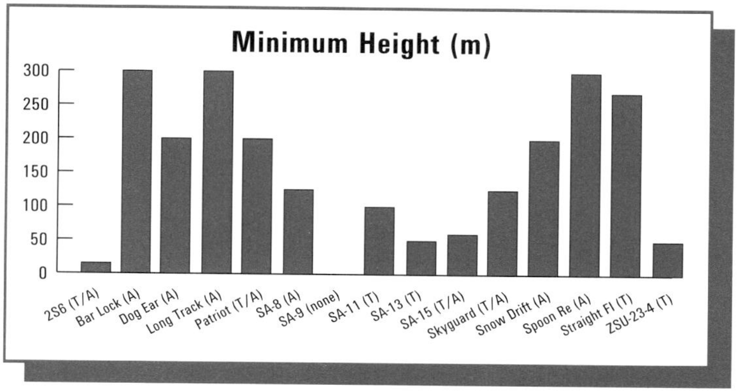

- You're harder to pick up if you are hovering.

If you're moving at all, your movement stands out against the returns from stationary ground clutter — the faster you are flying, the lower the altitude at which a radar can pick you up.

- When you're moving forward, you're easier to pick up from the front and aft than you are from the side.

This is due to Doppler shift — as you move toward or away from the radar, you generate a Doppler shift in the radar waves which can be picked up through ground clutter. If you fly perpendicularly to the radar's radius, you don't generate this shift.

- There is a "reaction time" delay between acquiring a target and firing the first missile.

Reaction time includes the time it takes for a system to acquire a lock on its target, pass information to a tracking radar, track the target, aim the launcher and fire a missile. (Reaction times for IR systems are shorter than those of radar systems because TR systems can skip the tracking phase.)

Reaction times vary greatly according to the situation. In general, targets at close range can be engaged sooner than faraway targets, and subsequent missiles are fired faster than the first missile. The chart below gives you a rough idea how different systems compare, but again, exact times differ according to the situation.

SAM	Reaction Time
Skyguard	10s
Avenger	4s
Patriot	9s
SA-6	20s
SA-7[1]	6s
SA-8	8s
SA-9	8s

SAM	Reaction Time
SA-11	12s
SA-13	6s
SA-14[1]	8s
SA-15	6s
Stinger[1]	4s
2S6	5s

[1]Manportable

Detection Tables

For a detailed explanation of what these statistics mean and how to use them to your advantage, see **Avoiding Detection**, p. 26. All game statistics were closely modeled on Jane's statistics — however, a few had to be "tweaked" here and there to make objects perform realistically in the game.

RADAR DETECTION STATISTICS

Radar Type. Lists whether the radar is used to find and acquire targets (Search), track targets that have already been acquired (Track), or both (S/T).

Linked With. (For radar vehicles only) lists the SAM systems the radar *can* be linked to. (See **Avoiding Detection**, p. 26, for more information on missile guidance.)

Max Range. Farthest point that a radar can detect an aircraft. (Some restrictions, such as altitude of the aircraft, apply — in general, the farther something is from a radar, the harder it is pick up.) For launchers with Search and Track capabilities, the ranges listed are for the tracking radar.

Min Range. Closest point to the radar at which an aircraft can be picked up.

Min Height. The lowest altitude at which an aircraft can be detected when it is 10km from the radar system.

Unit	Radar Type	Linked With	Min Range (km)	Max Range (km)	Min Height (m)
2S6	S/T	–	0.1	13	15
Bar Lock[1]	Search	–	0.5	150	300
Dog Ear	Search	SA-9/SA-13/ZSU-23-4	0.4	35	200
Long Track	Search	SA-6/SA-8	0.5	150	300
Patriot Radar	S/T	Patriot	0.2	170	200
SA-8	Search	–	0.1	15	125
SA-9	None	–	–	–	–
SA-11	Track	–	0.5	70	100
SA-13	Track	–	0.2	12	50
SA-15	S/T	–	0.5	25	60
Skyguard Radar	S/T	Skyguard	0.1	20	125
Snow Drift	Search	SA-11/SA-6/SA-8	0.5	100	200
Spoon Rest[1]	Search	–	0.5	150	300
Straight Flush	Track	SA-6	0.4	28	270
ZSU-23-4	Track	–	0.1	4	50

[1] **Note:** These are EW (Early Warning) radar and are not in any way connected to SAM or AAA sites.

VISUAL DETECTION STATISTICS

Only units with Surface-to-Air detection capabilities are listed.

Visual Range. Maximum distance at which unit can detect an aircraft.

Night Vision Range. Maximum distance at which unit can detect an aircraft.

Unit	Visual Range (km)	Night Vision Range (km)
2S6 (cannon)	2	0.7
Avenger SAM	4.5	2.25
BMP-2	0.8	0.7
BMP-3	1	0.7
BRDM	0.8	0.7
BTR-80	0.8	0.7
LAV-300 12.7mm	1	0.5
LAV-300 AAA	2	0.7
M2	1.5	0.75
Patrol Gunboat	1.5	0.7
POW Guard Tower	1.5	0.7
SA-9	2	1
SA-13	4	2
Skyguard (cannon)	2	0.7
Soldier	0.4	0.2
ZPU-4	1.5	0.75
ZSU-23-4	2.5	0.7

Disabling SAM & AAA Sites

Different missiles require different detection systems and locks. For example, radio command missiles, such as the SA-6, require a *search radar* to find a target, and a *tracking radar* to track the target until the missile hits. In the SA-6 system, these two systems are on separate vehicles. On the other hand, IR-guided SA-14s require only that the soldier carrying them see the target. Understanding the search and track systems used by each weapon will help you deal with them — in the examples above, taking out either radar would disable the SA-6, but you'd have to take out the soldier in order to disable the SA-14.

RADIO-COMMAND SAM SYSTEMS

In order for a radio-command missile to engage you, four things must happen:

1. A search radar must detect you and download your position to a tracking radar.
2. The tracking radar must lock on to you, and pass target info to the launcher.
3. The missile must be fired.
4. The tracking radar then tracks both the target and the missile, and directs the missile via radio command to its target. (The missiles usually have antennae in the tail end which receive these commands.)

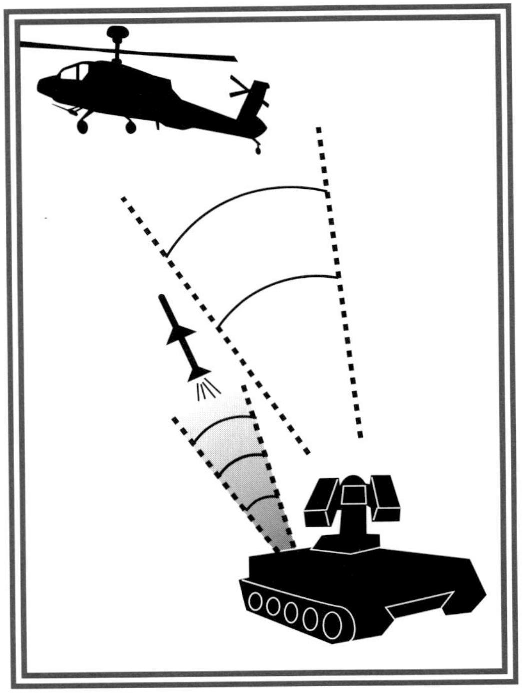

Radio-Command Missiles. *These missiles are guided toward a target by a radio commands from a tracking radar. This radar must track the target until the missile impacts.*

Most of the SAM systems in the game launch active radio-command missiles. Many of these of have separate radar vehicles connected to the launcher vehicles by data links. *Taking out the radar vehicles at one of these sites will render the entire site blind and therefore helpless.*

If you take out a search radar that has already downloaded target information to a tracking radar, the launcher can continue to fire at you. Blowing up a tracking radar will cause the missiles it was guiding to self-destruct.

Also, in addition to reducing a missile's chance of hitting you,your radar jammer can often "break" a radar lock by sending the radar false signals and confusing it. The farther away you are, the more likely your jammer is to break the lock. If the radar loses its lock, missiles on the way lose their target as well.

Radio-Command SAM Systems

2S6 (SA-19)	Search/tracking radar on launcher
SA-6[1]	Long Track or Snow Drift search radar, Straight Flush tracking radar
SA-8	Search/tracking radar on launcher (might use Snow Drift or Long Track to increase search range)
SA-11	Snow Drift search radar, tracking radar on launcher
SA-15[2]	Search/tracking radar on launch vehicle
Patriot	Patriot search/tracking radar

[1]Switches to semi-active radar homing mode at the end.

[2]Although a radio-command missile in real life, in the game, the SA-15 has actually been modeled on a active radar missile to simulate its high resistance to ECMs. Even for a active radar missile however, the tracking radar in the missile nose is necessarily so small that it has a range of only 2-5km, and the missiles are command-guided by a tracking radar for the first part of their trajectory. The SA-15 in this game switches to active radar about 2km away from its target. If you destroy the launch vehicle before this, you destroy the missile as well.

SEMI-ACTIVE RADAR-GUIDED SAM SYSTEMS

These missiles perform similarly to radio-command missiles, but the nature of their guidance systems is a bit different. A semi-active missile has a "seeker" in the nose of the missile that guides the missile toward a target painted by a tracking radar. So, semi-active radar missiles also require the tracking radar to maintain a lock on its target until the missile impacts.

Semi-Active Radar-Guided SAM System

Skyguard (AIM-7F)	Skyguard search/tracking radar vehicle

Semi-Active Radar-Guided Missiles. *These missiles are guided toward a target by a radar beam projected by tracking radar. This radar must track the target until the missile impacts.*

IR-GUIDED SAM SYSTEMS

IR missiles home in on a target's heat signature. IR missile launchers may use radar to find you, but they don't require a lock in order to fire. However, if they have a tracking radar and can lock on to a target, they can fire beyond their visual range (within the tracking radar's range). Missiles launched after the radar is destroyed can still home in on you.

The key to dealing with IR missile systems is avoiding detection.

IR Missile Systems

FIM-92C[1]	No radar
SA-7[2]	No radar
SA-9	Dog Ear search radar
SA-13	Dog Ear search radar, tracking radar on vehicle
SA-14[2]	No radar

[1]SA version of the Stinger, launched by Avenger SAM or manportable launcher

[2]Manportable

Note: *Detection for manportable SAMs is limited to the visual range of a soldier (see* ***Visual Detection****, p. 28). They also have only one missile — once they've fired it, they're left with only an AK-47. However, soldiers will not appear on your radar, so you may wander into their visual range without knowing it. Switch to TADS target acquisition mode to find these guys.* ***At least one in every four soldiers is carrying some kind of a SAM.***

IR Missiles. *Infrared missiles home in on the heat generated by a target.*

CANNON

Cannon don't need a radar lock to fire, so they can fire at you even if you are at low altitudes and partly obscured. However, radar locks increase their range and accuracy, so if you are within their radar range, there's a better chance they will hit you. This is especially true for night missions — all visual detection ranges (and thus, effective cannon ranges) are significantly reduced at night, but guns with a radar lock can fire up to their max range.

Anti-Aircraft Cannon

Skyguard	Skyguard radar vehicle
2S6	Search/tracking radar on vehicle
ZSU-23-4	Tracking radar on vehicle, Dog Ear search radar
ZPU-4	Visual range only
LAV-300 AAA	Visual range only

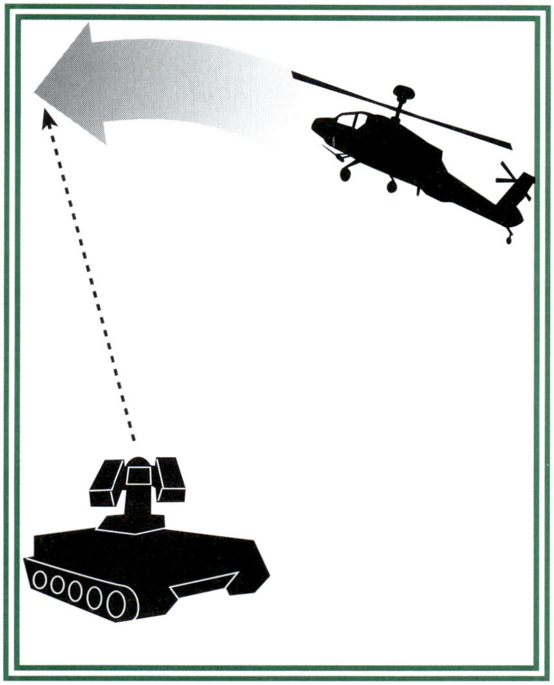

Cannon and Dumbfire Missiles. *These projectiles follow a flight path that can't be altered once they've left the gun or rail. Radar guidance increases their accuracy by automatically calculating leads.*

MISSILE PROFILES

Radio Command **Semi-Active Radar Guided** **IR-Guided**

Fire Methods/Helicopter Gunnery

The two methods of fire that can be used on the AH-64 are diving fire and running fire; each method has its own particular weapons employment techniques. The paragraphs that follow discuss the diving and running fire when employed on the AH-64.

The higher altitudes used with diving fire provide greater stand-off from small arms weapons. However, altitudes will vary with the situation.

Before the dive is begun, the CPG will acquire the target with the TADS to cue the pilot to the target. Since the pilot will fire the rockets from a dive, no laser ranging is necessary for the rockets. The dive is entered at 100 knots. At this airspeed, the pylons will be in flight stow and will remain so during the dive. The pilot will have a broken I-beam for a rocket steering cursor in the HMD.

Starting at an altitude of 3,000 feet, an airspeed of 100 knots, and a dive angle of 15 degrees, the pilot will have about 10 seconds to conduct the attack. The pilot must acquire the target, align the rocket steering cursor with cueing from the CPG's TADS, maintain constant torque, keep the aircraft in trim, employ the flares, and fire the rocket during this 10 seconds. At the end of the 10 seconds, the aircraft speed with be approximately 150 knots begins a 2- to 2.5-G pullout. During the pullout the CPG engages the gun. If a steep dive angle of 30 degrees is used, engagement time will decrease.

Running fire is an effective diving method to use during terrain flight. It also offers a good mix of aircraft survivability and weapons accuracy.

Switchology. (Except for the additions discussed in this paragraph, switchology remains the same as for diving fire.) Switchology for running fire begins when the CPG enters a grid location for the target into the FCC and the doppler. This gives the aircraft a rapid prepoint to the target using the TADS, steering information, and the range read-down for the pilot. The CPG lases for range information, but the pilot should also enter a manual range of 4 to 5 kilometers as a backup into the ARCS. The pilot uses a cooperative rocket engagement when the CPG acquires the target with the TADS and the pilot aligns the rocket steering cursor over the TADS LOS. The pylons articulate in elevation below an airspeed of 100 knots. (This should be verified in advance.)

Methodology. The starting point for a running fire attack is an IP located about 8 kilometers from the target. The IP should be a terrain feature recognizable either during the day or at night. Before departing the IP, the CPG prepoints the TADS to the target and selects the doppler entry for the target. For security at the IP, the pilot enters into a low orbit and keeps masked from the target.

The pilot departs the IP at 80 knots and flies contour to the target. At 6 kilometers from the target, the pilot performs a bump to gain intervisibility with the target. A bump is a gradual climb that allows the CPG to sight the target with the TADS. Once the CPG has the target, the pilot stops the bump and stabilizes the airspeed at 80 knots.

During the day the CPG can use DVO then switch to DTV for cooperative fire, or he can use DTV throughout. Going heads-down for the DVO may be required if the target is identifiable by color.

At 5 to 5.5 kilometers from the target the pilot aligns the rocket steering cursor with the CPG's TADS LOS and begins engagement. Since the airspeed is 80 knots, the pylons articulate and the pilot uses laser ranging. A 3- to 5-degree dive angle is all that is required. At 3.5 kilometers from the target, the rocket engagement ends and the aircraft is accelerated to 120 knots for a follow-up gun shot and turns off away from the target.

During acceleration, the pilot can remask the aircraft and bump up at 3 kilometers for the gun attack. At 2 kilometers from the target, the pilot begins his turnoff and positions the aircraft for another attack or returns to the IP.

When a Hellfire missile is fired against a high-threat target using running fire, the IP should be moved back 2 kilometers and the bump started before 8 kilometers is passed. While airspeed between 40 and 80 knots is maintained, the missile is fired at 8 kilometers using LOAL-Direct. The missile will impact the target at 7 kilometers when the aircraft is flown at 40 knots and 6.3 kilometers at 80 knots. The aircraft should break off from the target before crossing 6 kilometers and set up for another attack.

HELICOPTER STATS

Player
Friendly
Enemy

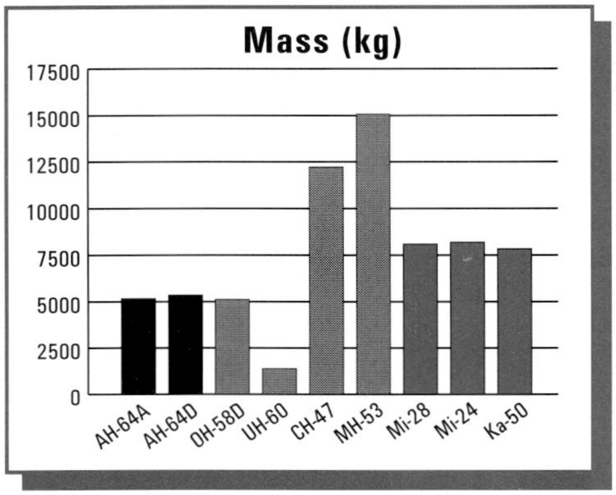

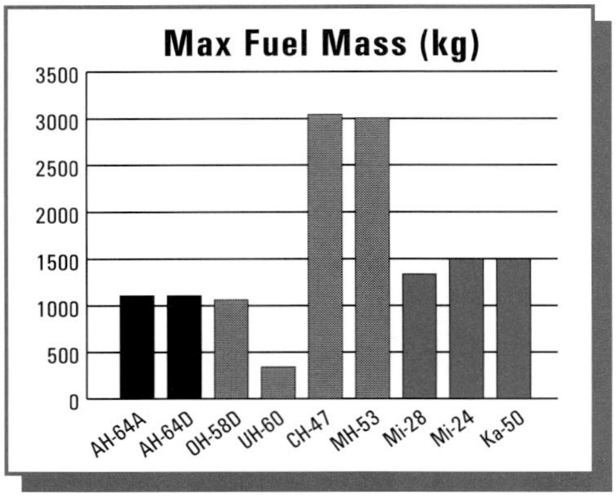

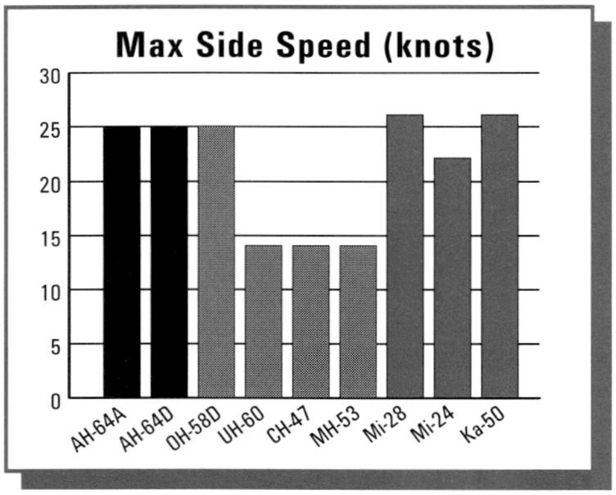

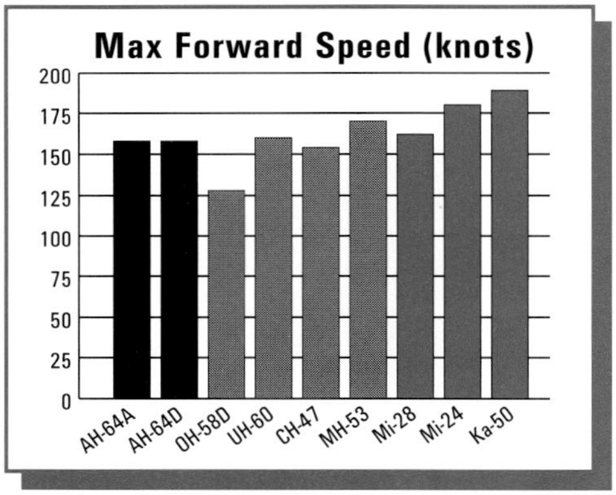

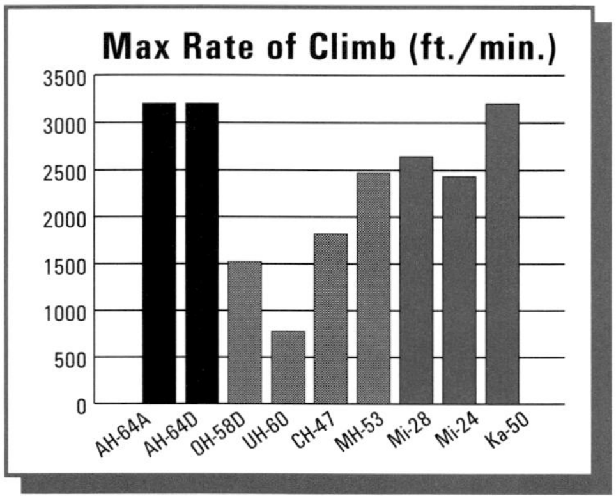

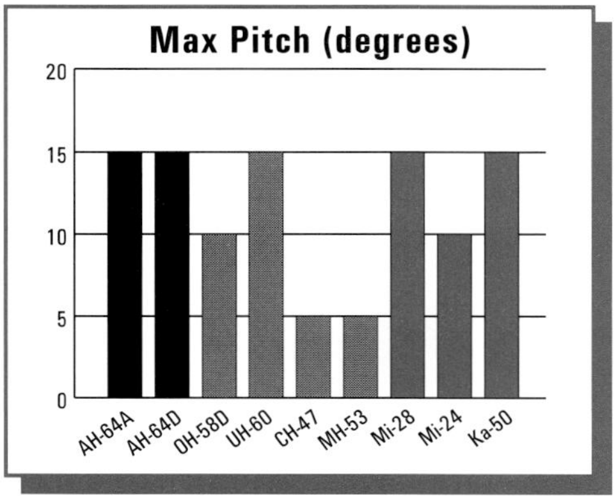

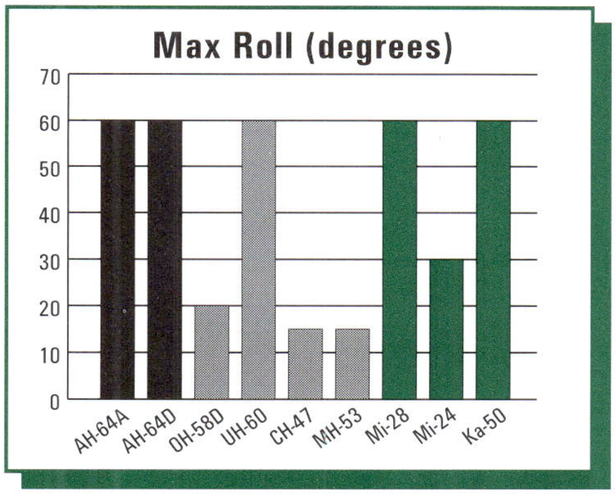
Max Roll (degrees)
70
60
50
40
30
20
10
0
AH-64A
AH-64D
OH-58D
UH-60
CH-47
MH-53
Mi-28
Mi-24
Ka-50

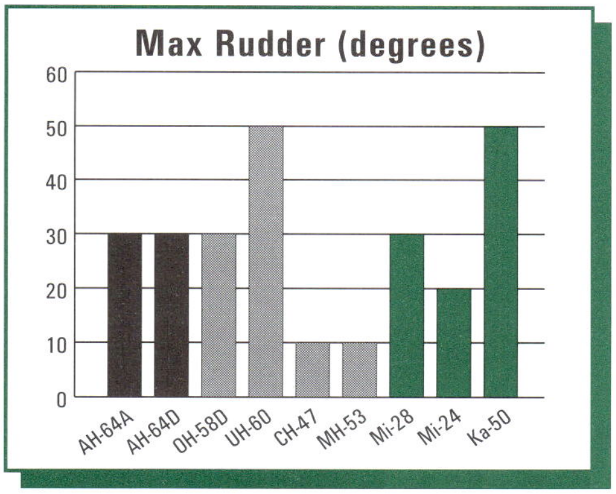
Max Rudder (degrees)
60
50
40
30
20
10
0
AH-64A
AH-64D
OH-58D
UH-60
CH-47
MH-53
Mi-28
Mi-24
Ka-50

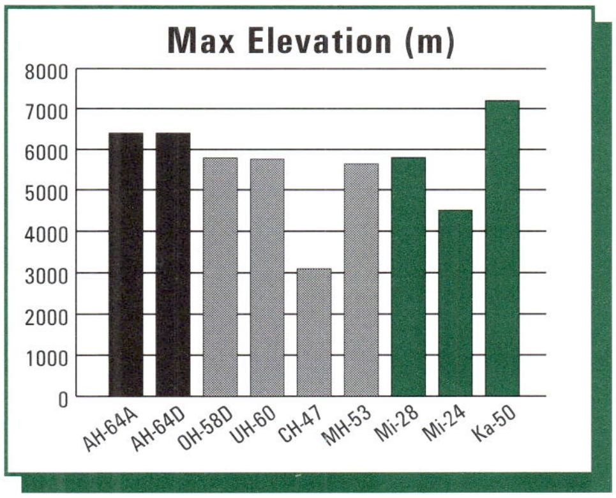
Max Elevation (m)
8000
7000
6000
5000
4000
3000
2000
1000
0
AH-64A
AH-64D
OH-58D
UH-60
CH-47
MH-53
Mi-28
Mi-24
Ka-50

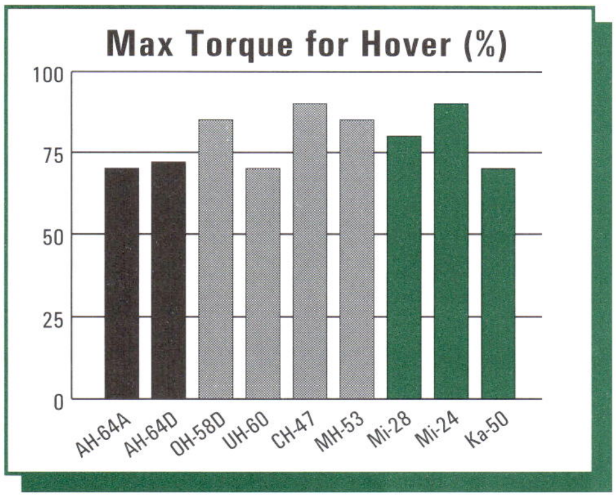
Max Torque for Hover (%)
100
75
50
25
0
AH-64A
AH-64D
OH-58D
UH-60
CH-47
MH-53
Mi-28
Mi-24
Ka-50

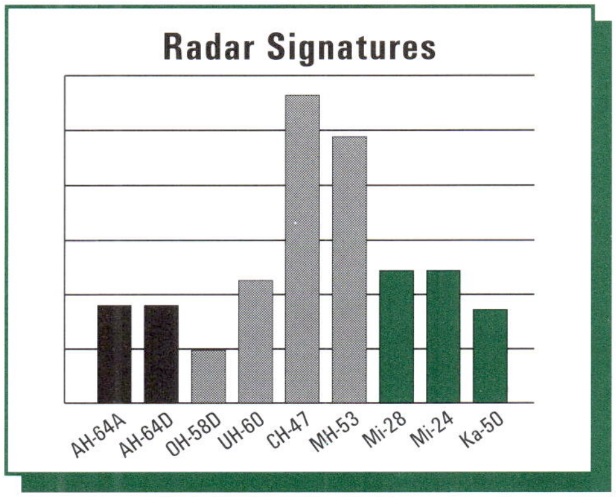
Radar Signatures
AH-64A
AH-64D
OH-58D
UH-60
CH-47
MH-53
Mi-28
Mi-24
Ka-50

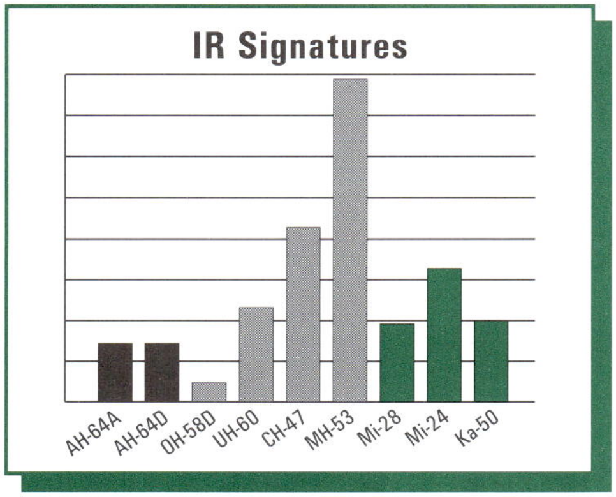
IR Signatures
AH-64A
AH-64D
OH-58D
UH-60
CH-47
MH-53
Mi-28
Mi-24
Ka-50

OBJECT STATS & LOADOUTS

Structural points. The number of structural points an object has determines how much damage it can take. An object with 100 structural points can take 100 points worth of damage from a weapon before it is destroyed. Numbers in parentheses are structural points for ground objects when dug-in, or aircraft when grounded (given only when they differ from the object's normal structural points). (Damage points are listed under **Cannon and Machine Gun Stats**, p. 40 and **Missile, Rocket and Bomb Stats**, p. 42.)

Armor. Every object has an armor rating — Lt (Light), Med (Medium) or Hvy (Heavy). Every weapon is rated for its chance of direct hit against these different armor types. (Chance of direct hit stats are listed under **Cannon and Machine Gun Stats**, p. 40 and **Missile, Rocket and Bomb Stats**, p. 42.)

Kill Points. These points are added to your score when you dispatch the object. (See **Scoring**, p. 48.)

Loadout. Lists the weapons each object carries in the game. The number in parentheses is the number of rounds loaded. See pp. 38-39 for statistics on the weapons. Weapons for surface-to-surface artillery (such as the SCUD) do not affect gameplay and are not included.

	UNIT	STRUCTURAL POINTS	ARMOR	KILL POINTS	LOADOUT		CM CH/FL	MAX V
HELICOPTERS	AH-64A/D	85 (80)	Med	-100	M230 (1220)	FFAR (8)	30/0	158
	(default)				AGM-114B (8)	AIM-92C (4)		
	CH-47	70	Lt	-100	(n.a.)		0/0	154
	MH-53	120	Lt	-100	Vulcan (5000)		120/60	170
	OH-58D	80 (40)	Lt	-100	(n.a.)		30/15	128
	UH-60	60 (40)	Lt	300	(n.a.)		–	160
	Ka-50	100	Med	300	2A42 (500)	AT-12 (12)	128/64	189
					S-8 (40)	SA-14 (2)		
	Mi-24	100	Med	300	VSPU-24 (1470)	AT-6 (16)	0/96	180
					S-8 (64)			
	Mi-28	80 (70)	Med		NPPU-28 (250)	AT-6 (4)	128/64	162
					S-8 (40)			
AIRPLANES	A-10	100	Med	-500	GAU-8 (1174)	AGM-65G (6)	120/60	381
	C-130	250	Med	-500	(n.a.)		120/120	321
	Su-25	100	Med	500	AO-17A (250)	S-8 (64)	256/128	513
					AS-14 (4)			
SAMs/AAA	2S6	75 (85)	Med	250	A38M (1904)	SA-19 (8)	–	52
	Avenger SAM	25	Lt	-100	FIM-92C (8)		–	60
	LAV-300 AAA	100	Med	100	Vulcan (2280)		–	50
	SA-6	60	Lt	100	SA-6 (3)		–	–
	SA-8	70	Lt	250	SA-8 (6)		–	38
	SA-9	70	Lt	200	SA-9 (4)		–	36
	SA-11 Launcher	60	Lt	100	SA-11 (4)		–	–
	SA-11 Command	60	Lt	200	(n.a.)		–	–
	SA-13	70	Lt	200	SA-13 (4)		–	–
	SA-15	70	Lt	250	SA-15 (8)		–	–
	Skyguard Gun	25	Lt	100	35mm (238)		–	–
	Skyguard Launcher	25	Lt	150	AIM-7F (4)		–	–
	ZSU-23-4	70	Lt	150	AZP23M (2000)		–	48
	ZPU-4	40	Lt	150	ZPU-4 (4800)		–	–
RADAR	Bar Lock	30	Lt	200	(n.a.)		–	–
	Dog Ear	70	Lt	200	(n.a.)		–	56
	Long Track	40	Lt	200	(n.a.)		–	–
	Patriot Radar	25	Lt	200	(n.a.)		–	–
	Skyguard radar	30	Lt	200	(n.a.)		–	–
	Snow Drift	60	Lt	200	(n.a.)		–	–
	Spoon Rest	50	Lt	200	(n.a.)		–	–
	Straight Flush	60	Lt	200	(n.a.)		–	–

CM (Ch/Fl). Countermeasures — Chaff/Flare, lists the number of chaff pods or flares an aircraft carries.

Max V. Maximum speed a vehicle is capable of attaining in this game. For helicopters and aircraft, this figure is given in knots. For all other vehicles, it is given in miles per hour.

TERRAIN CANDY

Blowing up non-military objects — civilian buildings, houses, bridges, etc. — adds nothing to your score. Many of them are destructible, however, so if you find yourself with an extra round or two ...

Structure	**Structural points**	**Armor**
Bridges, whole	90-200	Med-Hvy
Houses/Small Bldgs.	100	Lt
Factories, Nuclear Silos	500-2000	Lt

Basically, the number of damage points roughly corresponds to an object's size, and most civilian buildings have light armor.

UNIT	STRUCTURAL POINTS	ARMOR	KILL POINTS	LOADOUT		CM CH/FL	MAX V	
BM-25	40	Lt	150	(n.a.)		–	–	ARTILLERY/SS
SCUD Launcher	60	Lt	200	(n.a.)		–	34	ARTILLERY/SS
SO-122	60	Lt	150	(n.a.)		–	–	ARTILLERY/SS
US MLRS	50	Lt	-100	(n.a.)		–	–	ARTILLERY/SS
BMP-2	60	Med	100	30mm (500)		–	50	APCs/IFVs
BMP-3	60	Med	100	30mm (500)		–	50	APCs/IFVs
BDRM	40	Med	100	(n.a.)		–	–	APCs/IFVs
BTR-80	50	Lt	100	Heavy MG (2500)		–	–	APCs/IFVs
LAV-300 12.7mm	100	Med	100	Heavy MG (1400)		–	52	APCs/IFVs
LAV-300 90mm	100	Med	100	90mm (8)		–	–	APCs/IFVs
LAV-300 Command	100	Med	100	(n.a.)		–	–	APCs/IFVs
M-109	60	Lt	-100	(n.a.)		–	–	APCs/IFVs
M-113	40	Lt	-100	(n.a.)		–	40	APCs/IFVs
M1A2	250 (300)	Hvy	-100	120mm (55)		–	45	TANKS
M2	70	Med	-100	25mm (300)		–	50	TANKS
T-72	200 (225)	Hvy	150	125mm		–	27	TANKS
T-80	225	Hvy	150	120mm (39)		–	43	TANKS
CIS Fuel Truck	15	Lt	50	(n.a.)		–	56	OTHER VEHICLES
CIS Truck	40	Lt	50	(n.a.)		–	56	OTHER VEHICLES
HUMMV	25	Lt	-100	(n.a.)		–	60	OTHER VEHICLES
URL Jeep	40	Lt	50	(n.a.)		–	50	OTHER VEHICLES
US Truck	40	Lt	-100	(n.a.)		–	56	OTHER VEHICLES
Barracks, 8-pack	2500	Lt		(n.a.)		–	–	MISCELLANEOUS
Barracks, single	400	Lt		(n.a.)		–	–	MISCELLANEOUS
Bunker, Airport	600	Hvy	150	(n.a.)		–	–	MISCELLANEOUS
Bunker, Sandbag	185	Med	150	(n.a.)		–	–	MISCELLANEOUS
Bunker, Concrete)	600	Hvy	150	(n.a.)		–	–	MISCELLANEOUS
Bunker, Command	600	Hvy	150	(n.a.)		–	–	MISCELLANEOUS
Buildings, Airport	350	Hvy		(n.a.)		–	–	MISCELLANEOUS
Control Tower	250	Med		(n.a.)		–	–	MISCELLANEOUS
POW Tower	60	Lt	150	Heavy MG (1000)		–	–	MISCELLANEOUS
Prisoner Block	500	Lt		(n.a.)		–	–	MISCELLANEOUS
Prisoner Buildings	2000	Med		(n.a.)		–	–	MISCELLANEOUS
Patrol Boat			0	Heavy MG (2000)		–	22	MISCELLANEOUS
Tent	45	Lt		(n.a.)		–	–	MISCELLANEOUS
*Enemy Soldier	1	Lt	40	AK-47 (500)	SA-7 (1)	–	2	MISCELLANEOUS
				SA-14 (1)	FIM-92C (1)		–	MISCELLANEOUS
US Soldier	1	Lt	-100	(n.a.)		2		MISCELLANEOUS

* Soldier will only carry AK-47 and possibly a hand-held SAM. (On average 1 in 4 carries a SAM.) Some soldiers may be unarmed.

CANNON & MACHINE GUN STATS

The most important statistics for cannon and machine guns are *max range, probability of direct hit* and *damage points*. Max range tells you from how far away the gun can hit you. (You can target an object and check your range to target at the bottom left of your IHADSS to find out how far away you are from it.) Probability of direct hit and maximum damage points give you a rough idea of how powerful a gun is.

Caliber. Diameter of the gun's ammunition, in millimeters.

Targets. Air and/or **G**round — lists the type of targets the gun can attack in the game.

Maximum range. The farthest point at which a target can be hit. The check for maximum range is made when the gun fires.

Probability of direct hit. Since gun ammunition is unguided once it leaves the barrel, you will get hit if you remain in the path of the bullet. If you are hit, *probability of direct hit* is the chance that this hit will be a direct hit and not a glancing blow.

For example, an M230 has a 31% probability of direct hit against light armored vehicles and can inflict 30 points total. This means that *if* the cannon hits a light-armor target, it has a 31% chance of inflicting a direct hit (up to 30 points). It has a 69% chance of causing only fractional damage.

Damage points. Total number of damage points a projectile can inflict on its target. Probability of direct hit ratings and maximum damage points are roughly based on the caliber of the gun.

Maximum pitch. Maximum angle (relative to the horizon) that the gun can fire.

Minimum pitch. Minimum angle (relative to the horizon) that the gun can fire.

Maximum yaw (aircraft cannon only). Degrees that a gun can pivot. (For a nose-mounted gun, 90° would mean the gun could pivot 45° to either side from the nose of the aircraft.)

Rate of fire. Number of rounds fired in a second.

	2A42	AK-74	A38M	AZP-23M	GAU-8/A	M230	NPPU-28	Skyguard	VSPU-24	Vulcan	ZPU-4	Hvy. MG	25mm[1]	120mm[2]
Caliber (mm)	30	30	7.62	23	30	30	30	35	12.7	*	14.5	*	*	*
Targets (Air/Ground)	A/G	A	A/G	A	A/G	A/G	A/G	A	A/G	A	A	A/G	A/G	G
Maximum range (km)	4	4	0.4	2.5	4	3.5	3.5	3.5	1.5	1.5	1.5	1.5	2.5	3
Prob. of direct hit														
Light armor	35%	47%	8%	47%	79%	31%	31%	35%	47%	47%	31%	20%	31%	100%
Medium armor	20%	24%	1%	24%	55%	20%	20%	24%	16%	20%	16%	8%	16%	100%
Heavy armor	3%	3%	0%	2%	24%	2%	3%	4%	1%	1%	1%	1%	2%	100%
Damage points	30	30	5	23	120	30	30	35	12	20	12	12	50	250
Maximum pitch	0°	80°	80°	85°	5°	11°	13°	90°	20°	80°	90°	80°	60°	20°
Minimum pitch	-30°	6°	10°	4°	5°	60°	40°	5°	60°	10°	10°	10°	10°	10°
Maximum yaw	5°	n.a.	n.a.	n.a.	5°	100°	100°	n.a.	60°	n.a.	n.a.	n.a.	n.a.	n.a.
Rate of fire (rd/s)	15	66	10	66	70	10	10	18	76	50	40	10	3	1

[1] These stats apply to both 25mm and 30mm cannon.

[2] These stats apply to 90mm, 120mm and 125mm cannon.

* Caliber is as appropriate to the weapon.

2A42 (KA-50 HOKUM)

This single-barreled, gas-powered automatic helicopter cannon evolved from a prototype designed in the mid-1970s. The Tula design bureau adapted it to increase combat effectiveness of the BMP-1. Its manufacturer is believed to the Moscow Aggregate Plant Dzezhinets.

A38M (2S6 TUNGUSKA)

The A38M cannon are water-cooled, gas-powered, electrically-fired weapons. Each barrel has an automatic velocity measuring device that feeds data to the fire-control computer. Cranes reload ammunition containers through the turret roof.

AK-74 ASSAULT RIFLE (INFANTRY)

Avtomat Kalashnikov 1947g — The rifle was named after the man who designed it during Russia's Great Patriotic War. It is estimated that well over 20 million have been manufactured, making this one of the most widely distributed weapons in the world.

AZP-23M (ZSU-23-4)

The first prototypes were completed in 1961; the ZSU was accepted for service the following year. It was first seen in public during a 1965 parade held in Red Square, Moscow. *Zenitnaia Samokhodnaia Ustanovka* is Russian for "self-propelled anti-aircraft mount"

GAU-8/A AVENGER (A-10A THUNDERBOLT II)

This cannon was designed specifically for destroying tanks and other hard-skinned ground objects. The A-10A Thunderbolt with GAU-8/A system saw extensive service during the Gulf War. It is believed that the AO-17A cannon mounted on the Su-25 is similar to the GAU-8/A.

NPPU-28 (MI-28 HAVOC)

The NPPU-280 gun turret was developed by the Dzerzhinets design bureau of Moscow. The turret was developed to provide a self-contained, single-barreled, 30mm weapon system for use on attack helicopters.

SKYGUARD/OERLIKON (SKYGUARD)

This gun was intended to improve the defensive capability of medium-caliber air defense guns against high technology weapons. Successful demonstrations, in conjunction with a Skyguard fire-control system, were carried out in Austria in 1993. This cannon is used against air targets that are too close to be engaged with missiles.

VSPU-24 (MI-24 HIND-D)

The VPSU-24 is the designation for the under-nose turret specifically designed to be slaved to the Mi-24 Hind's sensor systems.

VULCAN (LAV-300, MH-53 PAVE LOW)

Vulcan series are externally powered Gatling-type cannon that have been steadily evolving from a study begun in 1946. Of these, the M61 was the first, although the Gatling principle of multiple barrels was first used in the mid-19th century.

ZPU-4 (ZPU-4)

The ZPU-4 entered service with the former Soviet Army in 1949. Although no longer in front-line service, it is still used by second-line units defending airfields and other high priority targets. The ZPU-4 is manufactured in China.

MISSILE, ROCKET & BOMB STATS

Warhead. Mass and type of explosive material contained in the missile. **HE b** and **HE c** stand for HE blast and HE contact explosives, respectively.

Targets. Air and/or **G**round — lists targets the missile can be used against in the game (if air is not listed, missile system can only detect and fire against ground targets).

Minimum range. The point closest point at which a target can be hit. (The check for minimum range is done only at launch time — if the target isn't too close, the missile is launched.)

Maximum range. The farthest point at which a target can be hit. (The check for maximum range is done only at launch time — if the target is within range the missile is launched.)

Accuracy percentages. This number is used twice. Before the missile fires, this is the chance the missile system will be able to get a lock on a target that it has located and is tracking. Once the missile has left the rail, this is the base percentage chance that it will hit its target. Even if a missile has a 100% accuracy percentage, the target can still evade it by leaving its field of view (FOV), dropping out of sight, and so forth — if the target is an aircraft, it can also turn on jammers and drop chaff and flares, which reduce the chance that it will get hit.

ECCM/IRCCM strength. Measurement of a missile's ability to counteract jamming. All aircraft targets have a radar and an IR jammer strength rating (see page 27 for a list of these). If a target's jammers are on, its jammer strength rating modifies the accuracy percentages defined above. A radar missile's ECCM or IRCCM strength rating in turn modifies these jammer strength ratings. For example, if a missile has 100% accuracy, but its target's radar jammer rating is 40% and the missile's ECCM rating is 20%, then the missile's accuracy is reduced to 80% (100% + 20% - 40%).

Decoy rejection. Every time a target drops a decoy (chaff for radar-guided missiles, flares for IR-guided missiles), the missile has a certain chance of rejecting the decoy. (If a missile has a decoy rejection rating of 94%, then there is a 94% chance it will ignore the decoy.) If the missile ignores the decoy, it continues on its path toward the target.

Probability of direct hit. Each weapon is rated for its probability of direct hit, or the percent chance that it will inflict full damage against different armor types once it has hit its target. See example, page 40.

Damage points. Total number of damage points a missile can inflict on its target. Size and type of warhead are used to determine probability of direct hit and damage point figures. (A HEAT round is more powerful than HE contact, which is more powerful than HE blast.)

FOV angle (Field of View angle). Total angle the seeker in the nose of a missile can "see" (a missile with a 90° FOV can see objects 45° to either side of its nose).

Maximum speed. Highest speed the missile is capable of attaining, in meters per second.

Maximum acceleration. The missile's max acceleration, in meters per second^2.

Turn rate. Degrees a missile can pivot in one second.

Maximum pitch of launcher. Maximum angle (relative to the horizon) that the launcher can fire.

Minimum pitch of launcher. Minimum angle (relative to the horizon) the launcher can fire. For aircraft launchers this number can be negative. For ground vehicles it will be positive.

	TV-GUIDED		RADAR-GUIDED								
	AGM-65G	AS-14	AIM-7F	AGM-114C	AT-6	MIM-104 A	SA-6	SA-8B	SA-11	SA-15	SA-19
Warhead: Mass (kg)	136	317	39	8	7.4	73	59	40	70	15	9
Type	HEAT	HEAT	HE b	HEAT	HEAT	HE b	HE b	HE b	HE b	HE b	HE b
Targets (Air/Ground)	G	G	A	A/G	G	A	A	A	A	A	A
Maximum range	n.a.	20	20	8	5	160	24	15	30	12	8
Minimum range	n.a.	1.5	1.5	0.5	0.5	1.5	3	1.5	3	1.5	1.5[2]
Accuracy percentages											
Front	100%	100%	75%	99%	79%	91%	67%	71%	75%	75	75%
Aft	100%	100%	71%	99%	79%	87%	63%	67%	71%	71%	71%
Left/right	100%	100%	59%	99%	87%	83%	51%	55%	60%	59%	59%
Top/bottom	100%	100%	79%	99%	91%	94%	71%	75%	79%	79%	79%
ECCM/IRCCM strength	n.a.	n.a.	40%	n.a.	n.a.	60%	20%	35%	55%	50%	40%
Decoy rejection	n.a.	n.a.	87%	n.a.	n.a.	94%	63%	70%	87%	79%	79%
Probability of direct hit											
Light armor	100%	100%	100%	100%	100%	100%	100%	100%	100%	100%	100%
Medium armor	100%	100%	100%	100%	100%	100%	100%	100%	100%	100%	85
Heavy armor	100%	100%	31%	94%	100%	57%	46%	31%	55%	12%	7%
Damage points	6800	6800	780	400	500	1460	1180	800	1400	300	180
FOV angle	20°	20°	120°	50°	40°	120°	80°		60°	180°	120°
Maximum speed (m/s)	350	350	875	350	400	1750	952	840	850	850	900
Maximum accel. (m/s2)	19.7	19.7	240	135	19.6	250	195	250	250	300	250
Turn rate (°/s)	24	24	12.8	25	15	9.6	8.8	15°	13.2	20	12.4
Max. pitch of launcher	n.a.	n.a.	60°	0°	n.a.	60°	60°	60°	80°	85°[1]	80°
Min. pitch of launcher	n.a.	n.a.	0°	0°	n.a.	0°	0°	0°	0°	n.a.	6°

1 This missile is vertically-launched. The launcher will always fire 85° above the horizon.
2 Actual minimum range is probably much shorter than this, but this is the range at which it will switch to guns.

	IR-GUIDED						LASER-GUIDED		UNGUIDED ROCKETS & BOMBS		
	AIM-92C	FIM-92C	SA-7b	SA-9b	SA-13	SA-14	AGM-114A	AT-12	Artillery	FFAR	S-8
Warhead: Mass (kg)	3	3	1	2.6	4	2	8	n.k.	n.a.	4.5	4.5
Type	HE c	HE c	HE c	HE b	HE b	HE c	HEAT	n.k.	n.a.	HE b	HE b
Targets (Air/Ground)	A	A	A	A	A	A	A/G	A/G	G	A/G	A/G
Maximum range	4.5	4.5	3	8	5	4.5	6	8	n.a.	3	3
Minimum range	0.2	0.2	0.26	0.56	0.8	0.26	0.5	0.5	n.a.	n.a.	n.a.
Accuracy percentages											
Front	91%	91%	16%	43%	60%	63%	94%	87%	99%	n.a.	n.a.
Aft	94%	98%	47%	60%	71%	79%	94%	87%	99%	n.a.	n.a.
Right/Left	79%	79%	4%	31%	47%	51%	94%	94%	99%	n.a.	n.a.
Top/Bottom	86%	87%	8%	40%	55%	59%	99%	98%	99%	n.a.	n.a.
ECCM/IRCCM strength	75	75	0	20	40	40%	n.a.	n.a.	n.a.	n.a.	n.a.
Decoy rejection	95	94	20	55	71%	63%	n.a.	n.a.	n.a.	n.a.	n.a.
Probability of direct hit											
Light armor	94%	94%	31%	63%	94%	63%	100%	100%	100%	100%	100%
Medium armor	70%	71%	24%	25%	38%	47%	100%	100%	100%	47%	47%
Heavy armor	12%	12%	4%	2%	3%	8%	94%	94%	100%	4%	4%
Damage points	90	90	30	52	80	60	400	400	*	100	100
FOV angle	80°	40°	10°	50°	50°	80°	50°	50°	90°	90°	90°
Maximum speed (m/s)	770	770	500m	630	700	470	350	400	n.a.	n.a.	n.a.
Max. acceleration (m/s2)	250	250	150	200	150	150	135	195	n.a.	n.a.	n.a.
Turn rate (°/s)	18.2	18.2	14	13.9°	17.8	17.8	25	28	n.a.		n.a.
Max. pitch of launcher	n.a.	70°	60°	80°	80°	50°	0°	0°	n.a.	4°	4°
Min. pitch of launcher	n.a.	10°	0°	-20°	5°	10°	0°	0°	n.a.	-15°	-15°

***Artillery damage points.** Shell: 500; Rocket: 250.

TV-Guided Missiles

AGM-65G MAVERICK (A-10A THUNDERBOLT, DROPPED DURING AIR STRIKES)

The AGM-65 Maverick family has been steadily improved since the mid-1960s. Designed for use against tanks and hardened targets, the later versions have a larger penetrating warhead specifically to attack ships, bunkers and hardened aircraft shelters.

AS-14 "KEDGE" (SU-25)

The AS-14 "Kedge" (Russian designation Kh-29T/L) is a third-generation tactical air-to-surface missile. Developed in the 1970s, it is believed to have entered service around 1980.

Radar-Guided Missiles

AIM-7F SPARROW (SKYGUARD)

The AIM-7F model was the first Sparrow missile to use all-solid-state electronics. Advantages included a condensed the guidance section which, by allowing the warhead to be moved forward on the wings, made room for a more powerful motor. Speed and range were therefore dramatically improved.

AT-6 "SPIRAL" (MI-24, MI-28)

The AT-6 was developed in the 1970s and first seen in an air-to-surface role in the early 1980s. It purportedly has the Russian name Kokon and the designation 9M114. The Russians use ground-launched AT-6 "Spiral" missiles against mobile armoured targets and helicopters.

MIM-104 A PATRIOT (PATRIOT LAUNCHER)

The MIM-104A Patriot missile is shipped, stored and fired from its rectangular box-like container-launcher. The missile requires no testing or maintenance outside the factory; instead, occasional lot-sampling of missiles in the field provides assurance of the weapon's capability.

SA-6 "GAINFUL" (SA-6 LAUNCHER)

Development of the SA-6 began in 1959. Initial service entry was in 1965, but the system (known as *Kub* or "cube" in the CIS) had a prolonged and troubled trial period. It entered full operational service in 1970.

SA-8B "GECKO" (SA-6)

The system, known as *Osa* (Russian for "wasp") or *Romb* ("diamond"), entered service in 1973. It was first seen in public during a parade in Moscow in November 1975.

SA-11 "GADFLY" (SA-11)

Known in the CIS as the *Buk* (Russian for "beech"), and believed to have entered service in 1979-80, significant numbers were not deployed until the late eighties. The complete system, including the radar and support equipment, has the Russian Industrial Index number 9K37.

SA-15 "GAUNTLET" (SA-15)

The SA-15 entered limited service in 1988 and is replacing SA-8 systems at divisional level. The SA-15 is capable of engaging not only aircraft and helicopters, but also remote-piloted vehicles, precision-guided weapons and various types of guided missile. Its CIS designation is *ZRK Tor* (Russian for the Norse folklore god, Thor).

SA-19 "GRISON" (2S6)

The Shipunov design bureau developed this hypersonic, low altitude SAM for use on its 2S6 hybrid tracked air defense gun/missile system. The tube-launched, two-stage missile is mounted in elevatable launcher tube pairs on either side of the turret, and is designed primarily for use against NATO anti-tank helicopters.

IR-Guided Missiles

AIM-92C STINGER (AH-64A AND -D APACHE)

The air-to-air program for the second-generation IR-guided Stinger entered full-scale engineering development in 1984. The missile entered service with the US Army in 1988.

FIM-92C STINGER (AVENGER SAMS, MANPORTABLE LAUNCHERS)

The surface-to-air version of the Stinger missiles have been widely exported, and used with particular success in Afghanistan.

SA-7B "GRAIL" (MANPORTABLE LAUNCHER)

SA-7 "Grail" is the NATO code and designation for this first generation missile (Russian designation 9M32). Development started in 1959, with the SA-7a first entering service in 1966. The "Grail" has been progressively developed since then — in 1971 they introduced the SA-7b "Grail" (Strela-2M) with improved seeker, warhead and motor.

SA-9B "GASKIN" (SA-9)

This first generation IR missile system attained operational status in 1968. Its first combat use was in May 1981, when a Libyan SA-9 battery engaged Israeli aircraft over Lebanon. No hits were made, and the battery was destroyed in a retaliatory airstrike.

SA-13 "GOPHER" (SA-13)

Second-generation IR SA-13 (Russian designation 9M37) missiles are believed to have entered service in 1978. Missiles captured in Angola in 1987 were designated 9M37M — an improved system, including better IRCCM capabilities and a long ranged seeker.

SA-14 "GREMLIN" (KA-50, MANPORTABLE LAUNCHER)

Development purportedly began circa 1970. A successor to SA-7 "Grail," the missile first entered service in 1974. Exports of the SAM version have been widely reported.

Laser-Guided Missiles

AT-12 (KA-50)

A missile first seen at the 1991 Dubai Air Show with the Russian name *Vikhr* (designator 9M120) is believed to be the NATO-designated AT-12. An alternative Russian name might be *Ataka*. The Russians were displaying the missile for export and described it as an Anti-Tank Laser Beam Rider.

Unguided Rockets & Bombs

S-8 (KA-50, MI-24, MI-28, SU-25)

This family of 80mm rockets was developed in the late 1970 to provide the Russian armed forces and their former allies a wide range of ground attack options. They were designed to be fired from at least two known launchers carried by either fixed- or rotary-winged aircraft.

TAKING HITS

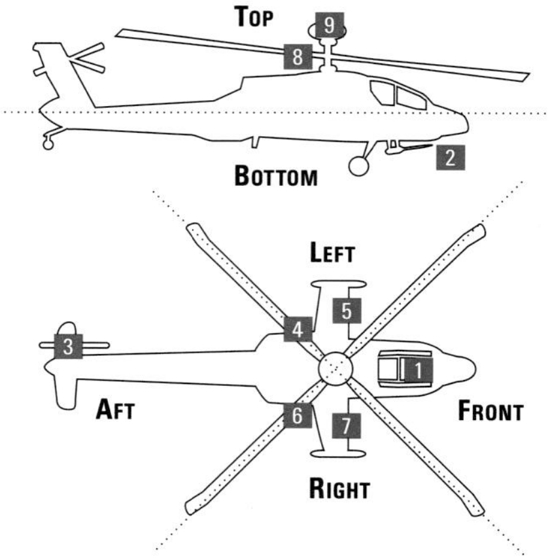

Your helicopter is divided into six sections — front, aft, left, right, top and bottom. Each of these sections houses some of the helicopter's systems and components. The damage done to these components determines the extent of damage done to the helicopter.

When a missile hits you, it hits a particular section. There is a certain percent chance that it will do damage to a component in that section. If it does not do damage to a component in that section, it will do damage to a randomly chosen system somewhere else on the helicopter.

Let's say a soldier standing directly in front of you fires an SA-7 at you, and this SA-7 hits the front of your aircraft. There is a 16% percent chance that your cockpit will be damaged by this hit. There is an 8% chance that your cannon will be damaged. There is a 76% chance that something else on your aircraft (chosen at random) will be damaged.

The following table lists the percentage chance that a system will be damaged *when its section is hit*. The information in the table applies to both the AH-64A and AH-64D, except that since the A-model does not have a radar dome — for the A-model there is no chance that the Longbow Radar will be hit.

Hit Location	Systems/ Components	% Chance System is Damaged
Front	1 Cockpit	16
	2 Cannon	8
Aft	3 Tail Rotor	20
Left	4 Left Engine	39
	5 Left Wing	20
Right	6 Right Engine	39
	7 Right Wing	20
Top	8 Main Rotor	39
	9 Longbow Radar	8
Bottom	10 None	0

If a system is already destroyed, there is no chance that it will get hit again.

How much damage can a system take?

Each of the systems on the aircraft can withstand a certain maximum amount of damage.

System	Max Dam Points
Cannon	10
Cockpit	50
L/R Engine	60
L/R Wing	40
Longbow Radar	20
Main Rotor	50
Tail Rotor	40

If a system is hit by a missile delivering more damage points than the system can take, then 10% of the remaining damage points are distributed randomly to another system. For example, if a Stinger with 90 points of damage hits your left engine, which can take up to 60, 10% of the remaining 30 points (or 3 points) is applied to another system, picked at random.

HOW DAMAGE AFFECTS PERFORMANCE

The System MFD page lists the status of each of the systems. Systems with up to 50% damage are listed as OK. At over 50% damage, a system is listed as MARGINAL. At 100% damage, it is INOPERABLE.

Cannon. When MARG, it stops tracking targets. When INOP, it stops firing. The chance that your gun will overheat increases slightly as your gun takes damage.

Cockpit. At the INOP damage level, you die.

Left/Right Engine. Once one of your engines reaches INOP, it stops. Engine torque on the remaining engine increases, since it is having to work harder. Your rotor RPM will drop unless you reduce your collective to about 50% (hit [5]). Reduce collective further if rotor RPM continues to drop.

It is best if you disengage your rotor completely (hit [R]) and make an autorotational landing if one engine goes out completely. Land while you still can.

If both engines go out, disengage your rotor immediately and begin an autorotational landing. Your rotor RPM, and thus your lift, will quickly drop to zero if you have dead engines connected to your rotor.

Left/Right Wing. With MARG damage, your Stinger station stops firing. At 75%, your outboard pylon stops firing. Once INOP, your inboard pylon stops firing. Also, above MARG damage to the left or right you will notice the aircraft begin to roll slightly in toward the damaged side. Rolling will increase as damage increases, and there's not much you can do to counteract it.

Longbow Radar. Once INOP, you lose your radar. Your sensor systems switch to TADS target acquisition mode, and you will no longer be able to switch back to FCR mode or fire RF Hellfires. The Radar MFD page goes blank. (If you try to fire RF Hellfires, INVALID MODE will appear in the Weapon Inhibit Field of your IHADSS.)

Main Rotor. You lose lift, control and forward thrust as you take damage. With MARG damage your main rotor rpm will begin to drop and the helicopter will begin to pitch towards the ground. This will increase as your damage increases. Once INOP, you're operating at about 70% of normal lift and control.

Tail Rotor. As you take damage, your chopper will begin to yaw to the right. To reduce this effect, lower your collective. Once INOP, you won't be able to turn to the left at all when you're hovering. The yaw to the right is reduced somewhat by airspeed — higher speeds might help you maintain straight flight.

SCORING

There are two "career tracks" for a Longbow pilot. There is the campaign, where success means you've survived and met your campaign mission objectives, and there is a running cumulative score, which determines your eligibility for promotion and certain medals.

You earn a score for every campaign, historical and single mission you fly. These mission scores are tallied, and a cumulative score is kept for each pilot you create.

MISSION SCORE

Your score for each mission is based on your Kill Points for that mission, modified by other factors.

MODIFIERS

- Realism Modifier (RM)
- Flight Model Modifier (FM)
- Enemy Modifier (EM)
- Landing Modifier (LM)
- Success Modifier (SM)

EQUATION

$$\textbf{Score} = \frac{(\text{Kill Points} \times \text{RM} \times \text{FM} \times \text{EM} \times \text{LM} \times \text{SM}) + \text{Bonus Points}}{\text{Number of FARP Landings}}$$

In order to get the highest score, you not only need to rack up as high a kill total as you can, but you want to score as close to 100% as you can in the modifier categories and earn your bonus points, without coming back to refuel.

Kill points for objects are given in the following section. The modifier categories and how to up your score in them are explained in detail on p. 50-52.

Note: *The options used to calculate your Realism Modifier, Flight Model Modifier and Enemy Modifier scores can be changed during flight. Your modifier scores in these categories change when you change these options, and your mission score from that point on is calculated with the new modifier scores. See* ***Realism Modifier, Flight Model Modifier*** *and* ***Enemy Modifier****,* *p. 50-52* *for more details.*

Kill Points

You earn points during a mission for every object you destroy. The values of objects differ.

- You earn kill points for every enemy you and your wingman destroy.
- You don't earn any points for enemies destroyed by air strikes or artillery strikes that you call in.
- Aircraft on the ground are worth 100 points (-100 for friendlies), regardless of type.
- You lose points for every friendly that you or your wingman destroy. You lose 500 points for any A-10 or C-130 that gets shot down, and 100 points for any other type of friendly object destroyed (including infantry and structures).
- You don't lose any points for friendlies destroyed by enemies.
- You lose 100 points for killing each friendly (except A-10s and C-130s which cost you 500 points) no matter what options you have chosen.

ENEMY POINT VALUES

Helicopters

Ka-50	300
Mi-28	300
Mi-24	300

Planes

Su-25	500

Radar

Dog Ear	200
Bar Lock	200
Spoon Rest	200
Long Track	200
Straight Flush	200
Snow Drift	200
Skyguard Radar	200

Artillery

BM-25	150
SCUD-C	200
SO-122	150

SAMS/AAA

2S6	250
LAV-300 AAA	150
SA-8	250
SA-9	200
SA-13	200
SA-15	250
ZSU-23-4	150
SA-6	100
SA-11	100
SA-11 Command Post	200
Skyguard Launcher	100
Skyguard Gun	150
ZPU-4	150

Tanks

T-72M	150
T-80U	150

APCs/IFVs

BMP-2	100
BMP-3	100
BRDM-2	100
BTR-80	100
LAV-300	100

Trucks

Truck	50
URL Jeep	50
Fuel Truck	50

Infantry*

Soldier	40

*Includes infantry armed with manportable SA-14, SA-7 and Stinger SAM launchers.

Structures

Bunker (any type)	150
POW Tower	150

Realism Modifier

The more realistic options you choose, the higher your score. Your level of realism is computed for each kill based on the options you have active on the REALISM option menu. This modifier can range from 0 to 100% (0 to 1.00)

Note: *If you set WEAPONS LOAD to UNLIMITED AMMO or INVULNERABILITY to ON at any time during the mission, your score for that mission will not be added to your pilot's cumulative score. You will see the score on the chalkboard at your debrief, but it won't count toward medals or promotions.*

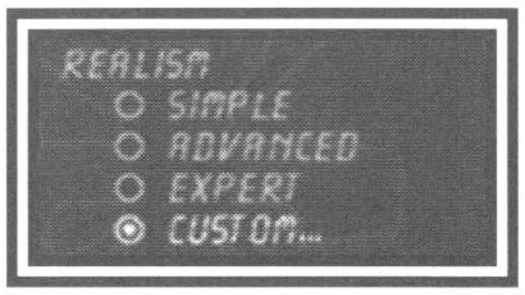

1.00 EXPERT (or all custom options on)

.86 ADVANCED

.66 SIMPLE (default)

If REALISM is set on CUSTOM, subtract the following from 1.00 for all that apply:

-.10 If LANDINGS is set on EASY.

-.20 If LANDINGS is set on NO CRASHES.

-.02 If REALISTIC JAMMERS is off.

-.02 If REALISTIC TADS TARGETING is off.

-.30 If REALISTIC WEAPON DAMAGE is off.

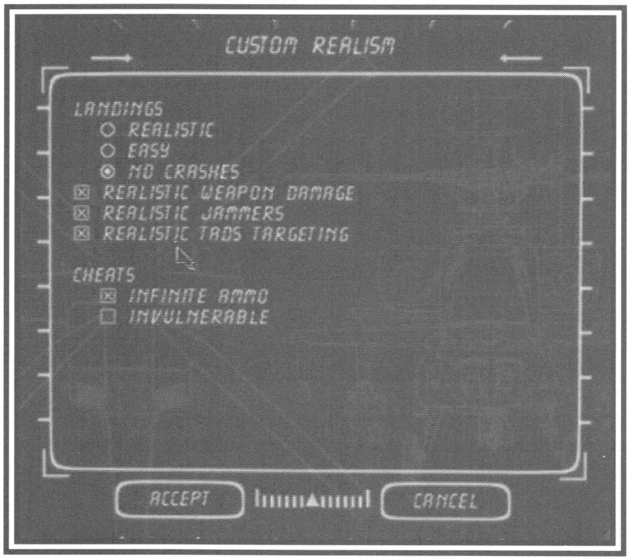

The remainder is your realism modifier. In other words, if you are flying with LANDINGS set on NO CRASHES and everything else set on realistic, and your destroy a Spoon Rest radar vehicle, you earn 160 points (200 x .8).

Flight Model Modifier

You are also rewarded for flying with a realistic flight model, but the stakes aren't quite as high. Your flight model score is determined by the flight model options you have selected on the option menu and can range from 83% to 100% (.83 to 1.00)

1.00	EXPERT (or all options under custom are active)
.94	ADVANCED
.83	SIMPLE (default)

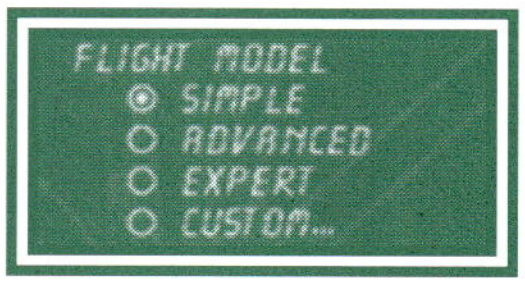

If FLIGHT MODEL is set on CUSTOM subtract the following from 1.00 for all options that are ***off***.

-.03	REALISTIC COLLECTIVE
-.01	GROUND EFFECT
-.01	WEIGHT EFFECTS
-.01	TRANSLATIONAL LIFT
-.04	FULLY AEROBATIC
-.04	FULL DYNAMICS
-.01	ALTITUDE EFFECTS
-.01	WIND
-.01	TURBULENCE

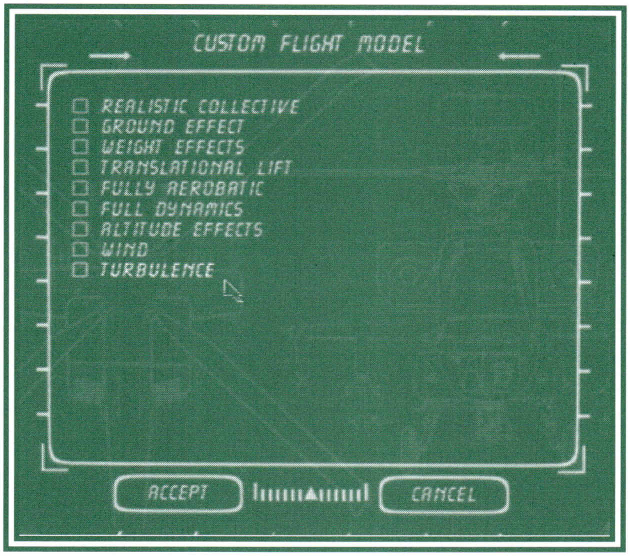

Enemy Modifier

The category of enemy you have active on the menu is also factored into your score for each kill. Your enemy's skill level is determined by a sliding bar on the GAMEPLAY option menu; the percentages marked show the score modifier for a killing an enemy at each level.

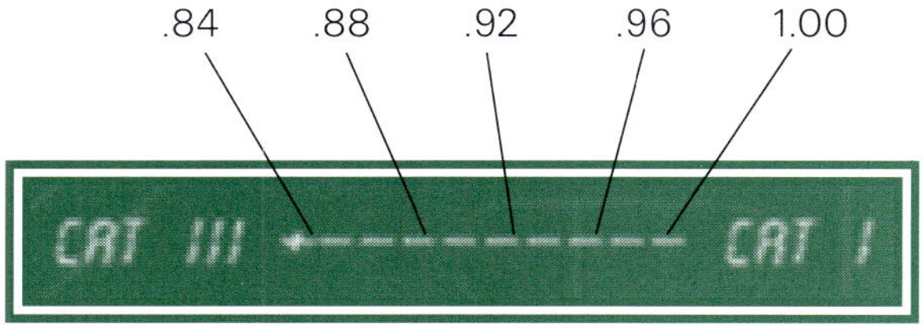

Landing Modifier

To get a 1.00 Landing Modifier, land at a FARP — as close to the tents as you can without hitting them.

1.00	You finished the mission at a FARP.
.80	You finished the mission anywhere else (including crashes, captures or even quitting out of the mission).

Success Modifier

You are rewarded for achieving your mission objectives. Your objectives may be to kill, sight, rescue or defend a certain number of primaries. How many primaries you actually kill, sight, rescue or defend determines whether you succeed or fail. A rough idea of the success/failure categories is given below, but these can vary greatly from mission to mission. See the individual mission notes, p. 66-169, for exact numbers for each mission.

1.00	SUCCESS+ (S+)	More than 90% of primaries
.90	SUCCESS (S)	60-90% of primaries
.50	FAIL (F)	Less than 60% of primaries
.25	FAIL– (F–)	*No* primaries

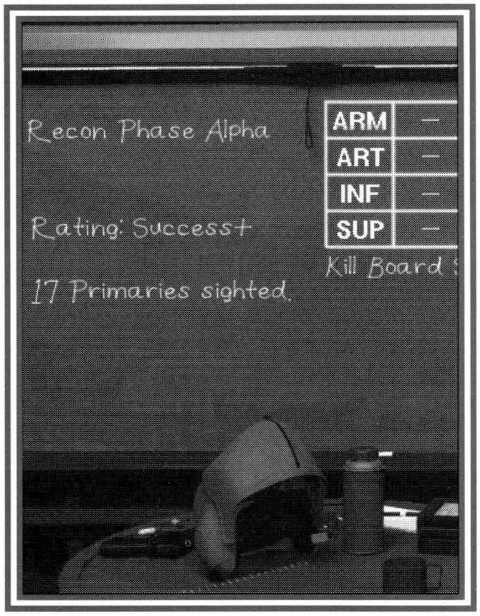

Bonus Points

You get 1000 bonus points for flying a SUCCESS or SUCCESS+ mission. This score is added *after* all of the modifiers so you get the entire 1000 points, no matter what enemy skill and realism levels you flew with. It pays to meet your objectives.

Number of FARP Landings

Once your points are tallied as described above, this total is divided by the number of times you landed at a FARP. Think about that — your entire score is cut in half if you return to refuel or re-arm only once (1 rearming landing + 1 final landing = 2 landings). *Get the job done the first time out.*

Example Equation

Let's say you fly an entire mission against CATEGORY 1 enemies, with Realism and Flight Model options set on ADVANCED. You kill 1 Spoon Rest radar vehicle and 3 2S6s, without coming back to re-arm or refuel. You land at your final waypoint, and your superiors declare that you have flown a SUCCESS (but not SUCCESS+) mission.

SCORE FACTORS

Kill Points	950 (1 Spoon Rest = 200, 3 2S6s = 3 x 250)
Realism Modifier	.86
Flight Model Modifier	.94
Enemy Modifier	1.00
Landing Modifier	1.00
Success Modifier	.90
Bonus Points	1000
# of FARP Landings	1

EQUATION

$$\frac{(950 \times .86 \times .94 \times 1.00 \times 1.00 \times .90) + 1000}{1} = 1691$$

PROMOTIONS

You begin your tour as an Apache pilot with the rank of Warrant Officer (WO1). Your career path follows a simple, linear pattern — assuming you make the cut. You are promoted to the following ranks as you earn the cumulative scores listed.

2000	Chief Warrant 2 (CW2)
6000	Chief Warrant 3 (CW3)
10,000	Chief Warrant 4 (CW4)
16,000	Chief Warrant 5 (CW5)
22,000	2nd Lieutenant (2nd Lt.)
30,000	1st Lieutenant (1st Lt.)
40,000	Captain (Capt.)
75,000	Major (Maj.)
100,000	Lieutenant Colonel (Lt. Col.)
150,000	Colonel (Col.)

Game Commendations

The table below lists the commendations awarded in the game and the criteria for earning them. A history of the medals follows.

Important Note: *To earn an award for a mission, you have to successfully complete it. Scoring 9000 in a mission won't earn you a Distinguished Flying Cross if you can't meet your mission objectives.*

Award	Single Mission Score	Additional Requirements
1 Congressional Medal of Honor	11,000	100,000 cumulative score
2 Distinguished Service Award	10,000	75,000 cumulative score
3 Silver Star	9000	
4 Legion of Merit	8000	
5 Distinguished Flying Cross	6000	Awarded no more than once every 3 missions
6 Bronze Star	4000	Awarded no more than once every 4 missions
7 Air Medal	2000	Awarded no more than once every 5 missions
8 Army Commendation	1000	Awarded no more than once every 7 missions
9 Army Service Ribbon	N/A	Every pilot you create begins with this ribbon – it means you've graduated flight school
10 Purple Heart	N/A	Successful return (to any friendly FARP) with 3 or more parts of your chopper damaged
11 Armed Forces Expeditionary Medal	N/A	1 Overseas Service Ribbon in every theater
12 Overseas Service Ribbon	N/A	3 successful missions in Desert Storm or Just Cause, or 5 successful in Baltic Hammer
13 Liberation of Kuwait	N/A	6 successful missions in Desert Storm
14 SW Asia Service Ribbon	N/A	3 successful missions in Desert Storm
15 Baltic Hammer Service Ribbon	N/A	Successfully completing campaign

Medals

1. CONGRESSIONAL MEDAL OF HONOR

Initially created by Congress for the Navy in 1861, this is the only medal worn around the neck awarded in the Armed Forces. It was officially adopted by the Army in 1904 and is the highest decoration given to personnel in the Armed Forces. It consists of a blue neck ribbon and one of several anchors or trophies affixed to a bronze, five-pointed star. In the star's center is the Roman goddess of righteousness and wisdom on the battlefield.

The Congressional Medal of Honor may be awarded during war or peacetime to anyone who risks his or her life above and beyond the call of duty. A person may receive this medal one time only — subsequent medals are gold stars pinned to the original ribbon.

2. DISTINGUISHED SERVICE AWARD

The Distinguished Service Award was first authorized in 1918 by the United States Army as a replacement for the Certificate of Merit, which was awarded to private soldiers not eligible for commissions or brevet promotions. The Navy and Air Force adopted the Distinguished Service Award in 1919 and 1947, respectively.

The award is given to soldiers who demonstrate exceptional heroism and risk their lives during combat, although some have been given to those performing several acts of merit off of the battlefield. Subsequent awards are gold stars.

3. SILVER STAR MEDAL

First presented in 1918, the Silver Star replaced the original silver citation stars, which were pinned onto service ribbons for specific campaigns. In 1932, wearers of the citation stars were authorized to trade them in for a Silver Star. Today, this decoration recognizes individuals who demonstrate singular or successive acts of extraordinary heroism during combat. The Silver Star is the third-highest ranking award, just below the Congressional Medal of Honor and the Navy Cross. Successive awards are oak-leaf clusters.

4. LEGION OF MERIT

The Legion of Merit award was first established by Congress in 1942 and is awarded to soldiers of any rank whose meritorious conduct and excellent service distinguish them from their fellow soldiers. This decoration is given both during war and peacetime operations.

For foreign and high-ranking officers, the award has four different degrees of merit according to rank: Chief Commander, Commander, Officer, and Legionnaire of the Legion of Merit. Badges are sometimes placed on the service ribbons to designate the rank of the recipient.

5. DISTINGUISHED FLYING CROSS

Established in 1926, the Flying Cross is awarded to aircrew members who voluntarily perform an exceptional act of heroism or achievement during combat or non-combat flight. (Unlike the Distinguished Service Cross, this award cannot be used to reward extended bravery in combat.) Subsequent Army awards are bronze oak-leaf clusters; in the other branches they are gold stars. In some cases, the Distinguished Flying Cross has been given to foreign airmen serving with American forces in wartime conditions.

6. BRONZE STAR

Specific to the Army since 1944, the Bronze Star is given to soldiers who demonstrate heroism during combat, or to civilians or foreign personnel not directly involved in combat. The Bronze Star falls just behind the Legion of Merit and the Silver Star. It parallels the requirements of the Silver Star to a lesser degree (the act does not need to be quite as heroic). Multiple Bronze Star awards denoted by oak leaf clusters.

7. AIR MEDAL

The Air Medal was established in 1942 and is awarded to airborne Army individuals that perform meritorious acts in combat or non-combat situations. The Air Medal award ranks below the Distinguished Flying Cross but is nearly equal to the Silver Star.

This award was often given in Vietnam to crews who flew many combat-support missions, and some airmen received dozens of them. Successive awards are denoted by bronze (Arabic) numerals pinned to the ribbon.

8. ARMY COMMENDATION MEDAL

In 1944, the Navy became the first service branch to implement a medal and a letter of commendation for notable acts during combat. The other armed forces followed suit, and the Army Commendation Ribbon was adopted in 1945. Later, a medal was added to the ribbon and the award was redesignated as the Army Commendation Medal.

This decoration can be awarded to any armed forces member serving with the Army who exemplifies remarkable heroism or meritorious service. It may also be given to soldiers in friendly, foreign forces who significantly contribute to an operation. Succeeding awards consist of oak-leaf clusters (ground soldiers and air crews) or gold stars (sea-borne soldiers).

9. ARMY SERVICE RIBBON

The Army Service Ribbon was implemented in 1981 and is awarded to Army, Army Reserve or Army National Guard soldiers who complete basic training. Those pursuing a specialty skill or Military Occupation Skill (MOS) are eligible after four months' service. The five colors on this ribbon denote the completion of initial training in several areas.

10. PURPLE HEART

This popular honor evolved from the Badge of Military Merit, which was established during George Washington's presidency in 1782. A new version bearing Washington's likeness was reinstated by Congress on the 200th anniversary of his birth (1932), replacing the gold chevrons worn by wounded soldiers during World War I.

Anyone seriously wounded during combat is awarded this medal. The wound must be a result of an outside enemy or force. Subsequent wounds (but not multiple wounds during the same incident) are recognized by Gold Stars.

Campaign Awards

The military awards campaign medals (also called service medals) to all members of the armed forced who actively serve in major American wars and engagements. They may be awarded to anyone participating in a campaign, regardless of whether or not that person was directly involved in combat. American servicemen participating in Korea, Vietnam, Panama and Desert Storm all received one or more campaign awards for their involvement.

Sometimes, additional medals are authorized for certain campaigns. Several of the awards discussed in the next section were awarded for service in Vietnam, Korea, Grenada, Panama and the Gulf during specific dates.

11. ARMED FORCES EXPEDITIONARY MEDAL

Implemented in 1961, this medal is given to soldiers who participate in U.S. military operations or support United Nations activities. The operation may have a number of purposes, including administration, military maneuvers, training, strategic defense, or direct combat.

Soldiers who served in the Persian Gulf after July 24, 1987 or in Panama between December 20, 1989 and January 31, 1990 are eligible for this medal. Those who receive expeditionary medals in two different arenas receive a bronze star as their second award.

12. OVERSEAS SERVICE RIBBON

Established at the same time as the Army Service Ribbon, this ribbon is given to Army, Army Reserve or Army National Guard soldiers who complete an overseas tour. The Overseas Service Ribbon is not given, however, if a service medal already exists for that tour (such as the Southwest Asia Service Medal for the Persian Gulf conflict). Persons receiving multiple Overseas Service Ribbons are awarded bronze Arabic numerals.

13. KUWAIT LIBERATION MEDAL.

Recipients of this award must have served in Kuwait, Iraq, Saudi Arabia or surrounding war zone areas during Operation Desert Storm/Desert Shield. The award was established in 1992.

14. SOUTHWEST ASIA SERVICE MEDAL

This medal was established after the conclusion of the Gulf War. It is awarded to those U.S. military personnel who served in the defense of Saudi Arabia, the liberation of Kuwait, or the cease-fire campaign.

15. BALTIC HAMMER SERVICE RIBBON

(Fictional award) The **Operation Baltic Force Award** was recently proposed by the Sec. of Defense for ground and airborne units deployed for more than 10 days in Ukraine or on the Crimean peninsula. It has not yet been approved, but is expected to enter distribution by early 1997.

Cav Pocket TACSOP
Annex G (AH-64 Considerations)

Revised August 1994

5. Rules of Engagement:

A. If a target commits a hostile act it will be engaged immediately.

B. If a target cannot be visually identified as hostile, it will be engaged until confirmed as a hostile by at least one report from US or Allied forces in contact with the target.

(3) Deep attack operations assume all military assets on the enemy side of the FLOT to be hostile unless otherwise briefed.

C. Engagement Priorities:

(1) Immediate treat to self
(2) Immediate threat to team members
(3) Immediate threat to ground forces
(4) Other targets in priority

D. Target Priority:

(1) ADA
(2) Command and Control
(3) Armored/Anti-Tank
(4) Artillery/Lt Armor
(5) Combat Service Support
(6) Dismounted Troops

6. Air-to-air operations:

A. General: The principals of ATA combat are to avoid detection, see the threat first, recognize the threat, decide to engage, fire first, and be unpredictable. A minimum of two aircraft, flying in a mutually supporting formation, are required to avoid detection, and support each other if attacked by enemy aircraft. Good terrain flight techniques, continuous observation of all sectors, and crew coordination can preclude being surprised by enemy aircraft.

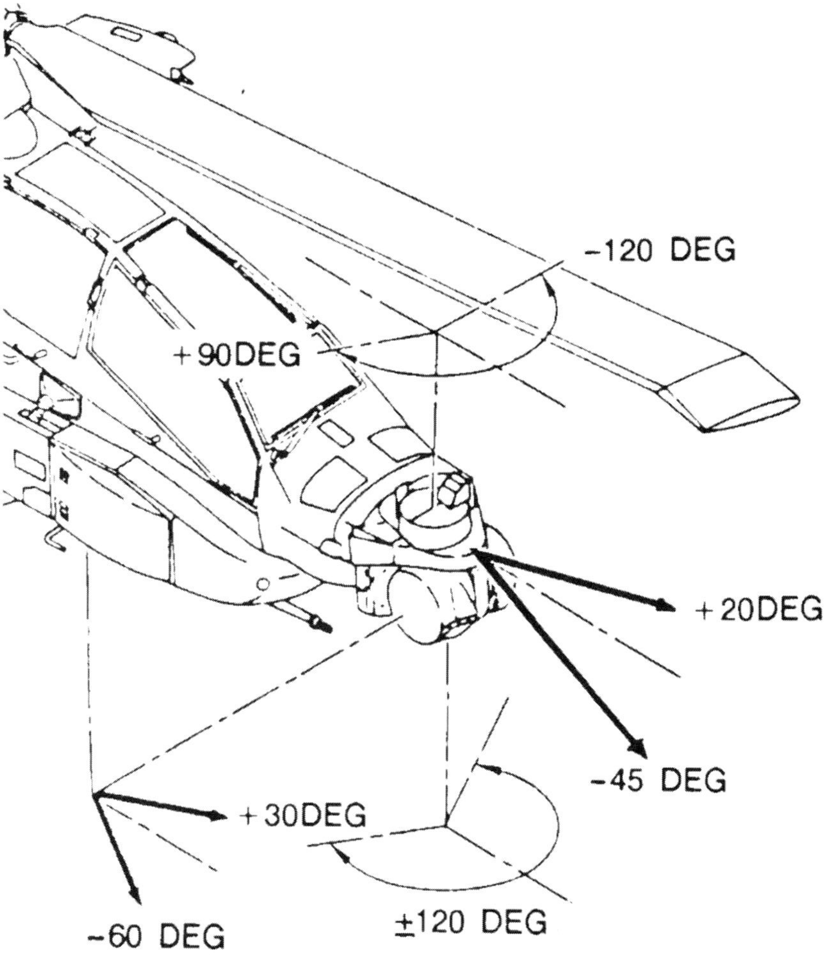
-120 DEG
+90DEG
+20DEG
-45 DEG
+30DEG
-60 DEG
±120 DEG

MISSION ANALYSES

The box at the top of each analysis details important information about the mission:

Mission. Lists your objective. *Recon* — sight your primaries without firing; *Attack* — destroy your primaries; *Escort* — prevent friendly primaries from being destroyed; and *Rescue* — cover transport choppers and troops being rescued.

Environment. Lists weather conditions and time of day for the mission.

Primaries. Lists the number and type of all primary objective targets. These are the targets you have to defend, sight or destroy in order to win the mission.

Air/Artillery Strikes. Lists how many you can call during the mission.

Mission Rating. Tells you what the definitions are for a Success+, Success, Failure and Failure– ratings in the mission.

Maps

Each mission analysis has two types of maps. The **gray map** at the top is an unzoomed shot showing all waypoints, friendly FARPs and SAM detection range circles. Key areas on this map are enlarged and detailed in the green maps.

This symbol marks additional friendly FARPs on the gray map.

WAYPOINT 2(3) **Waypoint Number**

The green bar at the top of each green map corresponds with a waypoint description in the text. If you have been advised to create additional waypoints in the mission text, the original waypoint number will be followed by a number in parentheses — the parenthetical number is the new waypoint number if you created all of the additional recommended waypoints. A shot of the map with the new player waypoint tells you where the recommended waypoints should go.

Zoom Factor

The number in this box tells how many times the zoom button on the mission planning screen was clicked for the map shown. The basic briefing map is 50km across. Scales for zoomed maps are as follows:

Zoom Factor	1	2	3	4	5	6	7	8
Scale Across	25km	12km	6km	3km	2km	1km	0.8km	0.5km

On some systems, 1 click (25km) is as far as the map will zoom in.

Map Symbols. Boxes are used to mark the locations of objects and key terrain features on the maps. The boxes are color-coded:

☐ Enemy primaries ■ Other enemies ☐ Friendly primaries ☐ Other Feature

The numbers in the boxes correspond to the key beneath the map — the key lists the number and exact type of object or feature marked by the box.

A white arrow shows the direction an object is moving. (You may not encounter objects exactly where they are marked on the map.)

Notes

One of the greatest dangers for a helicopter unit is dated intelligence. Our goal is to provide you with an accurate idea of what's out there — including current intelligence on enemy positions and an understanding of the local terrain.

The text of the mission notes describes what you can expect at each waypoint and along your flight path. Your flight path is not fixed — part of your job is to plot your best course to the target. In some missions, there are suggestions for creating additional waypoints to take advantage of hills and valleys. When additional waypoints are suggested, the new waypoint numbers will be in parentheses after the original numbers.

Any mention of scoring is made with the assumption that you are flying with REALISM, FLIGHT MODEL, and ENEMY options set to EXPERT and CATEGORY I (these options are on the GAMEPLAY screen of the **IN-FLIGHT OPTION** menu). The default settings are much lower, but having them low reduces your score. (A certain percentage is deducted if you have simpler settings active — see **Scoring**, p. 48, for more info.) If you're after a high score, press [Alt][O] to get to the **IN-FLIGHT OPTION** menu and set the options on harder settings.

CAMPAIGN FLOWCHART NOTES

The flowchart on the next page is a schematic of possible ways to progress through the campaign. There are three "paths" in the campaign — the winning path (missions 1-29), the losing path (missions 30-38), and an intermediate path (missions 50, 60, 70 and 80) that connects them. You can move back and forth between these paths — if you end up on the losing path, it's usually possible to get back on track and still win the campaign.

Missions listed together in a box belong to a series. At the end of the series, the number of missions you've won determines where you go next. (The only exception to this is the first mission — if you lose it, you get court-martialed, and your pilot's career is over.)

(2-4) The green circles at the lower left corners of each box point out where you go after *winning* the number of missions specified — 2-4 means winning 2 to 4 missions.

Crucial missions are worth double — if you win them, it's counted as winning two missions; if you lose them, it's counted as two losses. (This doesn't affect your score in the mission, just your progress in the campaign.) Missions worth double have a 2 in parentheses after them.

(*CIS Threatens Stability*)

Inside the white ovals are the names of the movies you will see as you progress through a series. The movie is listed right after the mission it will follow. (You will only see *SCUD Threat Eliminated* if you win mission 15; otherwise, you will see each movie no matter how well you do in the mission before it.)

BALTIC CAMPAIGN FLOWCHART

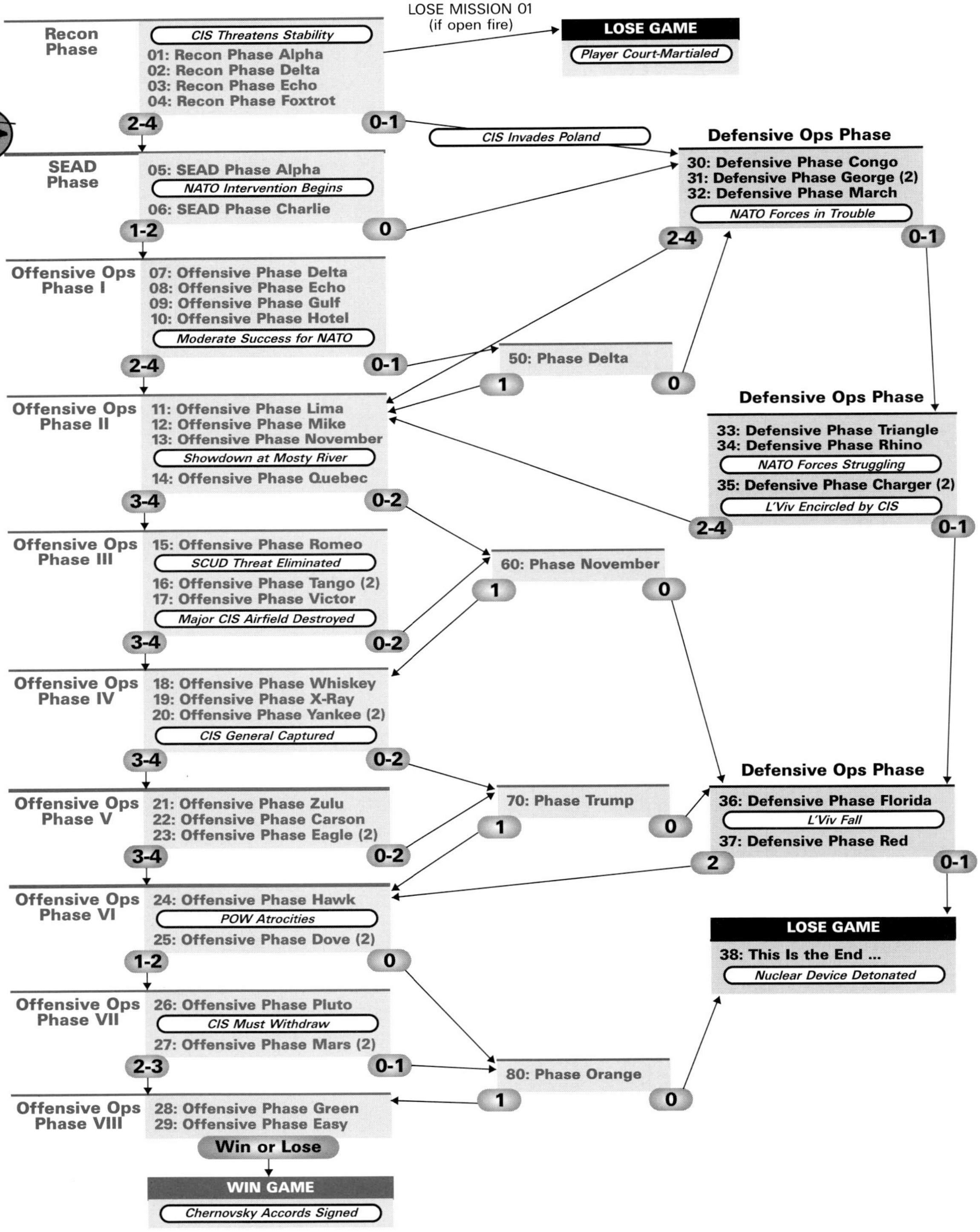

Campaign Missions Chart

Winning Missions		Environment	Objective	F-	F	S	S+
1	Recon Phase Alpha	Day/Clear	Recon Tanks	0[1]	1-6	7-15	16+
2	Recon Phase Delta	Night/Clear	Recon Armor	0[1]	1-5	6-7	8+
3	Recon Phase Echo	Night/Cloudy/Hazy	Recon Artillery	0[1]	1-3	4-6	–
4	Recon Phase Foxtrot	Night/Clear	Recon EW Site	0[1]	1	2-3	
5	SEAD Phase Alpha	Dawn-to-Day/Clear	Attack EW Site	–	0	1	–
6	SEAD Phase Charlie	Dusk-to-Dark/Clear	Attack SA-11 Site	0	1-4	5-8	9
7	Offensive Phase Delta	Day/Clear	Attack Armor	0	1-7	8-9	10+
8	Off. Phase Echo	Night/Cloudy/Haze	Attack Convoy	0	1-5	6-9	10+
9	Off. Phase Gulf	Night-to-Dawn/Clear	Attack TAC Post	0	1-3	4+	–
10	Off. Phase Hotel	Day/Clear	Attack Commo Site	0	1-6	7	–
11	Off. Phase Lima	Day/Clear	Escort US Armor	0	1-3	4-5	6
12	Off. Phase Mike	Night/Clear	Attack MLRSs	0	1-2	3-5	–
13	Off. Phase November	Night/Clear	Attack Choppers	0	1-3	4-5	6
14	Off. Phase Quebec	Dawn-To-Day/Clear	Attack Enemy FARP	0	1-4	5	–
15	Off. Phase Romeo	Night/Clear	Attack SCUDs	0	1-2	3-4	5
16	Off. Phase Tango	Night/Clear	Escort US Armor	0	1-7	8-10	11
17	Off. Phase Victor	Dawn-To-Day/Clear	Attack Airfield	0	1-4	5-7	8
18	Off. Phase Whiskey	Day/Clear	Attack Depot	0	1-5	6	–
19	Off. Phase X-Ray	Night/Clear	Destroy Convoy	0[2]	1-3[2]	4[2]	–
20	Off. Phase Yankee	Day/Clear	Attack TOC Post	0	1-3	4	–
21	Off. Phase Zulu	Day/Cloudy	Rescue US Pilot	–	2[3]	2[3]	–
22	Off. Phase Carson	Dusk-to-Night/Clear	Attack Convoy	0	1-4	5-8	9
23	Off. Phase Eagle	Day/Clear	Attack Choppers	0	1-3	4-5	6
24	Off. Phase Hawk	Dusk/Clear	Attack Airfield	0	1-6	7-8	9+
25	Off. Phase Dove	Dawn/Clear	Rescue POW	0	1[4]	2[4]	3-4
26	Off. Phase Pluto	Day/Haze	Destroy MRLSs	0	1-6	7	–
27	Off. Phase Mars	Dawn-To-Day/Cloudy	Attack Units in L'viv	0	1-5	6	–
28	Off. Phase Green	Day/Clear	Attack SAM Site	0	1-4	5	–
29	Off. Phase Easy	Night/Clear	Attack Maint. Site	0	1-4	5-6	7

Losing Missions		Objective	Environment	F-	F	S	S+
30	Defensive Phase Congo	Day/Cloudy	Attack Artillery	0	1-3	4	–
31	Def. Phase George	Night/Clear	Attack Armor	0	1-9	10-17	18
32	Def. Phase March	Dawn-To-Day/Cloudy	Attack Mobile SAMs	0	1-7	8	–
33	Def. Phase Triangle	Night/Clear	Attack Choppers	0	1-4	5	–
34	Def. Phase Rhino	Day/Clear	Attack SCUDs	0	1-3	4-5	6
35	Def. Phase Charger	Dusk/Cloudy	Attack BMPs	0	1-9	10-18	19
36	Def. Phase Florida	Day/Clear	Attack Armor	0	1-7	8-10	11
37	Def. Phase Red	Dusk/Cloudy	Attack Choppers	0	1-2	3	–
38	This Is the End ...	Day/Clear	Retreat	Automatic Fail		–	–

Intermediate Missions		Objective	Environment	F-	F	S	S+
50	Phase Delta	Night/Cloudy	Destroy Ammo depot	0	1-8	9	–
60	Phase November	Day/Cloudy	Attack Tank Column	0	1-6	7-10	11
70	Phase Trump	Dusk-to-Dark/Cloudy	Attack Refueling Depot	0	1-3	4	–
80	Phase Orange	Dawn/Clear	Attack Choppers, FARP	0	1-3	4	–

[1]Failure if you shoot any enemy targets
[2]Number of friendly helicopters that survive
[3]Failure if MH-53 or pilot killed, success if both survive
[4]Number of friendly SAR helicopters that survive

CAMPAIGN DESIGN

The Ukraine campaign was designed by Mike Francis. In designing the missions, Mike drew on experience he gained in fifteen years as a Military Intelligence Analyst. He served in Desert Storm and was involved in planning operations for Just Cause. He comments:

I wanted to simulate a Soviet combined-arms army facing an American corps in the field. The phases are simple — there's a Recon Phase, a Suppression of Enemy Air Defense (SEAD) Phase, and the actual Offensive Phase. These are basic phases of any offensive operation.

Although commanders have satellite-intercept and other types of intelligence information, it might be hours or even days old. A commander wants to *see* what's in front of him, and that's the purpose of the Recon Phase. Using a helicopter like the Longbow Apache is one of the best ways to get this information in a timely manner. One of its primary duties is looking for air defense units along the axis of attack.

After this comes a SEAD Phase. The Apache's role here would be conducting pinpoint strikes against air defense installations. This provides a clear path for other Division units to move in, and it also aids the Air Force by clearing areas in which the risk of sending in a jet is great.

In this game, we are using the Apache in the role of *force multiplier* for the Offensive Phase. The Apache can be considered a force multiplier because a couple of Apaches can do what an entire company of tanks would be able to do in the same amount of time. The Apache has the potential for destroying at least eight targets (eight Hellfires, so eight targets) and it can be moved in and out of areas very quickly. It can spearhead an offensive, fight a rear guard, do pinpoint strikes, and even hold ground to a certain extent.

In an Air-Land battle — which is basically what is being simulated here — doctrine states that once the battle is joined, it is no longer the Corps Commander's main concern. He uses his tanks to wage the battles at the front, but his major concern is the enemy's follow-on force, positioned maybe 25-30km behind the front. He's concerned with reinforcements, artillery positions, logistic positions, re-supply convoys, etc. — the concept is, if you disrupt the flow of supplies and reinforcements, then your enemy will have no reserve to bring forward into battle, and the advance will move faster. At least, that's the theory. Does it always work like this? No.

This doctrine is simulated in the game. If you will notice, many of the missions in the Offensive Phase require you to fly past the front line to engage your targets and then fly back out.

In this game, as in reality, you don't always know everything. In a lot of computer games, if something is supposed to be at a certain place, when you get to that place, it's there. This isn't very realistic. In many of our game briefings, I'll tell you that something is in a particular *area*, but you'll have to go out and actually locate it. I tried to make the enemy almost as smart as you are. He's not going to sit around and wait for you to come blow him up; he's going to keep moving.

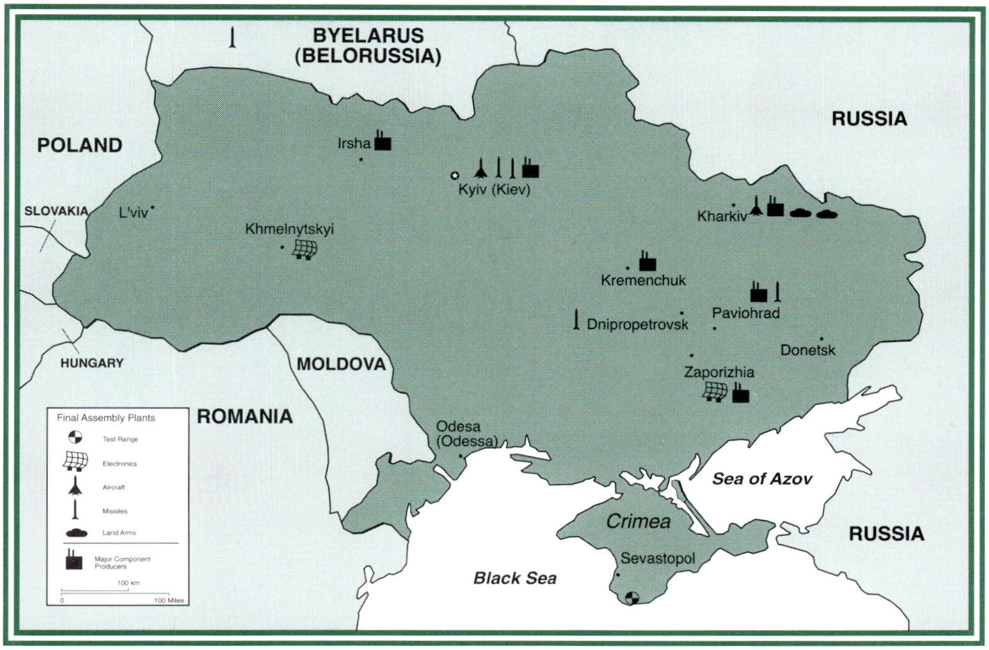

I also tried to simulate *air parity* — the idea that there is a constant battle for the skies over the battlefield at high, medium and low altitudes. In any serious fight for air parity, medium and high are highly contested — they go after your AWACS, you go after theirs; they bomb you, you bomb them. In several missions, you'll see A-10s engaging Su-25s. These aircraft have the same mission, really — they just happen to run into each other and it's a free-for-all.

Don't get distracted by things like this. I simulate the fact that there are other units all around you carrying out different missions at the same time. Although you might be tempted to go after everything you see, you want to keep your head down. If you get involved in every tank battle along your flight path, you may end up flunking the mission.

If you fly some of the losing path missions, you will see the Defensive Phase of this operation. In a Defensive Phase, your orders typically become less clear. You are no longer in control of the battlefield, and you have to react to whatever the enemy does. Targets aren't where they are supposed to be. Your FARP is suddenly very close to the front and you have to fight your way in and out in addition to carrying out your mission.

About the losing endgame — at the local level, every unit has the ability to fire a nuclear weapon. Even artillery units have nuclear-capable rounds. Also, Soviet doctrine states that, if a force is advancing, its goal should be to surround the opposing force. If the area held is large enough, and the enemy force is offering stiff resistance, the Soviets can nuke it. So, in the final stage of the losing path, you are told over and over that the goal of your mission (and others) is to prevent your unit from being surrounded. If you can't do that ... well, the question is, "Would an American general allow a unit of this size to be surrounded and killed?" I don't think so. So, who set off the nuke? It's a State secret ...

Campaign 1: Recon Phase Alpha

Mission Recon Tanks

Environment Day/Clear

Air Strikes 0

Artillery Strikes 0

PRIMARIES	MISSION RATING
21 T-80Us (dug in)	16+ sighted....S+
	7-15...........S
	1-6............F
	0[1] ....F-

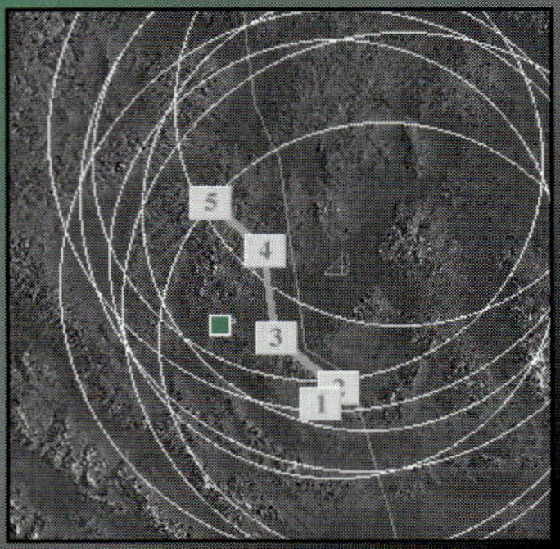

Getting Ready. You've finally made it into the cockpit, and you're anxious to try out the Longbow, its weapons and its avionics suite. But like all new pilots, you're going to have fly a few missions in which combat doesn't play a part. A "few" in this case means four reconnaissance missions. And before you can do that, you have to learn to fly a helicopter. (The training missions on the Base are a good start.)

You should have some kind of flight control in your hands by this time. An advanced joystick with multiple buttons and a throttle wheel is preferable, but if you don't have one, the keyboard will have to do. If your stick has a hat switch, you can program all of your flight controls onto the joystick, freeing up one hand for controlling avionics and targeting keys on the keyboard. (See p. A.1 of the **Reference Manual** for instructions.)

ALTIMETER

Cockpit. Before you lift off, take a look at your cockpit. That big mass of green numbers in front of you (the IHADSS) is important, but you only need to know a couple of things about it for now. First, look at the vertical altimeter bar on the right side of the cockpit. It's going to be your most vital instrument — most of the time, you'll be flying below 150 feet of altitude. The box to the left of this bar gives a digital readout of your altitude as well.

A similar box on the left side of the screen gives your airspeed in knots. This can be pretty important, especially when you start approaching target areas.

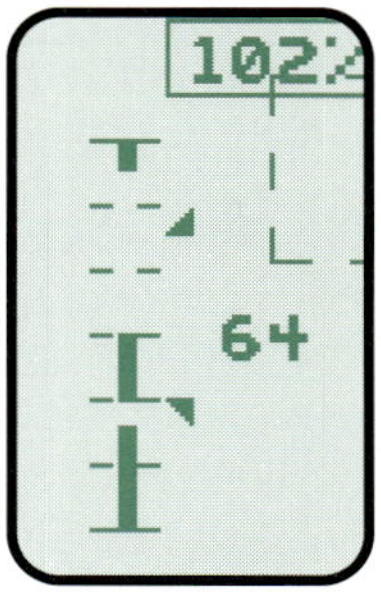

AIRSPEED

[1] Or if player kills an enemy threat. In that case, the player is court-martialed.

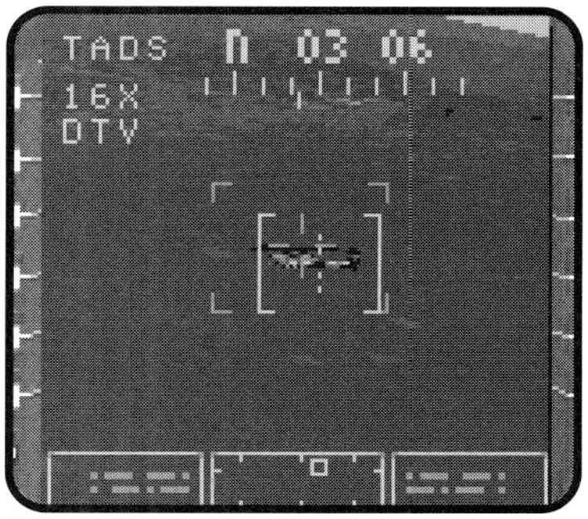

MFD PAGE (TADS SHOWN)

Next, check out the large, square boxes on the bottom of the screen. These are called MFD pages. You've got seven different ones available, and you can manually adjust which ones appear. Check out pp. 2.22-2.33 in the **Reference Manual** that came with the game to find out exactly what each page does.

Go ahead and press the following keys: Shift 8, U, ,, Del, Ctrl M and Home, then press Pg Dn three times. You'll learn how to configure your cockpit, but this is the most efficient method for now. To find out what each one does, see the **Reference Card.** One of them — Ctrl M — puts your weapons on "safe" mode, which keeps you from firing (Do this for the next three missions as well. You won't need to fire your weapons until the fifth mission.)

Helicopter Flight. If you're used to jet sims, forget everything you know about flying. Helicopters don't leave vapor trails — they hover, and you rarely ever fly faster than 140 mph.

That said, here's a quick overview of your helo's flight controls. The directional pedals (rudder pedals, or [and]) control your tail rotor. This basically spins your helicopter around in circles if you're flying under 60 knots.

The cyclic (your joystick or keyboard arrow keys) pitches and banks your helicopter. Use it to move forward, backward or sideways and steer the helicopter during flight.

The last control, the collective, is the most important one. In pilot jargon, you "pull" or "drop" collective" when you want to change altitude. What this does is collectively change the angle of the rotor blades, which adds or decreases lift. If you're using a throttle stick, or if your joystick has a large throttle wheel on one side, you'll move that to control your altitude. If you're using the keyboard, you'll have to press + and -.

Note: *If you manage to crash your helo and haven't adjusted any landing/crash settings in the* ***OPTION*** *menu, you can re-fly the mission. After you see the crash/rescue/fail flick, click on the flight helmet in the Debrief area to give it a second go.*

Waypoint 1 (Takeoff). This is a recon mission, so if you rise high enough, you can see everything you need to see without leaving your FARP. (Of course, you can cruise to all of the waypoints if you're confident in your abilities.)

Before takeoff, you need to engage your rotors (press R). You'll hear a "whomp whomp" sound as they start to spin. Next, add collective by pressing +, or by moving the throttle wheel/device forward. (You can reverse the direction in the **IN-FLIGHT OPTION** menu.) In a few minutes, your helo will rise. Watch the altimeter bar ... it grows taller until 200 feet, then disappears. This is because you'll do most of your cruise flights under that altitude.

Whatever you do, don't move the joystick. You don't really want to fly anywhere right now. As you climb, look at the boxed display labeled TSD. Icons appear as targets come in view of the radar that sits atop the helicopter.

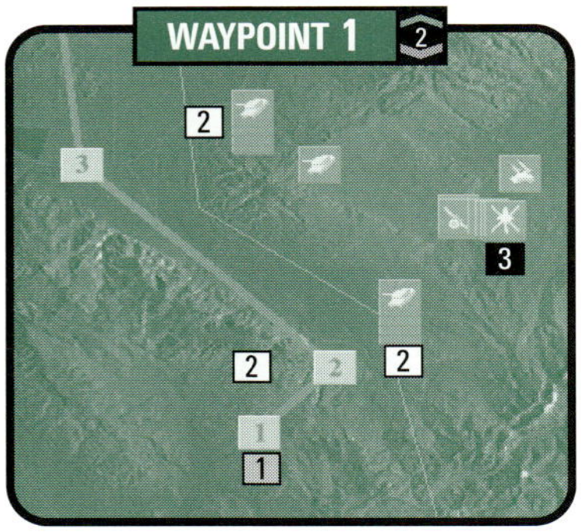

1 FARP Archer
2 T-80U Tanks
3 Enemy FARP

TSD MFD. The TSD is basically an electronic view of the battlefield. (see p. 2.22 of the **Reference Manual**). You'll need to master it pretty quickly to survive. In a nutshell, icons represent threats, large circles indicate enemy SAM ranges, and little circles with numbers describe your waypoints.

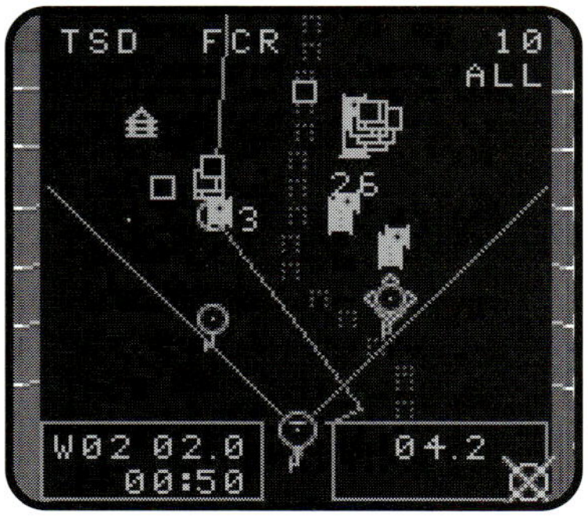

TACTICAL SITUATION DISPLAY (TSD) MFD

When you reach about 1000 feet, press H to activate auto-hover. You'll quit climbing. (Normally, you wouldn't go over 300 or 400 feet, but this height is appropriate here because nothing's going to shoot at you.)

Now, use the tail rotor (pedals or [and]) to make a 360-degree turn. More things should show up on the TSD, and you should get a *Mission Successful* message from your CP/G (that's pilot-speak for co-pilot/gunner).

Use T to cycle through targets, and watch the long, rectangular display. The current target name shows up there. The mission is considered successful if you detect 7 primaries, but if you want to find all 16 targets and get a super-successful mission, you can climb higher.

Waypoint 1 (Landing). When you've achieved the objectives and want to land, drop collective. Again, don't move the joystick — if you move away from the FARP, you'll have to maneuver over it again.

When your altitude drops below 200 feet, the analog altimeter bar reappears. Increase collective until you're descending slowly. Go down to about 30 feet or so, then press H. Once you're settled into a hover, *gently* drop collective and drop down onto the FARP. Then, choose to END MISSION. That's all there is to it.

Campaign 2: Recon Phase Delta

Mission Recon Armor	**Air Strikes** 0
Environment Night/Clear	**Artillery Strikes** 0
Primaries	*Mission Rating*
7 T-80Us	8+ SIGHTED.....S+
2 2S6s	6-7............S
	1-5............F
	0[1] ....F-

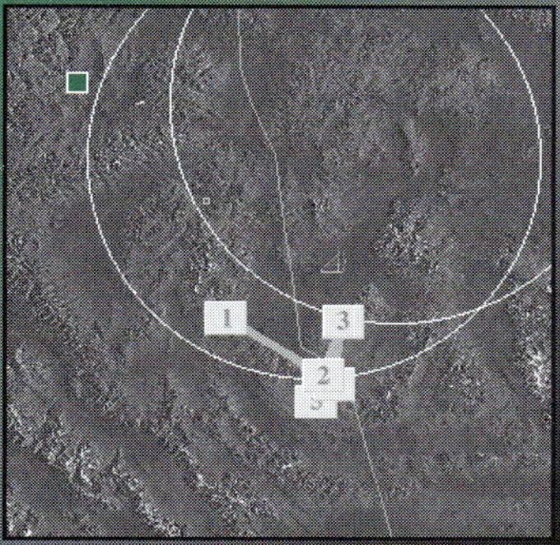

Waypoint 1. So you're refreshed and refueled, and ready to take on your second mission? Good ... this one may be tough if you're a first-time helo pilot. Not only does this mission occur at night; it's also the first mission that requires you to fly somewhere.

The first thing you need to do is sharpen your eyesight. Your Longbow has a Pilot's Night Vision System you can activate by pressing [P]. The PNVS superimposes a green, infrared camera image over your viewscreen with the help of a camera mounted on the helicopter's nose. This allows you to see green thermal images of terrain and objects and gives you lethal night-attack capabilities.

Before you head off into the night, make sure you've got your FCR active (press [Home]) and that you've opened the Upfront target display (press [U]). You might also want to increase your TSD range to 10km (press [Pg Dn] once).

CLOSE-UP OF IHADSS DISPLAY

Navigating to Waypoint 2. Look at the rectangle at the bottom of the IHADSS. "wo2" appears just to the left of that rectangle, and indicates that Waypoint 2 is your current destination. You can manually cycle through waypoints by pressing [W] or [Shift][W], but you don't need to. When you reach one waypoint, the computer automatically sets the next one as your current waypoint.

Look at the heading tape at the top of your viewscreen. It's got all sorts of indicators, but the only one you need now is the carat (it looks like an upside down "V"). Lift off (press [R], then add collective) and use your tail rotor to center this carat on the tape.

[1] Or if player kills an enemy threat.

The next step takes coordination, and it might take a while to perfect it. You're going to transition (more pilot slang) into forward flight. Come to a hover at about 180 feet of altitude using the collective and the [H] key. Then, dip the nose of the helicopter by pushing the cyclic forward gently (or pressing [↓]). This is how you induce forward speed.

Keep a close eye on the altimeter. If you start losing height, add a little collective or pitch up slightly. If you rise above 200 feet, reduce collective or nose down slightly. The objective is to keep your forward speed anywhere from 50-100 knots and your altitude between 30 and 100 feet. In cases where SAM threats are nearby, you may have to fly as low as 20 feet if there's no terrain to hide behind. Getting the correct combination of cyclic and collective takes some getting used to. Just remember — the slower you go, the more time you have to react.

Waypoint 2. Head straight toward the second waypoint (if the carat is in the middle of the tape, you're flying in the correct direction). You can tell how far you've got left to go by looking at the number next to WO2 — it indicates the distance to the waypoint in kilometers. The estimated time to arrival appears just below that number.

Once you get pretty close to Waypoint 2 (within 2km), stop and go into a hover. Pop your bird up (rise to about 350 feet) and make a quick scan of the area to update your TSD.

ASE MFD. Now, press [,] (once) and [Del] (twice), if you haven't already, and spare a minute to look the boxed display on the left side of the cockpit. The Aircraft Survivability Equipment MFD page (ASE) keeps track of threats that are scanning or acquiring a radar lock on you. This is going to be a lifesaver for you during your career as a pilot. The large dashed circles indicate the effective range of SAM missiles (SA-11s and 2S6s have the largest circles). Consider them fair warning ... when you move inside the circles, you're vulnerable.

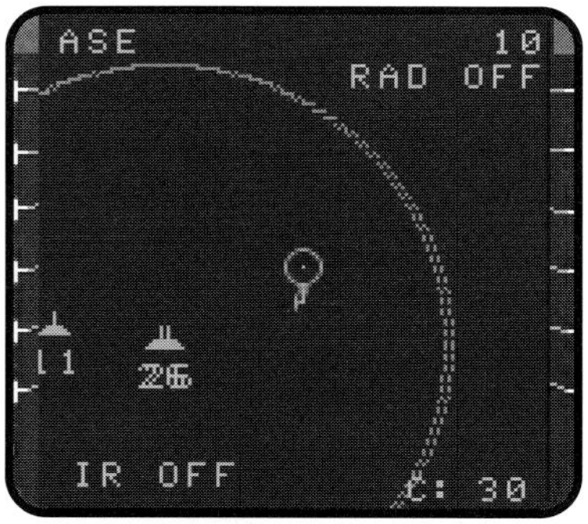

AIRCRAFT SURVIVAL EQUIPMENT (ASE) MFD

Circles only appear when the threat is scanning the area with radar. If the circle goes solid, you're being tracked by radar. A solid line will appear between the icon in the center of the display (your position) and the SAM that's firing at you. When this happens, drop like a rock. The next thing you know, you'll be dodging missiles (seen as bright green diamonds that appear on the ASE).

It takes nearly 10 seconds or so for a SAM to acquire a lock and launch a missile. This is to your advantage, because you can pop up to see what's around, then drop back down before SAMs have a chance to get a missile lock on you. Even if they have a lock on you, it gets broken when you drop low enough.You can't always avoid being shot at, though. It happens to the best pilots. (Keep in mind that the greater the ASE range, the earlier you can see what's out there. To cycle through its ranges, press [Del].)

When missiles are inbound, your CP/G will prompt you to move ("Evasive action, now!"). Do it quick, because the missiles close in in a heartbeat. If you've deactivated his countermeasure ability, you'll have to drop chaff manually by pressing [C].

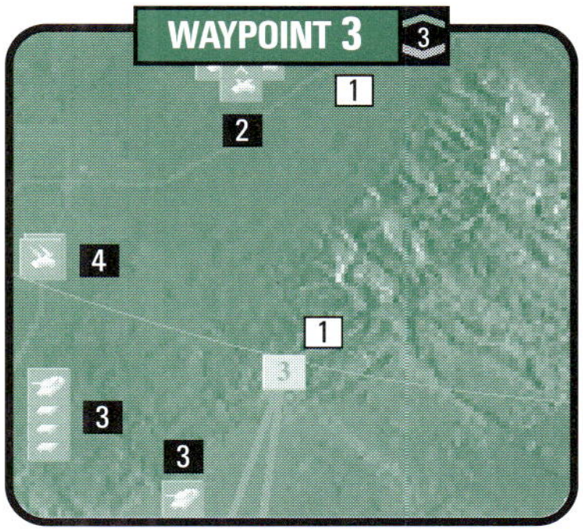

1 T-80U Tanks
2 Enemy FARP
3 T-80U Tanks
4 SO-122 Artillery

Waypoint 3. If you moved all the way into Waypoint 2, the WO2 you saw earlier automatically changes to WO3. If not, you need to change waypoints manually by pressing [W]. As you leave the second waypoint, adjust your altitude to under 100 feet while you're hovering, then turn toward Waypoint 3 by centering the carat on your heading tape. Stay low as you can as you cruise to Waypoint 3 (between 20 and 40 feet is fine). This is a difficult mission, and the lower and slower you are, the better.

You're going to have to pass by several SAM threats on the way. This is where your ASE is going to prove useful. Fly as low as you can, and briefly pop up every 4 or 5km to update your radar. You should find up to 8 T-80U tanks, which are your primary targets. they'll show up in the Upfront display as T-80U TANKS PRIMARY. Drop back down as soon as you can. If you fire at and kill a SAM, you lose the mission.

Once you reach Waypoint 3, break right to maneuver out of range of the 2S6 there. Hang around near the hills and use them to conceal your position. After the tanks roll in, you should soon get a mission success message, and then you can head to your landing FARP.

Campaign 3: Recon Phase Echo

Mission Recon Artillery
Environment Night/Cloudy/Hazy
Air Strikes 0
Artillery Strikes 0

Primaries	*Mission Rating*
5 SO-122s	4-6 sighted....S
1 Bunker	1-3............F
	0[1] ....F-

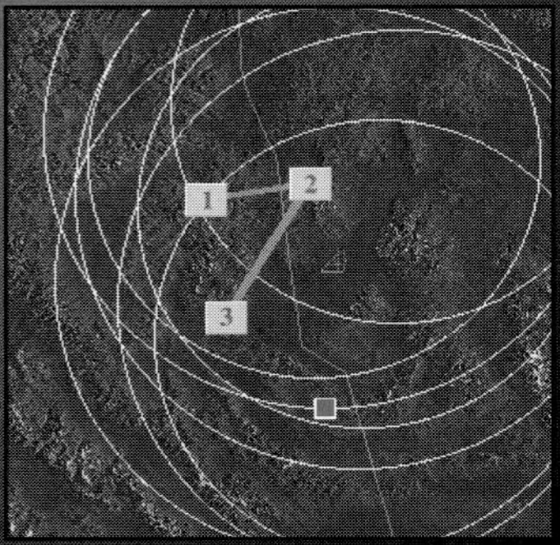

Waypoint 1. If you've made it through the first two missions, you're doing fine. It takes a lot of self-discipline to avoid firing at threats you see, especially if they're trying to lock you up with their weapons. If you simply can't wait two more missions to fire off your ordnance, you might consider taking a break from the campaign and playing an Instant Action mission or two.

This mission is another nighttime excursion. However, this time you're going to jump into the role of navigator and slightly reroute the mission. Open up the navigational map (press Alt N) and take a look at the current mapping. You'll notice a gray line running vertically down the map. This is the boundary between enemy and friendly lines.

Waypoint (2). Sometimes it's a good idea to add your own waypoints. You can use them to avoid certain threats, or just to mark landmarks. To add a new waypoint onto the map, left-click on the red line connecting Waypoints 1 and 2. A new one labeled USER WP will appear.

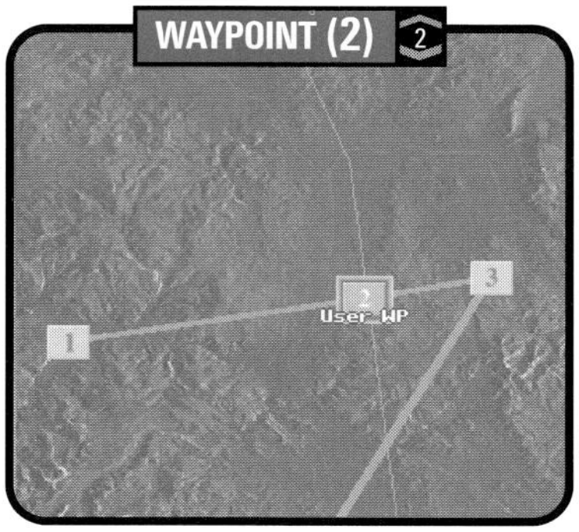

Notice that it's a different color than the default waypoints — this means that you can drag it. To do so, right-click-and-hold on the new icon and drag it on top of the gray line, keeping it in line with the existing waypoints. This will give you a visual cue as to when you're about to cross over into enemy territory. To delete a waypoint you created, select it and press Del.

1 Or if player kills an enemy threat.

Return to the cockpit and activate your PNVS system and all the usual cockpit setup keys. (By this time, you should have experimented with the keyboard and read the technical manual that came with the game.)

Climb to a hundred feet or so and make sure that FCR is the active target acquisition system. This updates your radar and memorizes targets within radar range. Next, drop down and cruise to Waypoint 2 at an altitude no higher than 50 feet.

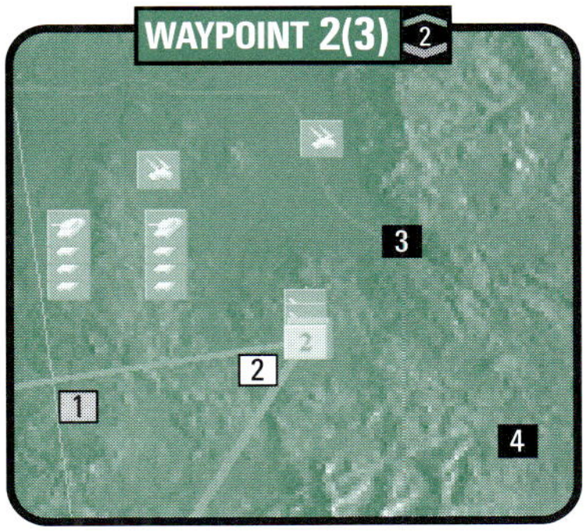

1 Border
2 SO-122 Artillery
3 2S6s, Bar Lock radar
4 SA-11s, Snow Drift radar

Waypoint 2 (3). You should be checking your TSD MFD periodically. When it shows a row of small U-shaped brackets, you'll know you're near enemy territory. Slow down and drop collective so you can come to a hover before you cross the battle line.

Pop up, as you did before, to detect as many threats as you can. Remember, this is a recon mission, and your assignment is to sight everything you can. If you go high enough and zoom out your TSD to 20km, you can get the *Mission Success* message without ever having to cross over into enemy territory. All you have to do is sight at least four primaries. Once you've done that, you can go back to your landing FARP and touch down.

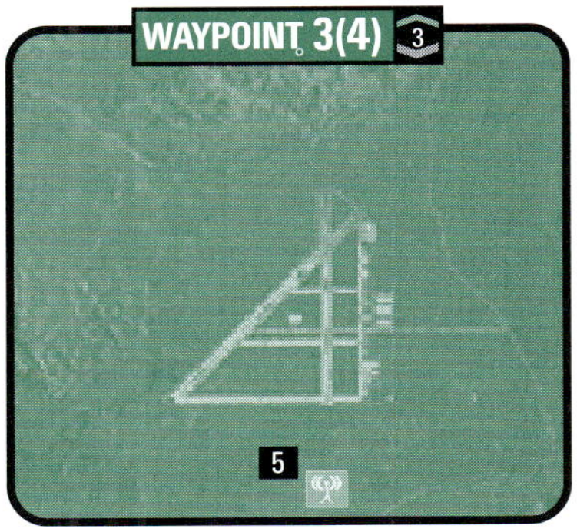

5 SA-11s, Snow Drift radar

Waypoint 3 (4). If you want the experience, continue on through the waypoints and stay low and slow. Watch out for the SA-11s on the way home, however. If you choose the latter method, you don't have to pop up at all during the rest of the mission — you've already succeeded.

Campaign 4: Recon Phase Foxtrot

Mission Recon EW Site **Air Strikes** 0
Environment Night/Clear **Artillery Strikes** 0

Primaries	*Mission Rating*
1 Bar Lock/Spoon Rest	2-3 sighted....S
2 Bunkers	1..............F
2 Tents	0[1] ....F-
1 2S6	....

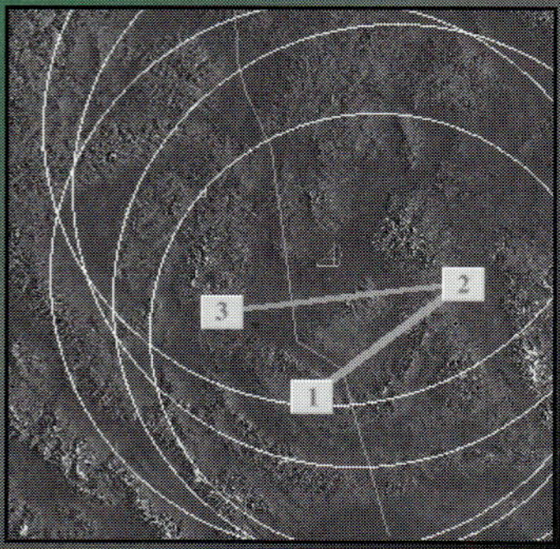

Waypoint 1. You should be turning into a night owl by now ... this mission occurs at night as well. Use PNVS.

Once you take off, take a cursory glance around your takeoff FARP by making a 360-turn using the tail rotor, just. to see what's immediately around you. You should spot a SAM. Once you do, open the nav map and reroute your flight path by adding and dragging a waypoint between the two ridges to the east.

Waypoint (2). Skirt around the ridge and come to a hover at Waypoint 2 (the one you added). Rise and acquire some more targets, then descend and head for Waypoint 3 (originally Waypoint 2).

WAYPOINT (2)

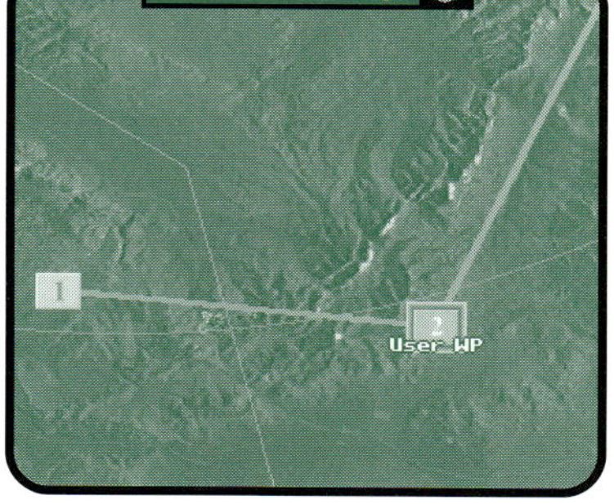

[1] Or if player kills an enemy threat.

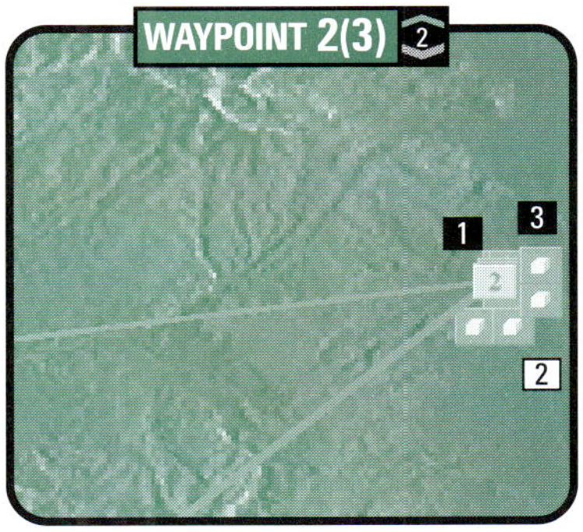

- **1** SA-8
- **2** 2S6s, Bar Lock radar,tents,bunker
- **3** SA-11, Snow Drift radar

Waypoint 2 (3). Be careful when you pass over the ridge on the way to Waypoint 3 — there's an SA-8 that will acquire you if you aren't below 50 feet or so. Once you do pop over the ridge and approach Waypoint 3, you'll sight your primary target, a Bar Lock radar.

Congratulations ... that's all there is to do in this mission. You can now backtrack and go out the same use way you came in. You can use autopilot (press [A]) to let the computer fly you home, but again, be wary of the ridge. Autopilot keeps you at around 100 feet of altitude.

If you're autopiloting, you must manually cycle through to the second waypoint (or first one, if you didn't add one). When you arrive there, select w01. (You must do this because autopilot will travel to the next *highest* waypoint by default.) When you're at the takeoff FARP, land.

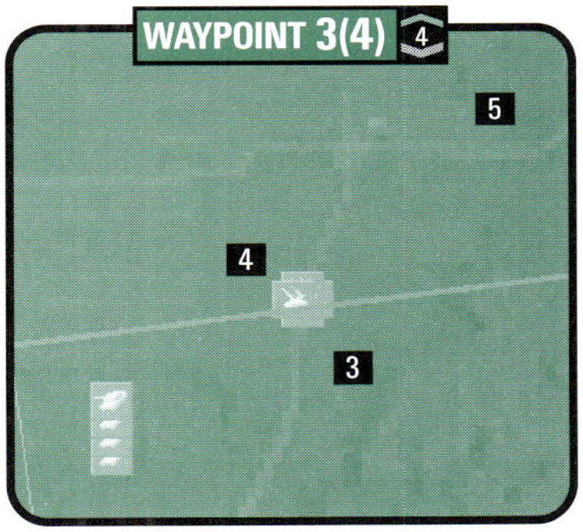

- **3** Bar Lock radar
- **4** Enemy FARP
- **5** 2S6s

Waypoint 3 (4). If you want to log more cockpit time, follow the default waypoint route. Between the target waypoint and your FARP, you'll see lots of enemies and 2S6s. Stay low and try to skirt around them.

One last note. Players seem to fall into one of four categories after flying a few missions — some use master modes extensively, some configure cockpit elements individually, others put all the keystrokes they use onto a programmable stick, and the rest flounder around and wonder why they can't win the mission. If you're in the final category, we strongly recommend that you master the basics before continuing on. From here, you're headed into combat.

Campaign 5: SEAD Phase Alpha

Mission Attack EW Site

Environment Dawn-to-Day/Clear

Air Strikes 0

Artillery Strikes 0

Primaries	Mission Rating
1 Bar Lock/Spoon Rest	EW destroyed...S
2 Bunkers	EW Site not
1 Tent	destroyed......F
1 2S6s	

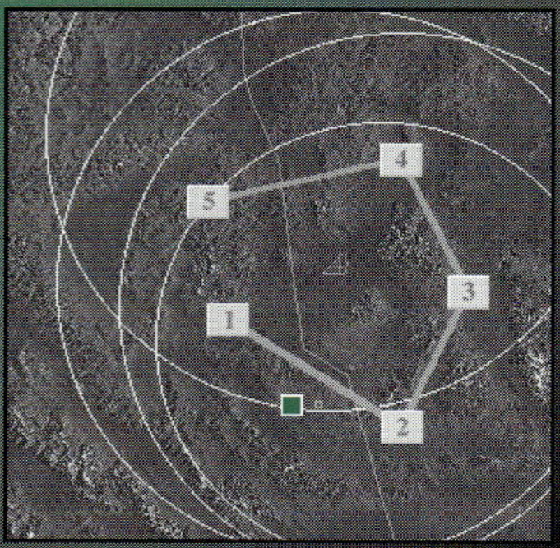

Waypoint 1. Now that war has broken out between the CIS and NATO forces, you actually get to attack something. Keep your ASE range at 25km and your TSD at 10km. Also, switch into FCR target acquisition mode (press [Home]).Pop up to 600 feet at after takeoff to ID what's near. (Popping up high across enemy lines, however, isn't always a great idea.)

As you cruise along to Waypoint 2, you'll see a SAM ring on the ASE. Swing outside of it — it indicates three 2S6 sites, accompanied by many other enemy threats. These guys are arguably the nastiest things you'll come up against — they've got a long radar range, they launch SA-19s, and they've got a powerful A38M Quad 30mm cannon, which they'll turn on when you're in gun range.

Keep an eye on the circles in your ASE. If one turns solid, the SAM radar has switched into tracking mode. If you hear your CP/G yell *"Evasive action, **now!**"* you'd better drop — a SAM missile is inbound.

Waypoint 2. Stop here, pop up, then yaw around to update targets in your TSD. If none appear, use [<,] to cycle through to the Radar MFD page. If you see concentric circles, switch to ground mode (press [Pg Up]).

Once you've acquired your targets, drop down and hover. There's a 2S6 around somewhere — cycle through your targets ([T]) to find him. Ignore the SA-8 and SA-11s you see ... they'll cause you trouble if you attack them. You can toggle the Upfront Display ([U]) to show the names of your targets. (Hey, it's a cheat, but it works, and it doesn't affect your score.)

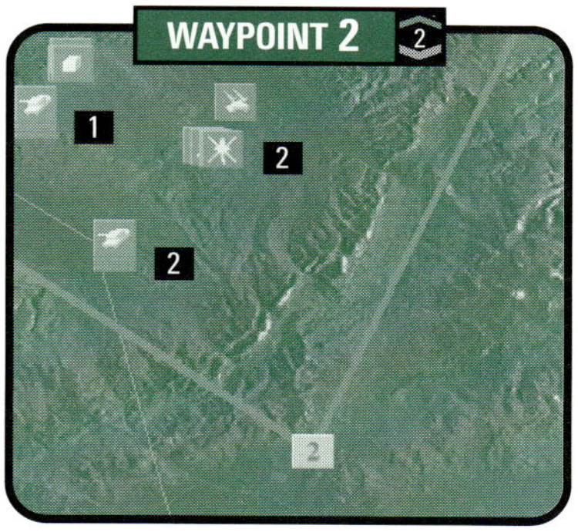

1 2S6s

2 SA-8, 2 Havocs

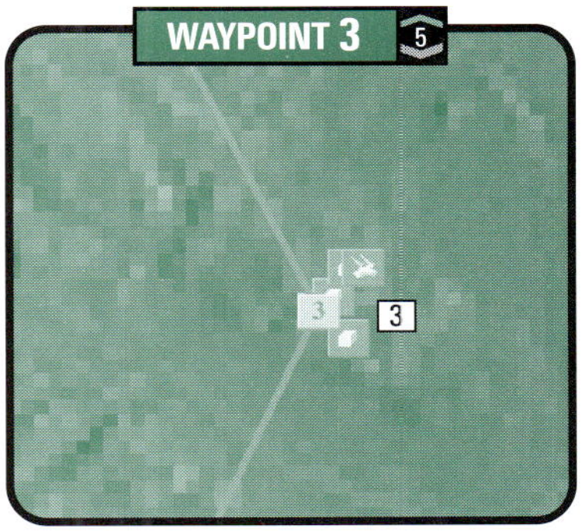

[3] Bar Lock radar, 2S6, tents, bunkers

Waypoint 3. Now comes the moment you've been waiting for. Somewhere on your TSD should be an icon with a green diamond around it —your current target. If you've cycled through the target list to him, 2S6 TUNGUSKA SAM/AAA should appear in the Upfront display.

Firing Missiles. Activate Hellfire missiles by pressing [Bksp] until MSL appears to the right of the high-action display box. To the left of the box, you'll see "A" plus some number. This indicates the distance to the current target and must be 7.9km or less to fire a missile effectively.

Yaw around until the 2S6 icon is appears in the TSD "pie" wedge. You should see a small or large box in the viewscreen, either dashed or solid. (There's two different launch modes, but it makes no difference right now.) That's a missile constraint box, and it indicates whether or not you have a valid missile lock.

Add collective until the box turns solid. Once that happens, VALID LOCK appears above the high-action display, and you can fire. Press [Enter] or your joystick missile fire button. If you want to watch your first Hellfire strike, press [F8] to assume the missile's view. (Press [F1] to restore the normal view.)

Once you've taken out the primary 2S6, repeat the process for other targets. Your other primaries are a Bar Lock radar, a couple of bunkers and a tent. If you want to score a lot of points, use Hellfires only against the 2S6s and radar sites (SAMs with radar become helpless after the radar is destroyed), then use guns or rockets on other targets. This conserves ordnance.

Try sending your wingman after other targets while you look for the Bar Lock. Select a target, then press [Ctrl][3] to send him after it. After all, it's his first weapons-free mission too.)

You may see 2 Havocs as well — check your air radar frequently ([Pg Up]). By now you know where ground threats are, so replace your ASE page with the Radar page ([,] or [.] toggles pages) and switch radar modes occasionally.

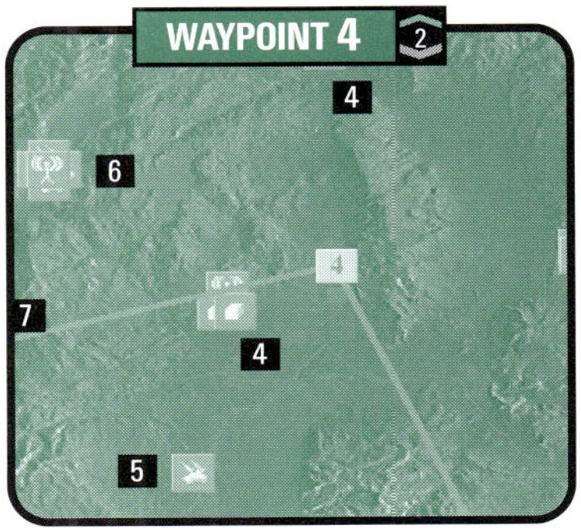

[4] SA-8
[5] SA-8 enemy
[6] SA-11s, Snow Drift radar
[7] SA-8, 2S6

Waypoint 4. No primaries here, only SAMs. Your best bet is to avoid the waypoint entirely. Fly back to Waypoint 1, then select Waypoint 5 (press [W] to cycle through waypoints). Fly slow and stay below 20ft on the way — any leftover 2S6s have short-range guns as well as missiles.

Campaign 6: SEAD Phase Charlie

Mission Attack SA-11 Site
Environment Dusk-to-Dark/Clear
Air Strikes 0
Artillery Strikes 0

Primaries	Mission Rating
1 Snow Drift	9 killed.......S+
4 SA-11 Gadflys	5-8............S
1 Tent	1-4............F
1 2S6	0..............F-
2 Soldiers	

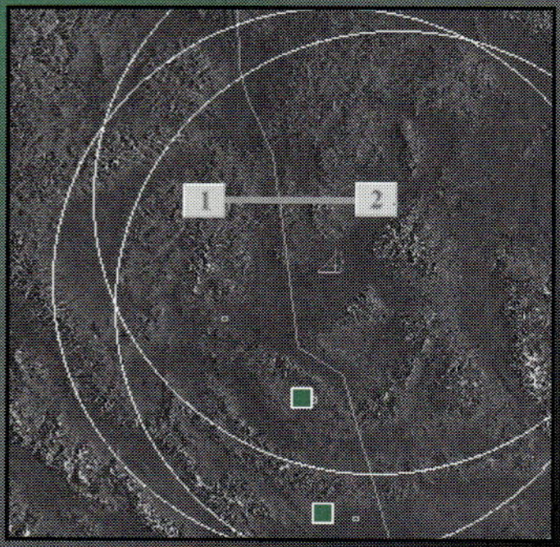

Waypoint 1. There's only one waypoint in this mission, but don't be deceived. Auto-hover when you take off and drag a PFZ around the 2S6 to the east, just across enemy lines (see below). Stay below 100 feet and take out the 2S6 and SA-15 on the way to Waypoint 2.

Creating Priority Fire Zones. PFZs are very useful targeting items that make life as Longbow pilot easier. Usable only with RF Hellfires, they allow you to ripple-fire missiles at targets in the box without picking out individual targets. Hellfire missiles are "smart" enough to attack anything that can be picked up by radar within the zone you create (including friendlies.)

To make a PFZ, right-click-and-drag a box inside the TSD MFD around the targets you want to include in it. You can transmit a PFZ to your wingman (Ctrl 3), and he'll attack everything in it.

To ripple-fire, make sure you have Hellfires selected and LOAL missile launch mode active. (Press Ins to toggle between LOAL (large constraint box) and LOBL (small constraint box) modes. Select a PFZ by left-clicking on the PFZ name in the TSD, then fire.

The Border. As you approach the border, you discover some enemy tanks on your side of the line.

Now you can play around with one of this game's fun features — an object camera. (Only do this if you've taken out the SAMs and can hover comfortably nearby.) Next Object View (F6) and Previous Object View (Shift F6) cycle through nearby objects, allowing you to watch

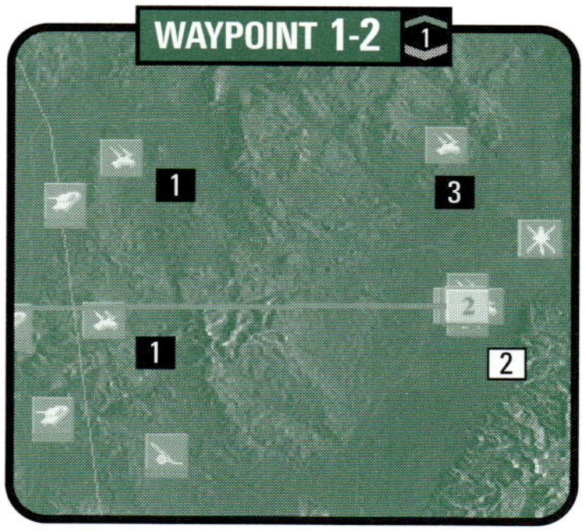

1 2S6s

2 SA-11s, Snow Drift radar, CIS soldiers, 2S6

3 SA-15

pitched battles between tanks, soldiers, etc. Sometimes it's fun to watch the grunts on the ground. F6 cycles through aircraft, ground vehicles and immobile objects (in that order). Use the arrow keys or your joystick hat to pan the view, F1 to restore the cockpit.

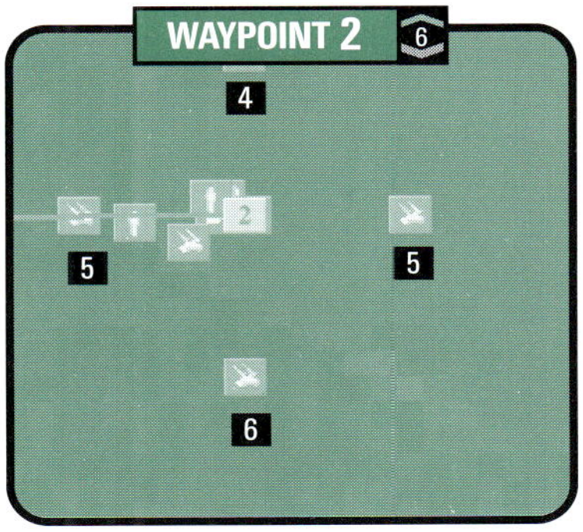

4 SA-15
5 2S6s
6 SA-11, Snow Drift radar

Waypoint 2. Veer left or right to avoid surprise SAMs placed just over a hill along the direct route to the waypoint. (Watch your ASE.) If you go left, you'll see a couple of helicopters. If you go right, you'll run into more tanks. Try sending your wingman after either.

This area is heavily defended by SAMs and AAA, and you need to worry about them before the choppers. You have two options here:

The John Wayne Method. Fly Nap Of the Earth (at 20ft and 50 knots) straight for your targets. Give your Wingman the Weapons Free (Ctrl 6) command. Send off your Hellfires as fast as you can, then switch immediately into ATA mode to take on the choppers. (Switching to ATA Master Mode (Shift 4) will switch everything — radar, target acquisition, weapons and MFDs — to ATA-friendly modes at once.)

The Textbook Method. Auto-hover about 5km away from the waypoint. Switch to FCR target acquisition mode (Home) and LOAL missile launch mode (Ins) if you haven't already. Bob up to get targets, then drop down and create a PFZ around the waypoint. You might want to create two PFZs and give one to your wingman.

(Go ahead and do the John Wayne thing — if you fail, you can always re-fly it textbook-style.)

Waypoint 1 (Landing). If you've taken out the choppers, it's an easy ride home. Keep an eye out for CIS soldiers with shoulder SAMs — you need to switch to TADS target acquisition mode to see them (press Home). If you have Hellfires left, consider using them. It may seem like a shame since soldiers only take 1 damage point, but it keeps you from having to move in too close. Otherwise, move in with guns.

Campaign 7: Offensive Phase Delta

Mission Attack Armor

Environment Day/Clear

Air Strikes 1

Artillery Strikes 3

Primaries	*Mission Rating*
10 T-80Us	10+ KILLED.....S+
	8-9............S
	1-7............F
	0.............F-

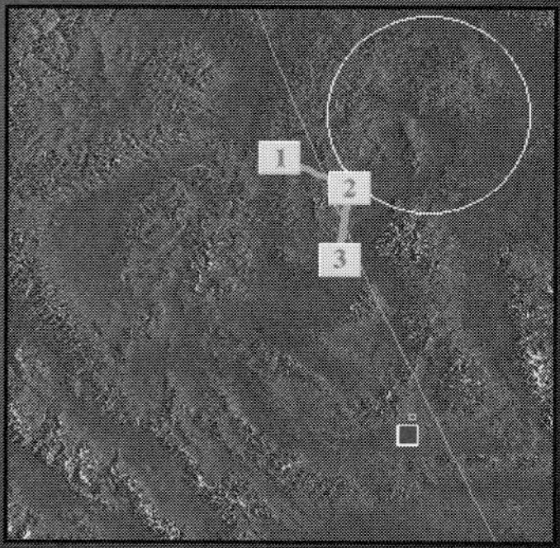

Waypoint 1. Don't bother setting up your cockpit before you go to the second waypoint. You're going to have to switch master modes there, anyway.

Waypoint 1-2. Slow down before you get to the second waypoint (5km or so) and switch to ATA Master mode (press Shift 4). This accomplishes a lot of things at once — it displays the RAD MFD, puts your radar into air mode, and selects Stinger missiles as the active weapon. And since you've got air targets coming in, it saves you a lot of key presses.

You've got an Su-25 Frogfoot coming in. You don't have to attack him, but you can if he comes in close enough. Target him using T, then swing in a circle until you bring him into forward view. Fire a Stinger at him when he comes at you head-on, and get your wingman to fire at him as well by pressing Ctrl 3. Between the two of you, you should be able to knock him out (500 points!). Save a couple of Stingers for Hinds that move into Waypoint 2. (You can also use guns or rockets against them if you think you're up for it.)

If you're using rockets, you can set your rockets to fire in salvos of 1, 2, 4 or 8. If your salvo size is greater than 1, you can fire multiple rockets with a single pull of the trigger. If you know you're going to use your rockets, do this before you take off — cycle through the MFDs to open the Weapons page, and press S to cycle through salvo sizes. The size of your salvo appears after RKT at the bottom of the Weapons MFD.

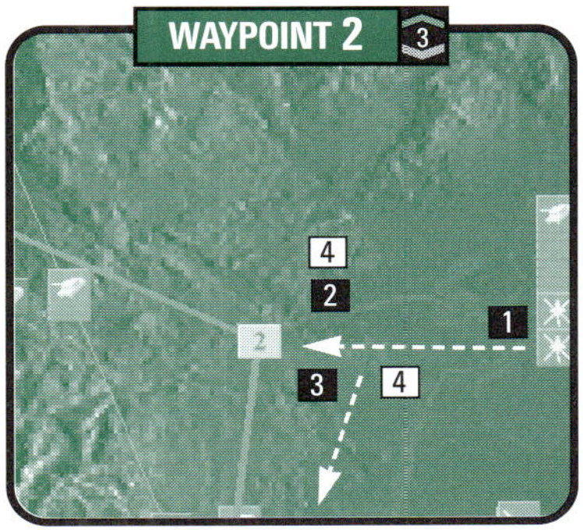

1 2 Hinds (heading west)
2 2S6s
3 2S6 (heading south)
4 T-80U Tanks

Slow down and pop up when you reach the enemy border to ID what awaits you. Then, drop down and move a little closer toward Waypoint 2. You can hover just past the border and kill all the SAMs.

Waypoint 2. There are lots of 2S6s around this waypoint. Drop below 40 feet once they start lighting you up (look for the circles on your ASE) and slow down a bit. If you don't have them on your TSD, bob up to acquire them and make sure you're in FCR target acquisition mode — (Home)). Then, drop back down and PFZ them from an auto-hover position about 2.5km away. Have your wingman take out 2S6 SAMs with his missiles (they're not objectives). Stay about 7km out and pop up to 80 feet to get a valid LOS on the 2S6s so you can fire off Hellfires at them.

Now, go after the primary tank convoy. Along with their mobile 2S6 escort, they're rolling south toward Waypoint 3. Two "bonus" primaries — T-80Us — appear north of Waypoint 2.

Waypoint 3. That not-so-friendly Frogfoot may reappear here if you didn't kill him earlier, along with more Hinds. You don't have to take them out. Just make it to the waypoint and land.

Campaign 8: Offensive Phase Echo

Mission Attack Convoy **Air Strikes** 0

Environment Night/Cloudy/Haze **Artillery Strikes** 1

Primaries	Mission Rating
7 Ural-375s	10+ killed.....S+
3 2S6s	6-9............S
	1-5............F
	0..............F-

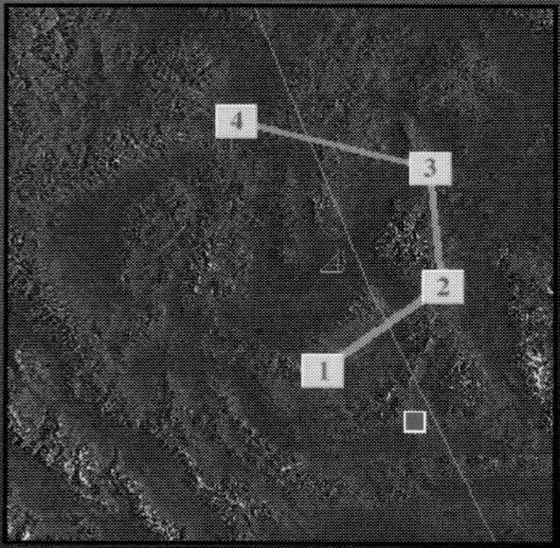

Waypoint 3. Take the programmed path for this mission, at least the first half of it. You won't find much en route to Waypoint 2, other than a distant 2S6. Between 2 and 3, the scene gets a little more hectic. The convoy you're to attack is off the map at first, but rolls in by the time you arrive. Fuel trucks are your primaries, but before you can get to them, you've got to take out the SAMs. Create a PFZ around them and start a ripple fire attack.

The hefty ridge halfway to Waypoint 3 won't do much good against the convoy. Approach low and stop about 5km out. The best way to prepare for the attack is to rise high enough to find the valid line of sight to the target. Then, you can get a valid weapon lock, and the constraint box for the active weapon — guns, rockets, Hellfires or Stingers — turns solid if you meet all the firing conditions. Once you've found the correct altitude, drop down only until the SAMs' ASE circles turn dashed, and hover there.

In some missions, you'll need to drop way down because several SAMs are threatening you. If that happens, count the seconds it takes you to descend to safety. If you're using LOAL mode for Hellfires, fire and then pop up that many seconds before your Hellfire missile timer runs out. This minimizes your exposure time, but gives you the time you need to get a valid lock before impact.

Here, the firing altitude is around 80 or 90 feet. There are a couple of targets you won't be able to lock up on unless you climb to around 380 feet. Once the SAMs are gone, give your wingman the go-ahead to attack the fuel trucks in the PFZ. Meanwhile, take out the Havocs. Once all targets are gone, backtrack the way you came.

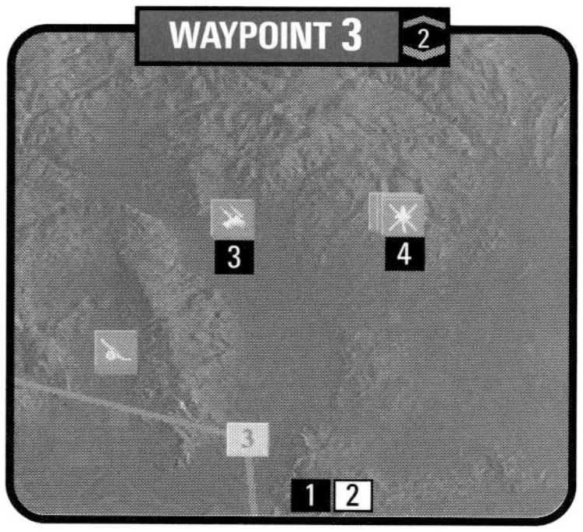

1 Havocs, convoy

2 2S6s, fuel trucks in convoy

3 2S6s

4 Enemy FARP, Havocs

Campaign 9: Offensive Phase Gulf

Mission Attack TAC Post **Air Strikes** 0

Environment Night-to-Dawn/Clear **Artillery Strikes** 0

Primaries	*Mission Rating*
1 Command Bunker	4+ killed......S
1 Bunker	1-3............F
2 2S6s	0..............F-
1 SA-8	
2 BMP-3s	

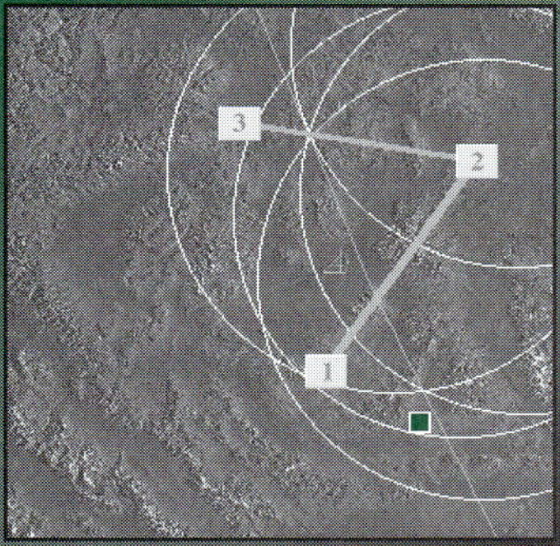

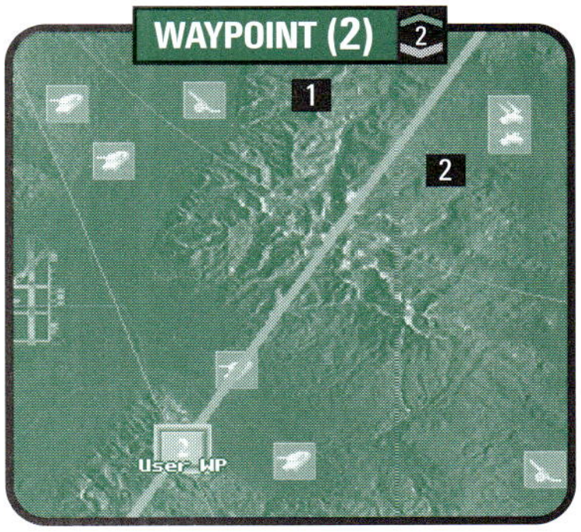

■1 2S6

■2 SA-8, 2S6, SA-15s

Waypoint 1. There's no point in re-routing your way around SAMs in this mission. The area surrounding the target waypoint is littered with them, and you won't be able to stay out of their range. It *is* useful, however, to place a waypoint in your flight path just before the border.

Waypoint (2). Head for your new waypoint. When you get to the enemy line, pop up before you cross it. This is the best vantage point for identifying a couple of nearby SA-15s SAMs and a 2S6 site. Take out the latter one first, but do it from a low hover (under 100 feet).

After the 2S6 is destroyed, pop up a little higher to launch Hellfires at the SA-15s. Then, climb to approximately 500 feet to uncover everything else that awaits.

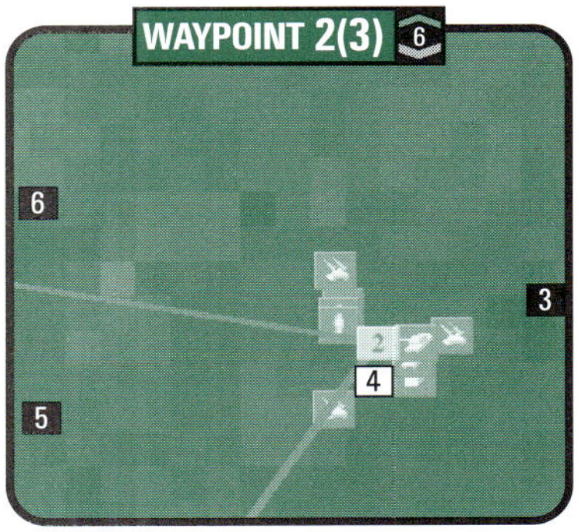

■3 2S6s, SA-15

□4 Bunkers, 2S6s, SA-8, BMP-3s

■5 SA-8, SA-15, 2S6

■6 2S6s

Waypoint 2(3). Here, your first task is to take out the primary, a 2S6. Then, you've got a pair of BMP-3s, a bunker and an SA-8 to take out as well. The big one, however, is the command post. You can use Hellfires or rockets against it, but not guns. Havocs may appear if you move directly over the waypoint.

That's it ... once you've gotten the "mission successful" message, you can either go to the landing FARP waypoint and rack up a few artillery kills, or play it safe and backtrack to your takeoff FARP.

Campaign 10: Offensive Phase Hotel

Mission Attack Commo Site | **Air Strikes** 2

Environment Day/Clear | **Artillery Strikes** 0

Primaries	Mission Rating
1 Long Track	7 killed.......S
3 Command Bunkers	1-6............F
4 2S6s	0..............F-

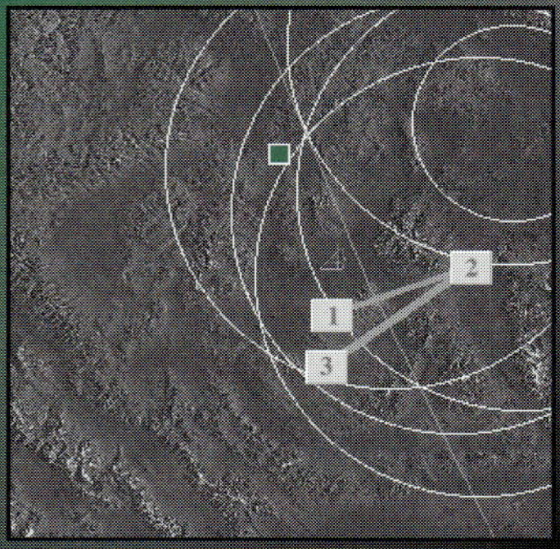

Waypoint 1. Be forewarned. This is a tough, tough mission. If you haven't yet mastered the art of taking out SAMs, get in some Instant Mission practice. (Even our expert pilots have trouble with this "pop-and-drop" mission.) The big challenge here is that you have to climb high enough to fire off your Hellfires, then quickly drop low enough to avoid getting shot down by a SAM.

It's good to keep your ASE range extended to 25km. It's very SAM intensive, and you want as good of a handle as possible on what's coming up. Conserve your Hellfires by clearing out the western side of your flight path first.

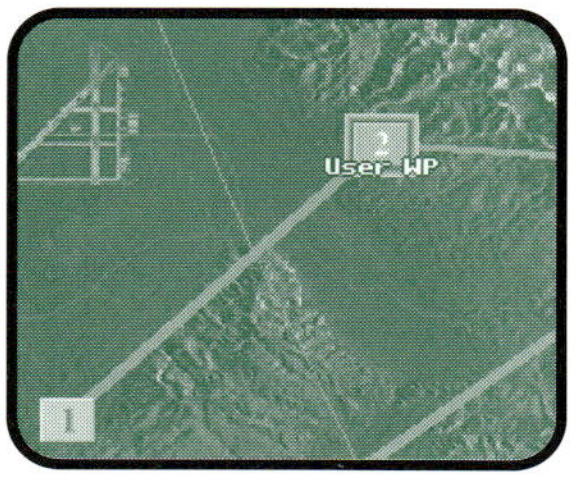

Create a new waypoint around the left side of the SAMs, and clear it out. This is usually a good move, because all of the SAMs threaten you at the primary waypoint. Place it at the foothills of the mountain northwest of the target waypoint. (Alternatively, another playtester suggests heading due southwest, then sneaking up through the valley south of Waypoint 2.)

Waypoint (2). When you're flying there, stay under 50 feet. In this mission, considering the number of SAMs you're about to face, it's imperative. Just as you cross the border, pop up and take out an SA-15 to the northeast. Then, continue on to the primary waypoint. At your new waypoint, take out all the SAMs you can (2S6, SA-15, SA-8, in that order). Get the first 2S6 manually, then PFZ the other ones on the way to Waypoint 2. (Just make sure that you cycle through to SAM targets so that you don't waste your Hellfires on tanks.)

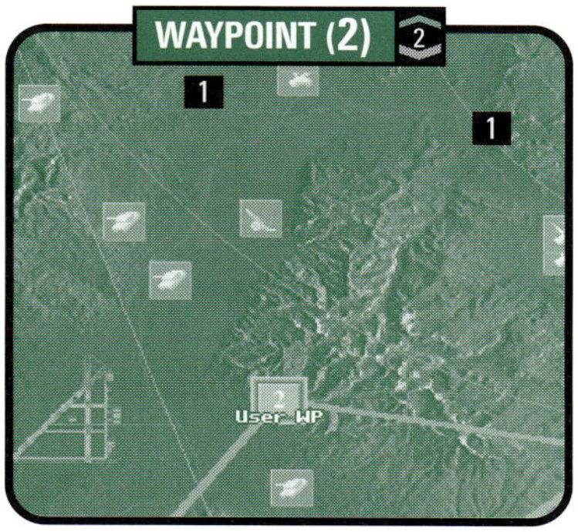

1 2S6s, SA-15, SA-8

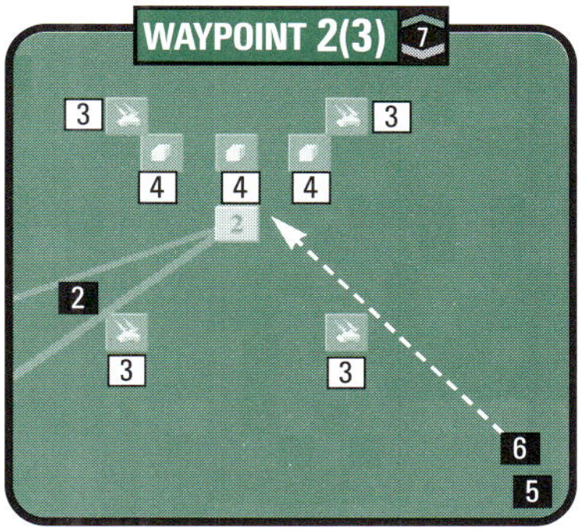

2 SA-15

3 2S6s

4 Command bunkers, Long Track radar

5 2S6s, SA-15, SA-8

6 Havocs, Hokum

Waypoint 2 (3). When you get about 8km out from the third waypoint, slow down and drop down low, to about 20 feet. Your LOS altitude is around 60 or 70, and you should be almost 8 miles out. Or, backtrack home to your takeoff FARP after the primaries are destroyed. Eliminate the 2S6, SA-15, SA-8 trio off your port (left) side. Next, move to a position six miles out from the waypoint and take out all the primary SAM targets first (2S6s) and then go in farther to take out two command bunkers.

A Hokum and two Havocs come to greet you at the second waypoint when you move closer, so take them out with Stingers or send your wingman after them. There's also a BMP-3 around that has some effective guns... give him to your wingman after the Hokums are history. Get everything at the HQ that shows up as PRIMARY in your Upfront display.

The Way Home. You may want to drag the custom waypoint you created to an area just northeast of the primary waypoint. There's a valley and ridge there that's disguising the presence of a few more 2S6s if you didn't kill them on the way to the primary waypoint. You can hide behind the ridge, then sneak in through the valley.

Campaign 11: Offensive Phase Lima

Mission Escort US Armor

Environment Day/Clear

Air Strikes 2

Artillery Strikes 2

Primaries	Mission Rating
6 M-1 Abrams, M-2 Bradleys	6 friendly tanks survive . . S+
	4-5 . . . . S
	1-3 . . . . F
	0 . . . . F-

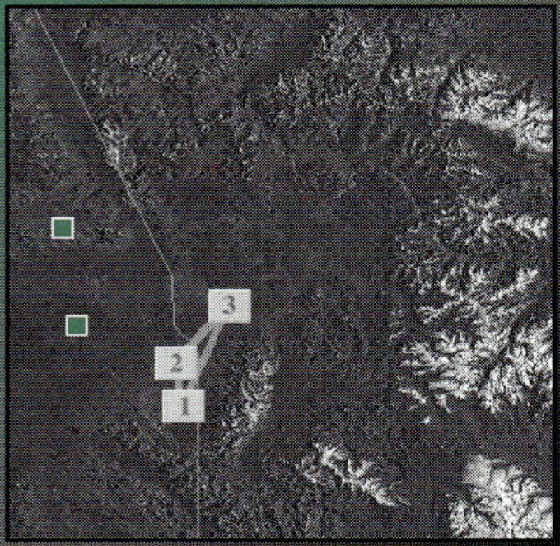

Waypoint 1. As soon as you lift off, transition into forward flight and bear left toward Waypoint 2. The point of this mission is to rendezvous with a section of tanks that are pushing their way to the third waypoint area. Your first plan of action, however, should be to detect a 2S6 site about 8 miles away from waypoint 3 and order your wingman to attack it, or call in an air/artillery strike. (You can sometimes ignore SAMs that aren't directly in your path and avoid detection by staying low. However, it's often harder to stay low in escort missions.)

Waypoint 2. Catch up with the friendly tank convoy at Waypoint 2, then fly scout ahead of them toward the third waypoint. The first threat you'll see, if you pop up, is an enemy tank ambush about halfway between Waypoints 2 and 3. Take them out, but don't use a PFZ (it doesn't distinguish friendlies from enemies).

After you take care of the tanks, go after the enemy Havoc choppers to the east. Engage them with Stingers, but only expend one per target and finish off each helo with gunfire. (More air targets will appear later.)

As tempting as those Su-25 Frogfoot look, ignore them and they won't mess with you. They're going after the advancing US tanks, but they won't kill enough of them for you to worry about. If you're a hotshot and want to score an S+, however, you might want to tangle with them head-on.

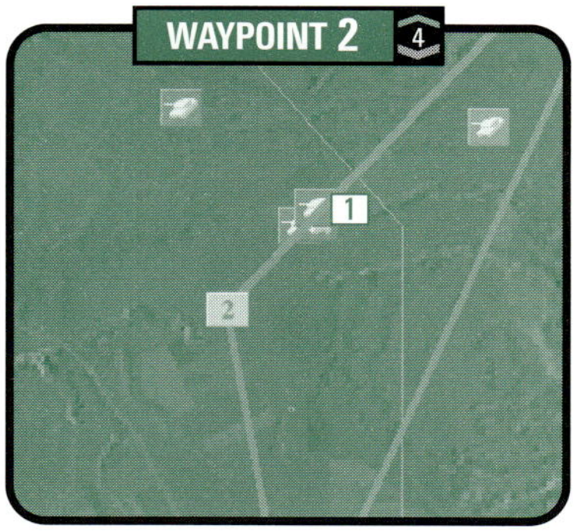

1 M-1 Abrams Tanks

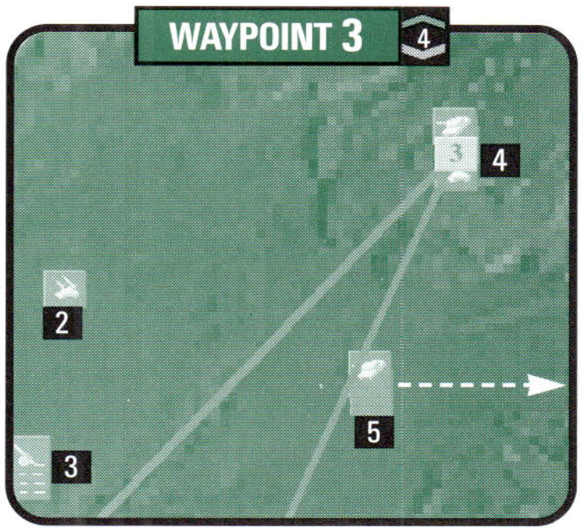

2 2S6s

3 Ambush (T-80U Tanks and SO-122 artillery)

4 2S6, T-80Us, SO-122 artillery

5 Fuel truck convoy

Waypoint 3. As soon as you've offed the Havocs at Waypoint 2, leave the tanks and make tracks to the third waypoint. PFZ the tanks and give them to your wingman while you go after the 2S6 (you can't miss it). It's important to quickly disable the SAM, because two more Havocs come at you from the east and attack the tanks. It's a lot easier to engage air targets when you don't have to worry about SAMs as well. If you're lucky, your tanks will clear out the SAM sites before you show up.

Finally, use your remaining Hellfires to take out any other targets of opportunity you see on the way home (anything you missed on the way into Waypoint 2). If you fly to the east when going home, you can take out a convoy of enemy fuel trucks.

Campaign 12: Offensive Phase Mike

Mission Attack MLRSs

Environment Night/Clear

Air Strikes 1

Artillery Strikes 0

Primaries	*Mission Rating*
4 BM-21s	3-5 KILLED.....S
1 SO-122	1-2............F
	0..............F-

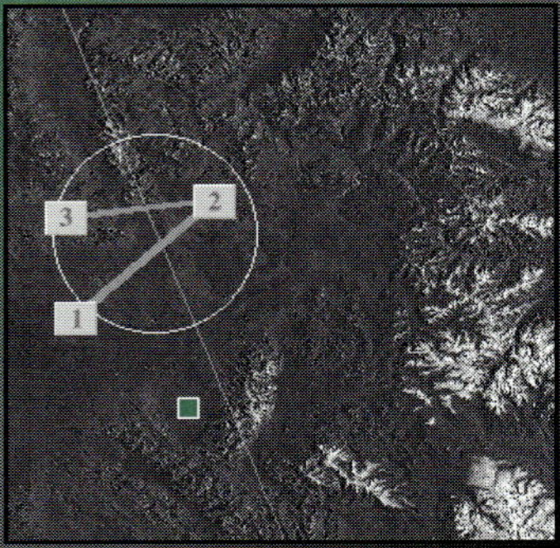

Waypoint 1-2. This mission works best if you stay with the suggested route. Although it appears that you're painting yourself as a target, it's not as bad as it looks. If you adjust your waypoints so that you go *over* the hills, you'll actually be pretty high when you pop up over the ridges. That's not a good thing, considering the fact that the SAMs will fire at you. The point is, fly low and slow.

After takeoff, two Su-25 Frogfoots make an attack. Hover low and shoot whichever one comes in first with a Stinger, followed by your guns. You'll have two aircraft to deal with later, so keep at least two Stingers on your pylons. There's a bonus primary SO-122 artillery site in the area as well (near the 2S6 northeast of Waypoint 1).

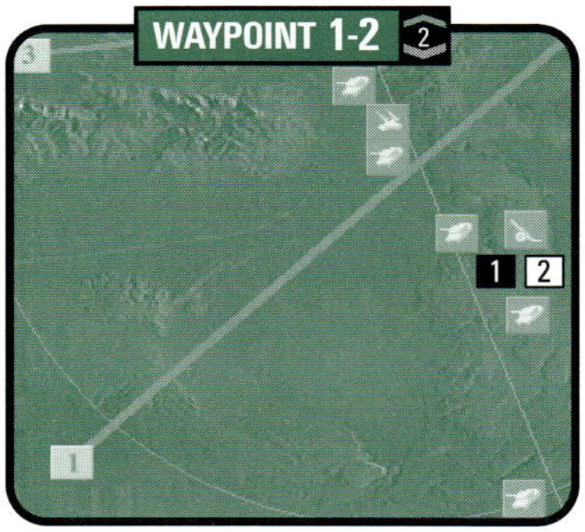

1 2S6

2 SO-122 artillery

Waypoint 2. Cruise at about 30 feet toward Waypoint 2 and take out other incidental 2S6 sites. Bob-up occasionally to update your FCR, but stay low. At the actual waypoint, make the two SA-15s a priority. Set up one PFZ around the ZSU-23 ground gun, and a second one around the SA-15s. Have your wingman attack one PFZ while you take out the other. Then, eliminate the SA-13.

You can handle this waypoint without a PFZ. If you prefer, select a single target and order your wingman to fire at it. Then, use one of your missiles to take out the next target. This keeps both of you from attacking the same target, and gives you authority over what your buddy is firing at.

After SAM duty, make your move against the four MLRSs. Two Havocs arrive on the scene as soon you start attacking them. With luck, you conserved at least two Stingers. If you're still loaded, use any leftover Hellfires on nearby tanks.

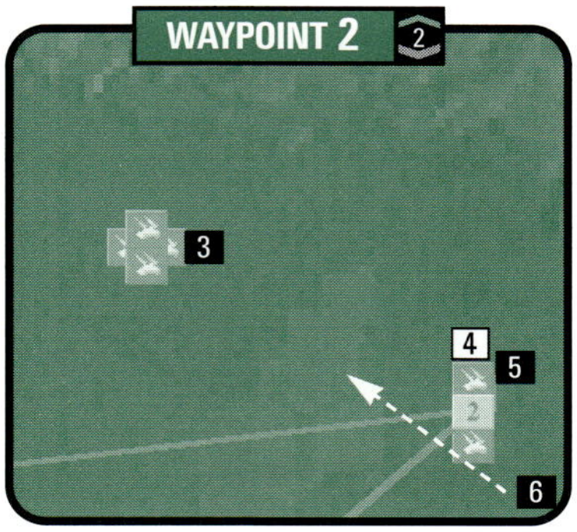

3 SA-15s

4 BM-21 MLRSs

5 ZSU-23, SA-13

6 Havocs (moving northwest)

Campaign 13: Offensive Phase November

Mission Attack choppers

Environment Night/Clear

Air Strikes 3

Artillery Strikes 3

Primaries	Mission Rating
4 Mi-28s	6 killed.......S+
4 Ka-50s	4-5............S
4 Mi-24s	1-3............F
	0..............F-

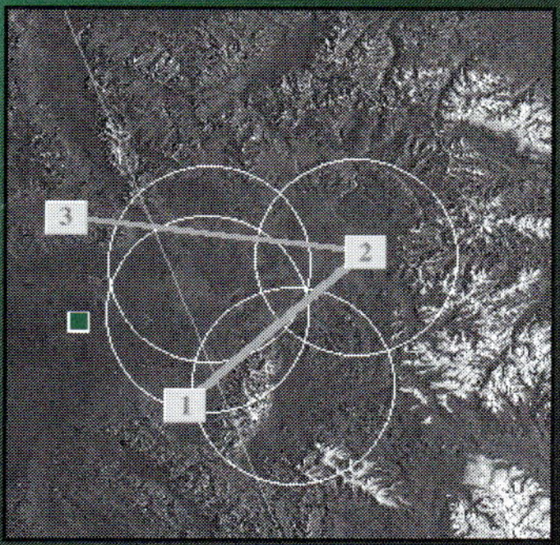

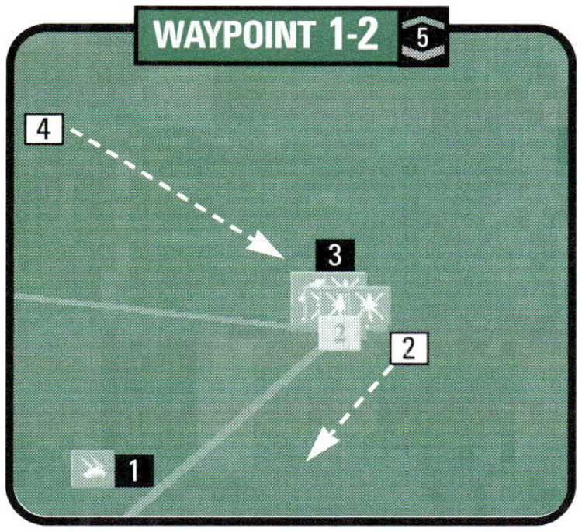

1. 2S6s
2. Hokums, Havocs, Hinds
3. 2S6s
4. Hokums, Havocs, Hinds (second wave)

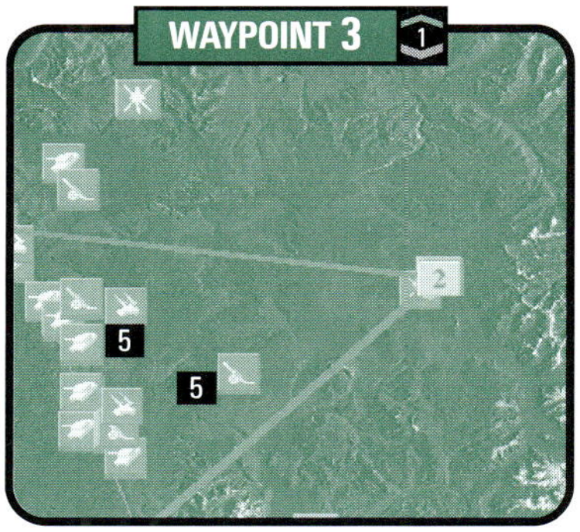

5. 2S6

Waypoint 1. (Rockets can be an asset in this mission. Take one bank of Hellfires, one of rockets.) After take off, fly at full speed north and take out the 2S6 sites near your takeoff FARP. Next, head east and prepare your cockpit by switching your radar to air mode by pressing [Pg Up]. That's the only way you're going to be able to find the primaries. It's also a good idea to display your Radar MFD page (cycle to it by pressing [<,]).

As soon as you run into the pair of Hokums, go in fast and low with a single Stinger. Get your wingman to fire on one of the choppers as well, then follow up with guns (if you don't, you'll later be wishing later that you had).

Midway to Waypoint 2, you're going to have your hands full with two Hokums, two Havocs and two Hinds. Of course, you'll want to take out the Hokums first – they fire air-to-air missiles at you – then the Havocs and Hinds. Use your wingman's weapons without regard. You won't have enough Stingers to accomplish the mission alone.

There's not much time for relaxation after you dispatch the initial wave. A second wave of the same variety appears. Use whatever Stingers you have left against the Hokums, and guns or rockets against the rest.

Waypoint 3. Fly toward your landing FARP and take out 2S6s on the way. Then, sweep out the other four helicopters that come along (two Havocs and two Hinds.) If you have any ammo after that, use it on any remaining tanks.

Campaign 14: Offensive Phase Quebec

Mission Attack Enemy FARP **Air Strikes** 3

Environment Dawn-To-Day/Clear **Artillery Strikes** 0

PRIMARIES	MISSION RATING
2 Bunkers	5..............S
2 Mi-28s	1-4............F
3 Tents	0..............F-
1 Ural-375	

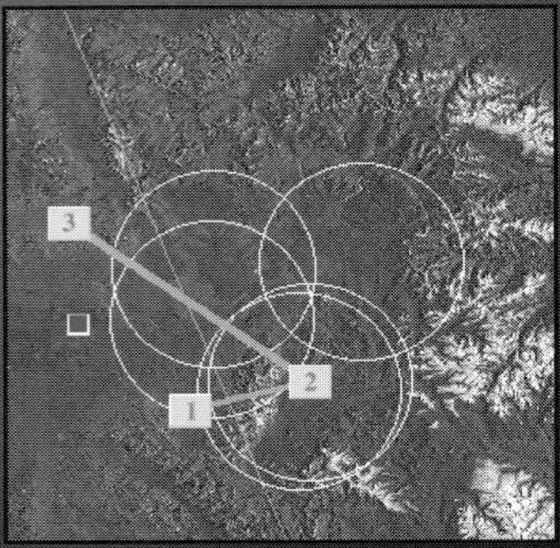

Waypoint 2. For this mission, it's back to the drawing board, or at least the mission planning computer. Create a new waypoint approximately halfway between 1 and 2, and drag it just below the snow-capped mountain. Doing so lets you approach what was originally the second waypoint from a valley position, instead of having to fly over a hill.

Activate your PNVS once you take off, and bring the carat for Waypoint 2 into sight. It's fairly close, which is why you'll want to stay low.

Waypoint 2(3). There's not much in the way of SAMs here, but you will find a couple of Havocs, along with some fuel tanks. Taking the helos out now is a smart move — even though they may hold off on attacking you, you can almost bet that you'll see them again later at Waypoint 3. Besides, they give you a point booster. Once the area is clean, bob-up to 400 feet or so to catch a glimpse of your surroundings (with FCR active).

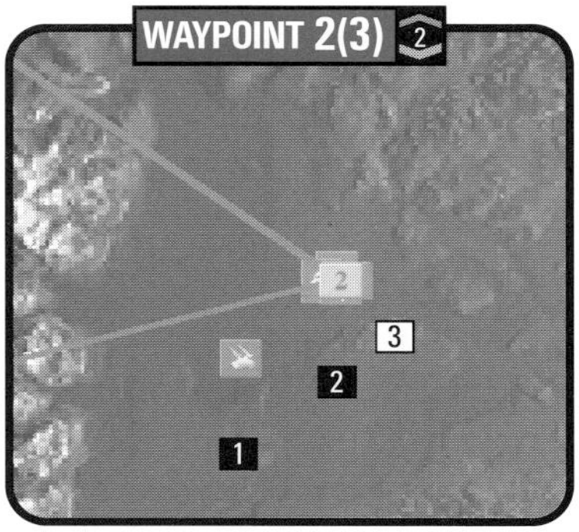

1 2S6s

2 2S6, CIS Soldiers (with Stingers)

3 Havocs, fuel trucks, tents, bunkers

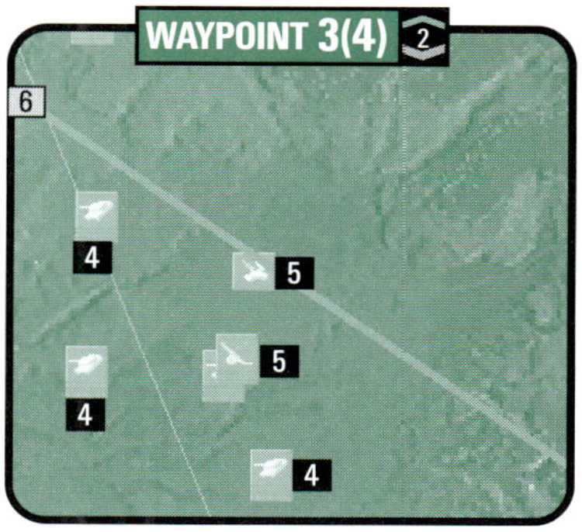

4 T-80Us

5 2S6s

6 To Waypoint 3(4)

Waypoint 3(4). As in the case of so many campaign missions, it's dangerous on the trip home. Keep your distance and go into an extremely low auto-hover when you're about 7 or 8 klicks away from the threats. Once you have everything in range, cycle through the targets (T) to select a SAM site.

Don't use a PFZ here if you want to assign targets to your wingman. It's not a good idea, because he'll waste his missiles on something that can just as easily be gotten with the Chain Gun later. The best way to designate single targets is to give the Attack My Target command (Ctrl 3) and keep that target locked until your wingman destroys it. Then, check out the destruction with TADS camera, and proceed to the next target.

Both of you are at the edge of the threat radii, so logically you want to take out the long-range 2S6s first. After it's history, you can kill everything else here. Although there are a minimal number of ground targets, everything you can sight are your primaries, including the tents. Use your wingman. Let him enjoy a kill or two, then take one for yourself. In this manner, knock everything out from the safety of your hover, but conserve at least three Hellfires for later.

Campaign 15: Offensive Phase Romeo

Mission Destroy SCUDs	**Air Strikes** 0
Environment Night/Clear	**Artillery Strikes** 1

Primaries	*Mission Rating*
4 SCUDs	3-4 . . . . S
1 Ural-375	5 killed . . . . S+
	1-2 . . . . F
	0 . . . . F-

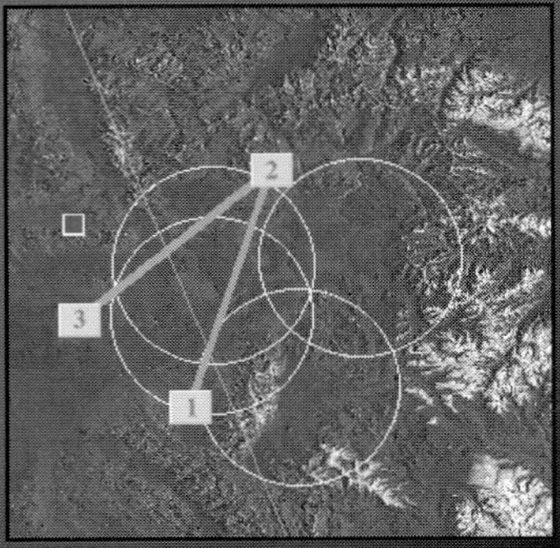

Waypoint 1. Waypoint manipulation is your main survival tool for this mission. Do the same thing that you did in the previous mission — create one new waypoint and drag it low, just below the mountain range. Add one more to make a zigzag path up the valley toward the artillery sites. (See the Waypoint 2-3 picture.) This flight path serves a dual purpose; you don't have to pop over ridges (and expose yourself to fire), and it keeps the central mountain range between you and the SAMs.

Waypoints (2-3). These are the two waypoints you created. Ordinarily, the Havoc helicopters that are here now, you'd see after you accomplished the mission and headed for home. This southern pitstop, however, lets you gun them down early. Luckily, the area isn't graced by the presence of SAMs, so you're not taking any large risks.

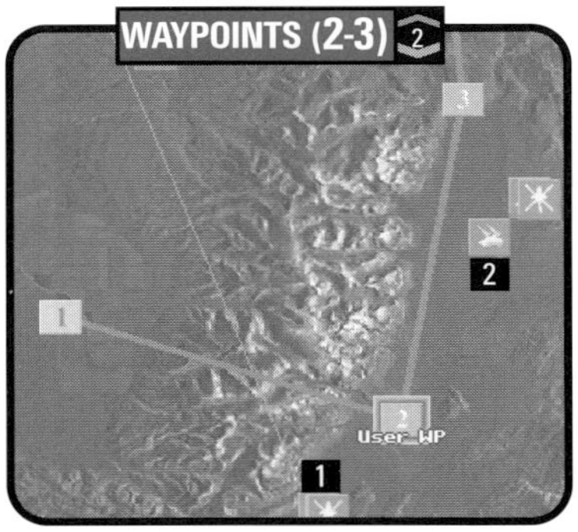

1 Enemy FARP 1

2 2S6, Enemy FARP 2

Next, head up the valley and attack a second enemy FARP. Use common sense and take out the 2S6 first. Had you followed the default waypoint path, the 2S6 and helicopters from this area would have ambushed you over the ridge. Instead, the Havocs are still grounded if you move quickly enough, which means that you can use your Hellfires against them. (Alternatively, save your Hellfires and use your guns against the Havocs.) Use your chain gun against anything else there, then move north.

Your next objective is to get the 2S6s and artillery near the third waypoint (one you created). They're expecting you from another direction. You, however, approach from the valley instead of popping over the hill. Eliminate the SAM and artillery units, then head for the next waypoint.

Take out the 2S6s and Havocs (yes, at yet another FARP — you should have FARP destruction down by now). Between the three FARPs, you should have accumulated quite a stash of mission points by now.

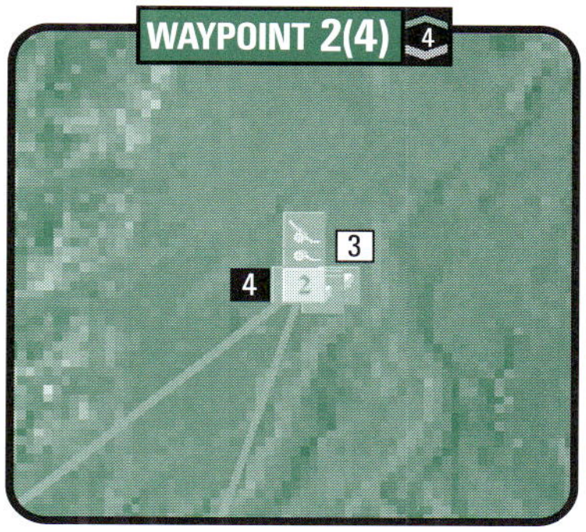

3 SCUD launchers, fuel truck

4 CIS Soldiers with Stinger missiles

Waypoint 2 (4). The fourth waypoint (or the second, if you didn't create any extra ones) contains the primaries. Sneak up within two miles, then make a quick ascension to update your FCR radar. Bend the rules a little and hover high — no SAMs are here to contest you.

When in TADS mode, you'll find several CIS Soldiers. If you move within 1km of them, be prepared to deal with their weapons. They can't hit you if you're not close, so staying far enough out negates this danger. They don't show up on radar, and therefore don't appear in the TSD when you've got FCR active. Keep an eye out for them whenever you're near FARPs, convoys and other likely soldier locations. Go into a hover, switch to TADS, and take out everything but the bunkers with your guns. Use your TADS camera to slew and lock onto targets you see in the TADS MFD.

Get the primary SCUDs, then destroy two more 2S6s on the way home if you've got any ordnance left.

Campaign 16: Offensive Phase Tango

Mission Escort US Armor

Environment Night/Clear

Air Strikes 3

Artillery Strikes 3

Primaries	*Mission Rating*
11 M-1 Abrams	11 friendly tanks survive . . S+
	8-10 . . . . S
	1-7 . . . . F
	0 . . . . F-

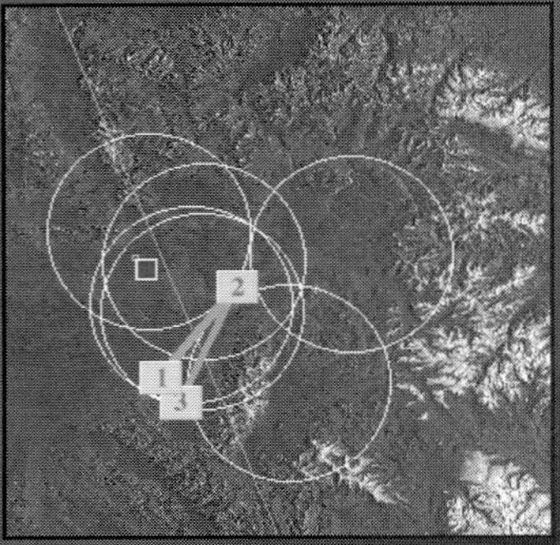

Waypoint 1. Escort missions almost always involve time restrictions, and this one's no exception. Pay no attention to the oddly decorated campaign building... it's just a minor pit stop on your way to victory.

Leave the waypoints as they are, and put on your night eyes as soon you're in the cockpit. Before you even worry about throttling up and lifting off, activate FCR and pick up a dangerously close 2S6. Take it out, then quickly head toward the second waypoint. In short span of time, you're going to have to take on enemy helo, as well as tanks that dare to threaten your friendly positions.

About midway to your second waypoint, you'll uncover a tank ambush and couple of SAMs. They don't pose much danger to you, but they *are* directly in the path of the tanks you're escorting. Set up a PFZ around them, and do it fast — two enemy FARPs to the south and west are in the process of sending in enemy helicopters. Call in a friendly artillery or air strike to attack the tanks and SAMS at the enemy line.

By this time, the Havocs will have spotted your position and made their approach from the outside FARPS. Take out the helos ... they're going after your tanks. Stay low... there are a few SAMs out there that you need to surprise before they find you. Use a quad of Hellfires to eliminate the four you're facing already, and two additional ones to get the SAMs to the rear of your tanks. Clear the entire area, and don't be afraid to use your wingman's Hellfires.

Next, face the Havocs and use your Stingers on them.

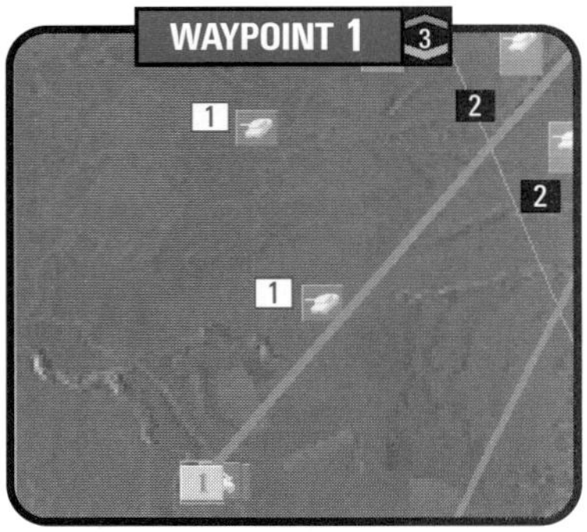

1 M1 Abrams
2 T-80Us

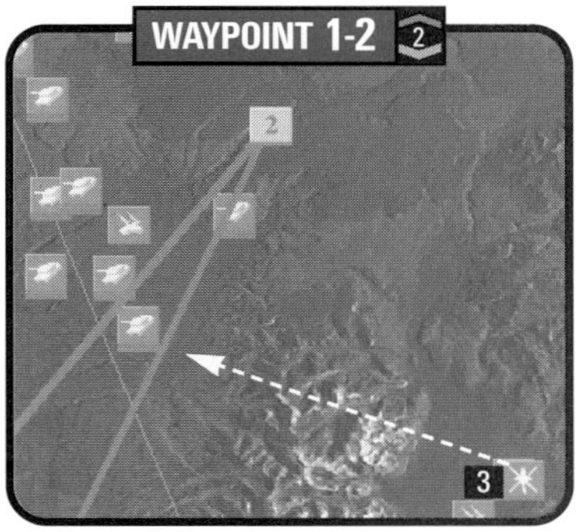

3 Havocs from FARP

Check on your tanks before you resume your original course to Waypoint 2, making sure they're not under attack by anything you might have missed.

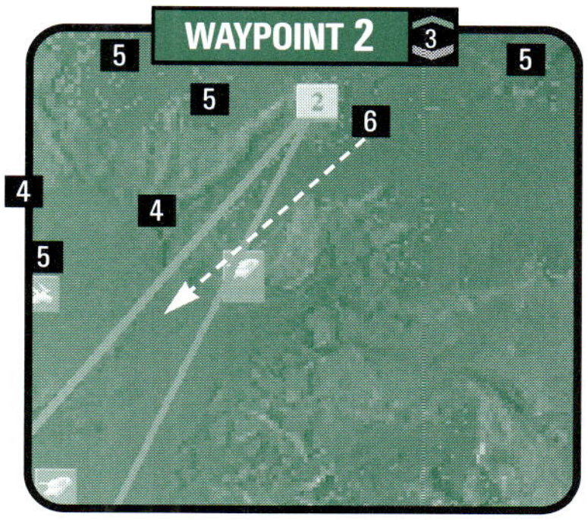

4 2S6s

5 2S6

6 Havocs

Waypoint 2. When you finally arrive, PFZ the tanks and send all your remaining Hellfires in ripple-fire style. Save one in your weapons bank for a lone 2S6 near this point. If you're Winchester, send your wingman in after it.

Once you mop up here, check on your tanks a second time and make sure nothing's attacking them. At this point you're free to fly low and corral the tanks over the hill. You still haven't reached the actual waypoint, but you need to ensure that the tanks do, and that they do so safely. Pop up every few minutes to make sure nothing's around. You can pretty much ignore the "Threat left" and "Threat right" messages from your CP/G. You're low enough that it won't matter.

When you're going home, swing west of the SAM from the Havocs' FARP. The SAM's arc touches your flight path between 2 and 3. You can avoid it entirely by back-tracking to Waypoint 1.

Campaign 17: Offensive Phase Victor

Mission Attack Airfield

Environment Dawn-To-Day/Clear

Air Strikes 3

Artillery Strikes 0

Primaries	Mission Rating
14 M-1 Abrams	8 killed.......S+
4 MI-28s	5-7............S
2 Ural-375s	1-4............F
3 Tents	0..............F-

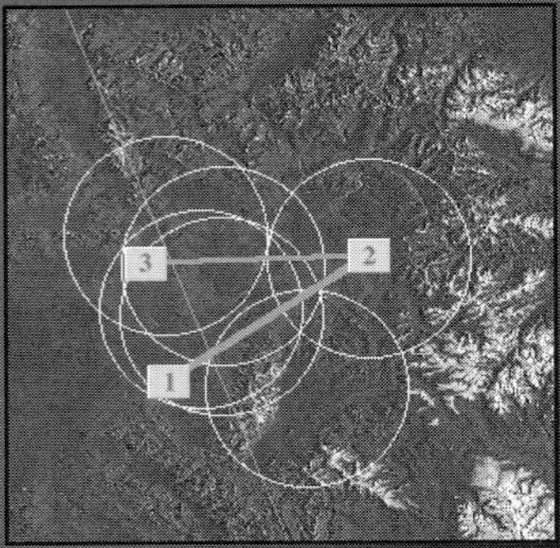

Waypoint (2). First things first ... create a new flight path by adding a waypoint between 1 and 2 that lets you bypass the mountain via the southern route. This new waypoint also leads you away from the SAMs, which is a good thing — they lock on you as soon as you lift off. You can deal with them later.

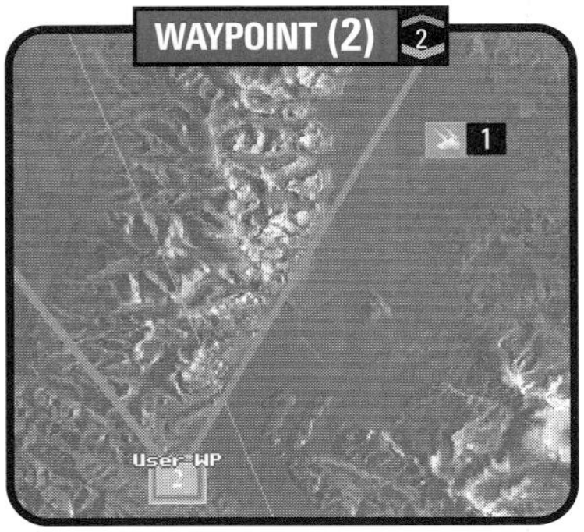

1 2S6

For now, activate PNVS and make a stealthy approach through the valley. Head north to the first actual waypoint (Waypoint 3 if you created an additional one, Waypoint 2 otherwise). Take out the 2S6 that lights you up on the way, and you've got clear sailing the rest of the way.

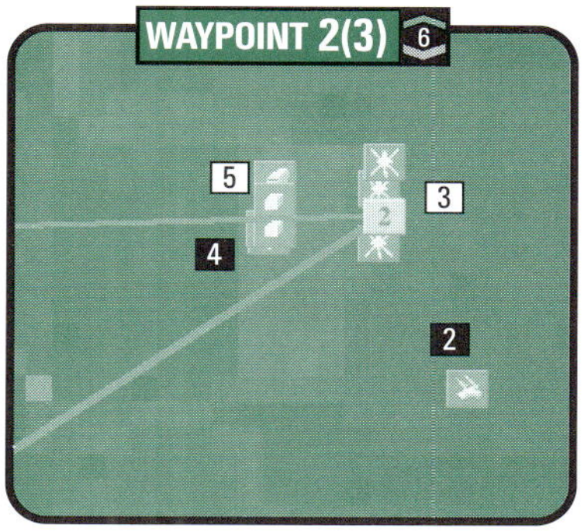

2 2S6

3 Havocs

4 Havocs

5 Tents, fuel trucks

Waypoint 2 (3). Here, you have multiple threats — a 2S6 and four Havocs. Move within 7km (just within Hellfire range), then bob up to acquire targets at the waypoint. Descend into an auto-hover and get ready for your attack.

The helos are your first primary targets... one or more of the Havocs may be grounded. Handle them yourself. Although your wingman can tangle with airborne helos, he won't use Hellfires against grounded ones, and he'll waste his Stingers.

On your ASE, you may notice the plethora of SAM ranges to the west and become concerned. Don't worry about them now, because you're shielded by the ridge. Get the Havocs out of the way, then take out the other targets at the FARP.The recommended method for attacking them is to switch to TADS and cycle through targets manually. Those little CIS infantry soldiers may be small, but they're well-armed with SAMs. To be really brutal, you can melt them with a Hellfire apiece, but it's a waste of ammo. The best takedown for a CIS soldier is to move over the center of action, switch to ground radar mode, and gun him down.

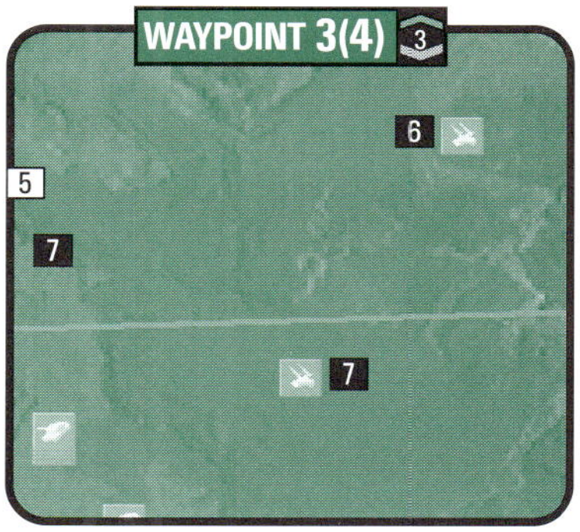

6 SA-15

7 2S6

Waypoint 3 (4). With the mission's primary targets eliminated (the airfield threats), you can head home. On the way, eliminate some of the SAMs that you originally saw over the other side of the ridge. Take out as many as you can with your remaining ordnance and head for the landing FARP.

Campaign 18: Offensive Phase Whiskey

Mission Attack Depot

Environment Day/Clear

Air Strikes 0

Artillery Strikes 0

Primaries	*Mission Rating*
5 Bunkers	6 killed.......S
1 Command Bunker	1-5 killed.....F
	0 killed.......F-

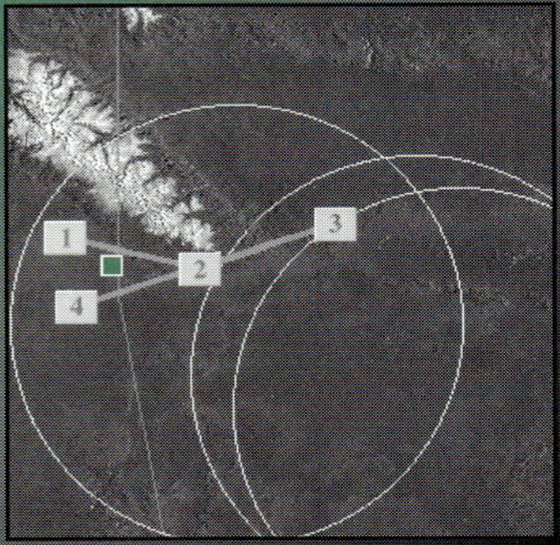

Waypoint 1. This mission is nasty — after you leave your takeoff FARP, you'll soon run into a pair of Sukhoi 25s. The best way to deal with them may seem cowardly, but it works. Hang out at the FARP in a low altitude hover, bring up your RAD MFD and the (Shift)(U) Upfront target screen. Next, activate air radar mode and time compression.

After a few minutes, the planes will appear on your radar. Restore normal time and get ready to fight. Your FARP has several Avenger guns that will hopefully down the Sukhoi. To give them a hand, swivel to bring the aircraft into view. Wait until one of them makes a head-on pass, then unleash a Stinger.

The initial wait for the Sukhois can consume a lot of fuel. If you get low, land and refuel/rearm. This detracts 50% from your score; however, there's enough stuff to blow up in this mission that you'll probably come out slightly ahead even if you do land.

From here, head to Waypoint 2. (Alternatively, consider skipping it entirely and flying directly to Waypoint 3.)

Waypoint 2. You don't *have* to destroy the pair of 2S6 sites on the way to Waypoint 2, but getting rid of them now makes it easier to return to your FARP — you can fly at higher altitudes on the way home without worrying about being spotted.

At Waypoint 2, you'll find lots of forward artillery. Good points, about 600. And since you get your wingman's points, assign them to him. Fly within 1km and tell your

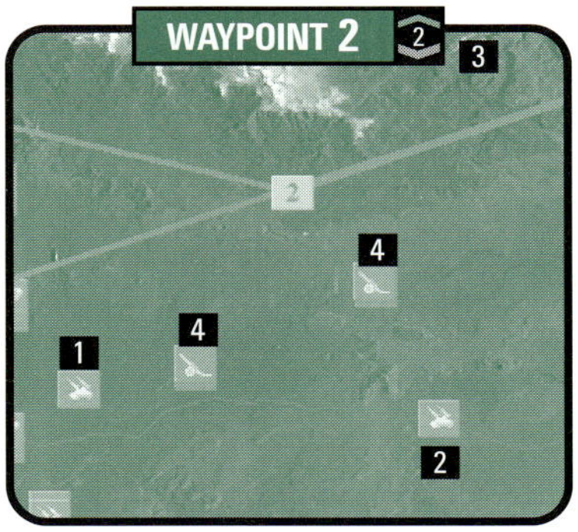

1 2S6
2 SA-8
3 SA-15
4 SO-122 artillery

wingman to engage your target. Keep your altitude low (15 feet or so) and transition into a hover. Move to another target and do the same thing until they're gone. You don't want to establish a PFZ here because you need to conserve his Hellfires for the mission targets.

A little northeast of the artillery, you'll encounter an SA-8. Take it out for points ... it's pretty easy to kill as far as SAMs go, especially if you sneak in within gun range.

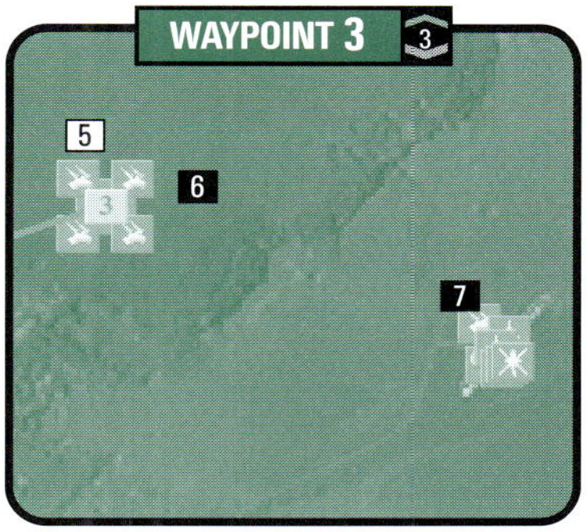

5 Bunkers
6 2S6s
7 Enemy FARP

Waypoint 3. Stay under 50 feet as you cruise to Waypoint 3, but bob-up occasionally to update your TSD. Weave around the circles on your TSD and ASE MFD displays. (The circles represent detection ranges for a couple of nearby 2S6s.) Once you near the SAMs, bob-up to get a valid LOS on them and launch a Hellfire. Give your wingman the other one.

A duo of Havoc helicopters come in after you start your attack on the 4 bunkers (your primary targets). Once you take out the aircraft, get the SAMs guarding the bunkers. There's also an SA-13 to the north that will toast you if you're not careful. Take him out with Hellfires before you go in after the targeted bunkers.

There's a FARP east of the waypoint with grounded helicopters. While you take out the airfield SAM site and use the hills as cover, send your wingman in after the helicopters. (This uses up some of his Stingers, but that's okay.) Then, establish a PFZ around the bunkers for your wingman. Let your wingman get them while you take out airfield SAMs and helicopter (they're grounded until they see you).

Use camera view to keep track of what targets your wingman has destroyed. Also use F11 inverse tactical. Delete PFZ after he's done. Once his bunkers are gone, go in yourself and demolish the rest of them.

The mission is accomplished after all bunkers are destroyed. For extra points, go back to airfield (which is now undefended). Get the Frogfoots, EW radar site and fuel tanks. Farther south, you'll also find an SA-11 and several SA-8s.

Waypoint 4. On the way home, if you and your wingman have missiles left over, go after other things you find to rack up points. There's some artillery and tanks that make excellent ripple-fire PFZ locations.

Campaign 19: Offensive Phase X-Ray

Mission Attack convoy

Environment Night/Clear

Air Strikes 0

Artillery Strikes 0

Primaries	*Mission Rating*
3 SA-8s	11 killed......S+
6 BRDM-2s	9-10 killed....S
3 2S6s	1-8 killed.....F
1 Ural-375	0 killed.......F-

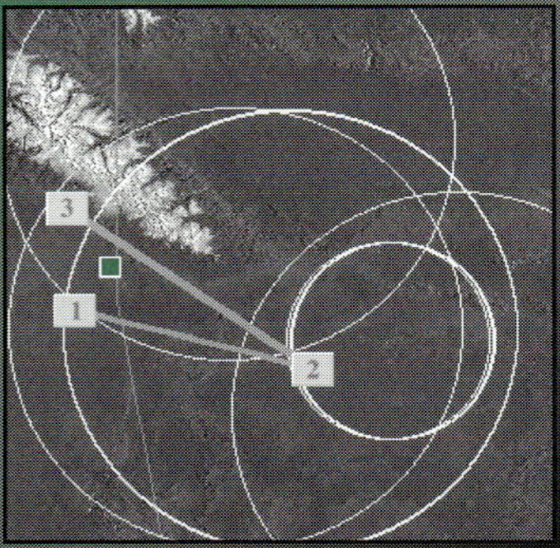

Waypoint 1. As soon as you take off, you're vulnerable to fire from two 2S6 sites on the battle line, about 6km east of your position. The very first thing you want to do is turn on your PNVS system — this is a night mission, and you won't be able to see much without it.

There's nothing too different about fighting SAMs at night. They can still see you with their radar, and you can still see them with your PNVS system and TADS FLIR camera. Approach the 2S6s cautiously, making sure you stay low and slow (and therefore, undetected). Target one of them and hand it off to your wingman (press Ctrl 3), while you handle the second site.

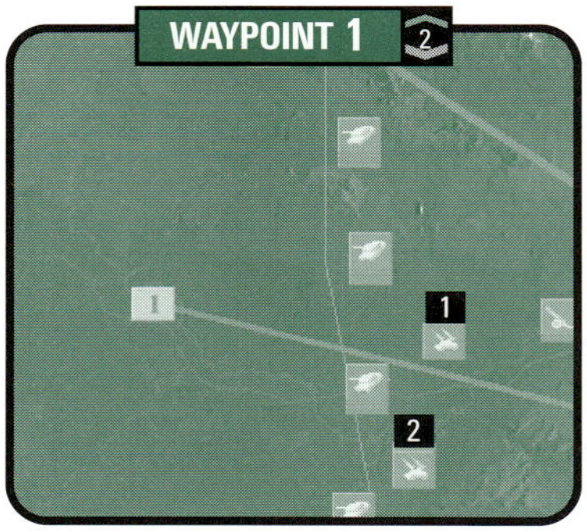

1 2S6

2 SO-122 Artillery, 2S6

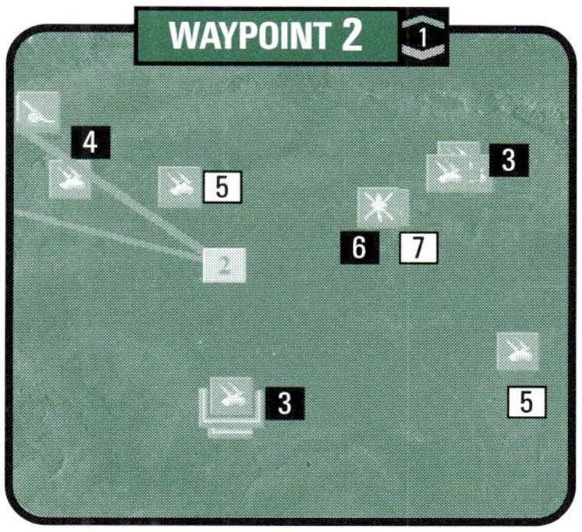

- **3** SA-11s, Snow Drift radar
- **4** SA-8
- 5 SA-8s
- **6** Havocs
- 7 2S6, BRDMs, fuel truck

Waypoint 2. On the way to Waypoint 2, take out the artillery sites (SO-122s) that are in your flight path when you cross into enemy territory. Use your Chain gun against the artillery — there's no sense in wasting any missiles before you reach the primary target.

Ignore the SA-11 warning your Bitching Betty broadcasts about this time. You've got bigger SAMs to fry. Instead, set up a PFZ and take out the two primary SA-8s south of artillery sites. You'll have to sneak up on them.

When you resume your journey to the waypoint, notice the 2 friendly Blackhawks on your radar (in air mode). They're also headed to Waypoint 2, but they're going to get shot down before they arrive. Don't feel too guilty about not helping them out... you're better off saving yourself. Keep tracking to Waypoint 2 — it's safer.

Near the actual waypoint, you've got an additional SA-8 primary and a couple of Havocs to take out. Get the SAM first — he shot down the Blackhawks and is hiding behind the hill. Stay low to keep from being seen, then go low over the hill and gun him. Hopefully, the Havocs won't have spotted you yet, either.

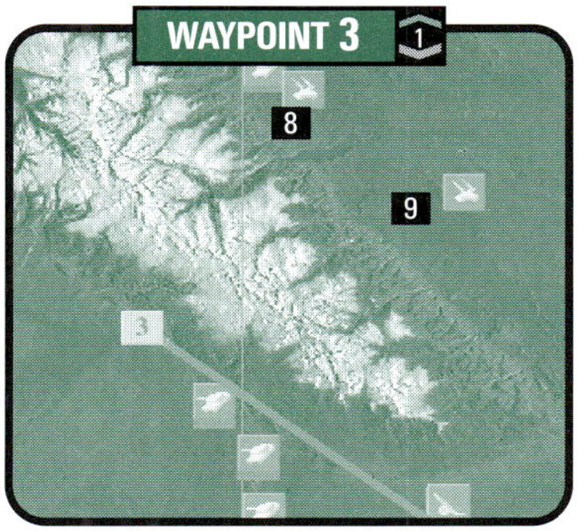

- **8** T-80Us, 2S6
- **9** SA-8

Okay, now you're ready to accomplish the mission objective. See that convoy? Try to stay about 7km away from it. It's heavily armed with 2S6s and BRDM-2s, both of which shoot liberally at you. The helicopters (Havocs you spotted earlier) will soon see you and initiate an attack. Finish off the helicopters with Stingers, maintain your current position to stay out of the convoy's range.

Next, use your wingman as extra firepower against the convoy SAMs. Assign him a single target and take another one for yourself. Fire Hellfires simultaneously with him, then bob-up to establish a valid LOS for the missiles at least 2 seconds before the timer runs out.

Once the 2S6s are gone, establish PFZ around the rest of the convoy, and another around the SA-11s. Use Hellfires against everything except the fuel trucks (gun them).

Waypoint 3. If your Longbow has taken damage at this point, fly directly home. You may encounter a few SA-11s on the way, along with a few T-80Us to the north. If you're not injured, take them out to use up your leftover weapons and rack up points.

Campaign 20: Offensive Phase Yankee

Mission Attack TOC post | **Air Strikes** 0

Environment Day/Clear | **Artillery Strikes** 0

Primaries	*Mission Rating*
1 Command Bunker	4 killed.......S
1 Bunker	1-3 killed.....F
1 Tent	0 killed.......F-
1 2S6	

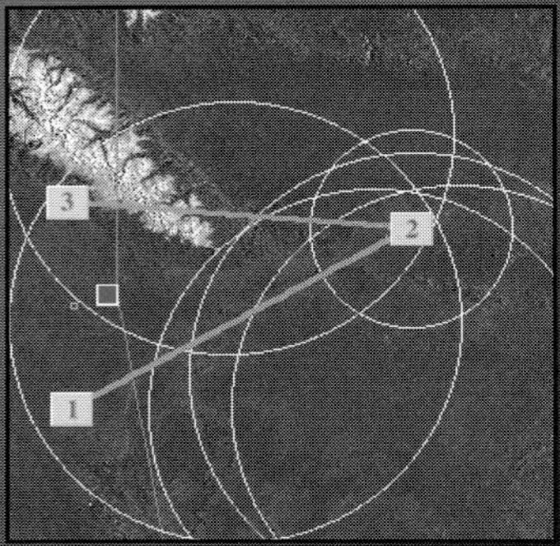

Waypoint 1. After you take off from your FARP and head for Waypoint 2, brace yourself for a tough ride. First of all, a duo of 2S6s are blocking your path. You need to take them out now, because you'll be busy later. Try handing one off to your wingman while you take on the second one.

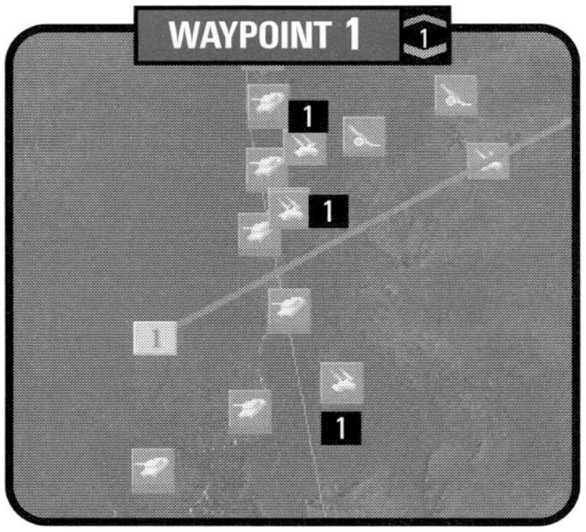

1 2S6

While you're in the neighborhood, use your guns to take out the small artillery units you see (after the 2S6s are gone, of course). Artillery almost always appears in a linear group of four. One effective approach to taking them out is to approach from one end of the line. Cruise along at about 70 knots and at an altitude of 70 feet and strafe them using your guns. You should be able to take them all in a single pass. If you're having trouble aiming, activate TADS target acquisition and manually pan the camera/gun.

Once the smoke settles from the artillery, two enemy Sukhoi 25s appear on the horizon. This is exactly why you're carrying Stingers. Go head-on with one of the approaching fighters and fire at him when he's within 4km. Also, reduce your speed to nearly a hover so that you can follow the fighter's turn if he continues the approach. (Although turning makes you more vulnerable, it also makes it easier to hit them.) Don't waste all your Stingers on the Sukhoi unless you're flying with unlimited ammo. You're going to face enemy choppers later and will need them.

Once damaged, the Sukhois may ignore you and head for your takeoff FARP instead (their original objective). Don't be fooled immediately, though — if the Sukhois appear to be running away, they may actually be making a second pass at you. Activate your air radar to get a 360-degree picture of where they're headed in relation to your current position.

After you destroy or discourage the aircraft, locate the nearby SA-8. Dropping low (and employing NOE flight) will cause it to lose its LOS and missile lock on you. Then, you can approach it with your guns.

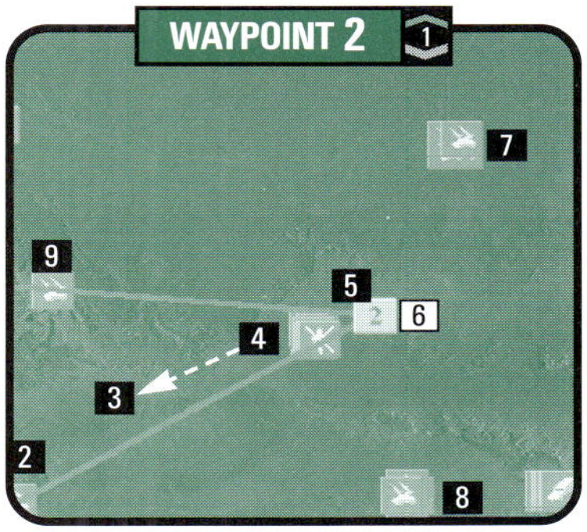

- 2 SA-8
- 3 Su-25 Frogfoot
- 4 SA-15, 2S6, Bar Lock radar
- 5 Havocs (grounded)
- 6 Bunkers, tent, 2S6
- 7 2S6s
- 8 SA-11s, Snow Drift radar
- 9 SA-15

Waypoint 2. Resuming your flight to Waypoint 2, you'll find an SA-11 and 2S6. Get the latter first ... remember, 2S6s pose the most danger because they have both long-range missiles and short-range guns. Unlike with other SAMs, there's no moving within their minimum range.

Finally, on to the enemy FARP (and your objective, the command post). Send your wingman after the SA-15 while you take out the grounded helicopters. (You'd be well-advised to do this first. Although you might be tempted to wait, they'll launch in a few minutes if left alone.)

Havocs out of the way, you can then turn your attention to the 2S6s surrounding the bunker complex and the command bunker. Any intact, grounded helicopters will then lift off in an attempt to defend the command bunker.

Before you make your gun run on the primary bunker, make a quick TADS MFD check to make sure no soldiers are around. Stay as low as you possibly can as you approach the 2 bunkers and the tent. At about 1km out, send your wingman in for the primary bunker and remain in a low hover. Once you verify that he's destroyed the target (check the TADS MFD), use your Hellfires liberally against any remaining SAMs and tanks around Waypoint 2.

Waypoint 3. On the way to the landing FARP, take out the SA-15 and as many artillery sites and tanks as your remaining weapons allow. You can make straight runs on them once the SAMs are gone, since they're the only thing that can really harm you.

Don't forget that you can establish PFZs for your wingman. He needs to use up his leftover ammo as well. You'll know when he's out of ammo when he says "We're Winchester ammo."

Campaign 21: Offensive Phase Zulu

Mission Rescue US pilot

Environment Day/Cloudy

Air Strikes 0

Artillery Strikes 2

Primaries	Mission Rating
1 Soldier (friendly)	MH-53J lands safely . . S
1 MH-53J Pave Low	MH-53J shot down . . F

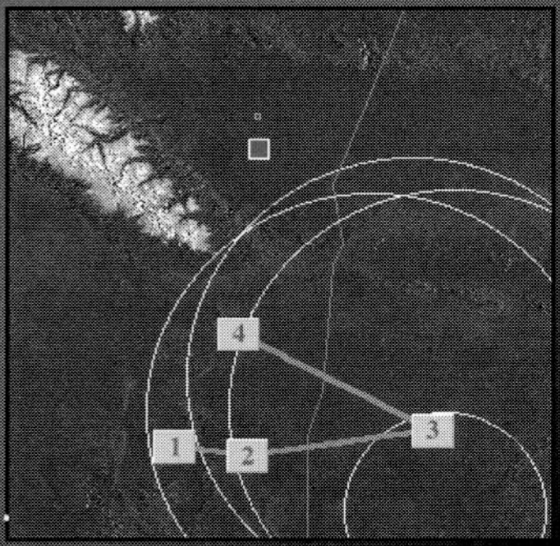

Waypoint 1. In most missions, you can take your time, firing at anything that gets in your way, and searching for cool stuff to destroy. This mission, however, tests your reflexes and gives you time restrictions. One of your flight buddies has gotten himself shot down behind enemy lines and needs a rescue lift. Although *you're* not going to pick him up, your duty is to escort a second aircraft that will. For this reason, you need to head straight for the second waypoint. Don't worry about points — your main concern is ensuring that the pilot and the rescue chopper stay alive.

Waypoint 2. The second waypoint is where you rendezvous with the rescue craft, an MH-53J Pave Low that takes off and follows you as soon as you approach the waypoint. Use your F6 external camera view to make sure he takes off, then make tracks to Waypoint 3. You and the Pave Low must rescue the pilot before a ground convoy with armed infantry arrives.

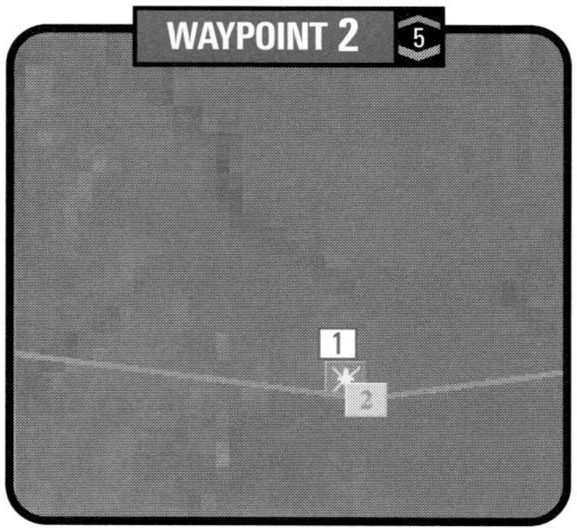

1 MH-53 Pave Low

Cheat: *If you want to eliminate the time element in this mission, you can fly using a shortcut method. Instead of approaching Waypoint 2, swing wide left or right and head directly for Waypoint 3. By doing so, you avoid activating the Pave Low. and are free to go search out and destroy every threat you find. You still have to make sure the pilot stays alive, but this method makes the rescue chopper's journey a lot safer. Once you secure the area, go back to Waypoint 2 and activate the rescue chopper. Then, go pick up the pilot and head for base.*

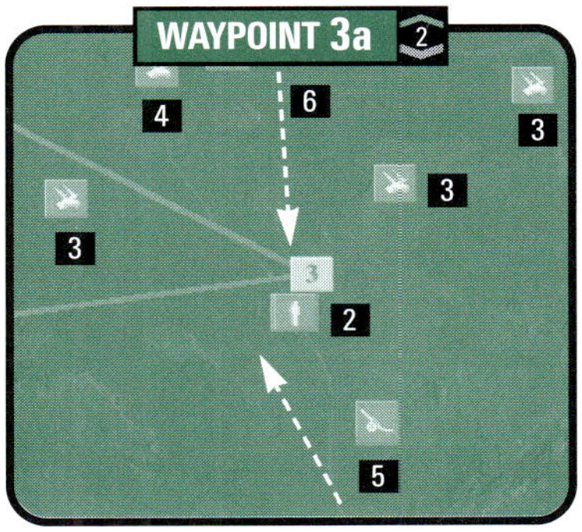

- 2 CIS soldiers
- 3 SA-8
- 4 SA-8, 2S6s
- 5 Transport trucks (with CIS soldiers)
- 6 Havocs, Hokum, Hind

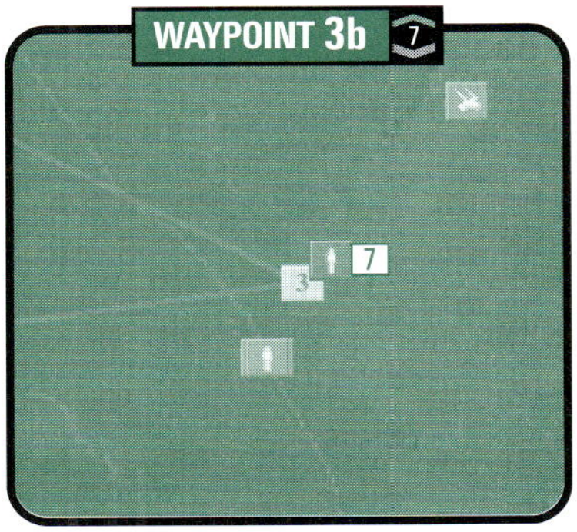

- 7 U.S. pilot

Waypoint 3. Don't stay too low once you're close to this waypoint... SAMs are there, and you want them to find you instead of the Pave Low. In essence, you're acting as a distraction. The first threat to detect you will probably be an SA-8. He's within threatening range of the Pave Low, so you need to take him out first. Next, go after the ground convoy near the downed pilot and take out its 2S6 and any troop transport trucks you can find.

This is where the mission gets tricky. Most likely, you're in FCR mode because you've been pounding away at the convoy with your Hellfires. The real enemies, however, are made of flesh and are carrying guns ... the CIS soldiers. And there's no detecting them with your radar. Instead, you need to switch to TADS mode and activate your TADS MFD. Cycle through the most threatening targets using Ctrl T, zoom in with Z, and gun down any soldiers that appear to be rushing toward the downed pilot. They've got handguns and plan to kill him.

While you kill soldiers that are jumping out of the transport trucks, your Pave Low should be landing near the pilot. By the time it lands, you should have cleared the battlefield of any armed infantry. Your next task is to eliminate a couple of nearby SA-8s and another 2S6. (You can use a PFZ if you so desire.)

The situation that just looked successful soon gets marred by the appearance of 4 enemy helicopters. Switch to ATA missiles and use one per chopper if possible. Your wingman can help you out as well. If you run out of Stingers, try your luck with the Chain Gun — it can track 220 degrees with your helmet's slewing capabilities.

As soon as the pilot is picked up and the Pave Low lifts off, head home. Even though there may be more things to destroy, only do so if they're directly in your way. To succeed in the mission, you need to escort the Pave Low and the rescued pilot safely to the landing FARP in friendly territory.

Campaign 22: Offensive Phase Carson

Mission Attack convoy
Environment Dusk-to-Dark/Clear
Air Strikes 0
Artillery Strikes 3

Primaries	Mission Rating
5 Ural-375s	9 killed.......S+
2 2S6s	5-8 killed.....S
	1-4 killed.....F
	0 killed.......F-

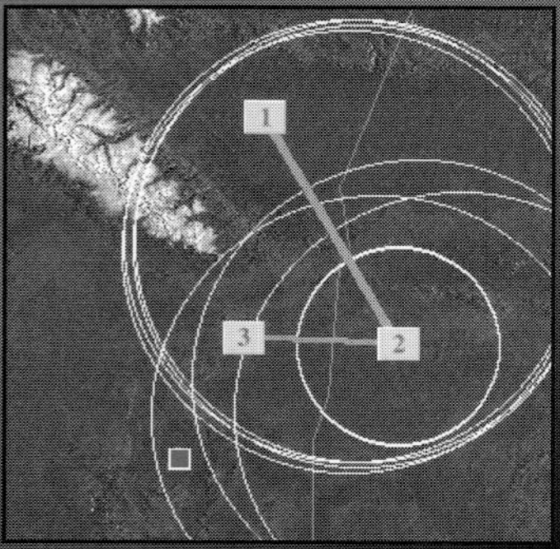

Waypoint 1 (FCR Mode). A new type of weapon has found its way into the battlefield — chemical. You're to intercept a convoy on its way to stock the front lines with the CIS' latest chemical weapon.

Cheat: *If you want to get through this mission quickly, simply fly to Waypoint 3, then toward the enemy border. The convoy will soon head toward the line, and you can pick them off there without ever having to break the border.*

Since this is a night mission, you'll want to activate your PNVS as soon as you take off. Once you start moving toward Waypoint 2, you're already within range of two SA-8s. Move within 8km and launch a couple of Hellfires from maximum range. Any closer, and you run the risk of getting hit. To reduce the chance of detection, keep your speed around 80 knots and your altitude near 70 feet.

As soon as you take out the initial SAMs, pop up to "see" the ambush that awaits you over the first hill on the way to SA-8. The big trap here is that if you're not extremely cautious, you'll run into a bunch of 2S6s and SA-8s. (As usual, take out the 2S6s first — they're the deadliest.) If you do get jumped and any of your weapons systems become damaged, you might as well start the mission over.... you'll need plenty of ammo for this one.

Assuming you survive the ambush, your next task is to find two enemy choppers that are grounded to the east. Take them out before they take off, or assign them to your wingman if you've already eliminated the SAM threats around them. (The choppers are likely to take off once you start attacking targets.) Then, head for Waypoint 2.

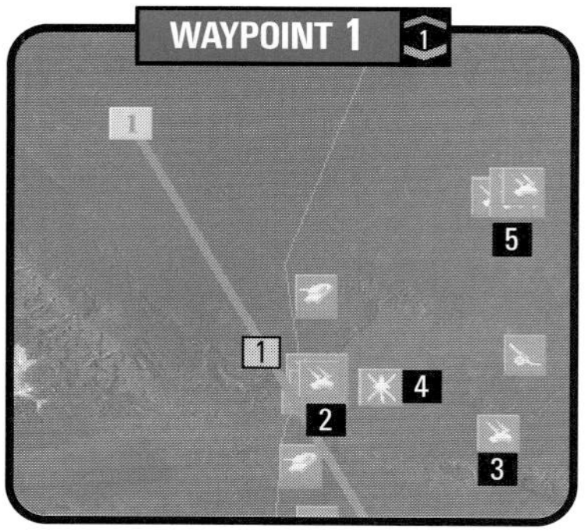

1 Pop-up site, border
2 SA-8s, 2S6s, Long Track radar
3 2S6
4 Havocs (grounded)
5 2S6, SA-11s, Snow Drift radar

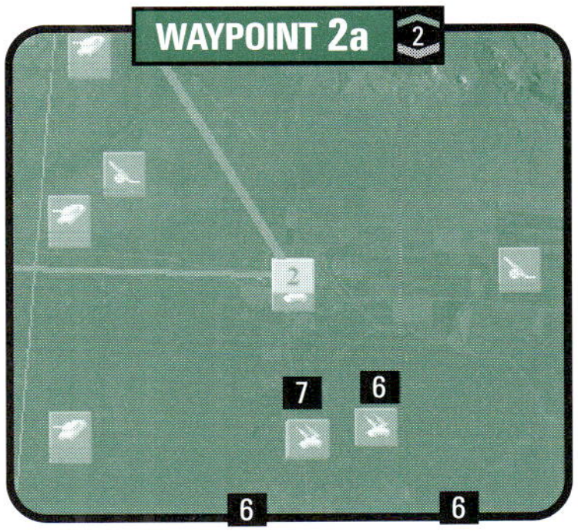

6 SA-8s
7 2S6

Waypoint 2. Waypoint 2 is actually a city, L'Viv. There's a convoy leaving the city, with a pack of mobile 2S6 SAMs. The trucks and their two 2S6 escorts are carrying the chemical weapons that are scheduled to be delivered to the artillery units — they're your primary targets.

Before you go after the trucks, eliminate the SAM sites south of the city. They'll detect and attack you as soon as you jump the convoy. Once that area is cleared out, follow the convoy as it heads down the road that leaves L'Viv. Establish a PFZ around the T80-U tanks for your wingman, and let him waste his Hellfires on them. (Don't forget to stay in a hover to make it easier for him to fire.)

Use your chain gun against the trucks as they approach your position. You can also pull Hellfires from your wingmen's stash. Destroying these primaries is imperative — once you do so, you win the mission.

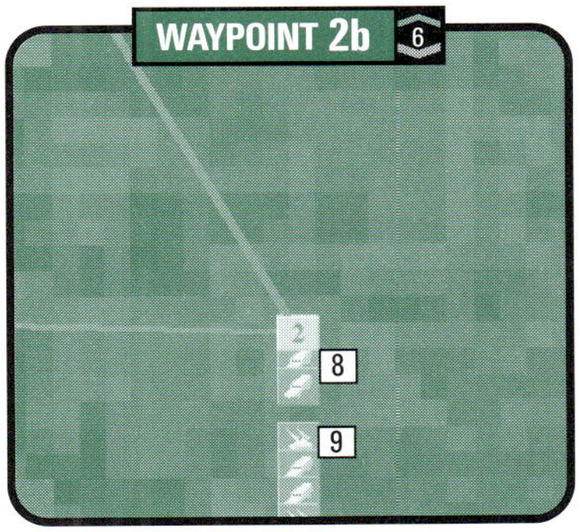

8 Truck (with chemical weapons)
9 2S6s

Campaign 23: Offensive Phase Eagle

Mission Attack choppers
Environment Day/Clear
Air Strikes 0
Artillery Strikes 3

Primaries	*Mission Rating*
4 MI-28s	6 KILLED.......S+
4 KA-50s	4-5 ....S
4 MI-24s	1-3 ....F
	0 ....F-

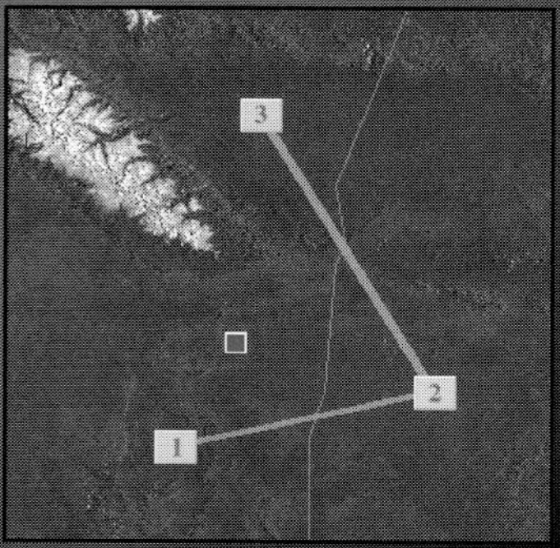

Waypoint 1. Before you even leave the FARP, activate your air radar and make sure your range is set to at least 10 kilometers in the RAD MFD. It's probably a good idea to arm your Stingers as well. (In case you haven't figured it out yet, Waypoint 2 is full of air threats.)

Waypoint 2. Opening up your Radar MFD allows you to see threats coming from Waypoint 2 — 2 Hinds, 2 Hokums and 2 Havocs. The Hinds and Havocs can only attack you with their guns and rockets, but the Hokums are carrying air-to-air missiles. You want to take them out first. Open up your ASE MFD (instead of the Radar page) and keep a close eye on it. If you see a bright, solid diamond, a missile has been launched at you (although air threats don't appear in the display, missiles do).

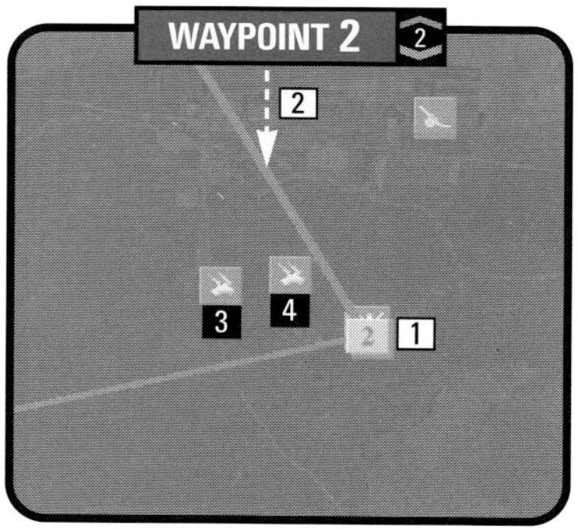

1 Hokums, Havocs, Hinds
2 Hokums, Havocs, Hinds (second wave)
3 2S6
4 SA-8

Evading missiles is tricky, but can be done. Listen to the missile tone. When it increases in frequency (repetition, not pitch), drop chaff and lose collective quickly. Make sure you're not too close to the ground, though, or else you won't have time to maneuver away from a potential crash. You can also try sharp turns to evade, and you should always activate IR jamming when you suspect that a missile is closing in. Don't make sharp right turns, however — you're likely to crash into your wingman.

Cheat: *As a cheat, you can activate time compression. This decreases the accuracy of missiles by effectively decreasing the number of checks the game makes for weapon impact.*

Hellfires have about 3 more miles of range than the Stingers, so you can try using them if you're finding it hard to get close enough to the Hokums with your Stingers. They fire IR missiles at you, so be sure you keep an eye on your ASE. If a bright diamond appears, that means the Hokum has launched a missile at you.

As for dogfighting, you want a lot of speed going into a helicopter fight. Try to tail the helicopter you're fighting, and keep your altitude low to avoid detection by the 2S6 that's just waiting for you to pop up high enough to be detected by its radar.

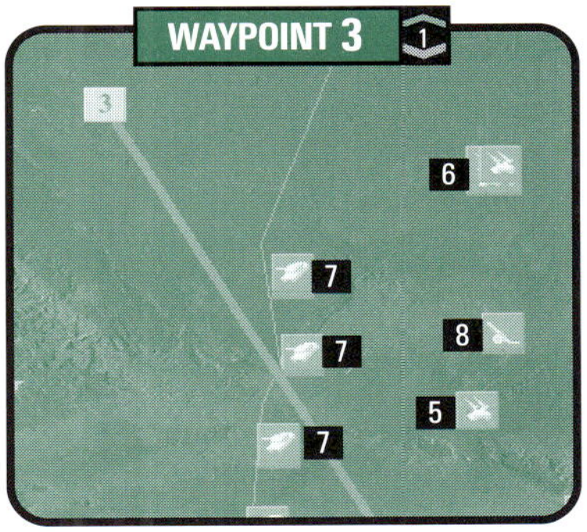

5 2S6
6 2S6s, bunkers
7 T-80U tanks
8 SO-122 artillery

Waypoint 3. After the helicopters and 2S6 are destroyed, you can rack up substantial extra points by attacking the T-80U tanks that are rolling nearby. Continuing over to Waypoint 3 yields some small artillery sites and stirs up several 2S6s that you can take out. (You can PFZ the entire area, and use [T] to cycle past the bunkers so that you hit only the 2S6s.)

If you're badly wounded at this point, go home. If you feel like taking on more helicopters, stick around near the destroyed bunkers. Several more helicopters activate if you wait long enough. You'd better be good, though, or else you'll have to re-fly the mission.

Campaign 24: Offensive Phase Hawk

Mission Attack airfield

Environment Dusk/Clear

Air Strikes 0

Artillery Strikes 0

Primaries	*Mission Rating*
1 Bar Lock	9 killed.......S+
1 2S6	7-8 ....S
1 SA-15	1-6 ....F
3 Su-25s	0 ....F-
2 Ural-375s	

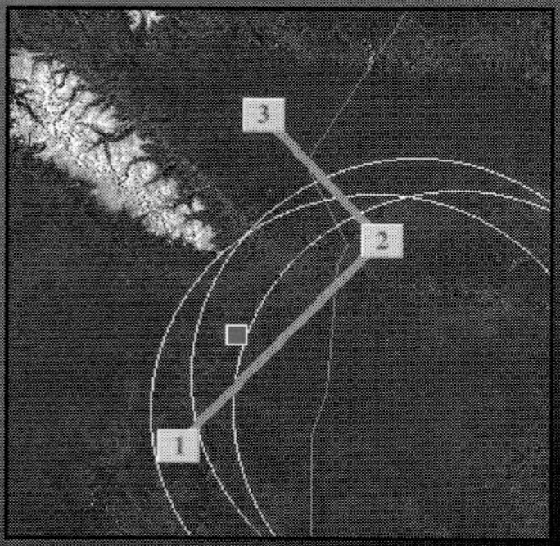

Waypoint 1. You're going to have to fly more aggressively than usual in this mission. There's lots of flat terrain, and not many places to hide. You'll need to make low, slow attacks — hovering or flying high makes you a sitting duck. Keep in mind, too, that you can run right into SAMs if you fly too fast.

After takeoff, turn on PNVS and pop up to see what's in store. Not far away, you'll discover a section of tanks good for points. Establish a PFZ around them and send your wingman in to make the kills. (Contrary to the rest of the mission, you can hover here — there aren't any immediate SAM threats. This may increase your wingman's accuracy.) Once he's destroyed all the tanks, autopilot to Waypoint 2.

Waypoint 2. You've probably learned by now to go after radar sites first whenever they appear, since they feed targets to surround SAMs. This airfield waypoint is a prime opportunity to exercise that skill. Your primaries are the Bar Lock radar and the grounded Sukhoi 25s at the airfield. Send a few Hellfires in to take out the Bar Lock radar. Next, deactivate the primary 2S6 and SA-15 SAMs guarding the airfield, and the primary fuel trucks.

On the ground, you'll find a collection of Su-25s that you can strafe. Activate the TADS target acquisition system and then fly over them at a low approach speed/altitude. Switching to the Shift F1 "no cockpit" view makes it easier to see where you're flying. The Shift F4 helmet view is also full-screen, but it automatically slews wherever your gun is aimed. If you use T to target, the gun and view automatically track the current target.)

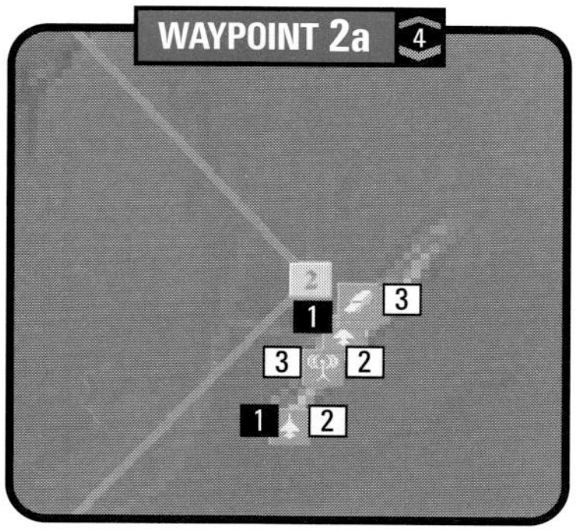

1 Su-25 Frogfoots

2 Su-25 Frogfoots

3 Bar Lock radar, fuel trucks, 2S6, SA-15

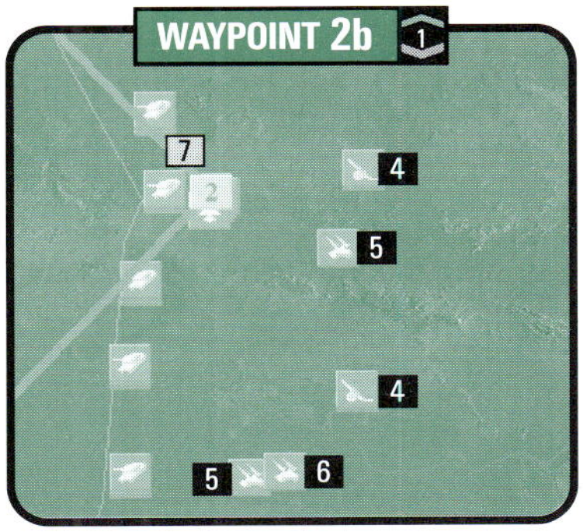

4 SO-122s
5 2S6
6 SA-8s
7 L'Viv

Just east of Waypoint 2, you'll find another 2S6. Take him out, then head for L'Viv. Near the town, there are a couple of 2S6s and SA-8s. You can fly between the buildings if you want to, but you can't use them to mask your position.

Northeast of town, you'll find a bunch of 2S6s. For points, take them on. If you're worried about dying, ignore them and head for Waypoint 3, or send your wingman into a PFZ you've established around them. From that point on, the mission's a cinch. Go home and land.

Campaign 25: Offensive Phase Dove

Mission Rescue POWs

Environment Dawn/Clear

Air Strikes 0

Artillery Strikes 0

Primaries	Mission Rating
4 MH-53 Pave Low Rescue Helicopters	3-4 helos survive .S+
	2 helos survive ...S
	1 helo survives ...F
	0 helos survive ...F-

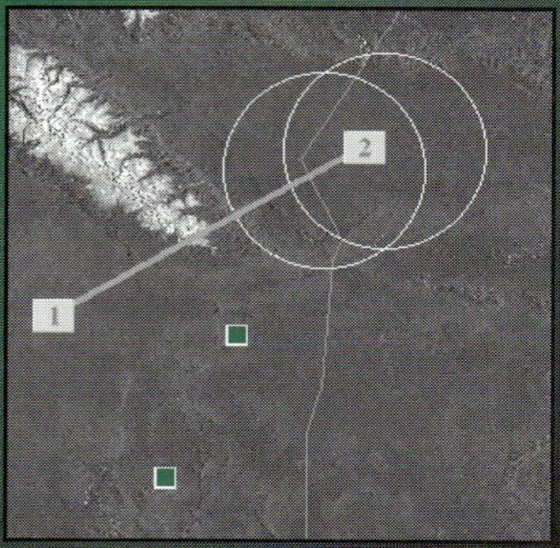

Waypoint 1. Like the downed pilot mission you flew earlier, this assignment has a time limit. Only this time, there's no cheat ... the fun starts immediately. Right after takeoff, you're tracked by a 2S6 that's encroached into friendly territory. Before you head for Waypoint 2, you need to take it out, or at least send your wingman after it.

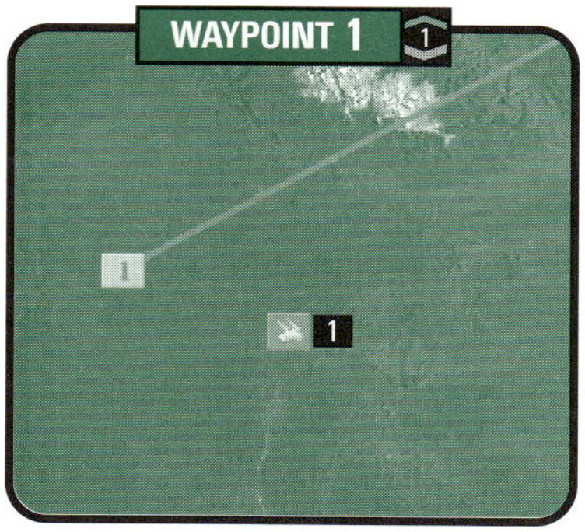

1 2S6

Waypoint 2. On the way, you'll have to eliminate several SAMs. One is a 2S6, another is an SA-15. At Waypoint 2, you'll be jumped by a lot of helicopters.

Cheat: *One covert way to "see" targets before they're in range of your avionics systems is to use the object view camera (F6). You can cycle through all the objects in the mission in this view. Although it doesn't distinguish between friendly/enemy/unimportant/important targets, it gives you an idea of what's in the area.*

You want to get to Waypoint 2 as quickly as possible, so don't spend a lot of time surveying what's out there. As soon as you approach the waypoint, drag a PFZ over the POW camp. Don't fly directly over the camp, though. This causes all kinds of raucous trouble and you may die.

Instead, stay as far out as you can, and pop the SA-8, SA-15 and 2S6 SAM sites. You'll need to take them out before you can move in any closer. Clearing out the SAMs opens up a safe area for the rescue choppers that will soon arrive, and frees you up to concentrate on eliminating the base's guard choppers. Five in all will come after you ... and a couple of them are Hokums. Deal with them as quickly as you can, Hokums first.

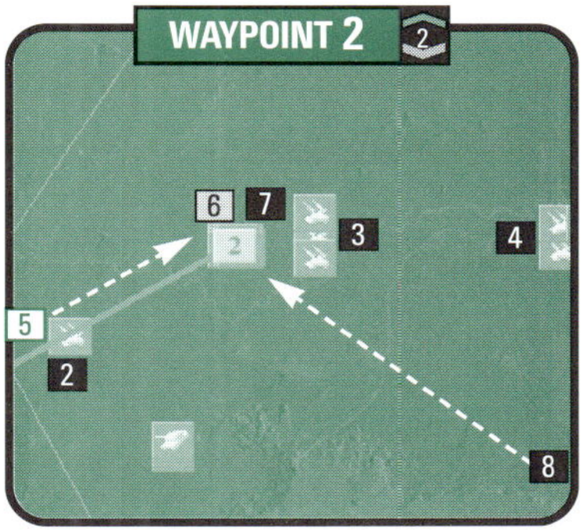

- 2 2S6
- 3 2S6, SA-15, SA-8
- 4 Enemy FARP
- 5 MH-53J Pave Lows
- 6 P.O.W. Camp
- 7 C.I.S. Soldiers
- 8 Hinds, Havocs, Hokums

One noteworthy comment — if you lose your wingman in this portion of the mission, consider starting over. You have to kill nearly everything you see, and it's hard to do on your own. Same with your gun — if it goes out, you're hosed.

Assuming your gun and wingman are still functional after the helicopter fight, switch to TADS target acquisition system and commence an attack against the ground troops at the POW camp. Display the TADS MFD and zoom in slightly.

After your attack on the camp is well underway, the rescue choppers come in to rescue the POWs you've broken out. You need to stick around until the choppers take off and then escort them home. Picking up the POWs shouldn't take more than a minute or two; While you're waiting, make sure you kill all of the CIS soldiers on the ground. Their purpose is to attack the rescue choppers. If you're severely damaged, you can go ahead and turn for home. However, if the rescue aircraft are shot down, you'll lose the mission.)

Make sure you fly slightly ahead of the rescue helicopters and ensure that nothing's in the flight path that can kill them. Chances are, if you've cleaned the area thoroughly, you'll succeed. The last things you really need to eliminate in this mission are the enemy helicopters you faced earlier ... any survivors attack your choppers. At least two rescue choppers must survive for you to succeed in the mission.

Campaign 26: Offensive Phase Pluto

Mission Destroy MLRS sites

Environment Day/Hazy

Air Strikes 0

Artillery Strikes 0

Primaries	Mission Rating
5 BM-25 MLRSs	7 killed.......S
2 Tents	1-6 ....F
	0 ....F-

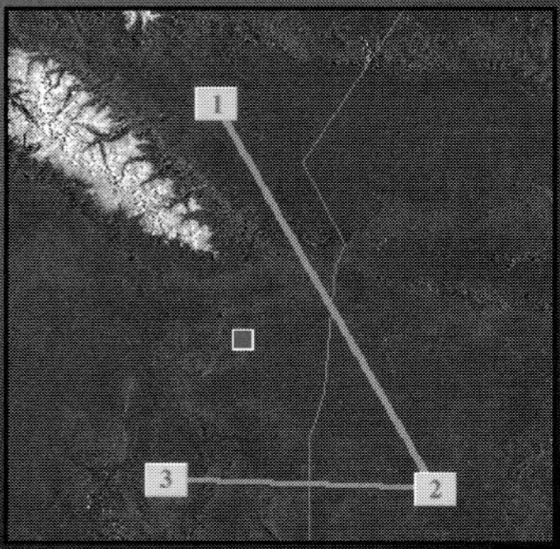

Waypoint 1. Four words should be running through your mind during this mission — Multi-Launcher Rocket System. Although it's tempting to attack everything at a FARP with your guns blazing after the SAMs are gone, remember that your mission is to get the MLRSs.

Once you cross over into enemy territory, move carefully to avoid being attacked by 2S6s and SA-8s. They're right in the middle of your flight path, and it's better to sneak up on them and take them out than it is to be detected by them. Once they're gone, continue on to Waypoint 2.

Waypoint 1-2. There's an enemy FARP just north of the SAMs that you also need to take out. It's defended by 4 helicopters (Havocs). If you fly slow and low, you can move in pretty close without being seen, and take them out with rockets or guns. If they detect you, however, all four will take off, and you'll find yourself in a hell of a dogfight.

Cheat: *If you can't get past this mission, switch to the simple flight model in the* **IN-FLIGHT OPTION** *menu, but leave everything else realistic. This will allow you to rack up a lot of points. Or, try unchecking the* REALISTIC WEAPON DAMAGE *option. This cuts your score by 30%, but you score enough extra points in the long run to make up for it.*

After you take out the air threats, fire on the other FARP elements ... tents, fuel trucks, etc. Then, resume your Waypoint 2 course. You'll find some artillery sites on the way, which will give you some more points.

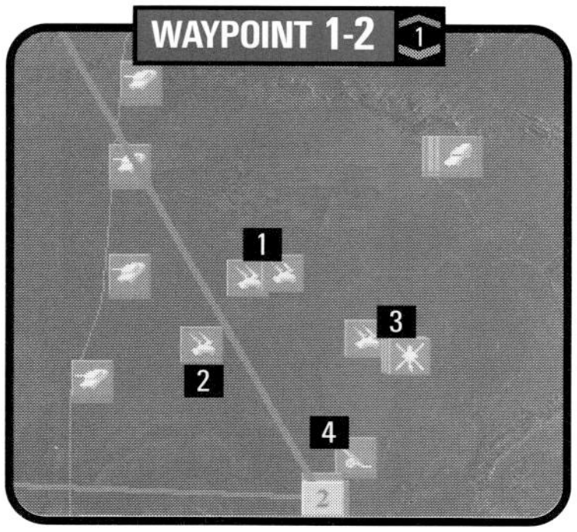

1 2S6, SA-8

2 SA-8

3 SA-8, Havocs at Enemy FARP (grounded)

4 SO-122 artillery

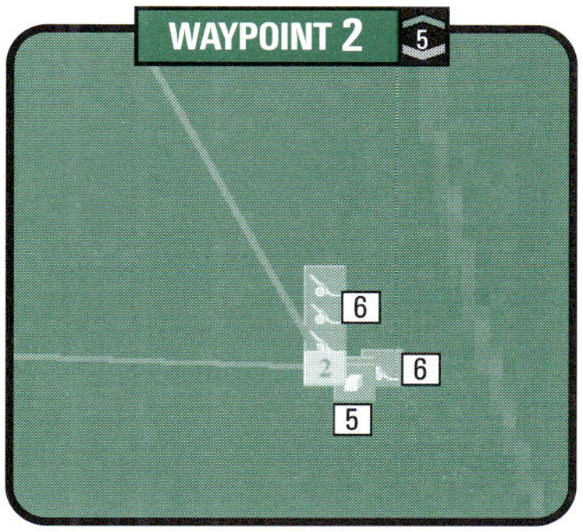

5 Tents

6 BM-25 MLRSs

Waypoint 2. Finally, you can attack your primary targets (MLRSs) at Waypoint 2. You must kill *all* of them to win the mission, so hopefully you didn't use up too many Hellfires at the previous FARP. Once the primaries are gone, use whatever you have left over to take out some T-80U tanks on the way home. (They're no threat to you, so you should always save them for last.)

Campaign 27: Offensive Phase Mars

Mission Attack units in L'Viv **Air Strikes** 2

Environment Dawn-To-Day/Cloudy **Artillery Strikes** 3

Primaries	*Mission Rating*
1 SA-8	6 KILLED.......S
6 BM-25 MLRSs	1-5 ....F
	0 ....F-

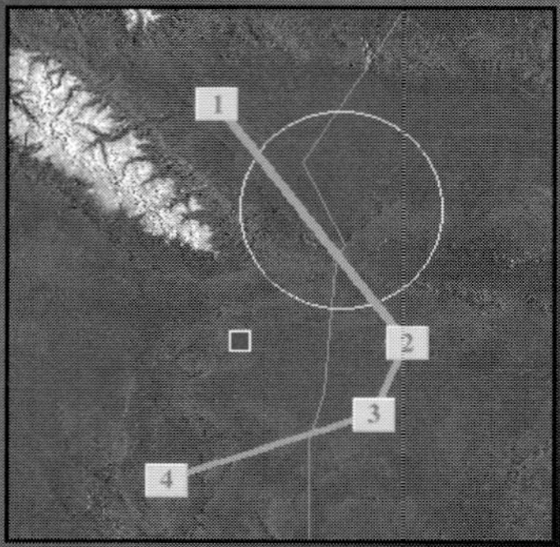

Waypoint 1. Better have some caffeine and a few donuts handy if you miss the action at the beginning of this mission. The best thing to do when you take off is activate auto-hover (or stay stationary on the ground) and turn around 180°. A section of two Sukhois are moving in on an attack against your takeoff FARP. If you move, your chances of survival decrease.

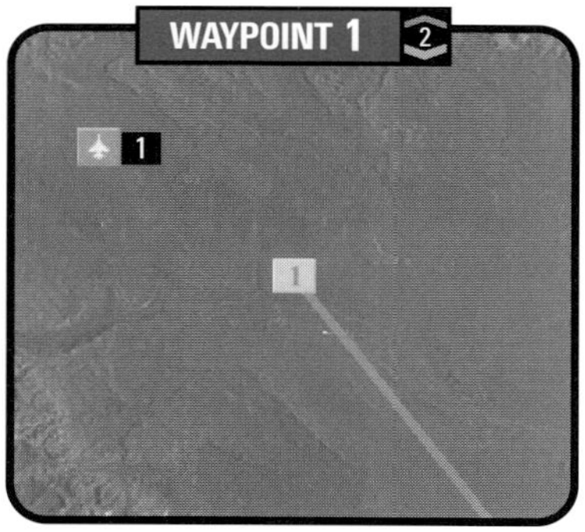

1 Su-25 Frogfoots

Pop open your Radar MFD and switch to air mode and a range of 10 miles. Then, swivel 180 degrees (the fighters will approach you head-on this way). Wait for the planes to move within 4 miles, then unleash a couple of Stingers. You might be tempted to fly toward them, but you should really stay at the FARP until they make their pass. They'll make an initial attack, then back off for a second one. If you manage to do enough damage to them on the first run, they may leave, which unfortunately means you'll have to deal with them later.

If you miss the first run, the coffee and donuts come into play ... it takes a while for the Sukhoi to turn around and make another pass at you. You'll burn a lot of time and fuel, but the 1000 points you'll get is worth it. And if you find you're low on fuel or weapons, you can land at your starting FARP and rearm/refuel. Although this costs points, the Sukhoi bonus should be more than enough to make up for the score penalty you incur for using the FARP.

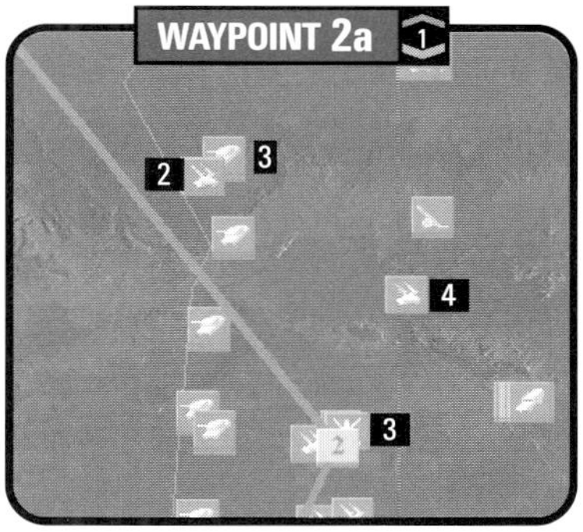

2 2S6s
3 Enemy FARP with 2S6
4 2S6

Waypoint 2. At some point in time, you'll take out the aircraft and head toward the second waypoint, where you'll run straight into a 2S6. Take it out and continue on. Once you cross into enemy territory, gun down the tents and fuel tanks for a few easy points. You'll find another 2S6 on the way to L'Viv.

Near the city lie your primary objectives, the artillery and SAMs surrounding the town. Start with the 2S6s east of your flight path. Hover at the outer edge of their threat radius as it appears in your ASE MFD page, and take them out with Hellfires. Establishing a PFZ is effective, as long as you cycle through your targets to make sure you're not wasting missiles. Whatever you do, don't send your wingman in after the SAMs ... he's sure to bite the dust.

Inside the city limits, there's a little hill just north of the city you can hide behind. Using it as a mask, you can attack the inner city targets — an enemy helicopter, MLRSs, SA-8s, 2S6s and buildings. If you have missiles to spare, stay behind the hill to attack your primaries. If you're low on missiles or have lost your wingman, fly into the city and rely on your guns for the smaller targets.

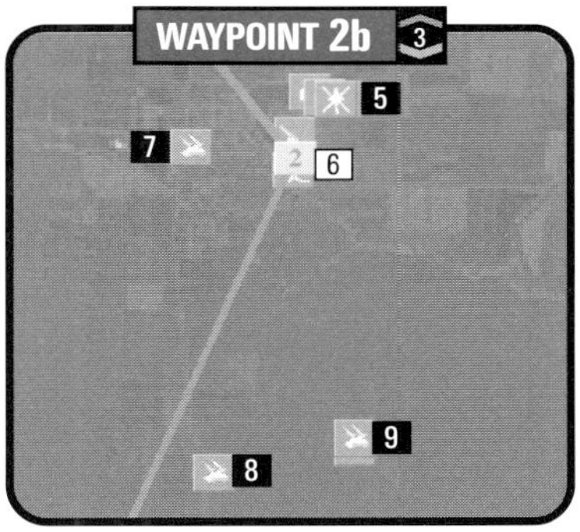

5 Havocs, tents
6 BM-21 MLRSs
7 SA-8
8 2S6
9 SA-8s

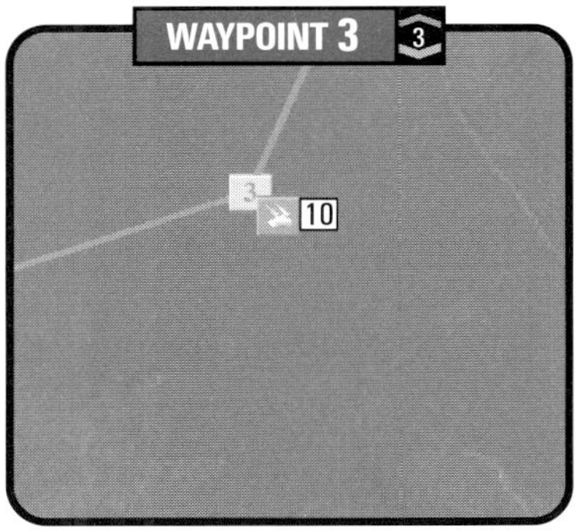

10 SA-8

Waypoint 3. This one's easy. All you find here is a single SA-8. Take him out, and you've got a clear shot home. Waste your spare ordnance on nearby tanks.

Campaign 28: Offensive Phase Green

Mission Attack SAM sites
Environment Day/Clear
Air Strikes 0
Artillery Strikes 0

Primaries	*Mission Rating*
1 Tent	5 killed.......S
1 Long Track radar	1-4 ....F
1 Snow Drift radar	0 ....F-
4 SA-11s	

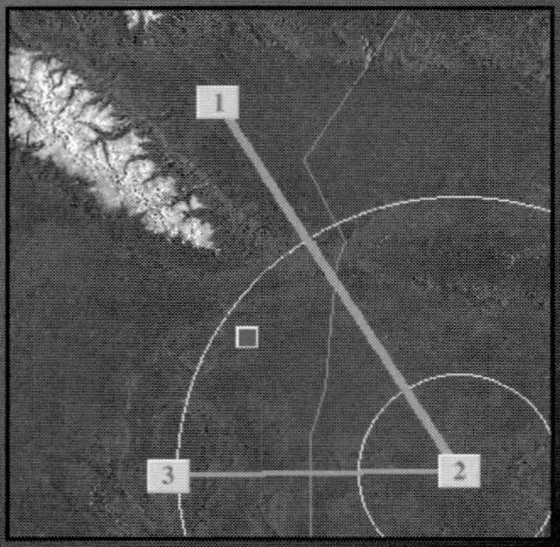

Waypoint 1. The missions are getting easier and easier. Toward the end of the campaign, the CIS is out of anything very dangerous. Head directly for Waypoint 2, and have your wingman attack some tanks on the way if you want extra points. He's got lots of weapons, so you don't have to worry about running out.

When you cross the battle line, fly east at low speed and altitude to surprise and eliminate a 2S6 site. You have time now, and if you don't eliminate him while you have the chance, he may make you miserable later. Near the 2S6 site, you can also knock out some artillery (extra points), plus a couple more 2S6s hidden around the bunker complex just north of the artillery units.

After you clean out the area, head toward the second waypoint. As you fly over the city, there are some SA-8 and 2S6 sites to the east that pose serious threats.

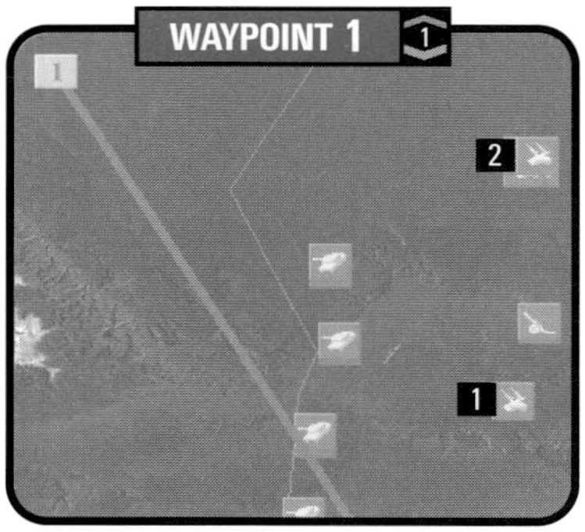

1 2S6
2 2S6s, bunkers

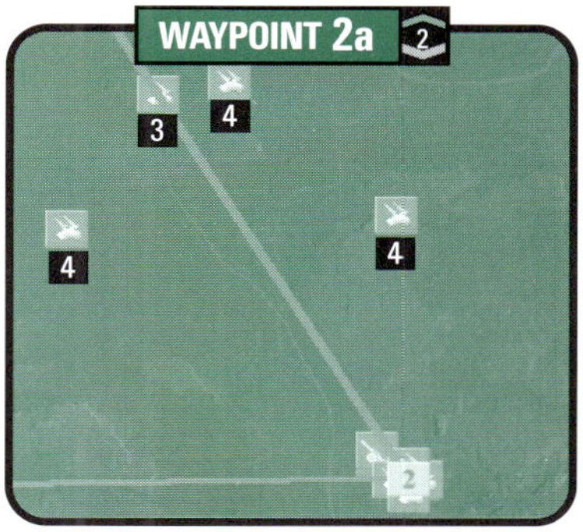

3 2S6

4 SA-8

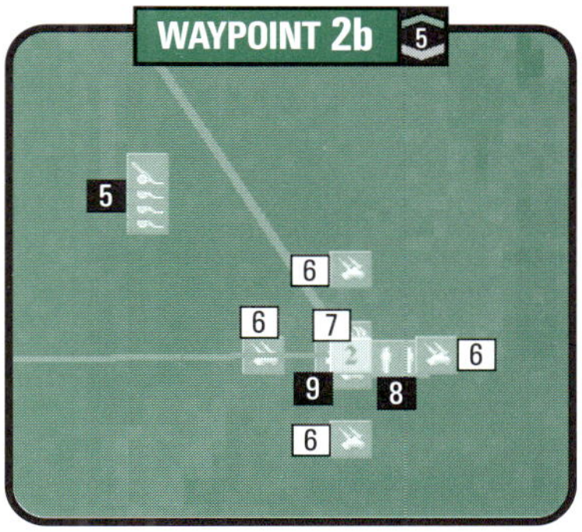

5 SO-122 artillery

6 SA-11

7 Long Track radar, Snow Drift radar, tent

8 C.I.S. Soldiers (one with an SA-14 SAM)

9 2S6

Waypoint 2. The second area can look intimidating until you realize that all you need to do is take out the two radar systems that are supplying targets to all the SAMs. Take out the Long Track radar first, from about 7 miles away. Then, have your wingman take out the 2S6 site while you take out the Snow Drift radar. With these elements destroyed, the site is no longer a threat and you can fly within visual range without being challenged.

Or so it seems. The enemy has a last-ditch ambush planned for you in the center of the site. If you're in FCR mode, switch to TADS about a mile or two out. That will allow you to see and take out the small soldiers with shoulder-mounted SAMs — the ambush. If you don't kill the troops quickly, you'll die a horrible death. Start shooting at them with your guns from about a kilometer out.

Once you've taken out the soldiers, take out the rest of the site with your guns. There's another artillery site to the west of the artillery site that you can take out if you'd like. Then, fly home, taking out whatever enemy you find as you go. Don't expect much more than tanks, however.

Campaign 29: Offensive Phase Grizzly

Mission Attack maintenance site **Air Strikes** 0

Environment Night/Clear **Artillery Strikes** 0

Primaries	*Mission Rating*
5 Bunkers	5-6 killed.....S
1 Command Bunker	1-4 ....F
	0 ....F-

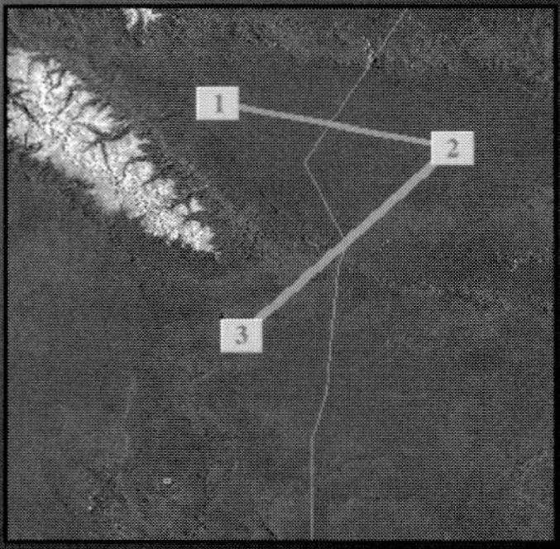

Waypoint 1. The final mission of the game is relatively easy. This makes sense, seeing as how you've penetrated the CIS' best defenses by this point.

Proceed to enemy territory.

Waypoint 2. At Waypoint 2, stay about 7km out, then come to a hover at 10 feet of altitude. Send your wingman in to attack the primaries, hardened bunkers (they take two Hellfires' worth of damage, and you might as well waste his instead of yours). Meanwhile, go after the 2S6 south of the target area.

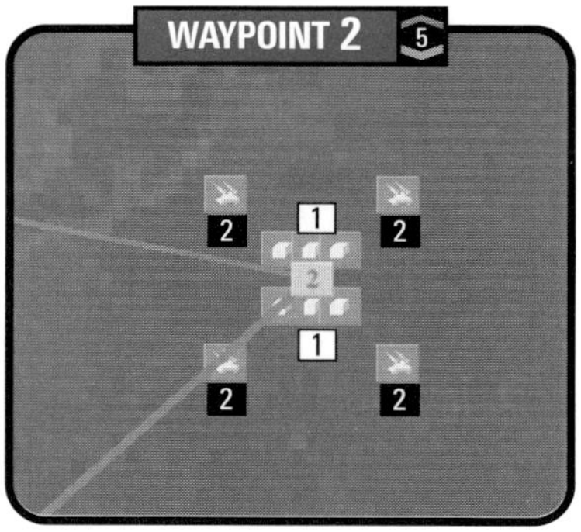

1 Bunkers

2 2S6

Keep an eye on your wingman's progress by using the F12 Death camera view, or with the TADS MFD. At the same time, turn your attention to the SAM sites. After you've sent your missiles in and destroyed all discernible targets, fly through the site to double-check that you've gotten everything.

There's some SO-122 artillery that you can mow down with your guns, but not much else. The war is nearly over. All you have to do is fly home, taking out the few straggler tanks you find along the way.

Campaign 30: Defensive Phase Congo

Mission Attack Artillery Sites

Environment Day/Cloudy

Air Strikes 0

Artillery Strikes 0

Primaries	Mission Rating
5 SO-122s	4+ killed......S
1 Bunker	1-3...........F
	0.............F-

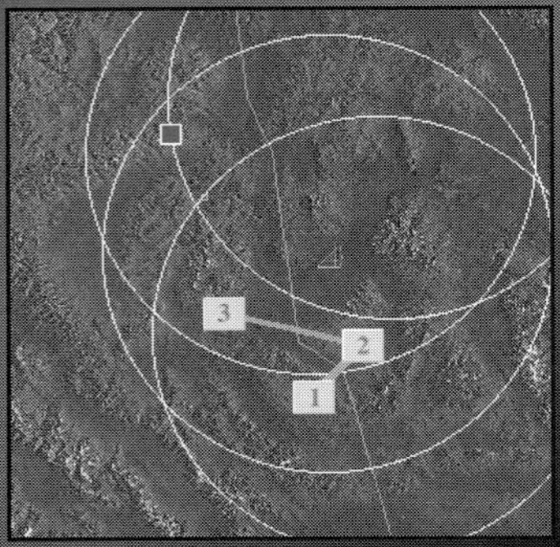

Waypoint 1. This is the first mission on the losing path, which means you failed two of the first four missions. Although this is a war game, war often involves reconnaissance. And that's just what you were supposed to do. Chances are, you probably shot at something or made yourself highly visible to enemy SAMs. You can either start over with a new pilot, or fly through a series of three missions that can put you back on the winning track. If you choose to fly this mission, you'll be taking out artillery units and some other accessory targets. The choice is yours ....

Waypoint 2. You've only got one waypoint to worry about in this mission, and it's not too far from your starting FARP. Once you take off, you'll find tanks and helos to the northeast. The only tricky part to attacking them is making your approach slowly enough. They're dug in just over the ridge, so your best bet is to come to a hover just before you cross it and bob up to several hundred feet. This lets you pick up the tanks on the TSD and prevents you from overrunning the lip of the ridge and getting shot down.

What are PFZs? Now for the difficult part — creating a PFZ. These useful little boxes let you define a target area, which you can then launch Hellfire missiles into. The missiles are smart enough to attack anything that can be picked up by radar within this zone. To make a PFZ, right-click-and-drag inside the TSD MFD. This draws a rectangle around the area you specify, and your Fire-Control Radar assigns priority to targets in this zone. Think of it as a square bullseye.

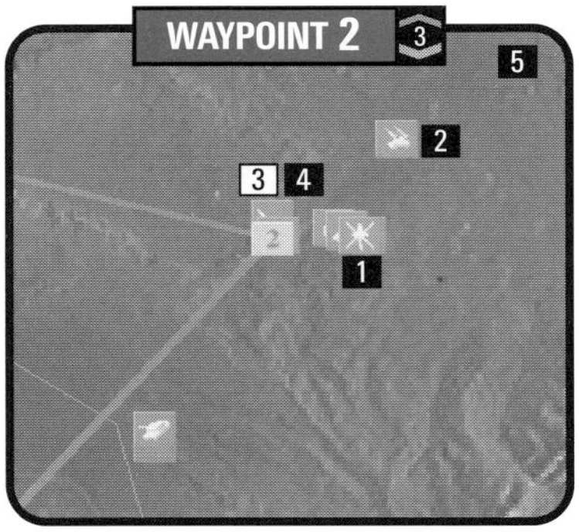

1 Enemy FARP (with Havocs)
2 SA-8
3 SO-122 artillery
4 C.I.S. soldiers (with small arms)
5 SA-11s, Snow Drift radar

The beauty of a PFZ is that you don't have to select a specific target. (But you should, just to make sure you're not wasting upward of $20,000 per shot on something like a tent.) You can keep your distance from the target and fire from as far as 8km away. You can also tell your wingman to attack everything there by pressing [Ctrl][3].

You need to have Hellfires selected and LOAL missile launch mode active to use PFZs correctly. This lets you fire missiles without a lock, which will become a staple tactic. Press [Ins] to toggle between LOAL (large constraint box) and LOBL (small constraint box) modes.

You may notice that the box is dashed sometimes, and solid other times. A solid box means that you have a valid lock on the target. It doesn't matter whether the box is solid or not when you fire, but it must be solid by the time the missile timer ("TOF" on the viewscreen) runs out.

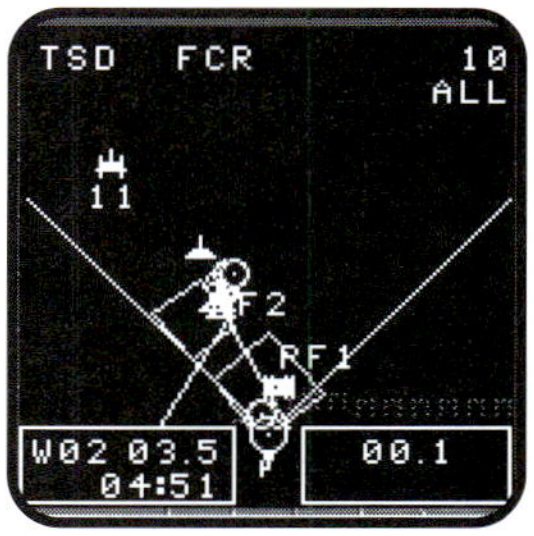

TSD MFD WITH PRIORITY FIRE ZONES

Creating PFZs. Test out a PFZ by drawing a zone around the tanks (H-shaped icons on the TSD MFD) at Waypoint 2. Make sure Hellfires are active and that you're in LOAL mode. (The current weapon and launch mode name appear at the bottom right of the IHADSS display.) Fire off two missiles. Now, bob up and watch the timer in the IHADSS. If the big missile box isn't solid, climb higher. It must be solid when the timer reads zero.

Both missiles are going after targets in the area you specified. The targets are put into a list in the computer, and each missile goes to the next target in the list. To cycle through targets in that list, press [T]. If all goes well, pretty soon you'll hear your CP/G say "Good Shot, Sir!"

You can draw multiple PFZs, but you don't want to clutter the display with them. Delete the zone once you've killed everything in it. To do so, click on it with the left and right mouse buttons simultaneously.

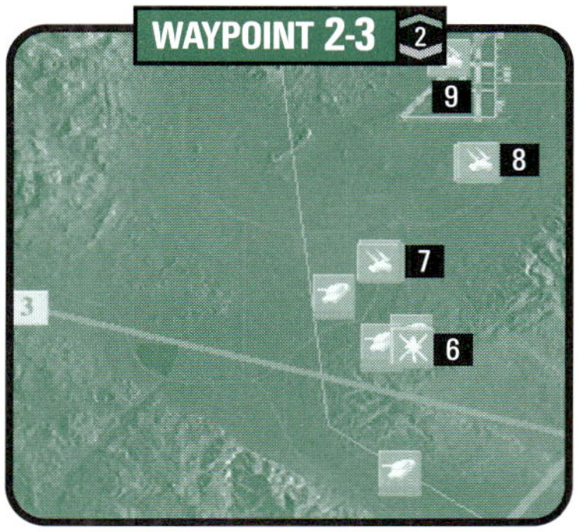

- **6** Hokums
- **7** 2S6s
- **8** SA-11, Snow Drift radar
- **9** SA-8

Now, try your luck again by drawing a second PFZ zone around the second waypoint and using it as you did before. Destroy the artillery primaries. Keep going ... just north of the waypoint, there are several SA-11s. Stay low, and they won't bother you. You can practice your PFZ skills with them, but don't send your wingman into any PFZ that contains SAMs — he's likely to get shot down.

Waypoint 2-3. Finally, there's AAA fire between the last two waypoints. You might want to retrace your route to your start FARP. (In losing path missions, you shouldn't concern yourself with getting points. Go to the waypoint, take care of the primaries, and then go home via the easiest route.)

Campaign 31: Defensive Phase George

Mission Attack Armor

Environment Night/Clear

Air Strikes 3

Artillery Strikes 3

Primaries	*Mission Rating*
19 T-80Us	18 KILLED......S+
	10-17.........S
	1-9...........F
	0.............F-

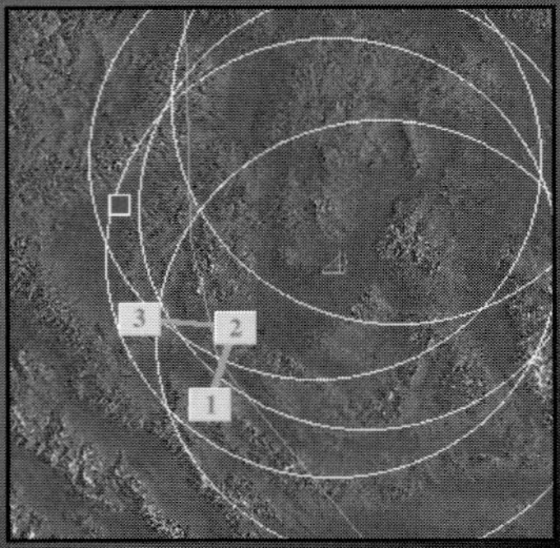

Waypoint 1. You've got many targets of opportunity in this typical search-and-destroy mission. Most of them are primary tank targets near Waypoint 2, but you'll have to search for the others. Follow the waypoint path and keep your TSD zoomed out to 10km. Before too long, you'll detect a column of tanks. Some are stationary; some are moving. It's slightly more difficult to hit the moving ones, but you shouldn't have too much of a problem taking them out.

Hellfires are the preferred ordnance against all tanks. Although you could conceivably use your guns to take them out, you'd expend a lot of rounds and energy. Rockets aren't that great — in fact, most of our playtesters only use rockets in one or two game missions and carry full racks of Hellfires the rest of the time.

Waypoint 2. Once you approach the second waypoint, a large arc appears on your ASE and TSD. Drop down so that you're flying below 50 feet. If the rings in the ASE are still solid, decrease collective and drop even more. A solid arc means you're being tracked by that SAM's radar and that he can fire missiles at you. 2S6s are the most threatening SAM sites you'll face. They've got long range and fire high-speed missiles and guns that are on you before you know it.

Your first task is to disable the 2S6 at Waypoint 2. All you have to do is stay low and maneuver within 8km of it. Track your range by checking the text to the left of the High Action Display. Pop off a Hellfire or two, and he's history.

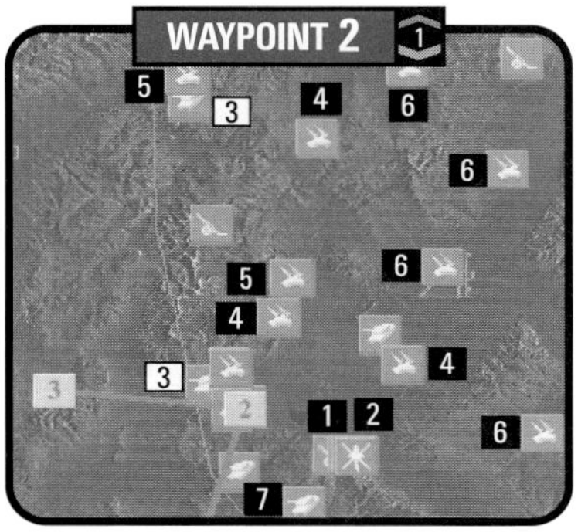

1 Enemy FARP
2 Havocs
3 T-80Us
4 SA-11s, Snow Drift radar
5 2S6s
6 SA-8
7 T80Us

The tanks are next. This time, establish a PFZ around them and try assigning the zone to your trusty wingman. Simply press Ctrl 3 to send an "Attack my Target" message to him. He'll go in and take care of everything for you, and you'll get credit for it (score-wise). You'll find that your wingman (or at least his ordnance) is a valuable tactical asset when you're using PFZs. Both of you can be attacking different zones simultaneously.

The remaining primary tanks are north of Waypoint 2, by about two or three kilometers. You should check your Hellfire load by cycling through the MFD pages (press , or .). The bright green boxes marked "R" indicate how many Hellfire rounds remain.

If you're low on Hellfires, assign the tanks to your wingman again. Otherwise, practice clicking on a single target (instead of drawing a PFZ). A good tactic is to click on something, order your wingman to fire at it with the Ctrl 3 command, click on a second target, and fire at it yourself. Trade targets in this manner until nothing's left to kill, then go to the nearest friendly FARP and land.

Campaign 32: Defensive Phase March

Mission Destroy Mobile SAMs **Air Strikes** 0
Environment Dawn-To-Day/Cloudy **Artillery Strikes** 1

Primaries	*Mission Rating*
8 2S6s	8 killed.......S
	1-7...........F
	0.............F-

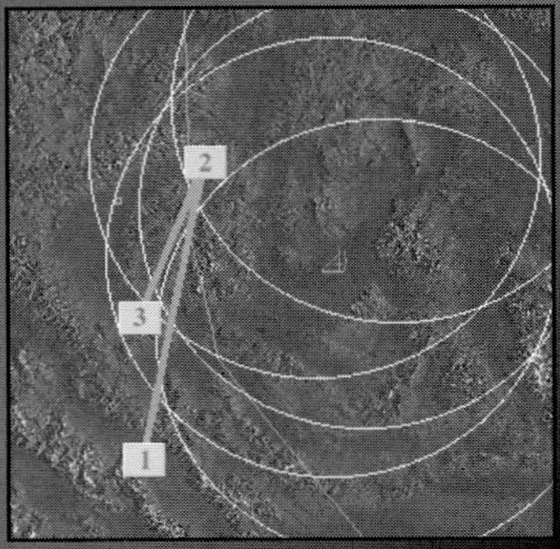

Waypoint (2). The enemy line running vertically through the mission planning map provides a good guide for your flight path. Add a waypoint between the first two stops, anywhere to the west of the the threats on the enemy's side of the border. You'll want to bypass as many of the non-primaries in this mission as you can. That's a general guideline for all of the losing path missions (30-37). At this point, score should be the least of your concerns — you simply need to survive to progress further in the campaign.

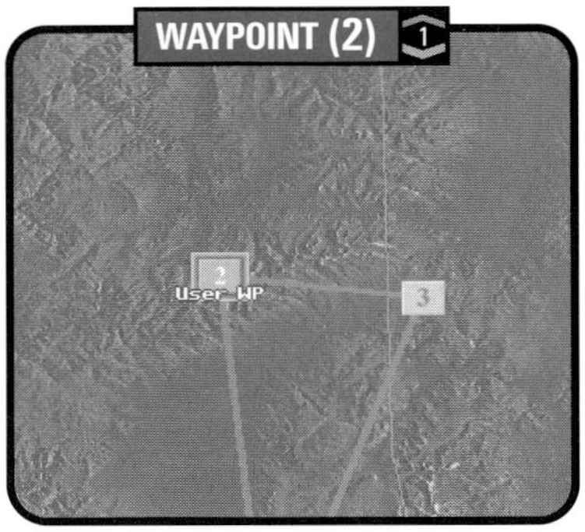

This is a dusk mission, so you'll probably need to turn on your PNVS system before too long (press P). Then use 8X autopilot to travel to the waypoint you added. If SAMs start popping up on your ASE, keep time compression active... your chance of getting hit are actually less. (The game checks for impact in real time, not in compressed time.)

Once you reach the waypoint you added, you'll be in range of several nearby SAMs (non-primaries). Transition into a hover and share them with your wingman by using your newly acquired PFZ skills and a few Hellfires.

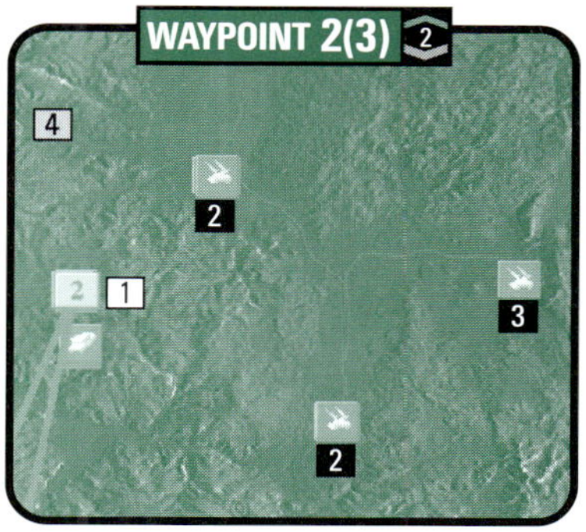

1 2S6s
2 Enemy
3 Enemy
4 Neutral

Waypoint 2 (3). When you near the target waypoint, take a moment to survey the terrain surrounding the primary targets. The targets — 2S6s — are corralled by hills you can use as cover. You don't really need to set another waypoint, although you can if you want one as a navigational tool.

Maneuver behind a hill with your Hellfires active in LOAL mode, and pop up just far enough to get a solid missile constraint box. Mentally take note of the altitude, and descend until the SAM circles on the ASE disappear (this means they lose their radar lock on you).

Left-click on a SAM target you want to hit, and fire off a single Hellfire. In this case, you don't really want to PFZ the entire area. Only specific 2S6s are primary targets, so you should take them out manually to avoid wasting your missiles. Save your ordnance for other primaries east of this waypoint.

Once all the primary SAMs are eliminated, you can land at the nearest FARP.

Campaign 33: Defensive Phase Triangle

Mission Attack Choppers

Environment Night/Clear

Air Strikes 0

Artillery Strikes 1

Primaries	*Mission Rating*
2 Mi-28s	5 killed.......S
2 Ka-50s	1-4............F
2 Mi-24s	0..............F-

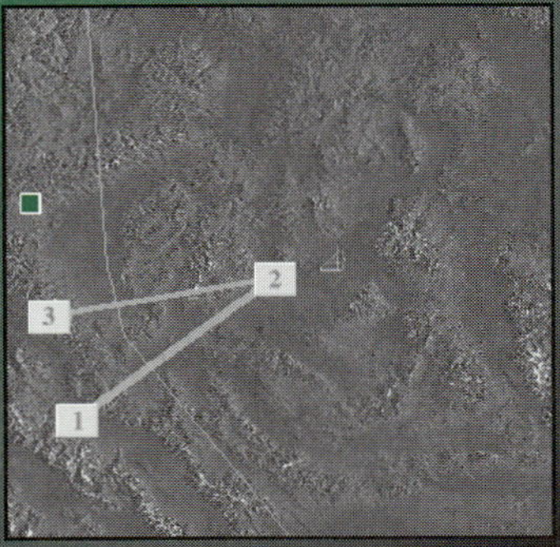

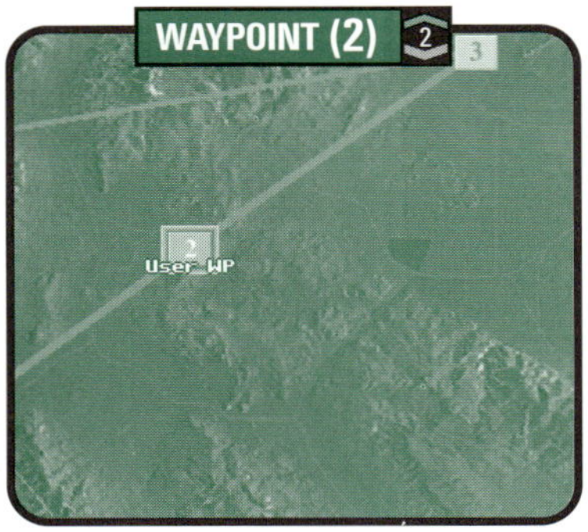

Waypoint (2). The name assigned to this mission is an apropos statement of its design. The default flight path takes you around a tall, triangular area that completely surrounds your primary targets. All the primaries are enclosed within the pie slice formed by your three waypoints.

Essentially, you can fly the entire mission by traveling halfway to the first waypoint. Use the mission planning computer to drop a marker waypoint exactly halfway between 1 and 2. You'll see why in a few minutes.

This mission occurs during the early dawn hours. You'll need to use your PNVS for a while, but you'll be able to turn it off midway through the mission. Fly toward the waypoint you created and come to a hover.

1 Enemy FARP

2 2S6s

3 SA-11s, Snow Drift radar

Waypoint 2 (3). Stopping and hovering here has a two-fold purpose. First, it gives you time to detect the SAMs and the horde of primary helicopters in this area before they see you and start attacking. Secondly, you can hide behind the ridge here to get the SAMs, and then slide into the primary target valley by following the pass that cuts through the mountain.

As soon as you come to a hover behind the ridge, pop up until you have a valid LOS on the target area. Several 2S6s and a cluster of enemy helicopters should display in your TSD MFD. (Make sure FCR is the active target acquisition mode so that it can memorize targets it sees when you drop back down.)

After you've taken a look at the threats and their positions, select the closest 2S6 as your current target. Move to an attack position 7.9km away from it, making sure you stay behind the ridge. Then, arm your Hellfires and bob up to around 100 feet. Toast the first one, and repeat the process until they're all non-functional. You might have to climb a bit higher to get the last few. If it makes you feel safer, take out the Snow Drift radar that serves SA-11s in the area as well. If you do so, you don't have to worry about altitude during the helicopter fight.

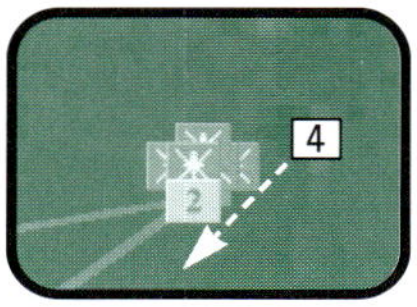

4 Havocs, Hokums, Hinds

Now, you've got to worry about the choppers. They've all seen you by now and are probably navigating for a pot shot at you. You've got Hokums, Havocs and Hinds to worry about. The Hokums fire both missiles and guns, so you'll want to tear them up first with your Stingers. The other birds can be lethal as well, but their guns aren't nearly as effective as the Hokum's missiles. Use your wingman to take out some of the helos. You don't have enough Stingers to do it all by yourself.

Pretty soon, the dust settles and another set of helicopters arrive from an enemy FARP to the north. They're not primaries, but you'll need to take them out anyway. If you were cautious with your shots earlier, you should have a Stinger or two left. Divide these final targets up with your wingman. If both of you are out of Stingers, you can try using Hellfires against the choppers, but they're not nearly as accurate as they are against ground targets. Guns are probably your best choice as a backup weapon.

Campaign 34: Defensive Phase Rhino

Mission Attack SCUDs
Environment Day/Clear
Air Strikes 0
Artillery Strikes 0

Primaries	*Mission Rating*
4 SCUDs	6 killed.......S+
1 Ural-375	4-5............S
	1-3............F
	0..............F-

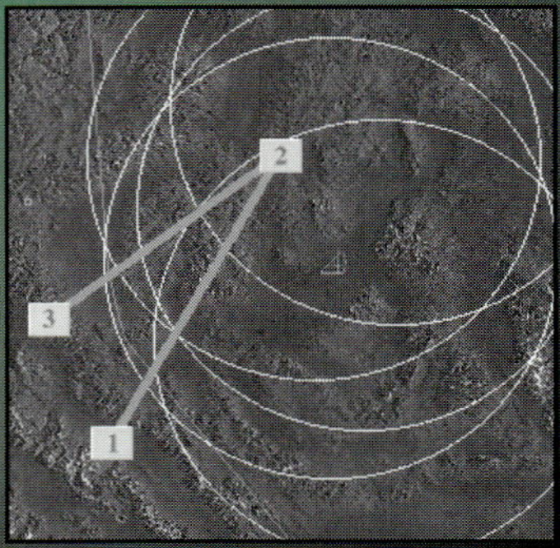

Waypoint 1. Finally, you get to sleep through the night and fly a day mission. You'll be surprised at how different the terrain looks during the day (the hills are much more visible).

This mission is comparatively easy — all you have to do is eliminate a couple of SA-11s and take out some SCUD primaries. The toughest part of it is that you're flying a deep strike mission, which means that you'll be flying awhile.

The Long Stretch. Whenever you have a long stretch of flight between waypoints, it's a good idea to stay low and pop up every 5km or so to update your FCR and TSD. In this mission, it definitely works to your advantage. You'll uncover eight — count them, eight — SA-11 SAM sites (two groups of four). SA-11s have a huge threat radius. In fact, it's so large that the circles rarely appear on the ASE. Unlike 2S6s, however, SA-11s don't have guns. If you move within a kilometer or two of them, they're defenseless.

There's a definite tactic to taking out a group of SA-11s. Target their Snow Drift radar. Each group of SA-11s — usually a group of four — has a single radar that provides target information. If you manage to take it out, the SAM sites don't have any way to lock you up.

The secret to attacking the radar itself is to stay extremely low, make a slow approach, and remain undetected. This takes finesse, but it takes you under their radar envelope. When you move within 1.5km, gun it down.

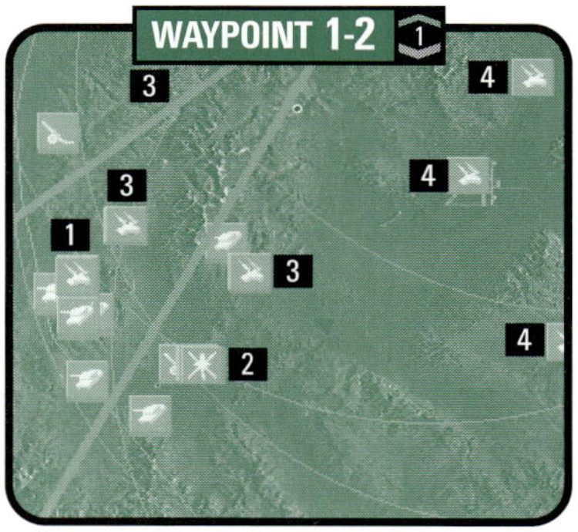

1 2S6s
2 Havocs
3 SA-11s, Snow Drift radar
4 SA-8

(Of course, you can always use a Hellfire or rocket from a distance to take out the radar, but that's not as fun. And it cuts down on the ammo you're going to need later.) With the radar destroyed, you can then move into close range and gun down the SAM launchers themselves.

You'll find a second set of SA-11s further along the path to Waypoint 2. There's also a 2S6 that pops up on your ASE, but you can skirt around him to the right and worry about him later when you're heading for home.

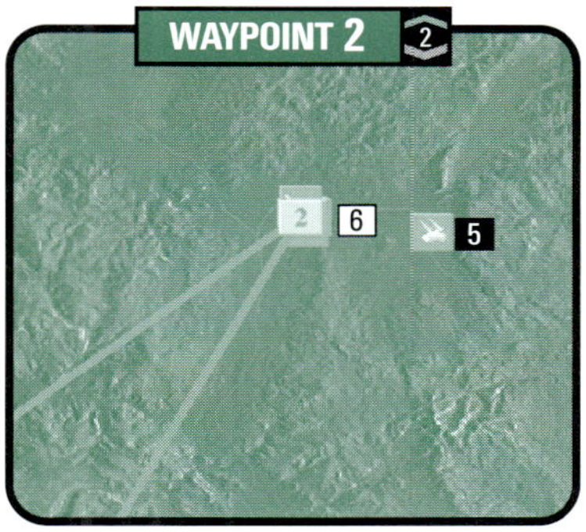

5 SA-11s
6 SCUD launchers

Waypoint 2. Near the second waypoint, you'll find your primary targets: SCUD launchers. You can fire at them while you're in a hover, about 120 feet above the ground. There's also a fuel truck or two marked as a primary, just to confuse you, along with some bunkers.

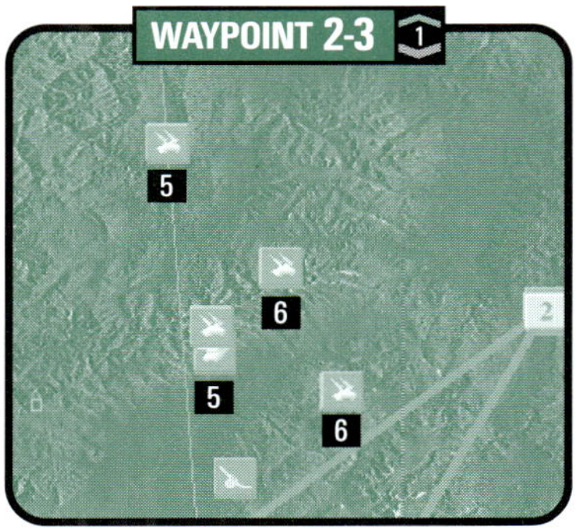

5 2S6s
6 SA-11s, Snow Drift radar

Waypoint 2-3. This part of the mission is fairly easy — it shouldn't take too long. When you undertake the long flight back to your base, use your remaining Hellfires to take out any targets you find (specifically, the SAMs you avoided on the way in). If you get into trouble with them, use time compression and autopilot to speed through their attack.

Campaign 35: Defensive Phase Charger

Mission Attack BMPs

Environment Dusk/Cloudy

Air Strikes 0

Artillery Strikes 0

Primaries	*Mission Rating*
19 T-80Us	19 killed......S+
	10-18..........S
	1-9............F
	0..............F-

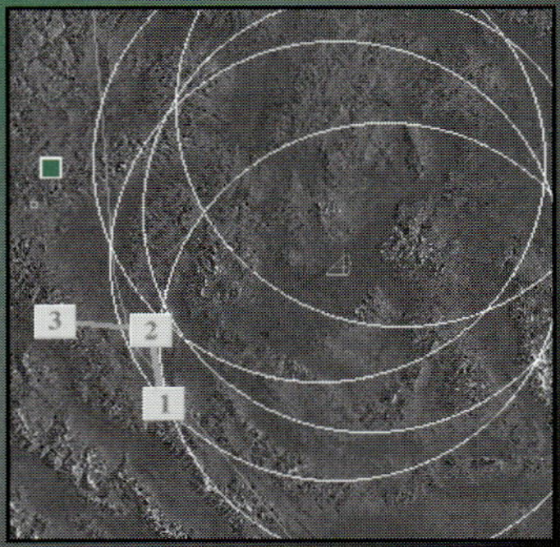

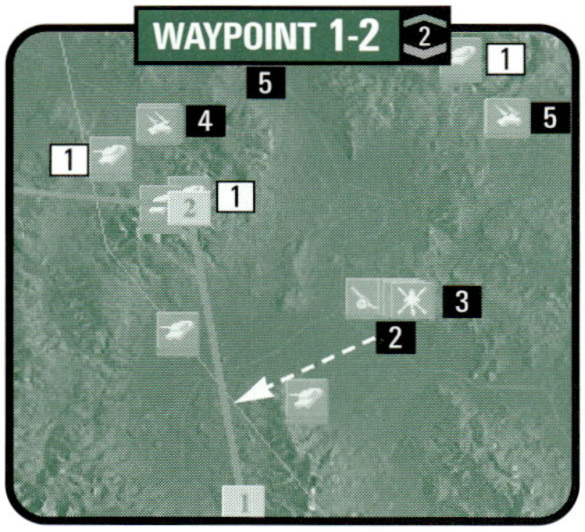

1 T-80Us
2 Enemy FARP
3 Havocs
4 2S6s
5 SA-11, Snow Drift radar

Waypoint 1. Nothing could be easier than the beginning of this mission. Picture yourself in the cockpit. Now, picture tanks within Hellfire range. It's not too difficult to guess what's next. As soon as you lift off and climb to over 100 feet, spin 180 degrees with your tail rotor and lay waste to one of the tanks with a Hellfire in LOAL mode. Keep doing this until you've gotten every primary possible from the takeoff FARP.

When that's done, head for Waypoint 2. Try to stay a little west of the battle line. It'll help conceal your presence from the SAMs. Luckily, there aren't too many to deal with in this mission.

Waypoint 2. North and east of Waypoint 2, you'll find a few targets to take out ... a pair of SA-11s and some primary target tanks. Remember, you can disable all the SAMs with a single missile by taking out the Snow Drift radar.

There's only one catch. At the second waypoint is a mesa-like hill. Just on the other side of it hill are your primary tank targets. They're protected by a couple of 2S6s that you can't see yet with your FCR. When you climb to get a valid LOS on the SA-11s, the 2S6s will have you for lunch.

You need to carefully think about your approach. Don't just pop over the hill... keep a good distance from it when you ascend. Don't climb any higher than you have to to get a valid lock. The 2S6s should show up on your ASE and TSD if you climb high enough. Take them out first, then go after the Snow Drift radar.

The Trip Home. On the way to your landing FARP, make a habit of checking your air radar frequently. You'll probably encounter Havocs from the enemy FARP on the way home. If you didn't kill them on the way to the target waypoint. Don't leave your radar in air mode, however. There are additional primary tank targets on the way home, and lots of them.

Campaign 36: Defensive Phase Florida

Mission Attack Armor

Environment Day/Clear

Air Strikes 0

Artillery Strikes 2

Primaries	*Mission Rating*
19 T-80Us	11 KILLED......S+
	8-10...........S
	1-7............F
	0..............F-

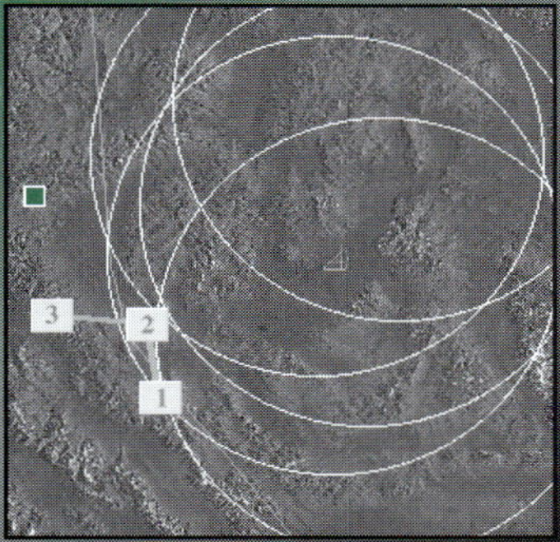

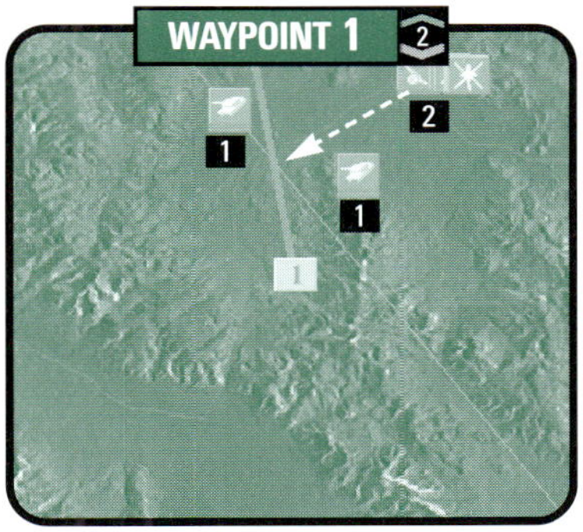

1 T-80Us

2 Enemy FARP (with active Havocs)

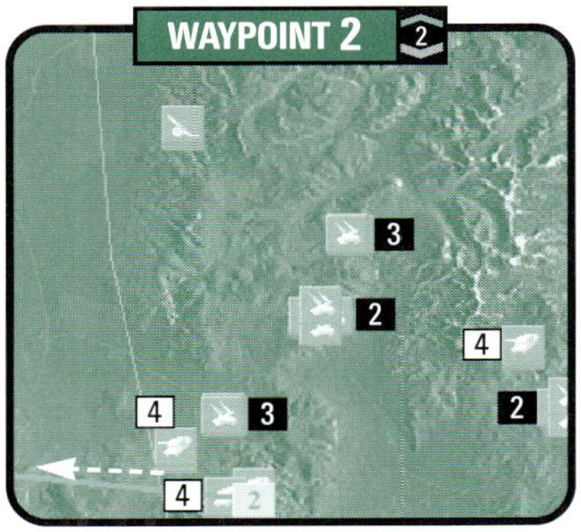

3 Havocs

4 T-80Us (moving west)

5 Enemy FARP

Waypoint 1. The navigation map for this daytime mission looks nearly identical to the previous mission. It's very similar, but this time, some of the primary tanks, 2S6s and SA-11s are moving. Take off and get whatever tanks you can see, then proceed to Waypoint 2. (Check out Mission 35 for more tactics. These two missions are very similar, except that tanks are moving in this one.)

Waypoint 2. On the way to and at the second navigation point, have a tank-killing spree with your wingman and take out all the T80-U primaries with Hellfires. Be sure to save a couple of missiles for the 2S6s you'll run across later.

About this time, you'll be jumped by several aggressive pairs of Havocs approaching from the north and the east. Loose your Stingers on them and give one or two choppers to your wingman.

Once you and your wingman are clear to proceed, search out more primary tanks just west of Waypoint 2. They'll be rolling, making them a little bit harder to hit. Before you can take pot shots at them, you'll have to eliminate a bunch of 2S6s. Do the usual approach — close in within 8km and get them with Hellfires.

From there, head for your landing FARP. Try to avoid SAMs if you're low on Hellfires, and stay slightly south of the flight path. You cleared out most of the stuff below your flight path on the way to the primaries. More SAMs lie to the north, and you probably haven't got enough ordnance to take them on now.

Campaign 37: Defensive Phase Red

Mission Attack Choppers	**Air Strikes** 0
Environment Dusk/Cloudy	**Artillery Strikes** 0
Primaries	*Mission Rating*
4 Mi-28s	3 killed.......S
	1-2............F
	0..............F-

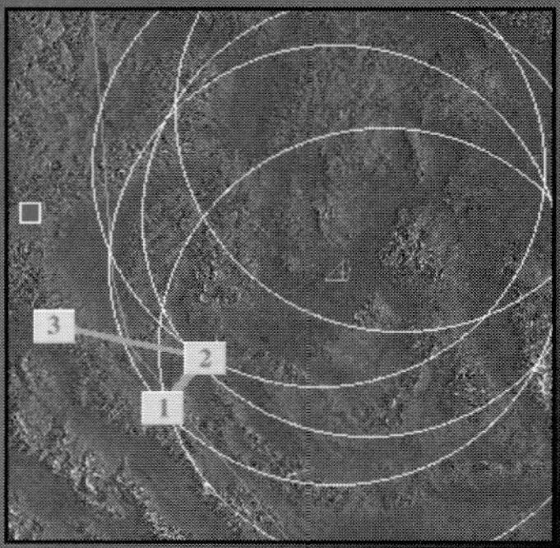

Waypoint 1. In this mission, you might get the impression that enemy pilots buzzed your FARP and challenged your entire squadron to a helicopter-helicopter showdown at dusk. It's almost true. There *are* a bunch of helicopters, and it *is* dusk outside.

If you ended up here, you have to win this mission and the one before this one to get back on the winning path. Otherwise, it's the end for you and all the NATO forces.

Waypoint 2. To meet up with the enemy, make tracks for the second waypoint as soon as you lift off. Arm your Stingers ahead of time — you'll be ambushed by Hokum helicopters before too long. The good news is that once you down at least two of them, you can go back to Waypoint 1 and land. There's no sense in flying all the way to Waypoint 3. It's a long ways off, and the path home is infested with SAMs (2S6s and SA-11s).

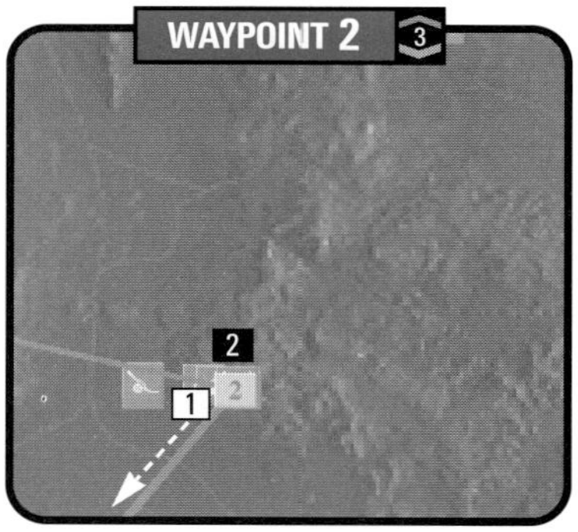

1 Havocs
2 SO-122 artillery

Campaign 38: This is the end ...

Mission Retreat

Environment Day/Clear

Air Strikes 0

Artillery Strikes 0

Primaries	Mission Rating
None	0 . . . . Automatic Fail

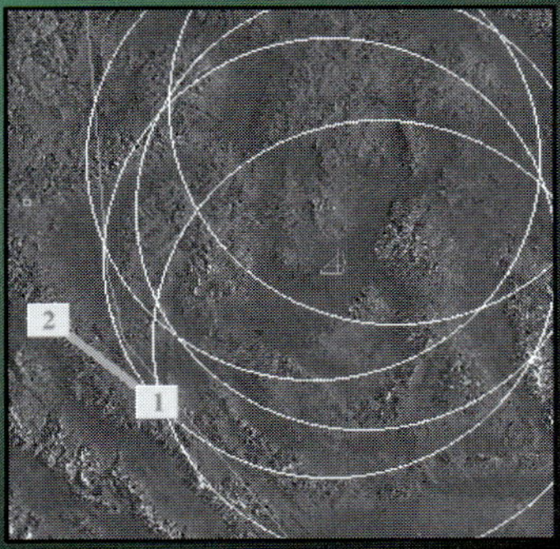

Waypoint 1. Well, you've gotten here by one of two means. Either you've heard how cool the endgame flick is and just had to see it, or you need some more combat practice (the training missions, for instance).

At least you're going to get to see some exceptional fireworks. The best advice we can give you is don't go here! There's no winning this mission. After a minute, it's all over ...

Note: *If you get to this mission, your active pilot dies and won't be available in the future. If you're watching this for fun, don't do it with one of your favorite pilots — take one you can afford to lose.*

Campaign 50: Phase Delta

Mission Destroy ammunition depot **Air Strikes** 0

Environment Night/Cloudy **Artillery Strikes** 0

Primaries	Mission Rating
5 Bunkers	9 killed.......S
1 Command Bunker	1-8............F
4 2S6s	0..............F-

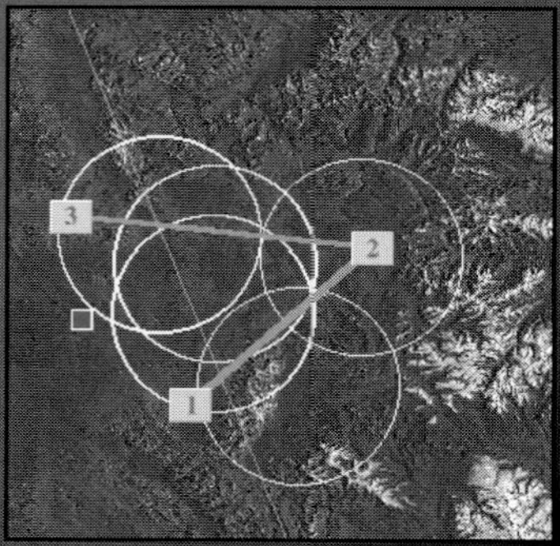

Waypoint 1. The only way to get here is to lose two of the previous four missions (the flowchart on p. 63). Compared to the winning path missions, the middle-path missions are a bit more difficult. You're not on the winning trail anymore, but you're not resigned to the losing path, either. In this and the other middle missions, you'll have to deal with SAMs, and lots of them. This one is by far the most difficult. Your mission objective is to destroy an ammo depot, and survive in the process.

In the mission planning computer, create a new second waypoint between Waypoints 1 and 2, but closer to Waypoint 1 (see facing page). Drag it slightly to the right so that you can cut through the pass in the mountain. Don't drag it too far — there are two enemy FARPs in this direction, and you only want to deal with one of them.

You don't have to go far to find something to shoot at when you take off. From this FARP, you'll be able to see four 2S6s if you bob up high enough. Turn so that you've got the closest 2S6 in front of you, then pop off a single Hellfire. You're out of range now, but if you center the waypoint in your heading tape and fly toward Waypoint 2, you'll be in range before the missile hits. However, make sure you have enough height to get a valid LOS.

Depending on how far your ASE is zoomed out, you may see additional 2S6s to the north. Normally, you'd attack them. In this mission, however, you've still got a ton of SAMs and primaries to take out and need to reserve your Hellfires. The most effective tactic against these threats is to veer outside their threat radii when you leave.

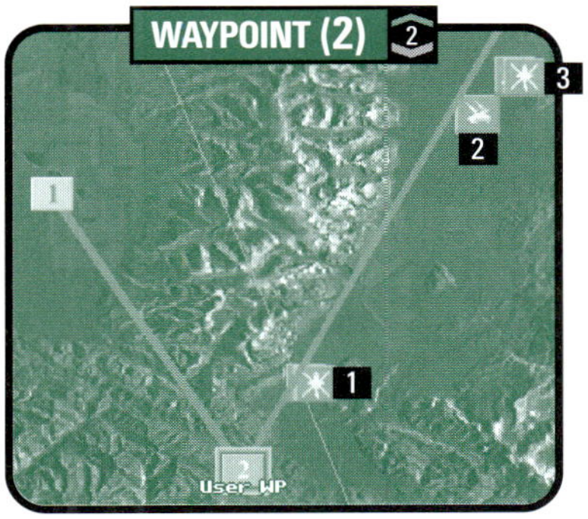

1 Enemy FARP (with active Havocs)
2 Enemy FARP 2 (with an active Havoc)
3 2S6s

Waypoint (2). This waypoint you created greatly increases your chance of survival and lets you bypass a lot of threats. Keep your speed low and go through the pass via the road that passes through the mountain range. Once you're almost through the pass and can see the valley, come to a hover and bob up briefly to ID what's around. If you don't see more 2S6s after rising a few hundred feet, go further down the valley (east) and try again. In this manner, you can see a pair of 2S6s at a FARP before they detect you.

Move toward the SAMs just enough to take them out with a couple of Hellfires, then drop down again and slowly push your way through the rest of the pass. As soon as you come out into the open valley, you'll find two Havocs. Clear them out with Stingers and follow the path to the third waypoint. You need to stay below 100 feet and weave through the low spots wherever possible. Using autopilot isn't recommended — you could penetrate further into SAM territory than you really want to.

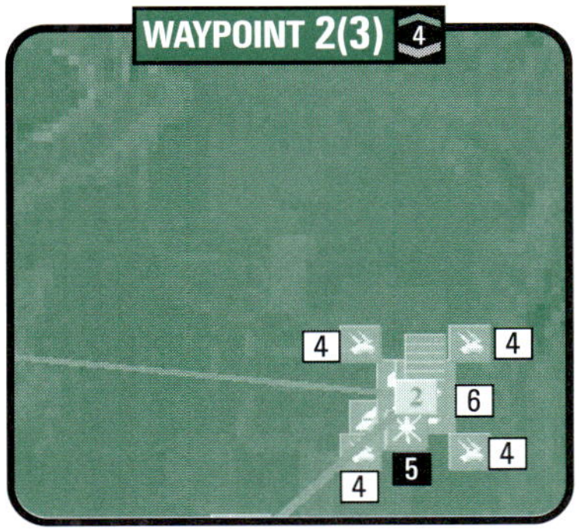

4 2S6
5 Havocs
6 Bunkers

Waypoint 2 (3). When you come within 9km the third waypoint, slow down and come to a hover. You're going to have to be patient and pick off the 2S6s one at a time. To target the one that's closest to you, cycle through targets with [T] until 2S6 appears in Upfront display, then check range in the IHADSS.

Creep in slowly until you're exactly 8.1km away from your target. If you maneuver just right, you'll be in detection range only for that SAM. Fire off a Hellfire, then move in to 7.9km of the threat to get inside your missile's range before it's timer runs out. Repeat these steps until all the SAMs are cleared out.

Once the waypoint is safe, move in to get the other FARP primaries. You'll also find two Havocs here, but they're grounded if you come in low enough. Send your wingman after the other standard FARP targets.

When heading for home, you may want to exit the exact way you came in. There's nothing else to kill on the way but additional SAMs, and you probably don't have many, if any, Hellfires left. (If your wingman's fully loaded and you want points, however, go for it. You can always activate 8X time compression to get past the 2S6s if you get into trouble.)

Campaign 60: Phase November

Mission Attack Tank

Environment Day/Cloudy

Air Strikes 3

Artillery Strikes 0

Primaries	*Mission Rating*
5 T-80Us	11 KILLED......S+
4 BMP-3s	7-10...........S
2 2S6s	1-6............F
	0..............F-

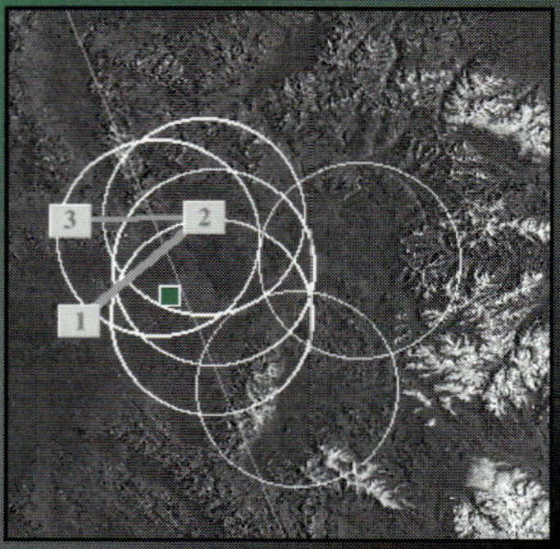

Waypoint 1. In this mission, you're to attack an armored column. You know what that means ... a full load of Hellfires for both you and your wingman. As soon as you leave your FARP, zoom your ASE out to 25 (press Del). This allows you to detect a group of 2S6s that will interrupt your journey to Waypoint 2. You won't be able to fly around them because their coverage extends all around the primary waypoint.

Finishing this mission takes patience. After you get the 2S6s on your TSD, you'll need to target the one closest to you using T. (Don't forget to press U to display the target name in the Upfront display.) Move to within 7.9km of the target, take out that 2S6, and then drift in a little closer to take out the next one. The SAMs are arranged such that you can take them out singly in this manner.

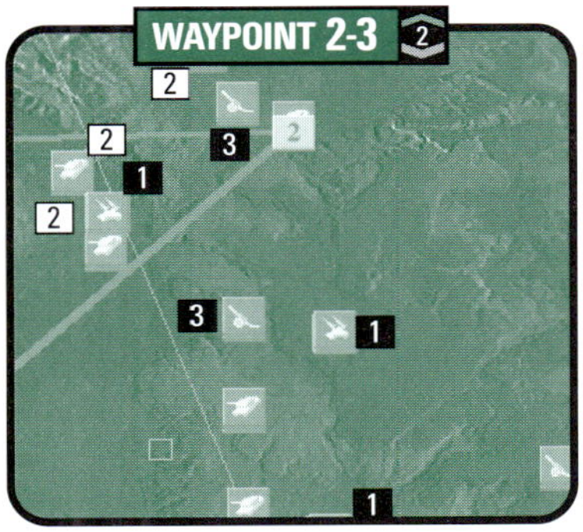

1 2S6s
2 T-80Us, BMP-3s
3 SO-122 Artillery

Waypoints 2-3. By the time you work your way through the SAMs, you may have forgotten that your actual objective is to ambush a column of tanks and infantry fighting vehicles. After you take out the SAMs, start looking for them. They'll be somewhat northeast of Waypoint 2, where you'll also find another complement of SAMs that are your primaries.

Now would be a good time to put your wingman to work. After you disable all the SAMs in the immediate area, let him take out the T80-Us while you catch the BMP-3s. The BMP guns can be lethal if you're not careful, which is why *you* should take them on instead of sending your wingman after them..

Once you get through the primaries, you've succeeded the mission and all you have to do is land safely at a FARP. There are a lot of tanks on the way home if you or your wingman have Hellfires left to spare. If you've only got guns, they really aren't worth the time it takes to destroy them.

Campaign 70: Phase Trump

Mission Attack Refueling Depot **Air Strikes** 0

Environment Dusk-to-Dark/Cloudy **Artillery Strikes** 0

Primaries	*Mission Rating*
4 Bunkers	4 killed.......S
	1-3...........F
	0.............F-

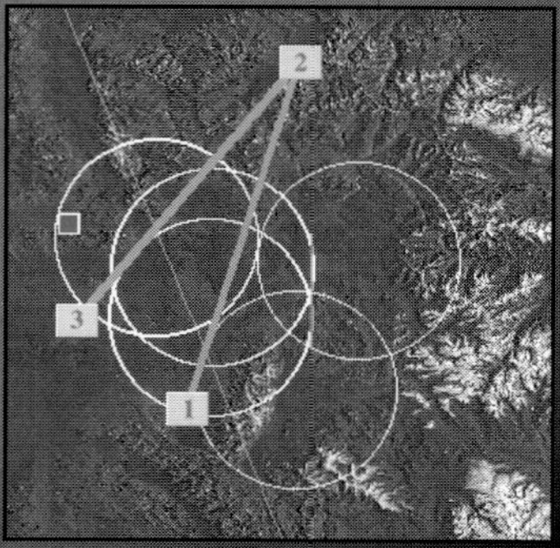

Waypoint 1. Grab a cup of java and run a few laps — you're going to be in the cockpit for awhile. It's not that the mission is extremely difficult, it's just that it's a deep strike mission, and it has a ton of SAMs. If you've flown any of the other middle-path missions, you'll be an expert by now at this type or sortie.

If you've looked at the briefing map, you know right away that you don't want to blow your cover on the way to the scheduled second waypoint. Use the mission planner and add a waypoint between 1 and 2. Drag it to the right so that it lies at the rightmost edge of the mountain range. Just east of that is a wide valley, at which point you'll want to stop and assess the situation before proceeding into the valley.

Activate PNVS and head for the mountains. It's especially vital in this mission to keep your TSD zoomed to 10km, and your ASE zoomed to 10km (preferably 25).

Waypoint (2-3). At your new waypoint, come to an autohover at around 50 feet of altitude. Bob up until you identify SAMs on your MFD, then draw a PFZ around the 2S6 icons to the north in your TSD. They're stacked four deep, so you'll need to expend four Hellfires here.

Now, you're free to go after the primary target, which is a fuel depot deep inside enemy territory at Waypoint 2(4) (assuming you added a waypoint earlier). On the way, you'll unveil additional sets of four SAMs, but you don't have to destroy them. Instead, weave your way around them by traveling through the narrow safety corridor that

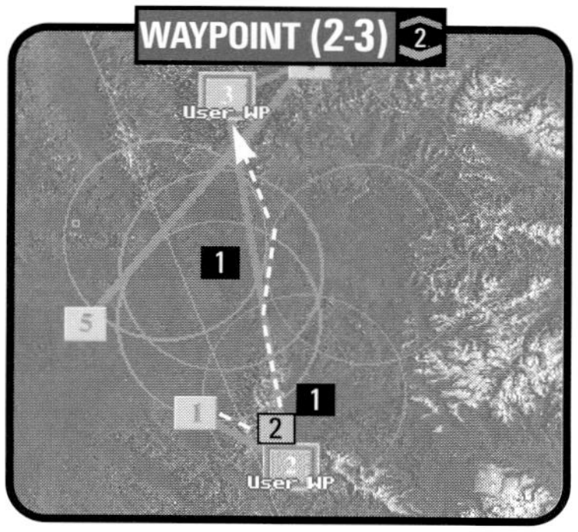

1 2S6 (destroy to open corridor)

2 Suggested Route

appears on the ASE. This frustrates the SAMs to no end — they can light you up with radar, but they can't touch you. Stay low, however, to avoid activating anything else that might see you.

Waypoint (3). This would be a good time to open up the nav map (Alt N) and add another waypoint. Create it between Waypoints 2 and 3, then drag it to the valley just southwest of the primary waypoint. (See the map on the previous page.) Use it as a landmark. When you reach this point, travel west through the valley and approach the primary waypoint from the protective west side of the ridge.

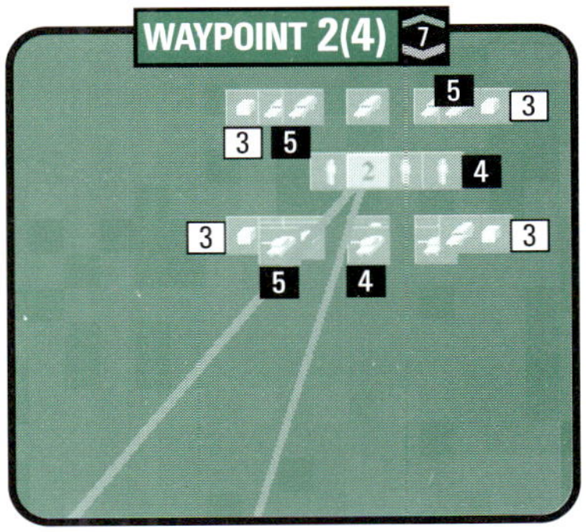

3 Bunker
4 CIS Soldiers
5 Fuel Truck

Waypoint 2 (4). Once you're about 5 miles away from the primary waypoint, hover and bob up so that you can detect the primaries (bunker buildings) with your radar. The actual waypoint is a turkey shoot. Although you've probably spent most of your Hellfires, your wingman should still be carrying a full load. Take out everything, and use your wingman's weapons to do it.

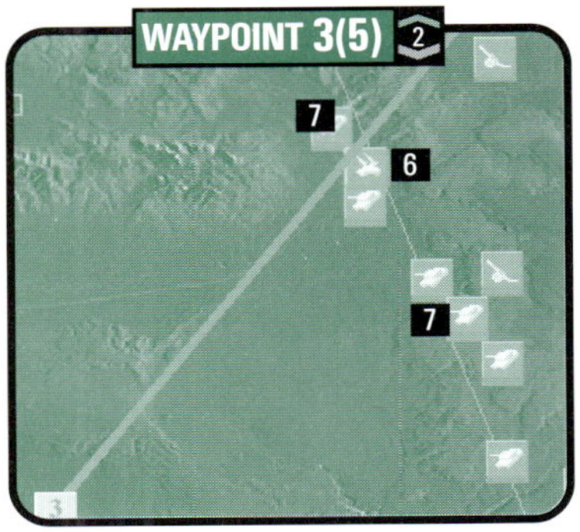

6 2S6s
7 T-80Us

Waypoint 3 (5). Follow the default route home. About 20km away from the landing FARP, you'll run across the outer range of four 2S6s. If you have missiles left, take them out, along with a bunch of tanks. If you're Winchester, stay low and slow.

Campaign 80: Phase Orange

Mission Attack chopper, FARP
Environment Dawn/Clear

Air Strikes 0
Artillery Strikes 0

PRIMARIES	MISSION RATING
2 Bunkers	4 killed.......S
1 Tent	1-3............F
1 2S6	0..............F-
1 Mi-24	

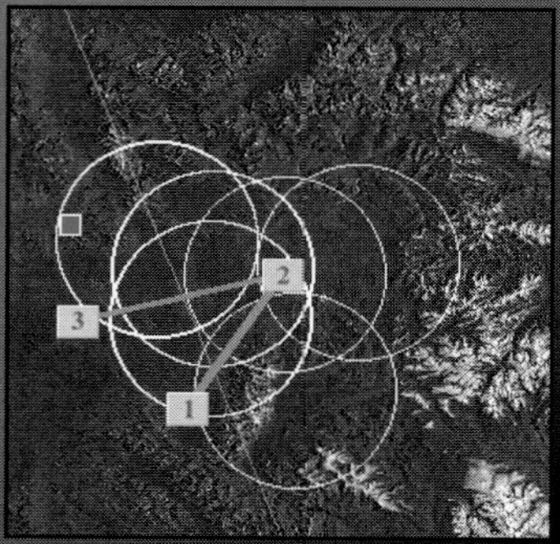

Waypoint (2). This is the mission that will make or break your career as a Longbow pilot. If you lose, you're destined for failure. If you succeed, you're two victories away from winning the war.

The first thing you can do to ensure your survival is create an additional waypoint. Put one between Waypoints 1 and 2 and drag it to the center of the rightmost SAM circle. This will bring you just outside the middle SAM's range once you destroy the rightmost 2S6s. By taking out the SAMs whose arcs appear on the right side of the map, you can totally bypass the SAMs in the **middle** of the map.

Next, you'll need to set your ASE to 25km and your TSD to 10km. This is a SAM-intensive mission, and as a general rule, you should use this range.

Immediately after you take off, you'll spot a couple of Havocs. Try to use your guns if possible — you'll need all four of your Stingers later, and it's really to your advantage to use guns now. Once the sky is clear, head for your new waypoint. Stay as low as you can, and bob up to about 300 feet every couple of kilometers. Soon, you should pick up four 2S6s on your MFDs. (It may look like only one, but they're actually just really close to one another.)

SAMs outside your flight path are normally indicative of an enemy FARP. Wherever you find stray 2S6s, there are almost always two or more helicopters. Send your wingman after the helicopters while you take out tents, etc.

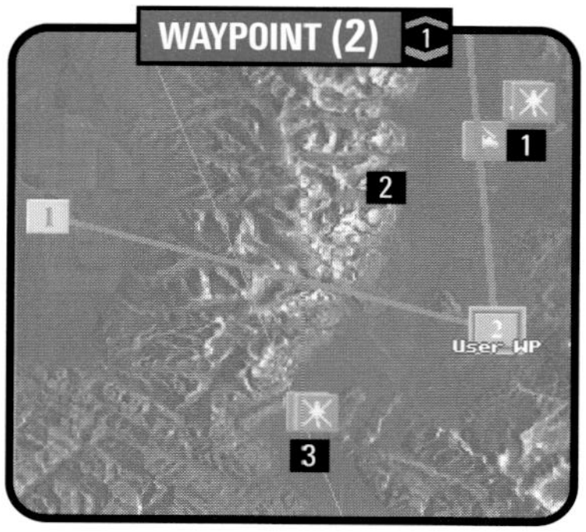

1 Havocs
2 2S6s
3 Enemy FARP

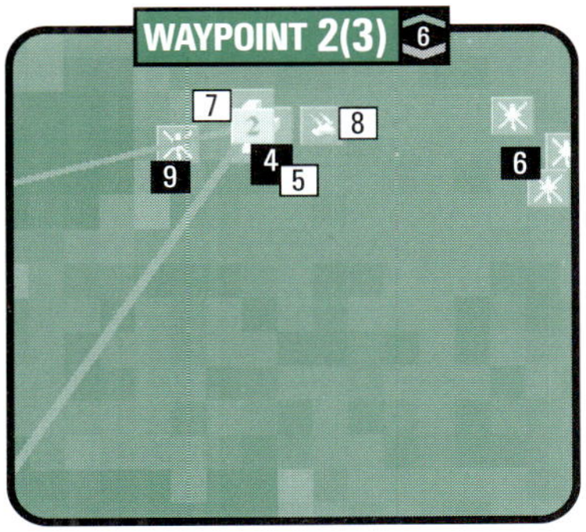

- **4** Hokums
- 5 Hind
- **6** Enemy FARP (with 2S6s)
- 7 Bunkers, Tent
- 8 2S6
- **9** Havocs

Switch back to air to air mode and make sure your wingman downed both of the helos from the south. If not, help him out with a couple of Stingers, then proceed on your normal course. You'll run across more 2S6s, but you can make short work of them by establishing a PFZ.

Waypoint 2(3). The Hind that appeared earlier was one of your primary targets. So is almost everything you see at the target waypoint. First, however, you need to take out the 2S6s at the enemy FARP directly east of the primary. Then, camp out there (approximately 8km away from the primaries) and toast the command post at will.Take out yet another 2S6 at the command post. (Although there are other SAMs around, you can get away with only taking out some of them if you stay between the SAM arcs in your ASE during the remainder of the mission.)

The rest of the mission is easy. Instead of clearing out a new path to your landing FARP, simply backtrack to your start position through the areas you've opened up already. Then, you can fly from Waypoint 1 to your landing FARP without having to kill anything else. (If you're going for points, don't do this. Just proceed normally and take out anything in your path.)

DESERT STORM MISSIONS

The Desert Storm missions were designed by Kevin Kushner and Mike Francis. Kevin recommends Lightning: The 101st in the Gulf War, *by Lt. Gen. Edward M. Flanagan, Jr. US Army (Ret.), as a good account of the Apache's role in the conflict. He comments on the missions below.*

DESERT STORM 1: DARKOVER

The first mission is based on the mission that opened the war. Two teams from the 101st set out to destroy two Early Warning sites deep inside Iraq. They succeeded, knocking out a huge ground control intercept and paving the way for conventional aircraft to go in and bomb Baghdad.

This was one of my favorites, because we found so much information on it. This mission was tactically very important, and a lot of planning went into it. We knew the exact layout for everything — where radar vehicles were, where the three trucks with the power generators were, etc.

At one point during the mission the teams passed a camp of Bedouins that fired small arms at them. One even had a shoulder-launched SAM, which he fired, but missed. We simulate this in the game.

We changed one thing — we shortened the flight time. The original mission was a deep strike, and so long the helicopters had to carry an external fuel tank on one pylon.

DESERT STORM 2: LIME FREEZE

This mission simulates one that took place after the air offensive had begun. Apache teams were sent in to destroy mobile SAMs, mostly SA-8s.

This was a very basic mission that suffered from poor intelligence. The SAMs were moving around more than expected, and when the Apaches reached the target area, the SA-8s had moved out and ZSUs had moved in, which was far more dangerous for the Apaches. This happens in the game too — ZSUs show up unexpectedly at the target waypoint. We weren't sure whether to inform the player of this, so in the briefing we mention that intelligence was spotty.

DESERT STORM 3: RUBY BLUE

This mission occurred during the opening days of the ground offensive. Coalition Forces had been stationed all along the Saudi Arabian border, and the goal for the first wave of the offensive was to move everyone up to Phase Line Smash. Apaches flew ahead to take out ground artillery, mostly SO-122s.

Mission #	Name	Objective	Environment	S+	S	F	F-
Desert Storm 1	Darkover	Destroy EW Site	Night/Clear	–	5 killed	0-4	–
Desert Storm 2	Lime Freeze	Destroy AA and SAMs	Night/Clear	–	5+ killed	0-4	–
Desert Storm 3	Ruby Blue	Destroy Artillery	Night/Clear	–	7+ killed	0-6	–
Desert Storm 4	Kitarin	Locate Armor	Day/Clear	–	10+ killed	0-9	–
Desert Storm 5	Restless Voyager	Destroy Air Defense	Day/Clear	–	6+ killed	0-5	–
Desert Storm 6	Seven Eleven	Destroy Armor	Day/Clear	–	10+ killed	0-9	–

DESERT STORM 4: KITARIN

This mission took place along Highway 8, or the "Highway of Death," before the Air Force blew up everything. The targets, T-72s and ZSUs (around 30) moving from As Samawah to As Nasiriyah, were brought in to replace the Republican Guard units destroyed in the first wave of the ground offensive. The Apaches went in and took out the AAA, and then basically took potshots at the tanks.

DESERT STORM 5: RESTLESS VOYAGER

In the final push to set up FOB Cobra (the "World's Biggest FARP"), the Apaches' mission was to destroy air defense (mobile SAMs and dug-in ZPU-4s) around As Salman airfield.

This was my favorite mission, because the ramifications were so great. After the opening mission, this was the second most important in the war — the Coalition Forces wanted to set up their airbase at this location. For the rest of the war, all air operations were based here.

DESERT STORM 6: SEVEN ELEVEN

This mission is based on one known as "The Battle of 73 Easting Line."

Tom Clancy provides a great account of this from a tank driver's perspective in *Armored Cav*. You're flying air support against the last Republican Resistance — there's stuff everywhere, and this is your opportunity to waste things. There are a couple of American tank companies mixing it up with the Iraqis that are fun to watch, too

Desert Storm 1: Darkover

Mission Destroy early warning sites **Air Strikes** 0
Environment Night/Clear **Artillery Strikes** 0

Primaries	Mission Rating
1 Bar Lock radar	5 killed.......S
1 Spoon Rest radar	0-4............F
2 Long Track radar[1]	
1 Straight Flush	

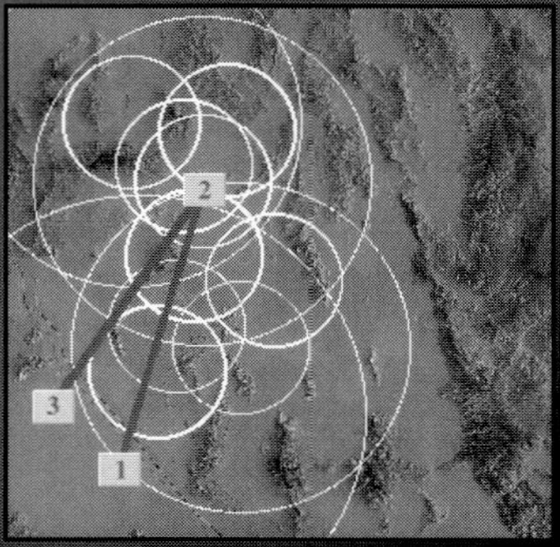

This is the mission that started it all. On January 16th 1991, AH-64A attack choppers went in to take out key Iraqi early warning radar installations. This is now your objective.

Waypoint 1. Be forewarned this entire area is crawling with mobile SAM sites and AAA. In this campaign, unlike most, you can fly high and fast. Even 100 feet up and 100 knots isn't too dangerous. Use your PNVS — it really helps in any hilly terrain.

Also, as often as possible, have your wingman engage targets. When you get to Waypoint 2, kill the different kinds of early warning radar sites — the Bar Lock, Spoon Rest, Long Track and Straight Flush radar. If you use your wingman to take out targets on the way, you'll still have ammo left on the way back. For the same reason, ignore any tanks or artillery on the way to your primary objective; you can sweep them up after you accomplish your goal. Don't spend ammo foolishly before you've done what you set out to do.

Take off and head for Waypoint 2. There are quite a number of surface-to-air threats, just waiting for you to fly by on your way to Waypoint 2. They do not appear on the briefing map; don't be caught off guard. Remember, your missiles can take out things up to five klicks away.

[1] Technically, one of these isn't a primary, but destroying it is vital to the success of the mission.

It's 26km to the next waypoint, and almost immediately you're going to run into bad guys. There's an SA-8 Gecko shooting at you before you've even gone one kilometer. As is usual for Desert Storm, ground threats are usually grouped in a diamond or square formation. Stay low to avoid detection by the ZSU-23s.

There you'll also find Bedouin soldiers in your path. Even though they only have machine guns, there are quite a few of them, and they will shoot you down.

About 3-4km away from Waypoint 2 (after the Bedouins), be careful! There is a SAM site at the bottom of a hill that will tag you if you aren't watching for it.

On the outskirts of where the early warning radar can be found, there are some sand dunes you can use as cover as you take out the few SAM sites nearby. Use them! Once you get past that group, the fireworks will begin.

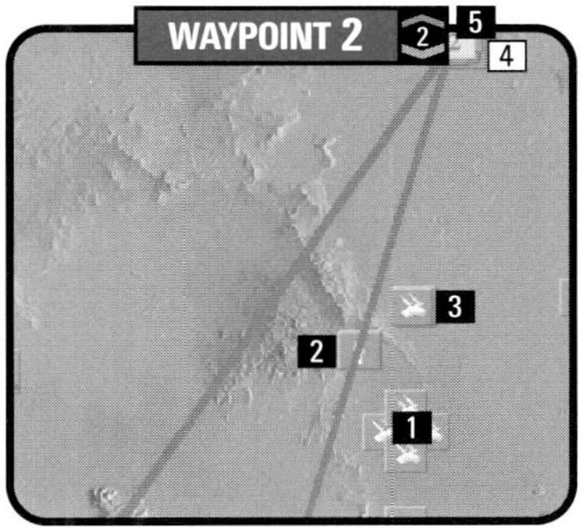

1 SA-6s, Long Track radar
2 Bedouin Soldiers
3 ZSU-23s
4 Bar Lock radar, Long Track radar, Spoon Rest radar, Straight Flush radar
5 ZSU-23s, SA-6s, SA-9s

Waypoint 2. When you are very close to Waypoint 2, give your wingman the "Weapons Free" command. Don't worry, he's not going to waste his ammo on anything unimportant.

The radar is heavily protected by mobile SAM and AAA defenders. You will also find a few Iraqi troops scurrying about. Take out the mobile SAM sites and radar first. The rest will be cannon fodder.

Destroy the AAA, troops and radar with your cannon, if possible. This will save the Hellfires for longer distance targets — like the mobile SAMs that are all over the place. There are at least 20 SAM and 12 AAA sites, along with many other threats. Watch out for the mobile SAMs and make every shot count!

It is unwise to fly past the waypoint or to go around it. There are plenty of enemies off the beaten path around here. Remember not to use all your ammo at the target site. You still have to get home, it's a really long flight, and yes, there are threats on the way back. You'll face as many as 25 SAM and 14 AAA sites plus 5 radar installations.

Desert Storm 2: Lime Freeze

Mission Destroy AAs and SAMs
Environment Night/Clear
Air Strikes 2
Artillery Strikes 2

Primaries	*Mission Rating*
2 SA-8s	5+ KILLED......S
5 ZSU-23-4s	0-4..........F

Waypoint 1. This time around, you are to clear the way for coalition airpower. Your opposition will be SAMs, AAA, BMPs, T72s and a few mobile radar installations. Wipe out the radar and SAM sites first; the rest will be sitting ducks for your cannon. (Except tanks of course. If you want to hunt tanks, save some Hellfires.)

This is an especially good mission for loading up on missiles. Your targets, after all, are surface-to-air missiles, so you want to be as far away as possible when you fire at them. More than that, however, is the sheer quantity of enemies: around 25 SAM and 14 AAA sites along with 5 radar installations. There are fortunately many sand dunes to hover behind while you get the job done. Remember, low and slow is the way to go! That is, until you're out of ammo. Stick to this particular flight path; there is nothing to be gained by changing your waypoints in this mission.

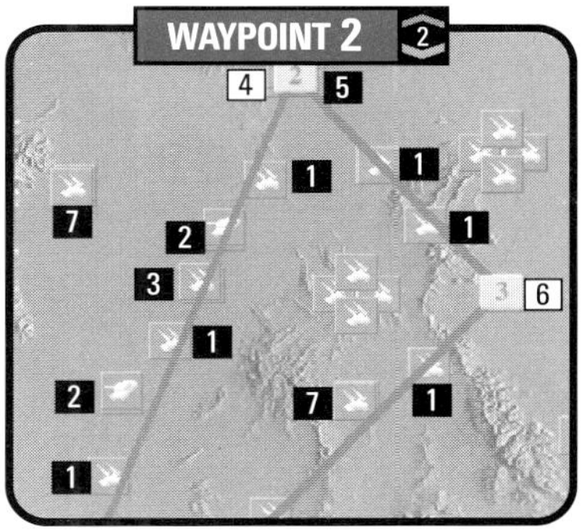

1 SA-8s
2 T-72s, BMP-2
3 ZSU-23s
4 SA-8s
5 T-72s, ZSU-23s
6 ZSUs
7 SA-9s, ZSU-23s

Waypoint 2. Here, completely ignore all the tanks and artillery. There are a *lot* of SAMs and AAA in the hills. They are designed to be a surprise, so be careful going over *each* and *every* hill. In particular, be careful just after Waypoint 2 and just before Waypoint 3.

You'll find some extra SA-8s, ZSUs and some tanks near Waypoint 2. You're going to have to kill everything but the tanks.

On your way to the next waypoint, there are some hills with an SA-8 nestled within them. If you cruise in fast, you're history. If you're ready for him, you can peek over the ridge of the hill and hit him before he launches at you.

Waypoint 3. Kill all SA-8s with missiles. That's the way to win this mission. Ignore everything else until the primary targets are all destroyed. You'll have noticed by now that this is an ammo intensive mission, so take out many of the AAA sites with your cannon as you can; the same goes for the mobile radar.

Near Waypoint 3, you'll see a ZSU-23. If you use the external view ([F7]), you'll find that there are actually three lying in wait for you. These guys have quad-machine guns — they're really feisty. If you get within a kilometer and a half of them, they'll snuff you like a candle. The good thing about ZSUs, though, is that you can shoot them from outside their range — just stay 1.5km away and kill them with your chain gun. You can outshoot them primarily because your targeting system is more advanced.

Be sure to remember, if things do get hot, you always have the option of calling in an artillery strike. Don't be afraid to use it. It sounds pretty impressive, and you'll really pity those guys once the shelling starts. In the meantime, send your wingman against ground threats and save the primary targets for yourself.

Waypoint 4. Watch out for bad guys sitting on the other side of hills and rolling terrain. Remember, if you're damaged or low on ammo, go back the way you came and *then* go to the last waypoint.

DESERT STORM 3: RUBY BLUE

Mission Destroy Artillery

Environment Night/Clear

Air Strikes 3

Artillery Strikes 1

PRIMARIES	*MISSION RATING*
10 SO-122s	7+ KILLED......S
	0-6............F

You will be faced with more than 21 SAMs and 15 AAA sites — this mission can be pretty hairy at times!

Waypoint 1. (Just for fun, at Waypoint 1, try shooting a fuel truck. See how many things are destroyed when it explodes. Then, start the mission over.)

Immediately after you take off, you find four SA-8s in a diamond formation. Take those out with missiles. The idea is to clear your path of hostiles, and using your missiles makes quick work of it. You can go ahead and use your guns on the artillery and tanks without wasting any time.

It's a very straightforward mission — no cat-and-mouse, no gimmicks. Everything you need to take out is right in your flight path, and anything that isn't, you don't need to worry about. Fly between 50-80 knots so you have time enough to react to any unexpected dangers. That's actually pretty slow, but you'll reach your waypoint in plenty of time.

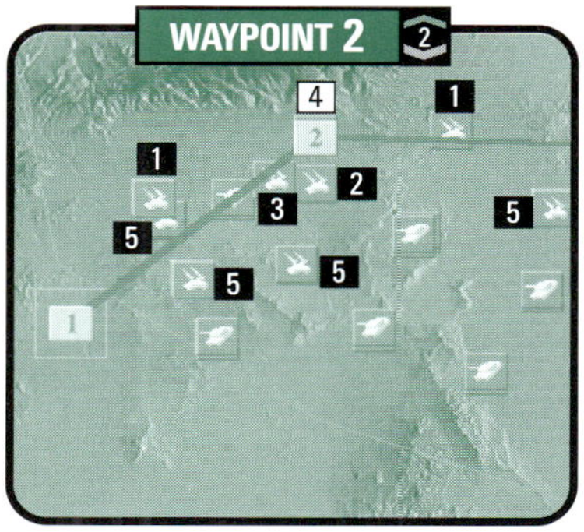

1 SA-8
2 SA-9, ZSU-23
3 ZPU-4
4 SO-122
5 ZSU-23

Waypoint 2. There are five artillery units at Waypoint 2. Fly until you are about 1 kilometer away from them and then just hold down your chain gun. If you've got lots of ammo, you can kill them from 3km away, but there's really no reason to waste bullets or time by staying so far out.

External cameras are a good way to see exactly what's out there. Watchout as you leave Waypoint 2. There's a ground threat lurking just over a ridge.

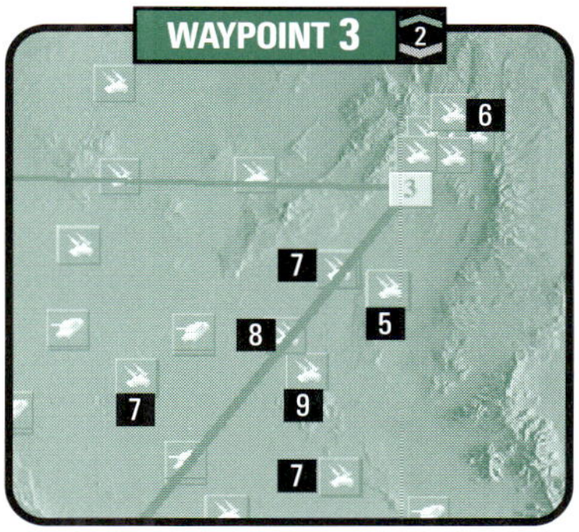

5 ZSU-23s
6 Anti-aircraft site
7 SA-9, ZSU-23
8 SA-8
9 ZPU-4

Waypoint 3. As you're coming from Waypoint 2 and are about to reach your primary objectives, there's an entire anti-aircraft site off to the left waiting for you to fly within range. To be safe, you'll want to approach these hills low and slow (under 30 knots and 30 feet). The AAA and SAMs are dangerous, so take due precautions on arrival.

Once you've cleared out your last primary objective, and you're ready to go home, you should switch to your weapons page and decide if you have enough ammo to make it there. If you've got a fair amount left, just head directly toward your next waypoint. (It also depends on how many points you want.) If not, go back the way you came.

Don't hesitate to give your wingman the "Weapons Free" command (Ctrl 6), and let him take out the remaining AAA sites while enroute to the FARP. Stay NOE and slow, and you should be fine. Keep in mind you can take out the AAA and SAM sites with your cannon, *if* you can get close enough. Just clear out any SAM sites first, and the other threats will be cannon fodder.

Desert Storm 4: Kitarin

Mission Destroy armor

Environment Day/Clear

Air Strikes 1

Artillery Strikes 1

Primaries	*Mission Rating*
12 T-72s	10+ killed.....S
	0-9 killed.....F

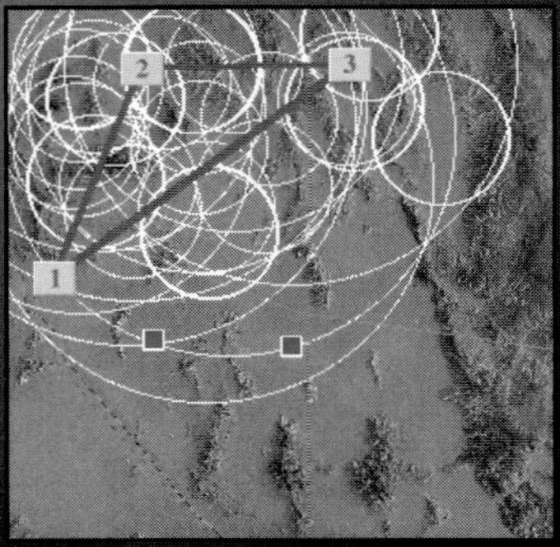

Waypoint 1. You'll need to clear a path, and as usual there are a couple of ZSU-23s lurking around. Gun them down. They'll give you trouble if you ignore them.

Waypoint 2. As you approach Waypoint 2, you will not find very much opposition. Expect, however, a few groups of mobile AAA, and a couple of mobile SAMs. Try dusting the AAA with your cannon (remember to dodge the flak), and try to save your Hellfires to take out the Republican Guard's T-72 tanks. Once you take out the first three mobile AAA , you will also find three more to the left of the airfield; you will pass them enroute to Waypoint 2. There are about 5 mobile SAMs altogether, so be on the lookout for them also.

Make sure you approach the hill just before Waypoint 2 carefully. As soon as you crest the ridge, you'll see them — about 5 ZSU-23s and 13 tanks. Attack the ZSUs first, and be cautious. Definitely send your wingman after them as well. Take out the T72s with your Hellfires, cut up the AAA with your cannon, and you should make quick work of them. Just sit back at a hover, over a ridge from behind them, and go to work. They will be on the move, but you can stop them dead in their tracks! Just be cautious on the way back to base, because there are a few more mobile AAA and SAMs along the way.

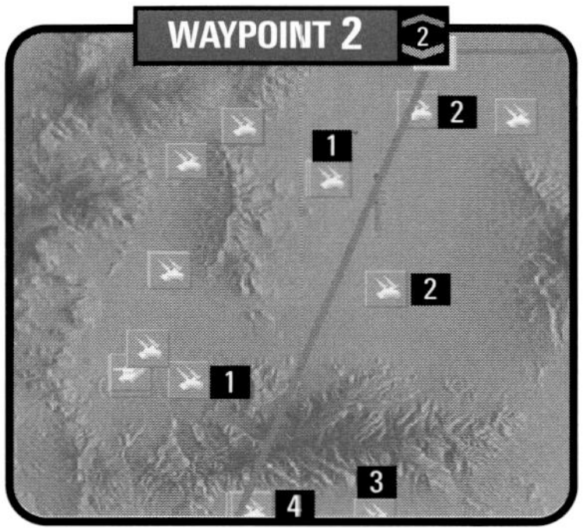

1 ZSU-23s
2 SA-8
3 ZPU-4
4 SA-9, ZPU-4

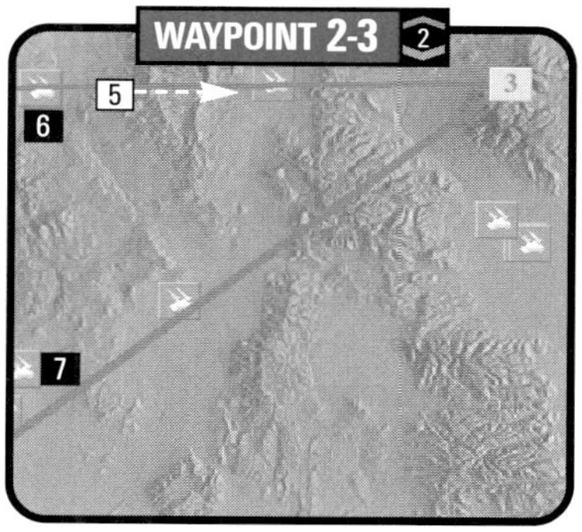

5 T-72s
6 SA-9, ZSU-23
7 T-72

Now notice that some of the tanks — depending on how soon you get there — are going over a hill. Don't send a missile after a tank that's going over a rise; you'll lose your line of sight on him. Keeping that in mind, pound them and pound them hard. Keep an eye on your altitude and try to hover around 25 feet. If you need to, rise to 60-70 feet momentarily, fire and return to a low hover position.

Remember, you're not alone! Give your wingman the Weapons Free command and he'll hover with you, toasting the T-72s with FFARs! It will take him a while, but you'll be glad he was there.

These are tanks, remember. Don't try to take them out with your guns; they're heavily armored and hard to kill. If you work hard at it, you might be able to gun down two or three. In fact, they are so hard to kill that you might have to return to a FARP to rearm. This mission is a big ammo-eater.

If you do find yourself taking a long time to stop the tanks, be very aware of your surroundings. If they can, they'll lure you near a SAM site, and the worst kind of trouble is missile trouble.

Waypoint 3. Keep it slow and low. There are almost always AAA sites hiding in the foothills.

Desert Storm 5: Restless Voyager

Mission Destroy air defense
Environment Day/Clear

Air Strikes 0
Artillery Strikes 0

Primaries	*Mission Rating*
7 ZPU-4s	6+ KILLED......S
3 SA-8s	0-5...........F

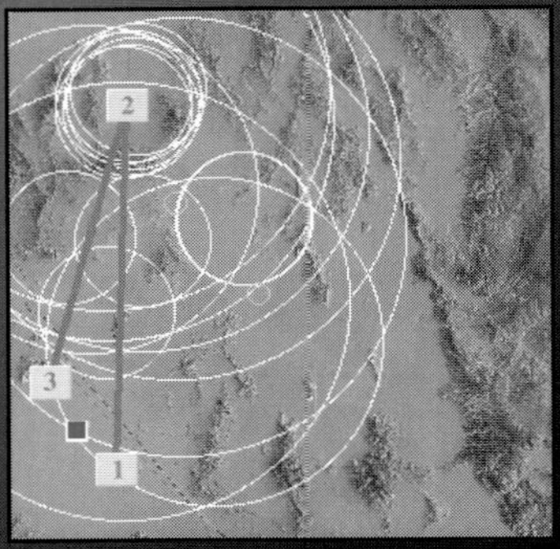

Waypoint 1-2. Now it's time to clear an airfield of SAMs and AAA. There will be many T-72s and BMPs between you and the airfield, and many mobile AAA sites, with a few SAMs where you least expect them.

There is nothing much to be concerned about near Waypoint 1. Keep alert while enroute, because there are a few SAM sites hidden in between the beginning of the enemy territory and the airfield. Shooting at anything around here would be a complete waste of ammo. This is a realistic aspect of the game, actually. Toward the end of a campaign you're winning, you've mostly mopped up the area of any serious threats. By the later portion of an action, it's simply a matter of Intelligence finding the remaining threats, your going after them, and then heading back home.

However, don't get complacent. As you get closer to Waypoint 2, there is an anti-aircraft site lying in wait for you at the foot of a hill. The trick is that not only is it on the far side, so you can't see it until you're almost on it, but there's also a tank on the horizon, and you might (understandably) focus on the tank to the extent that you forget to cycle through your targets.

Even this late in the show, be cautious around hills. The missions are long and the terrain is generally unvaried, so it's easy to overlook the small rises that SAMs and AAA can hide behind. Even in daytime, PNVS can provide a clearer contrast.

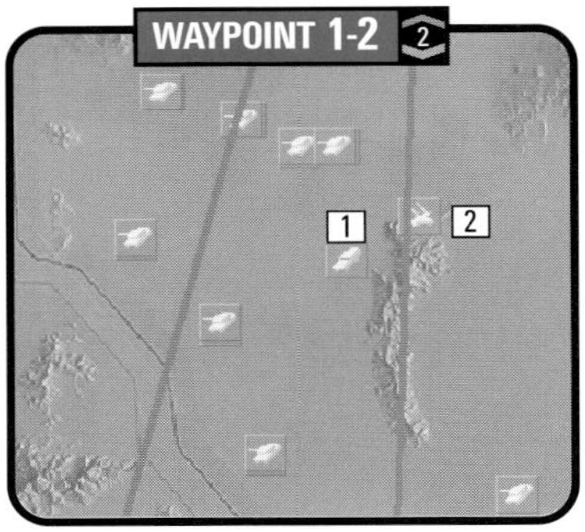

1 SA-8
2 ZPU-4

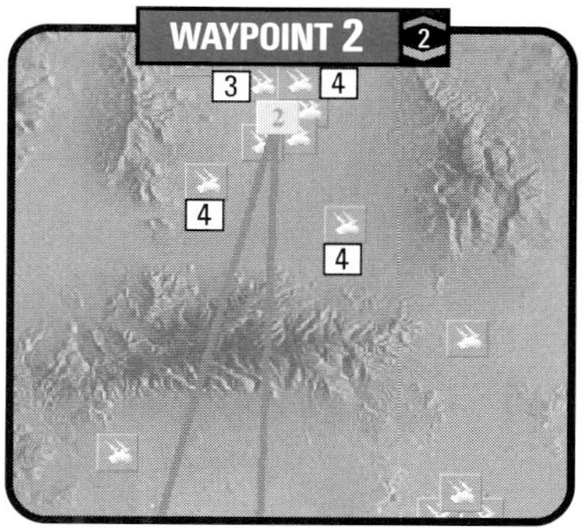

3 ZPU-4

4 SA-8

Waypoint 2. Close to the airfield is where the majority of the threats are tucked away. Just take your time, and you should be able to make it home without a scratch.

Don't try to strafe. Just kill everything from a nice position on top of the nearby hills. The target area is about 4km away, but since you're using missiles, that's no hindrance at all.

Your goal is to take out the air defense around the airfield. Note that the buildings are also marked as "enemy" — that doesn't mean you should shoot them. Repeat, do *not* take out the bunkers and hangars. This is a problem if you're firing simultaneous missiles; they'll happily go off and kill a hangar. Choose your targets wisely, since you don't want AAA and SAMs in the area when you're Winchester ammo.

You can stay high if you stay alert. Drop chaff and duck when a missile heads your way.

Make sure you mopped them all up. Don't forget to use your wingman. When travelling long distances, you can speed things up if you want: by hitting autopilot and time compression. You'll rush to the area in no time at all.

Waypoint 3. On your way back, watch out for the one SAM site over to the west. Just when it gets silent and the smoke starts to clear is when you should be most wary. Just for fun, you can also take out the BMPs with your cannon to make it easier on other troops that come through that area.

Desert Storm 6: Seven Eleven

Mission Escort armor

Environment Day/Clear

Air Strikes 1

Artillery Strikes 1

Primaries	*Mission Rating*
36 T-72s	10+ killed.....S
6 BMP-2s	0-9 killed.....F
14 ZSU-23s	
4 SA-8s	

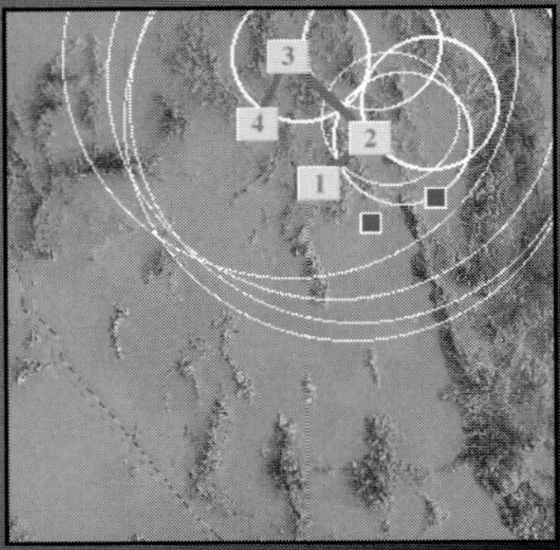

Your opposition will be mobile SAMs, AAA (Shilkas), T-72s, and BMPs. Save all your Hellfires for the SAMs and T-72s. Even the AAA can be defeated with your cannon. This mission can be tough or a walk in the park, depending on how you make your run. Just be sure to make every shot count.

Don't forget, if you get really torn up, you can always call in an A-10 strike to help you out.

Waypoint 1. This is essentially a tank bash. There are very few enemies in the hills on the way to Waypoint 2 because this is the last mission, and most threats have been eradicated earlier. Once again, take the battle low, and fly NOE once you are within 7km of Waypoint 2. Low and slow is the way to go! Try not to waste any Hellfires on the BMPs. They have lighter armor, and your cannon will cut into them just fine.

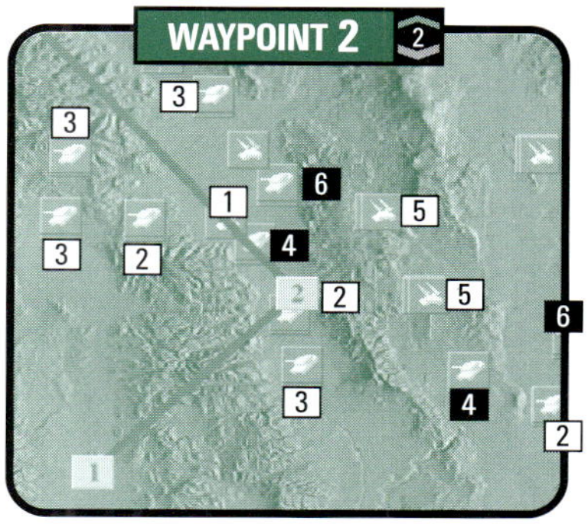

1 SA-8s
2 BMP-s2, T-72s
3 T-72s
4 T-72s
5 ZSU-23s
6 BMP-2s, T-72s

Waypoint 2. Stay in the hills. (To your left is an SA-8 or two, but they won't bother you if you don't fly near them.) Take out as many primaries as you can see. They're all hard targets, so expect them to be difficult to kill with your gun. Missiles are critical.

At Waypoint 2 you'll see some primary targets off to your right (east). You don't have to kill them, but it'll get you that much closer to success. Send your wingman after the non-primaries, if you want to keep the "real" targets for yourself.

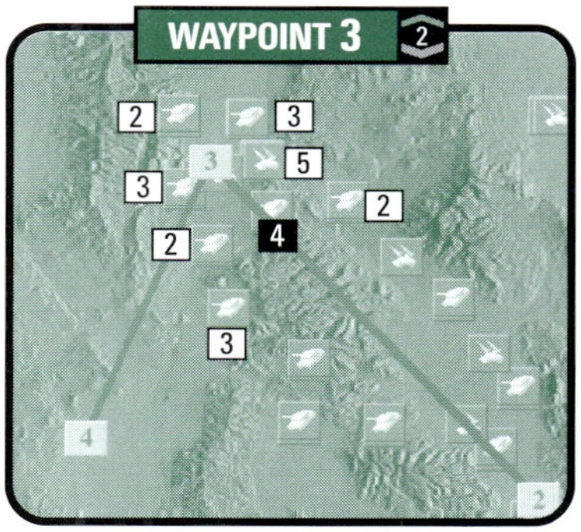

2 T-72s, BMP-2s
3 T-72s
4 T-72s
5 ZSU-23s

Waypoint 3. There's a little bit of a trap just after Waypoint 2, if you're not careful. Off to your left are a few SA-8s, about 9.5km from Waypoint 3. They are just on the other side of a rise. The longer you fly low, the longer it will take them to get a bead on you.

There are a couple of tanks left before you finish the mission. Just because it's a cake mission doesn't mean they can't kill you if you fly too fast and high.

JUST CAUSE MISSIONS

The Panama missions were designed by Mike Francis. Mike drew on first-hand experience in MI to create these missions, and gives some comments on them below.

Panama was the first combat use of the Apache, and it had a lot of problems. Apaches carried TOW missiles at the time that weren't working correctly, and the cannon also had a tendency to jam, so the Apaches were used mainly for recon. In the game, we use them as they were intended and send them in to blow up things.

JUST CAUSE 1: PINEAPPLE SLICE

This mission simulates the Ranger assault on Tocumen Airfield. There are two major airfields in Panama, Omar Torrijos International and Tocumen, a small military airfield nearby. Tocumen was a major objective, as it would be a primary escape route for Noriega and a potential seat of government for the PDF (Panamanian Defense Force).

I know about this one personally — I was involved in planning it. The key element in an operation like this is surprise. However, it's really hard to surprise anyone with 11 C-130s and C-141s that have to fly over mountains and through passes to get to the target area. In addition, this airfield had its own radar, and two things tend to make airport security personnel very suspicious — the Air Traffic Control Tower radar inexplicably going down, and explosions. In the game, it is the Apache's job to blow up air defenses prior to the C-130s' arrival.

JUST CAUSE 2: SUGAR CUBE

Another major objective was to secure the Panama Canal from terrorist attack. It was feared that Noriega loyalists would try to blow up the canal. The loyalists guessed this and planted mines and troops near several of the drop zones.

During this mission, helicopters covered the drop zones and there were a few fire fights. A Stinger was even launched at one of the Cobras, but it missed.

JUST CAUSE 3: TIGER CAGE

In this mission you are clearing out some LZs very close to Panama City.

In Just Cause, there was no discernable front line. No one knew how many of the PDF soldiers would end up being Noriega loyalists. Also, there were the "Dignity Brigades" — Noriega gave them a bunch of guns and told them to raise a lot of hell. Luckily they didn't do this to the degree they could have.

Mission #	Name	Objective	Environment	S+	S	F	F-
Just Cause 1	Pineapple Slice	Destroy SAMs/AAA	Dark-to-Dawn/Clear	–	3+ survive	1-2	0
Just Cause 2	Sugar Cube	Clear LZ	Night/Clear	11+ killed	10	1-9	0
Just Cause 3	Tiger Cage	Clear LZ	Dawn/Clear	15 killed	12-14	1-11	0
Just Cause 4	Ruby Seven	Destroy Airfield	Night/Clear	15+ killed	12-14	1-11	0
Just Cause 5	Rubik's Cube	Destroy Armor	Dawn/Clear	8 killed	7	1-6	0
Just Cause 6	Restless Stallion	Destroy Armor	Dawn/Clear	–	5 killed	1-4	0

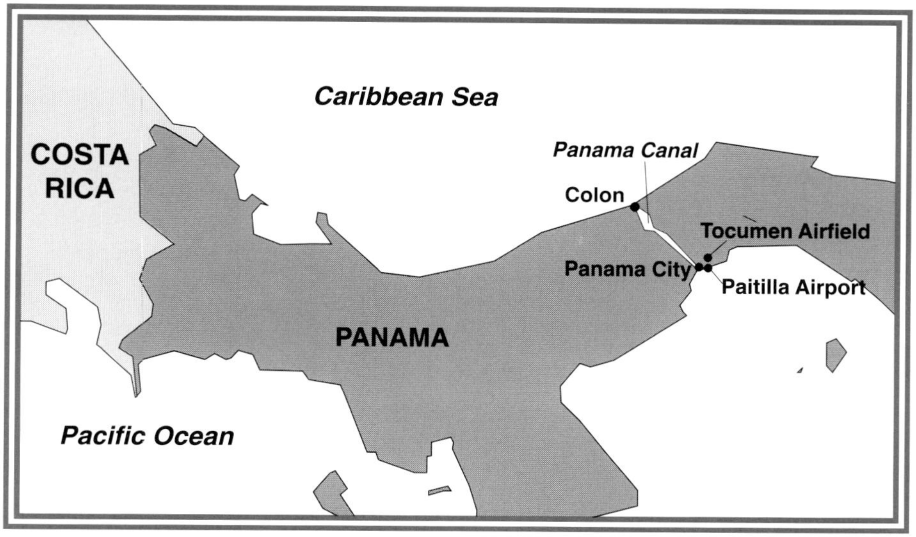

JUST CAUSE 4: RUBY SEVEN

Noriega kept a Lear jet at his personal airstrip — Paitilla Airfield — on the Pacific Coast. This was a potential escape route and thus an H-Hour objective. Seal Teams were to land on the coast and secure the airfield.

Your job as the Apache driver is to go in and make sure the helicopters dropping the SEAL team don't run into any nasty surprises — like the SAM and AAA units place around the airfield. You secondary objective is to prevent Noriega from leaving.

In real life, the Lear jet pilots did get nervous and attempted to take off. Noriega wasn't on board, but there was no way the US forces could be certain of this and the plane was shot down.

JUST CAUSE 5: RUBIK'S CUBE

During the operation, a small group of loyalists in LAV-300s decided they were going to make a run for Panama City. They were intercepted by Cobras.

In reality, this mission lasted maybe 2 minutes and 57 seconds. I don't know what the LAV drivers were intending to do, but they didn't get very far. I expanded this a bit to give the player the opportunity to fly around Panama City and blow things up.

JUST CAUSE 6: RESTLESS STALLION

Your waypoint for this mission is the bridge over the Panama Canal.

Again, the Canal Zone was a major concern throughout Just Cause. Cargo ships were everywhere and international shipping interests were at stake. And the last thing anyone needed was an international hostage incident, for other nations to become involved in the conflict.

Just Cause 1: Pineapple Slice

Mission Destroy SAMs/AAA **Air Strikes** 0

Environment Dark-to-Dawn/Clear **Artillery Strikes** 0

Primaries	*Mission Rating*
4 C-130s	3+ C-130s survive..S
	0-2............F

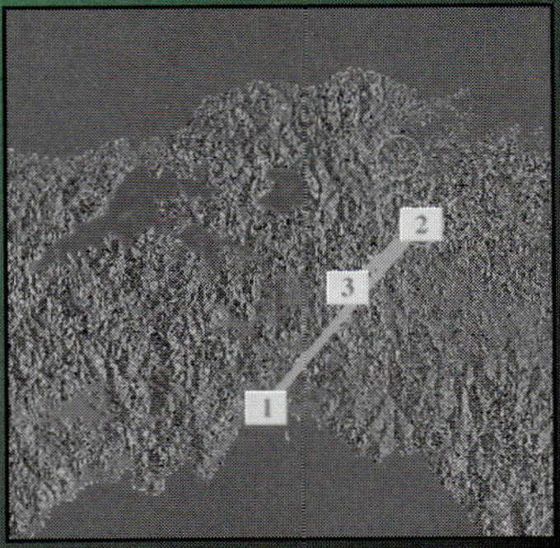

Just fly NOE with caution. You will be faced with APCs armed with AAA guns, Skyguard/Sparrow SAMs and converted AAA sites, along with a radar site and some PDF troops. Eliminate the radar and SAMs first, and the rest should be sitting ducks. Just don't waste any time, because those C-130s are enroute!

Waypoint 1. This is one of the toughest missions in the Panama campaign. One reason for the difficulty is because the time constraint is pretty fierce. If you hear "We are inbound at this time" *before* you've cleared the area, your mission is hosed. The second reason is because you may not recognize that you need to destroy the Skyguard radar and AAA north of the LZ. If you don't, the C-130's will get shot down.

Autopilot to Waypoint 2. There is nothing that can target you when you're going that fast and that high. Stop and hover when you are about 7 to 7.5km away from your destination.

1 LAV-300, PDF Troops, Skyguard SAM Site

2 Skyguard Radar

3 Skyguard SAM Site (radar)

4 C-130s

Waypoint 2. When you get around 7km from Waypoint 2, pull up your nose and drop down. There will be a radar site within range; take it out. Continue going forward slowly.

You should start to pick targets up on your radar about 6km out. Kill the two radar sites (always take out the radar first) and the AAA, then fly directly north. You'll find a Skyguard and AAA site there. They are essentially part of the same unit, but a little removed from the waypoint. You *cannot* win if you don't destroy those.

Circle around to the west on your way into the base. There are a couple of LAV-300s around there that have a formidable 20mm cannon that will shoot you down as you come over the ridge. You have to be careful ... careful and *fast*. You can't wait too long to start the attack, because there's a time constraint. The C-130s are already on their way; you must clear the area *before* you hear "We are inbound at this time." As soon as that happens, they're going to fly up, and if you don't have the area secure, they'll be shot down. If even *one* gets shot down, you've failed the mission. To track the C-130s, use [Y] (Target Friendly). That will give you an idea where they are.

Don't miss the opportunity to finish up all the little stuff. PDF soldiers are points, too, you know. Watch out for the ones that have shoulder-mounted Stinger Missiles — they *will* kill you. Hang out at the edge of the base and kill any people you see.

Just Cause 2: Sugar Cube

Mission Clear LZ

Environment Night/Clear

Air Strikes 0

Artillery Strikes 0

Primaries	*Mission Rating*
12 LAV-300 AAA	11+ KILLED.....S+
	10.............S
	1-9...........F
	0..............F-

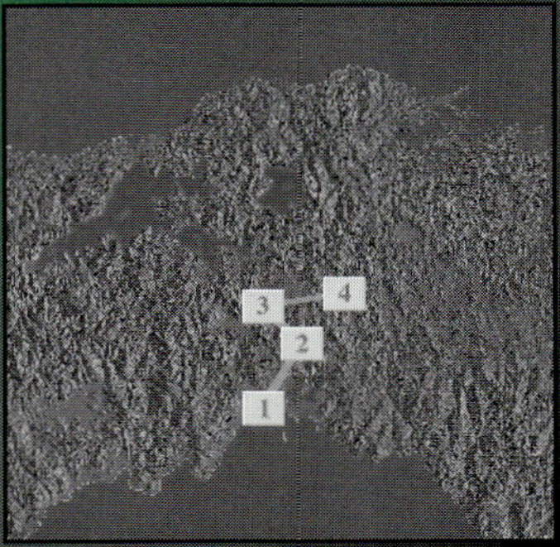

Waypoint 1. Threats for this mission are more APCs armed with AAA guns, and PDF troops armed with small arms.

This is more difficult than your standard Panama-style mission of fly here, kill everything, fly there, kill everything, go home. The difference is primarily in the number of soldiers carrying Stinger missiles, and the enthusiasm with which they fire them. Your only designated enemy targets are going to be LAVs, though.

If you fly in a straight line to Waypoint 2, you'll fly over some hills and come to a plain. There are some bad guys waiting for you in the flat area. Go low and slow over any hills, therefore, and be ready to hold down your chain gun. It's also wise to circle around hilltops and come from around the side. If you decide to crest the ridge, though, you ought to be going slowly — you should be able to survive being hit by an LAV-300 a time or two.

There are also some LAV-300s on the other side of the canal as well. You don't even have to cross the canal to face them — just fire Hellfires across the water until you've destroyed all the artillery pieces. Now you've got a choice. At least one of troops is carrying a shoulder-launcher. Do you waste missiles on soft targets, or risk your neck by flying across and using your machine gun in short bursts to pick off the rest of the soldiers? Your choice.

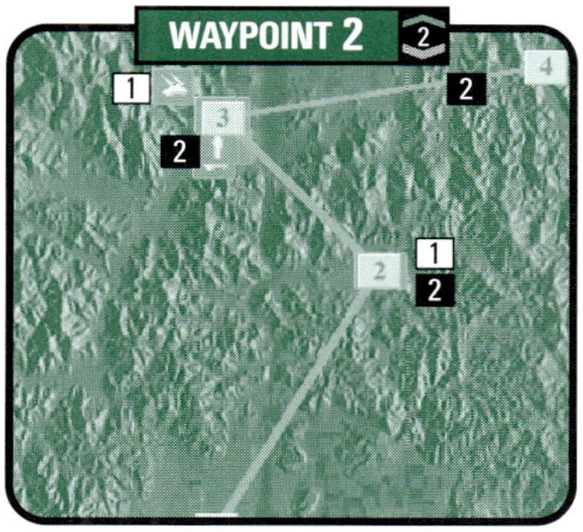

1 LAV-300,

2 PDF Soldiers

Waypoint 2. Waypoint 2 is right over a hillside, and if you fly over that hillside too fast, you will be in the enemy's lap. Slow to a hover, and start to pick off the assorted APCs. If you stay right at the ridge above the LZ, you should be fine.

Because the LAVs are surrounded by buildings, one Hellfire might not take out its target. The buildings take a lot of the collateral damage. Also, make sure that every target is really, truly dead before moving on. There are objects on top of objects down there, and just because you destroyed one doesn't mean that there isn't another one still there, ready to kill you.

Waypoint 3. The next stop, Waypoint 3, is once again a walk in the park. Once you get notification that the primary targets are in sight, drop to a hover, at about 600ft, and take out the APCs first. Use your Hellfires, and don't get too close. It's best if you stay on the near side of the canal until they're dispatched.

There isn't any enemy air power near here, so you can keep your altitude as high as you'd like. Use your machine gun on the troops, but watch out! Once again, there's a guy or two with Stinger missiles, and they'd like nothing better than to give you a dirt nap. It's against the Geneva Convention to use missiles on people, but sometimes fair is fair. Also, if you notice, one of the Stinger-toting troops is just barely on the far side of a hill, so if you drop too low to do your wipe-up, he'll disappear.

JUST CAUSE 3: TIGER CAGE

Mission Clear LZ
Environment Dawn/Clear
Air Strikes 0
Artillery Strikes 0

Primaries	*Mission Rating*
3 LAV-300 AAA	15 KILLED......S+
12 LAV-300s	12-14..........S
	1-11...........F
	0..............F-

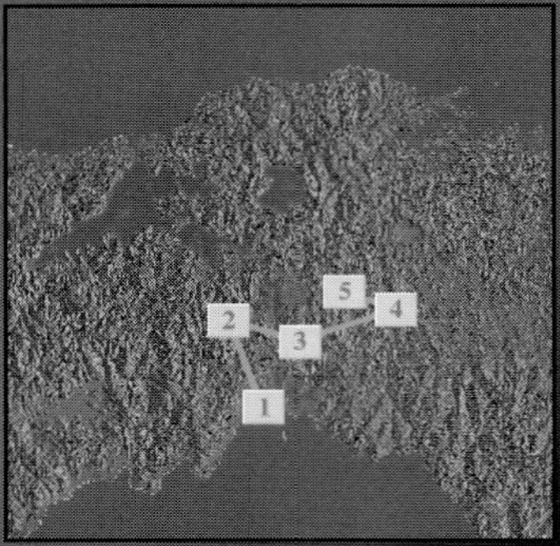

Your only threats will be APCs, but one of the units at each LZ is outfitted with an AAA gun! Go in, take a stance from a distance, and once again show these Panamanians who's the boss. Just be sure, at each LZ, to make it a practice to take out the APC outfitted with the AAA gun first. This ensures no allied casualties, as long as you aren't too close when you decide to hover. Once you are at a hover, alternate between shots with your wingman by assigning some of the targets him (Ctrl 3).

Don't waste too much time, since you're trying to clear the way for some folks who'll get shot down if you don't get there first.

Waypoint 1. During this mission, take time out to fly under the bridge near Panama City. It's fun. Also, go check out Panama City itself.

Waypoint 2. About 1km from Waypoint 2 there is a group of 5 LAV-300s — just over a small hill. They're just sitting and waiting for you. Go slow and low, and put your wingman on Weapons Free. That's the tricky aspect of this mission — go fast enough to beat your escort to the area, but slow enough that you don't zoom over the hill. When you're about 1.5km out from Waypoint 3, slow down and drop.

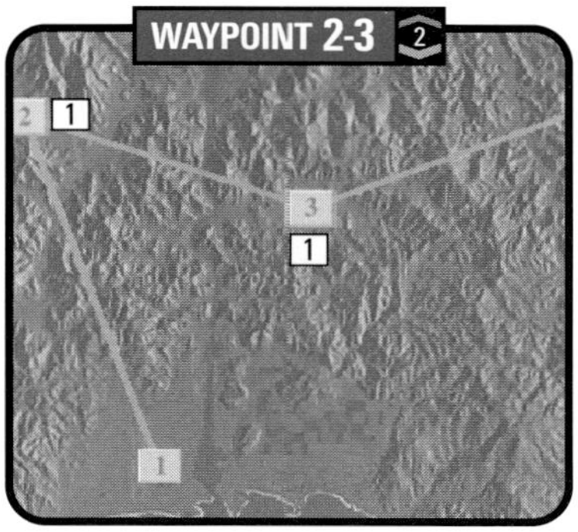

[1] LAV-300, LAV-300 AAA

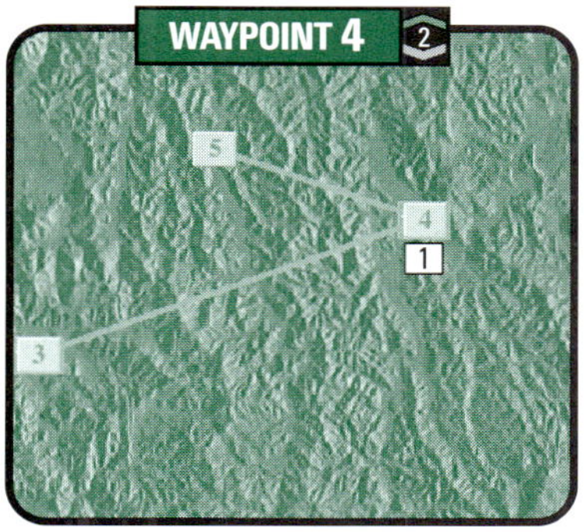

1 LAV-300, LAV-300 AAA

Waypoint 3. Here, there are 5 LAV-300s again. You can kill these guys before crossing the canal, as long as you stay around 1.5km away. (As far away as 5km is okay, but you're running the risk of missing your target.)

This mission is a breeze and should not cause you too much trouble. Just be certain to have your wingman take out a few of the targets. That's it. Quick and easy mission.

Waypoint 4. This is essentially the same as Waypoint 3.

Just Cause 4: Ruby Seven

Mission Destroy SAMs, AAA, hangar **Air Strikes** 0

Environment Night/Clear **Artillery Strikes** 0

Primaries	Mission Rating
3 MH-53Js	15+ killed.....S+
2 Skyguard Radar	12-14..........S
4 Skyguard AAA	1-11...........F
4 Sparrow SAMs	0..............F-
2 LAV-300 AAA	
3 LAV-300s	

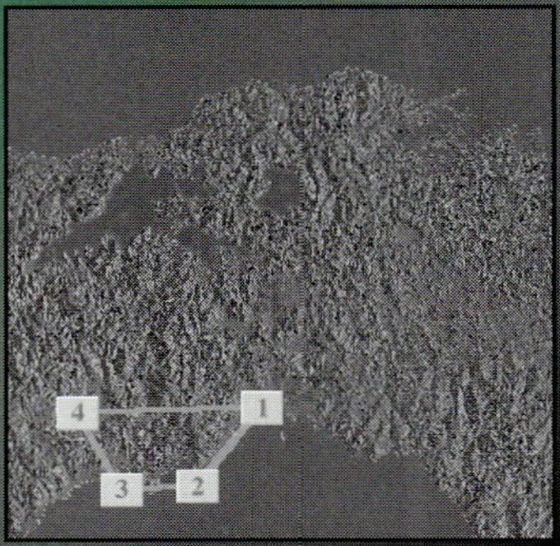

You must, must, must take as many missiles as you can. It's not easy to destroy a hangar; it takes a lot of pounding.

Waypoint 4. Once you get close to Waypoint 4, you must be very cautious. In this part of the mission you *must* fly NOE, more than ever before. Go around any hillsides and take it as slow as a turtle. Pop up over every hillside with *extreme caution.*

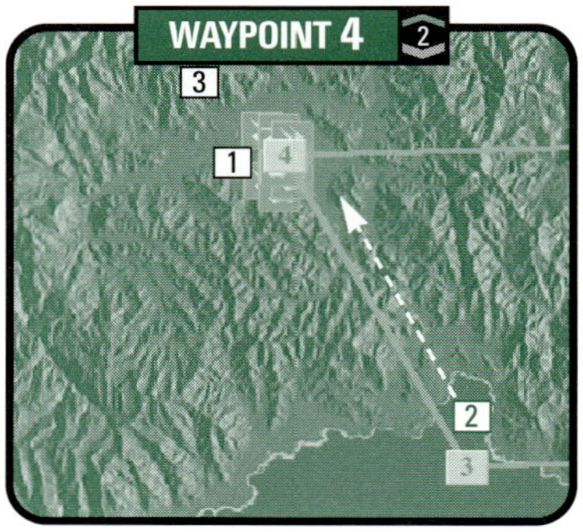

1 Skyguard radar, Skyguard AAA, Sparrow SAMs, LAV-300, LAV-300 AAA

2 MH-53Js (Pave Low)

3 Skyguard radar, Skyguard AAA, Sparrow SAMs

Once your co-pilot notifies you that the primary target is in sight, start to take out the more serious threats like the Skyguard/Sparrow AAA and SAM sites, as well as APCs with AAA guns. They are dug in well, so prepare for a few surprises! There are also two Skyguard/Sparrow SAM sites, located just before the airfield, over to the left. Those can catch you by surprise, but if you fly totally NOE and slowly, you should have more than enough time to react. Just don't get too confident when the firing ends. It may not be over.

Try to take out the Skyguards from around 4.5km away; don't get too close. Continue slowly until you are about 3km away from your next target. Take out the radar first, as always, followed by the SAMs and AAA. You don't even have to worry about the PDF soldiers, because the US troops have already arrived and engaged the infantry.

The hangar is not labeled a "primary" target, but you need to destroy it anyway. As you get closer to the waypoint and approach the hangar, be careful of the last set of hills. They hide a Sparrow missile launcher and an LAV-300.

JUST CAUSE 5: RUBIK'S CUBE

Mission Destroy armor
Environment Dawn/Clear
Air Strikes 0
Artillery Strikes 0

Primaries	*Mission Rating*
7 LAV-300 AAA	8 KILLED.......S+
2 LAV-300s	7..............S
	1-6............F
	0..............F-

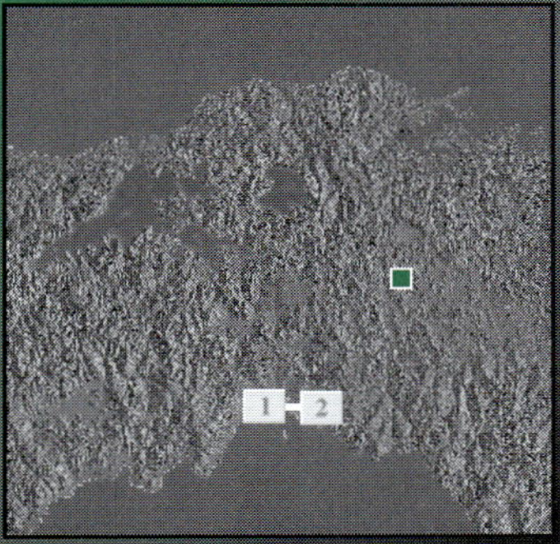

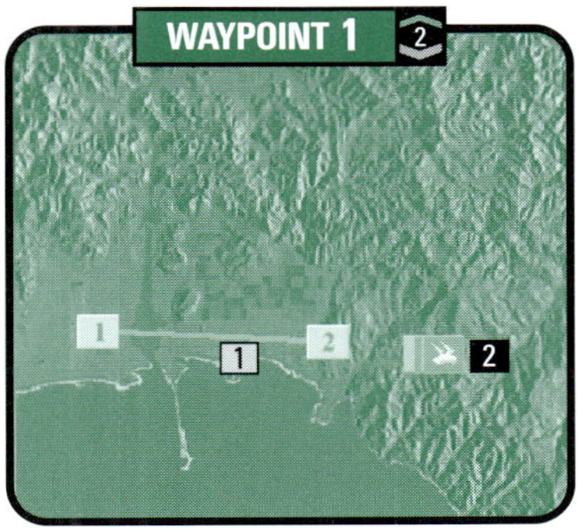

1 Panama City
2 LAV-300, LAV-300 AAA

Waypoint 1. This is an easy mission. How easy is it? This mission is so easy that you don't even have to go anywhere to win.

Easy Scenario 1. The next waypoint is 2.5km away, while your missiles have a range of 5-8km. All you really need to do is take off to an altitude of about 700 feet and kill everyone. When you drop down to the ground, you've won the mission.

Easy Scenario 2. They're coming your way, aren't they? You can wait for a while until they come to your base. It might take some time, during which you can use the F6 key to see where they are. When they come over the ridge, get a lock and start firing off your missiles. As each one clears the ridge, you can take another shot. There are about a dozen, and it makes an easy target practice session.

Waypoint 2. Okay, now for the regular scenario — your threats are APCs armed with heavy machine guns and 120mm cannon. Most of them are AAA guns, and only two are armed with the 90mm. When you get the "primary target in sight" notification from your CPIG, you'll be at a safe enough distance to engage the threats.

Go into a hover at about 600ft, right outside of Panama City. From there, you and your wingman can eliminate all the armored threats without breaking a sweat. Sometimes you may get a "Mission Complete" notification before *all* the threats are eliminated, but you can kill them all for good measure if you'd like and get an S+.

Just Cause 6: Restless Stallion

Mission Destroy Armor

Environment Dawn/Clear

Air Strikes 0

Artillery Strikes 0

Primaries	*Mission Rating*
5 LAV-300s	5 killed.......S
	1-4...........F
	0.............F

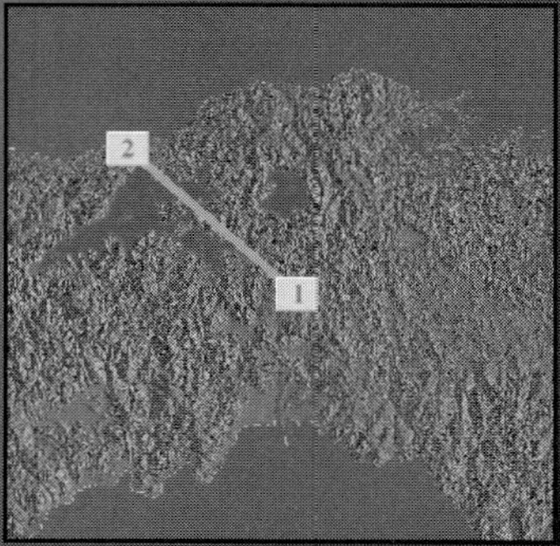

Waypoint 1. This is essentially the same as Mission 5, but because the waypoint is further out, you can't just climb and shoot. Your threats are LAV-300s, some armed with AAA guns, and 90mm cannon. You shouldn't even get close enough to them to find out what they're carrying.

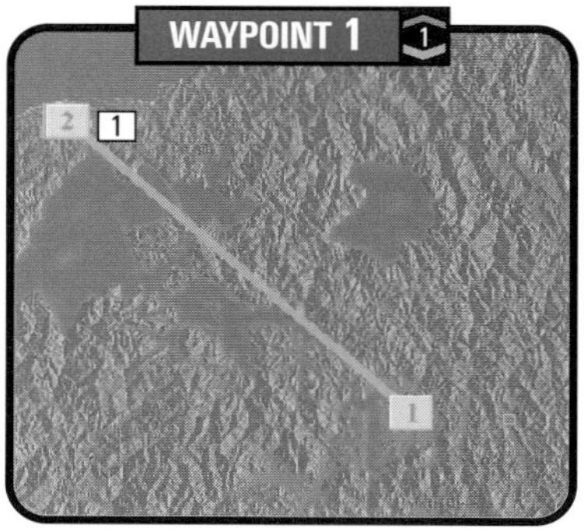

[1] LAV-300s

Waypoint 2. Autopilot to Waypoint 2. Go into a hover at about 100ft, and shoot all five of the armored threats with Hellfire missiles. When you get a "Mission Complete" notification, just turn around and autopilot home.

Hooray! You win. Go fly under the bridge again.

Cav Pocket TACSOP
Annex G (AH-64 CONSIDERATIONS)
Revised August 1994

4. Downed Aircraft Procedures:

A. General

(1) ue to the lack of the Army's lack of SAR capabilities, the responsibility for recovering downed crews falls primarily on the affected unit or its parent unit.

(2) Recovery takes precedence over all non-tactical missions.

(3) Prior to mission start, a mission outline should be sent to higher and /or the unit tasked with recovery responsibility. The outline should include as a minimum: Mission Start Time, Route of Flight, and Briefed pick-up points.

(4) When available HHT will provide one UH-60 for SAR operations. Secondary recovery will be the Air TAC. Tertiary recovery will be by AH-64.

(5) All ACP/SP/RP are designed as Downed Aviator Pick-up Points (DAP). Pick-up times will be briefed in the OPORD.

B. Crew Procedures - Deep Attack:

(1) If pick-up is possible by own unit remain on or near the aircraft. If terrain precludes pick-up move to the nearest suitable terrain. Ensure recovery aircraft is aware of your location.

(2) If immediate pick-up is not possible, begin movement to the nearest DAP.

(3) All radios, secure voice equipment and classified equipment and classified equipment will be secure d/destroyed, depending on the situation.

(4) If destruction is necessary, accomplish the following:

(a) Off tune all radios

(b) Zeroize KY-58/Kit-1-C.

(c) Fire a bullet through each radio/ KY-58/Kit-1-C.

(5) First aircraft arriving at the scene will extract crew, evacuate sensitive items, and if necessary, destroy the aircraft. Aircraft destruction authority is the squadron commander unless otherwise briefed.

(6) Tactical missions take priority over downed pilot recovery. AMC will brief recovery capabilities/procedures.

(7) Forward downed aircraft information in the following format. By secure means only.

(a) Acft ID (Tail number), Type

(b) Location

(c) POB

(d) Number of injuries by type

(e) Ammunition on board

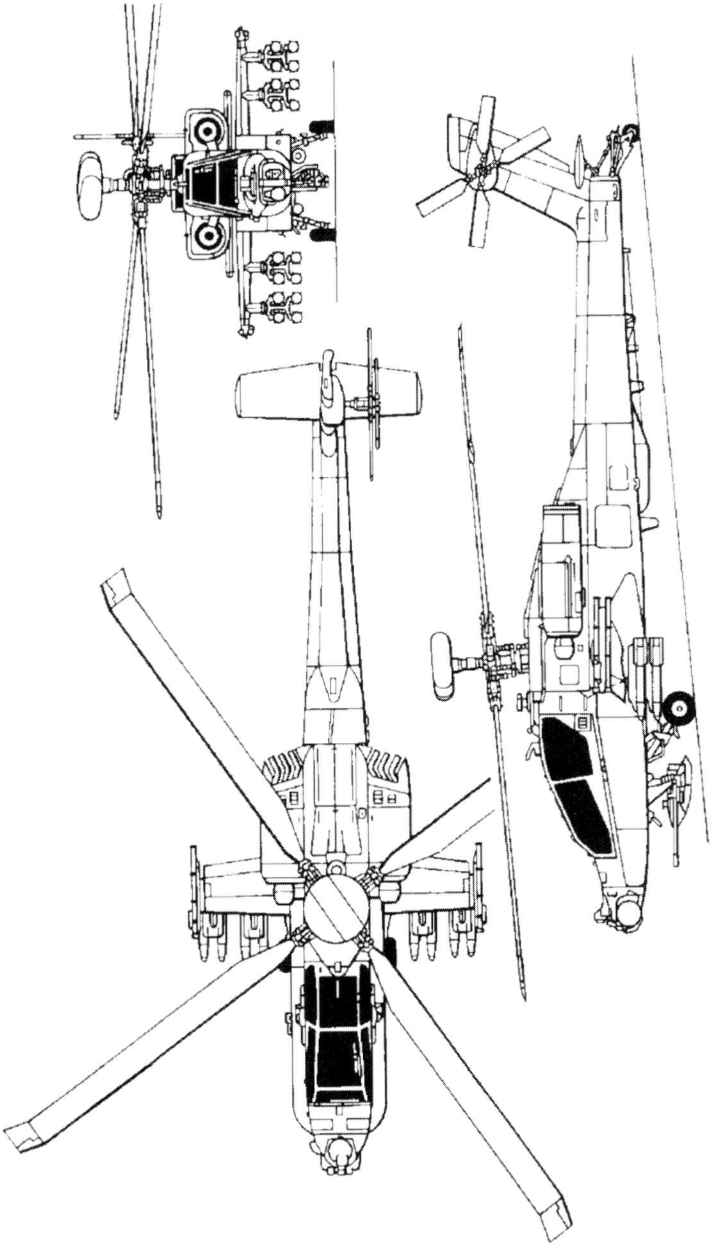

1 LT. (P) TROY EVANOVICH

Attack Platoon Leader, CP/G

Q: Your rank is First Lieutenant. Do you have a call sign?

A: Yes, Charlie One Six.

Q: How long have you been flying?

A: Six years.

Q: How many flight hours?

A: I've flown 500 hours since my start at Fort Rucker.

Q: That's in Alabama, right?

A: Yes. I'm currently stationed in Conroe, Texas, with the 7th Squadron, 6th Cavalry Regiment.

Q: What made you decide to become a helicopter pilot?

A: A lot of things, actually. A childhood dream, to begin with. And the fact that a helicopter can do so many things that an airplane can do, and more.

Q: Did you decide to go into the Reserves straight out of school?

A: No. Actually, right out of high school I joined the Air Force, then transferred into the Army and joined R.O.T.C. After graduating from there, I went on to flight school and learned how to fly.

Q: How long was flight school?

A: IERW, Initial Entry Rotor Wing, is one year. All student pilots — from Officer Candidate School, West Point and R.O.T.C. — train collectively at Fort Rucker. All pilots, both Commissioned Officers and Warrant Officers, have to learn more than just flying. We undergo more specialized training as Army Aviation officers, which adds more time to the overall training schedule.

Q: Tell us a little about your training. Are the instructors really rough on you?

A: It depends on your background. A lot of guys that went through training had no flight experience at all. And if you came in there with even a small amount of flight experience, you had the added edge you needed to be a little bit better than the other guys. Some guys were pilots before they got there, and those were the ones who were usually first or second in the class. The most difficult part was instrument flight training. The instructors expected more from you.

Q: *What made it hard?*

A: The instructor. When you walk into the class, he's sitting there staring you in the eye, wondering if you'd studied the required material. The chief instructor would stand up in front of the class and ask, "All right, Lt. Ketchum, stand up." You don't know what question he's going to ask you, but you'd better have the right answer, because if you don't, you have to take the time right there to open up your manual, find the answer and read verbatim from the book.

Instrument flight itself is pretty intense, too. You don't get the chance to see outside. You have to fly the aircraft, listen to your instructor, know all the different operating procedures, and understand the instruments and how everything correlates with the aircraft and where you are at over the ground so you don't get lost.

Q: *The Apache was designed to fly at night. What was your training for night flight like?*

Night flying was probably the second hardest. You don't see everything like you would during the day. In the OH-58 Scout Track, you fly with night vision goggles, which use the ambient light in the area to allow you to see. But getting into the Apache and going through night training is something different.

As your game showed, with the PNVS or FLIR, everything is monochromatic green — either dark green or an incredibly light green, depending on what you're looking at. So, off in the distance, you see a column of tanks. You can select two views, one "black hot," and the other "white hot," contrasting the tanks against the background. All of the instructor pilots recommend using white hot.

Q: *Was there a big transition from the training you did in regular helicopters to the training you did in the Apache?*

A: Flying is the same, but it's incredible the amount of power that you have compared to the Huey, the aircraft everyone starts out in. The Apache also has an onboard computer system to help you control the flight, which makes a world of difference.

The Apache will react instantaneously to any control input, whereas the Huey is slower in responding. And in the OH-58, if you even *think* about going left, you've already gone.

To coin a phrase, we like to say "You usually run out of armpit before you run out of collective." The aircraft has so much power that when you pull it up off the ground, it's like going up in an elevator at warp speed.

Q: *What happens beyond basic flight school?*

A: After IERW school, you get to your unit. Then, you go through a commander's evaluation and get to know the area you're flying in. You want them to get to know you as a pilot, and it's important that they understand you're capable of flying the aircraft and demonstrating good judgment. The majority of your time is spent training for missions, both on the ground and in the air.

Q: *Do you train separately to become a pilot or a CP/G?*

Initially, you're assigned to the front seat as a Co-Pilot/Gunner. Commissioned officers will usually remain in the front seat, simply because their duty is to control the mission. In fact, a large percentage of the pilots in the Army are Warrant Officers. They are the backbone of aviation, and without them, we'd be in trouble.

A Warrant Officer, about a good two years after he's proven that he's mature and has an exceptional understanding of the aircraft, may be recommended to progress to the back seat to become a Pilot In Command, or PIC.

Q: *How long was the Apache training program?*

A: The Apache course was about 12 weeks long. In the morning you are in classes learning about the aircraft's systems and capabilities. In the afternoon, you go to the flight line and practice what you've learned in class. You fly anywhere from an hour-and-a-half to two hours. Then you swap out with your stick buddy and usually end up getting home around 7 p.m.

Q: *What did you most worry about during training?*

A Three things you have to worry about — when a Warrant Officer says, "Hey, watch this," when a Lieutenant says, "In my experience ..." or when a Major says, "Well, I think ..." — then you know you are in trouble. So one time this Warrant Officer said, "Hey, watch this!" and that's about all I'll say ...

Q: *What was the hardest thing about your Apache training?*

I'd have to say the hardest part of training was going into "The Bag." This is where people usually wash out. It is the most stressful flying I've ever done. You are in the back seat, and the ground maintenance personnel install curtains or padding to block off the windows. You cannot see out of the cockpit, and your instructor is in the front seat and can see everything.

Getting used to the back seat takes awhile. You fly with your HDU — your Helmet Display Unit — which attaches to your IHADSS helmet and comes down in front of your right eye. Your view of outside is right there in this little reticle. You scan your environment with it, and you can see quite a bit. You also find yourself flying by the seat of your pants.

So you try not to get too distracted, although it happens, because you have what's called "binocular rivalry." One eye is focusing outside through the reticle, and you're trying to concentrate on flying the aircraft. Meanwhile, any bright light that enters the cockpit through the curtains may catch your eye. The next thing you know, you're looking at that light with your eye. You lose concentration, and your instructor says, "All right, concentrate on what you're doing, and don't get distracted."

He knows when you are looking at something, because you are trying to hover with no deviation from ATM requirements. And if you look at something, you fly in that direction. It's like driving a car — you look left, and the car moves left.

Q: Did you go on a lot of night training missions?

A: Yes, I did. The last half of the qualification course was all at night. Once the instructor thought you were comfortable inside "The Bag," he signed you off as a "go" for operating under the night vision system.

Q: Was that really different, flying at night? I've heard that your depth perception diminishes when you fly with PNVS.

A: Yes, it does. Your instructor asks you to look down, and you notice that you have little or no depth perception. A lot of it's just judgment, and using your FLIR cues.

While hovering, there is a small acceleration cue and velocity vector, called a "lollipop." It is extremely sensitive.

Q: What does the "lollipop" tell you?

You want the velocity vector to sit right below the acceleration cue, which means you are keeping nose-to-tail trim. If you are hovering through trees, you've got your tail sticking out 30 feet behind you to the left or right. And if you're not keeping nose-to-tail trim, the front end of the aircraft will go through the trees, but your tail will catch on them.

Q: So you want to keep the acceleration cue over the velocity vector?

A: Yes, you want to make your little lollipop. Keep nose-to-tail trim because it keeps the aircraft in a perfect straight line.

Q: How do you stay stationary during a hover?

A: You use the Bob-Up IHADSS mode when you are hovering to mark a reference point on the ground so that you can remain stationary. A box displays on your HDU reticle and helps you maintain your location over the ground. When you come up from a hover, you try to keep that box centered in your reticle. If the box starts drifting to the right, then the helicopter is moving to the left. So, you have to steer back to the right to re-center the box.

It's best to use Bob-Up mode when you want to remain at a stationary hover over one place on the ground. It allows you to concentrate on your primary mission without worrying about drifting.

Q: I've heard that helicopter pilots often use small openings in trees to hover and conceal their position. How can you judge whether or not your aircraft will fit in a hover-hole?

A: You have to use your judgment based on what you've learned in the past. Once you're know you can fit in a hover-hole, though, you can use the HDU Display to come back down into it after bobbing up. If you don't use Bob-Up mode, it's very difficult to come back down into the same location. The box keeps your place on the ground.

Q: *When do you want to be hovering, say, in a combat situation? When you are hidden behind something?*

A: The greatest challenge on the battlefield is avoiding detection. A large majority of your time is spent moving to the target with only minimal time spent locating targets and destroying them. So you actually will not find yourself hovering too often in a combat situation.

Hover mode is useful not necessarily to keep your place, but to maintain a stable hover — making sure you are not actually drifting too far. If that velocity vector saturates [moves] in any direction, then you know that you're not maintaining a stabilized hover, and you need to come back and keep your hover within constraints. You're not really concerned with staying over a single spot.

Q: *Which do you use when you are landing?*

A: I usually use Transition mode, because you have a horizon indicator on your HDU. Instead of having to look back down at your artificial horizon indicator, you've got everything right there in front of your eye. You can avoid having to focus out of the HDU image and then back in.

Q: *What kind of combat training did you get?*

A: Everything we do is training for combat.

Q: *Have you ever fired live missiles?*

A: Most of our combat missile training is actually done in the CMS, or Combat Mission Simulator, which is the *ultimate* virtual reality experience. You're networked in with your back-seater, who is in another simulator — we call them boxes. The CMS simulates all sounds and vibrations that you experience in the real cockpit.

Q: *How close is it to the real thing?*

A: It simulates flying and operating the weapon systems, but it is a lot different than getting into the real aircraft. The controls, although they do the same things, feel different.

Q: *When you train in the simulators, what exactly are you training for?*

A: We train to enhance our mission posture. There are multiple situations that you encounter on the battlefield and being trained to react to different situations in different flight environments increases your ability to respond to anything at a given moment. I can't get too specific here.

Q: *Any strategies?*

A: Avoid detection ... your survival and ability to accomplish the mission depend on it. Take out all of the radars — your top priority is to destroy radars first. You also want to smoke the weapons systems that can get you. 2S6s, ZSU 23-4s — we call them Zeuses — anything that's looking for aircraft.

Q: *What about helicopters? Do you face a lot of helicopters and fighters?*

A: It's not often that you get out there and go out against another helicopter or airplane — they are both out looking for other targets. If an aircraft sees a target opportunity, i.e. a helicopter ... we're taught different things to evade him.

If he's locked up on to you with his radar equipment and is picking you up, he's going to shoot you. When you see him coming down at you, you don't want to turn and run — you want to fly directly toward him. That forces him to increase his angle of attack on you, and it's only going to be down. Every adjustment he makes is lost opportunity for him to shoot at you. At a certain point, he has to break off so that he doesn't fly into the ground.

I don't have to worry about fighters too much, though. I'm more worried about the guy on the ground with the gun than I am anything else.

Q: *Any other interesting stories you'd like to share?*

Here's a "war" story — this really happened, out in east Texas. We were out there practicing image auto-tracking. You locate a moving target about two or three kilometers away, and engage the image auto-tracker. It throws up four gates around the target. The TADS bucket slews with the gates so you don't lose the target.

I was out there doing this, and the guy in the back seat — "Judge Roy Bean" we called him — said, "L.T., take a look at this!" And I said, "Whatcha got?"

"Look behind you. Take a look back at 5:00, on the ground."

I looked back, and there's this guy who had parked his black pickup truck and was walking up with what looked like a shotgun or a rifle, trying to sneak up on us. We were hovering in an authorized area, and I don't know if his weapon was loaded or not, but The Judge decided, "Let's get out of here."

He turned the tail toward the guy — this is a combat maneuver I learned: turn your tail toward the guy, because if he's going to shoot at you, he's going to hit the aircraft and not you — and we zipped out of there. We flew in a two- or three-mile circle and came back, and by that time he'd gotten in his truck and driven away. We got an eight-digit grid on his location and I called that in to the sheriff, but I don't know what they did with that.

Q: *What would you say are the least threatening targets? Tanks? They are all threatening, but if you had to rank them ...*

A: I would say my worst fear is being sighted by a 2S6, any hand-held surface-to-air missile and even a laser weapon. Tanks are a threat to you simply because of the speed of the rounds that come out of their muzzle. Field artillery is a threat, provided they can find you. Any air defense artillery can be dangerous as well, but again, you want to destroy their ability to see you. Although you wouldn't think that the infantryman is a threat, he's probably your *worst* threat, simply because he's capable of being anywhere.

Q: One of our guys upstairs has been telling that once we take out the radar equipment and the SAMS, the tanks are pretty much just target practice.

A: Yes, for the most part, but they're still very much of a threat. As I said earlier, striking the enemy's radar equipment first will virtually leave him blind. And, in doing this, you increase your chances of survivability.

Q: Do they teach you movement techniques? How to sneak up on targets?

A: Yes. Take a look at that mountain behind you. Would you see an aircraft if it was above it, or in front of it?

Q: Probably if it was above it.

A: Yes, because you silhouette yourself, and you *never* want to let that happen. Stay on the sides of mountains. Also, try to avoid flying with the sun directly in front of you because your aircraft can glare off the sun. Also, watch your shadow.

Rotor wash is another big signature. It's easy to detect a helicopter on the side of a hill with a lot of trees. He's got a large rotor wash signature, and it's going to push the tops of the trees down. It's easy to pick up. Especially if you are out looking with a pair of binoculars or another, more powerful device. The bottoms of leaves are usually lighter and stand out when they get blown over. That's how we tell what way is the wind blowing when we are out hovering around — we look for the whites of the leaves.

Q: So don't silhouette yourself, and be aware of your rotor wash. Anything else?

A: It's a green aircraft, so you want to try and stay against dark backgrounds. So being in front of a mountain is ideal. And above all else — stay low, and slow!

Also, you don't want to hover over dirt or anything that might blow up into the air. In our last combat training exercise over at Fort Hood, we were out there flying on line and an aircraft unexpectedly moved over a dirt road. All of a sudden, this big brown cloud appears. It's not bad for the engine, because it has its own filter system, but the signature! You can see it miles away, and it gets your attention.

Q: Do you train over different terrain?

A: Yes, we do. We try to expose ourselves to different types of environments. It allows up to experience a vast array of flight conditions and practice procedures in them. Each type of terrain we encounter provides us the opportunity to learn more about the aircraft, and increases our level of experience.

Q: Is landing in sand difficult? I know it was a problem during Desert Storm ...

A: On sand, we try to keep a forward momentum because if you land straight down, you brown out. Sand will get thrown up all around you, and then your visual orientation is lost.

Q: One last question. Going forward, what do you see as the next advancement in helicopters?

A: I'd have to say the Comanche helicopter. In the very near future, the Comanche will probably become the helicopter that will take on all combat helicopter roles within the military. It will serve as both a scout and attack aircraft. The Apache is filling this role now, but the Comanche will be more advanced in that it contains state-of-the-art systems.

The patch as worn by members of C Troop, 7th Squadron, 6th Cavalry Regiment under the command of Captain David W. Wilkinson.

Team Interviews

Andy Hollis, Producer

Q: *Where did you first see the AH-64D Longbow? What impressed you so much about it?*

A: It goes back to my involvement with a product called *Gunship* at MicroProse. It was a Commodore product, originally. At that time I was just learning about attack helicopters, and I didn't really have much knowledge of the subject prior to that. I learned a lot about it through that product. Then I followed it on with another product called *Gunship* for the IBM-PC, which was lot more than just a port. We did a lot of neat graphical things that we could do on the IBM that we couldn't do on the Commodore.

But the other interesting connection was that my dad worked for Westinghouse until he died recently, and he was quite interested when I was working on that *Gunship* project — more than he normally was. He used to take copies of it into work and show it to the guys. I wondered, "What's this all about?" A couple of years later, he came in one day and dropped a little ad on my desk — an ad for the Westinghouse millimeter-wave radar for the Longbow helicopter, which he had been working on in secret the entire time I was doing this A-model game. They had been developing this radar system for the Longbow helicopter. It was really a neat little personal interaction there. My dad worked on this thing in a big way. He used to go out west all the time during that period of time, and I had no idea where he was going. Well, I know now — he was going to Mesa, Arizona, to work on this stuff.

Q: *Why did you decide to produce* AH-64D Longbow*?*

A: As we do new products, we are always looking for the latest and greatest of whatever particular hardware we're modeling. And the other thing I always look for is the level of information that's necessary to do the kinds of simulations that I like to do — an in-depth, focused style of simulation where we are simulating everything on the aircraft the way it actually works, especially mission avionics.

And the AH-64D Longbow is, of course, the latest and greatest attack helicopter. At first we weren't sure we would be able to get the level of information that we needed, but through discussions with McDonnell Douglas we were actually able to get a lot of that. They were nice enough to let us come out for the Longbow rollout, back in 1993. And during that trip we spent quite a bit of time with some of their folks and they gave us all kinds of great information and pictures and video as well as some design documentation. From that point on, we knew what we were going to be able to do. We were psyched.

Q: It sounds to me like you were playing the role that Jane's usually does in getting that kind of information.

A: We were to a certain degree. In fact, some of the information we were looking for was data that Jane's wouldn't necessarily get — design docs or operator manuals or stuff like that. They're more interested in the specifications and mission employment — production numbers, when it's going to happen, what the variants will be, what all the equipment is — which is some of what we got. And this was all before the Jane's connection. So we had to locate this information on our own at that point in time.

Q: Did they seem impressed?

A: I think they were impressed with the professionalism of our operation and the quality level of the simulation that we were putting together. They were impressed with our attention to detail. Sure, our resourcefulness in getting those details certainly impressed them. But of course they were able to supply us with even more.

Q: Switching gears ... were you one of the many people watching Desert Storm?

A: I can remember where I was — at work at MicroProse. We had a big-screen TV that we turned on, and everybody emptied out of their offices and just stood there watching these reports come in with their mouths open. It was just amazing. And of course we couldn't believe it was really happening when it happened.

Q: Did the reports you saw during Desert Storm influence your approach to Jane's Longbow*?*

A: You've got to remember that during those days I had just finished *F-15 Strike Eagle II*, and I was working on something else. When Desert Storm happened we did a Desert Storm scenario disk for that game. We waited until the conflict was over, because we didn't think it was appropriate to be putting out a mission disk on something when these guys are over there dying. However, my interest then was more in the jets and things that were being used there.

What you heard about was all the air-to-air engagements, the strike missions, and things like that. Aircraft like Strike Eagles and Stealth Fighters that we had modeled in previous simulations, were the ones getting all the press. I guess the next sim I did was *Strike Eagle III*, which took in a lot of that Desert Storm experience. That was the first one where we got in-depth on the avionics of things, and spent quite a bit of time with pilots and the fighter pilot community. We had a retired F-15 pilot actually working for me at the time. We talked with those people and got their involvement, and also got the tremendous amount of documentation that we needed to do a hard-core in-depth simulation.

We went to Seymour Johnson AFB in North Carolina. That's were all the Strike Eagles, the F-15s, were then based. And that was during the period when they were still enforcing the fly zones, so they still had some of their aircraft over in Saudi flying missions. Some of their guys were still over there on active, trading off periodically.

Q: *I guess you found that a valuable source of information.*

A: Absolutely. It's all part of the evolution — *Longbow* really owes a lot of its heritage to that product, and one that I worked on a little bit before I left MicroProse, which was *F-14 Fleet Defender.* We did a lot of the initial research before I left. We went down to Oceana Naval Air Station, where we hung out with the F-14 pilots, crawled around their airplanes, got all the docs, and went through all that. So I had already been through that exercise with another product before leaving and coming down here. So *Jane's Longbow* really owes a lot to *Strike Eagle III* and to a certain extent to *Fleet Defender.*

Q: *Was it hard coming here from Baltimore?*

A: You've got to remember that when I came to ORIGIN it was in the aftermath of *Strike Commander.* It was a very different kind of product than the sort of things that I enjoyed. It was not the kind of product that I would have developed. But that's not to say it's good or bad — just not the type I would have developed.

And I basically had to assemble a team from scratch because the company did not have excess people on staff. That was very difficult, building a team from scratch. I was used to working with some of the best in the industry, with lots of experience. Assembling from scratch you might not get that grade of people — you have some trial and error involved — and you have to get the people motivated. ORIGIN, of course, was not the kind of company where people were coming out of the woodwork to create this type of simulation. I had to do a lot of that searching myself, and it was very difficult to put the team together. The team grew quite a bit, not just in size — people's abilities and interests grew tremendously throughout the process. Now it's an amazing group of people. I'm very proud of what they've accomplished with this product. And of course there is the personal growth, as well. So, yeah, it was hard to do that.

Q: *Why did you move to Austin? What was your original plan?*

A: In April, 1993, I came to ORIGIN to start up a new group to do simulations the "right way." At that time, ORIGIN had proven its ability to produce a game with the highest of production values in graphics and sound, but not necessarily the most realistic of simulations. My goal was to combine the authenticity of the "traditional" sims I had done at Microprose (*Gunship, F15 Strike Eagle II & III, F19 Stealth Fighter*) with these great productions values, to give the player the ultimate experience of really being there. Everything in the game would contribute to immersing the player in the world of combat aviation, suspending his sense of disbelief, and giving him the total experience of both the strategic and tactical decisionmaking a pilot faces on the modern battlefield. Piece of cake, right?

A product is only as good as the team of people who made it. I've always said "Take a great idea and give it to a mediocre group of people, and you get a mediocre product. However, take a mediocre idea and give it to a great team, and you get a great product." Imagine what you get when you combine a great idea with a great team! Fortunately, *Longbow* had such a team and such a vision. But it was not always that way ....

In the fall of '93, initial plans were drawn up for a game called *Chopper Assault* which would be playable on both the highly anticipated 3DO system and the PC. As such, the game would be a compromise in complexity, appealing to both the fast action crowd and the traditional sim audience. Of course, we all know what happened to the 3DO! Fortunately, with the demise of the 3DO came a more hardcore approach to the sim which coincided with certain key additions to the development team. All of our efforts then became focused on setting new high marks for PC combat aviation.

Q: So Andy Hollis arrives on the scene in Austin to do a flight sim. What do you do? You send out an e-mail saying, "Hey, everybody, do you like helicopters? Come to my office at five!" I mean, how exactly do you ...?

A: It was a lot more covert than that. Part of it was talking to some folks that I had worked with before, to see if they were interested, although I was somewhat restricted in how much I could do. I talked to contacts in the industry. We dropped ads in the paper, too, to try to get people who were interested. And we certainly talked it up to folks here at the company who were interested in that kind of product. There were a few of them here who knew my background and were very interested.

Q: Describe some of the people on your team.

A: The project director is **Will McBurnett**. He is responsible for day-to-day management of projects from an administrative and creative implementation standpoint, making sure that stuff is getting done and that they're doing it in the right way to maintain the common vision. At the same time he actually did a lot of that work himself. He did almost all of the avionics, both design and actual code for it. Will's a great guy for doing it, because he likes the same things I like. We share a very common vision on that. Of course we all work together on all this. But he is the most heavily responsible for that.

The second person who made a huge impact on this project was **Paul Stankiewicz**. Paul was Art Director on the project. He is responsible for the great look, all the elaborate terrains, all the intros. Paul pretty much did the whole Jane's intro, the one that comes out of the book, and the *Longbow* intro, and many of the other screens in the game. He was responsible for the overall look and maintaining that look. He acted as the mentor and tutor for the art staff, bringing them up to speed on *Alias* and teaching them how to do things in a realistic fashion to give a common look to all the product. He was responsible for us having a high production value. He was also the guy who completely arranged the whole video shoot, to get us all the vignette stock and all the newscaster stuff. We were really kind of concerned that it wouldn't fit right, but it slides right in perfectly. It matches so well with computer graphics that it looks real. We didn't want it to look campy. We're really thrilled that it didn't. It came out looking really, really good.

Putting together a team of people to do a traditional sim at a company without a strong reputation for doing so was not easy. There were plenty of comings and goings throughout the project, until personnel with the right mix of skills and interests were finally assembled. Two key defining moments came six months into the project. One was the hiring of Paul Stankie, our art director. Paul's influence is felt immediately as soon as you set eyes on the product. He is an absolute monster at 3-D work using *Alias* on the SGI and has a wonderful eye for animation. One look at

Longbow and you'll know what I mean. Paul also took ownership in our mini video shoot, organizing the whole affair and making certain that the footage integrated seamlessly into the computer-generated artwork. Best of all, he did it on a shoestring budget that would not have even paid the food bill for most PC-game video shoots.

The other key moment was bringing in Will McBurnett, our Project Director. Building a product like *Longbow* is a huge task from a creative side and from a technical side. But it is also a big deal administrative effort. Will served as the person with daily responsibility for who's doing what, when, and how. He helped keep the vision consistent and the team focused. In addition he also found time to design and program all of the cockpit and missions avionics. Best of all, Will's sense of what is important in a sim now parallels my own, allowing him to finally forget about his sordid past with *Pacific Strike*.

Two things really set apart the feel of a simulation and give it a "soul." One is the flight model and the other is the Artificial Intellience (AI) of both enemies and friendlies. Fortunately for *Longbow* players, **Tsuyoshi Kawahito** ("TK") joined the team midway through the development and immediately took ownership of these elements. Uniquely qualified for the task, TK holds a Master's Degree in Aeronautical Engineering with a speciality in Aircraft Control Systems and is an avid player of combat flight sims. Suddenly, *Longbow*'s flight model lost its "notchiness" and became appropriately smooth and bouyant. Working closely with real pilots from nearby Ft. Hood, TK worked tirelessly to get the model as accurate as possible, yet still be configurable for less experienced players. The result is simply amazing.

Equally amazing is the AI that controls both the friendly and opposition forces. TK worked miracles to create a realistic sensation of an active battlefield where things are happening all around, not just near the player. Try using the object views to scan the mission area and you'll see the result: tanks moving across the rolling terrain, advancing on opposition forces and attacking, A-10s doing Close Air Support attack runs to support the advance, Black Hawks dropping off ground troops who advance into a fire-fight, and more. And finally, wingmen who act like real pilots rather than just a bunch of mindless machines. Most importantly, all of this activity happens within the appropriate realistic capabilities of the equipment as defined by Jane's. Thanks, TK!

One of the longest tenured team members was **Wendy White**. In the early days of the project, Wendy was responsible for the overall program construction and managing the "virtual world." This included all computer-controlled AI and the physics of motion for all objects, including the player. Later, Wendy contributed greatly in the area of in-game sound, memory management and code optimization, as well as writing the mission system and the VCR replay.

Steve Muchow was also with the team from the beginning and was responsible for programming all of the wrapper screens. This includes all of the briefing and debriefings, the mission selection screens, the VCR interface, the mission planning, and the movie player. In support of this, Steve also had to process all of the animation footage and soundtracks, and program the mission flow and scoring.

The other *Longbow* old-timer was **Donavon Keithley**, aka "Mr. Visuals." Donavon was responsible for the terrain system and the object appearances that give the in-flight experience its very realistic look, even at the lowest altitudes. It was a long and arduous process, though, to finally settle on the system that is in the game today. Many blind alleys were travelled and many lessons learned, resulting in about four or five still-born (but very innovative!) terrain systems. In the end, though, I think you'll agree that the final result is quite good at both low-level sensation of speed and altitude, and higher altitude vision into the distance.

Equally important to the final look of the terrain was the contribution of **Jeremy Dombroski**, who generated all of the terrain data that was displayed by Donavon's system. Remember the old computer adage "Garbage in, garbage out"! Skilled both artistically and technically, Jeremy worked tirelessly to get the right mix of high resolution texture and huge mission area, yet still fit on the normal user's hard drive. Jeremy also contributed heavily towards building all of the 3-D objects in the world fighting tirelessly for more and more detail. He's the one who insisted on putting in the foot soldiers.

Also doing yeoman work on 3-D objects was **Vincent Lin**, who constantly pushed the performance envelope of the game engine in new and innovative ways. Vince also contributed heavily to the hand-painting of the terrain, and was joined in that pursuit by **Gary McElhaney** and **Carol Roberts**. You can thank all of them for the seemingly infinite variety of woods, farmland, roads, towns and cities in the mission areas. Carol and Gary's influence is also felt in some of the various wrapper screens, including Carol's ORIGIN Skunkworks logo. **Brian Smith** also made significant contributions to wrapper screen art and animation, but his biggest influence came in the form of the incredibly detailed 3-D models he built of the various military hardware in the game. These are used in all of the animations, and are the source of textures for the 3D objects in the real-time flight visuals. Absolutely stunning!

Another *Longbow* team member with unique qualifications for the job was ex-Army Intelligence officer and avid combat sim enthusiast, **Mike Francis**. As a Desert Storm veteran, Mike's knowledge of US Army procedures and mission doctrine was instrumental in establishing realistic battlefield scenarios and campaign progression. Mike set the rules for object placement and movement within the play area, and designed all of the campaign missions. He also researched and designed the historical missions. Just read the mission Op Orders and you'll know that Mike has "been there, done that."

The other mission "fragger" was late addition **Rob Irving**. Initially subbing-in as a pinch hitter, Rob quickly gained a reputation for generating missions that could easily kick the butts of the cocky *Longbow* QA team. Rob soon became a keeper, laying out the majority of the Single missions and all of the Instant Action.

From the beginning, one very clear vision of the project was the interactive training/tutorial system. The goal was that a new player who completed the training missions could then fly and win the first couple of regular missions without ever cracking open the manual (although I've got to say it's a great manual, with lots of information that's easy to read). The man responsible for making this come true was **Kevin Kushner**, who endured my constant scrutiny and commentary until the system performed just like a real instructor pilot. The results speak for themselves as our entire outside testing force was able to learn the game in very little time, just by using this tutorial because the manuals had not yet been finished! Kevin also performed admirably in coordinating all of the speech recording and processing, and he even found time to design some of the missions.

Longbow is an amazingly configurable product. It can be set up for the most inexperienced game player on a run-of-the-mill machine without even a joystick, to the most hardcore heavy-duty flight sim jockey with the fastest PC on earth and every realistic military input device known. Credit **Chris Norden** with providing the interface for setting all of this up, as well as the nifty install program and the Jane's object viewer/database. Chris's heaviest influence came throughout the last stages of the product as he became "The Version Builder." At work for more than 24 hours at a time, he meticulously integrated and tracked everyone's changes, verified everything, and burned and tested the CD's. Thank goodness someone had a clear head.

No contemporary sim product comes to market without lots of other support personnel, in addition to the primary development team, I would be remiss without mentioning our **Quality Assurance** group (headed by **Reece Thornton**), **Language Translations**, **Creative Services**, **Publications**, **Product Marketing**, and everyone else whose names are all spelled out in the credits. We could not have done it without you.

Will McBurnett, Director

Q: *What's your background with the company, and with helicopters?*

A: I came to ORIGIN in September, 1990, with Brendan Segraves and Phil Sulak. Phil somehow got in contact with a guy here at ORIGIN, and we offered to do a Macintosh port of *Ultima VI* for free as our senior software project at Trinity University. Richard Garriott heard about it and he, being a longtime Apple fan, decided, "Oh, cool!" We got all the source code and worked on it for about nine months. Come June, when the project was over, we were about 80% of the way to having a shippable product. We got a lot farther than we or ORIGIN ever thought we would. So they started negotiating to actually finish the game and pay us for it, but that fell through. What they did was hire us. Which is much better, I think.

So I started at ORIGIN in July of 1991. I worked on the libraries for *Strike Commander*, which are still being used on *Wing Commander IV*. Then I worked on *Serpent Isle*, and then Eric Hyman started *Pacific Strike*, which was turning *Strike Commander* into a World War II game. I'd always been big on the flight sims — I'd been flying *Microsoft Flight Simulator*, the stuff Andy did at MicroProse, even the obscure stuff like *ATP, Airline Transport Pilot*, any flight simulator I got my hands on. I took pilot lessons when I was in high school. My dad owned an ultralight and I got to fly it a couple of times.

So now, working on *Pacific Strike*, I got into aviation and military history. I watched the movies. I watched everything on Discovery Channel that they ever did. *Strike Commander* was a good game, but it wasn't really a flight simulator. With *Pacific Strike* we were trying to make it into a flight simulator. That was the big learning experience for me, about how things worked in flight sims. When I finished up, Andy got hired and it was obvious that ORIGIN was going to make a big effort to do a real flight simulation. This is before the Jane's thing ever happened. And I was being recruited by Andy to come work on the jet game they had, because he was having trouble finding people who actually believed in flight simulators and enjoyed them.

It soon became evident on the jet game that I wasn't really needed. I'm a project director, but I'm also a programmer, and the people they had were perfectly capable of programming it without me. So I looked over the Chopper product, and that was back when it was *Chopper Assault*, a multi-platform arcade game: 3DO, PlayStation and PC. It was nowhere near what it is now. And I asked if I could go work on that one, and he said, "Sure." Because that one was kind of floundering too, without leadership. So I went over there and took charge of that and slowly morphed it from an arcade game to a true flight sim.

The first thing we did was we got rid of the 3DO, so we didn't have simultaneous multi-platform development. We could start using a keyboard, and doing more sophisticated things. Then we got the Jane's license, which is a big coup. I'm still extremely proud and glad that Paul Grace out at Electronic Arts in San Mateo got that. That helped so much. Not only did we have a hope of getting information to use in the product, but it also helped in getting other people to take us far more seriously. The Jane's name carries a lot of weight. We started getting materials and we set out to make a game that would satisfy me and TK (programmer Tsuyoshi Kawahito). We're both the hard-core flight simmers. We also wanted to make Andy happy, as a middle-growth flight simmer. And we wanted to make some of the other people on the team happy who like to fly and blow things up and have fun. So, by having a spectrum of people on the product working on it we were able to try to please everybody. I think we crossed the spectrum.

Q: *How do you motivate people?*

A: The big thing is, when people come to you with an idea you basically say, "OK, that's a good idea." You make them think of how it will affect the other difficult parts or the more sophisticated parts of the product, and whether it will make things easier for the product. How will this integrate into the entire spectrum of things? What kind of options? If you want to add a feature like a new weapon that will change play balance, how would you put options on that so it will still be difficult on the high end and still be fun? The big thing is letting people try out their good ideas. That's an easy thing to do. That kind of clashes with any sort of schedule realism. But it always happens, especially with a green team, because on all this project, (programmer) Steve Muchow, Andy and I are the only ones who have done anything of this sort before. None of the others — twelve people — had done this before. So it took us a long time to get the experience to know when something was worth trying out.

Most of the good ideas on a project come in the last half. You try to put as much as you can down on paper at the beginning, but once you actually get into the game, once you start flying it, once you are really playing it, that's when the ideas come, because that's when you think, "What if I did this? What if I did that?" There's a context to design within. It's very hard to design from nothing. I can't do it. That's why I like flight sims so much. There's already a context there. You have a vehicle. You know what the vehicle does. You take that and do something with it. At that point, the big thing at the beginning is the team's experience. They motivate themselves. They know what they can do. They know what the other people around them can do.

Q: *It must have been quite a challenge to stay in a group of folks who did not necessarily share your passion for ultra-realistic sims.*

A: I came in pretty late on the project, so there were only two or three people who came in after me. Everyone else ... yes, there were some people who were not terribly into what we were doing. But most were. A flight simulator is one of the most broad, difficult products to do because it has to have a little bit of everything. It's got physics. It has to have a lot of really good artificial intelligence about how the world reacts to the player. It's got to have a very sophisticated graphic and sound system to get feedback to the user. You also have to have all the military stuff ... how the weapons work, whether they're realistic, how things work together to meet goals. There's AI, and then there's all the military part of it, too. And then there's an incredible amount of art — huge truckloads of art. The artists worked on this game for two years. Every bit of it was used. There's also the movie production stuff that people like to do. There's movie player technology.

There's so much stuff to do ... it's such a broad product that you can find something in there that each person likes. A person may not necessarily be really, really, really interested in the fact that there is a helicopter flight simulation, but would really, really, really like to do the graphics system for it. The work itself becomes the reward.

And then when it starts coming together, then people begin to realize that the whole of it is actually larger than they thought it was going to be, because of what everyone else has been doing with it. And that was a great moment — it happened last July when we finally got everything put together and we were flying a helicopter with spinning rotors and a shadow over terrain and weapons that were blowing things up. And everyone was just, "Oh, this is so much more than I thought it would ever be." That was right about when we had the Jane's introductions.

Q: *So that's what it's like to be a director, to motivate and meet schedules and run three things at once.*

A: I like doing that. I'm never really bored. Even right now at the end of a project I still have 500 things I have to do. And I did all the cockpit displays, all the avionics and stuff. That's one of the things I really like. I like digging through the design documents and manuals and figuring out how the pilots really use everything; and designing — I did the graphics for the cockpit and put it on the display. So that was my little payoff. I got to program and do all that stuff, and then my other job as Project Director was to make sure everyone else was doing their stuff. Andy and I also shared responsibility for a lot of things, because it's really too much of a job for one full person.

Q: *What's the breakdown of the team? How many artists? How many programmers?*

A: Right now at the end we have five pure artists and two design artists (they did the objects in the game vs. the movies and screens and stuff — they actually did the game art and the terrain art), so that's seven artists. Two designers. An Assistant Producer, who is also a designer. Our graphics programmer. Three systems programmers. Game flow programmers. Me. We had a sound guy for a while, but he went to go work for another company and we haven't replaced him. Right now we just use the company-wide resources in Jason Cobb's Audio group. Barry Leitch and Stretch Williams did a lot of the music.

Q: *Is there a story behind the song at the end of the game?*

A: Stretch played guitar and Micael Priest sang the song on the end credits. I went down and played them the song "Red Neck Mother," by Jerry Jeff Walker, and told them, "I want something just like this." I wanted to get that, but we couldn't afford it. "Can I have money for a country western song to go over the credits?" Andy's like, "And you're asking me this question?" So we tried to emulate that song's attitude. I think we did a pretty good job of it. That gripping music over the credits is one of the things I'm proud of. So stupid. It's so out of place, and it's also so very Austin, Texas.

Paul Stankiewicz, Art Director

Q: *You are the Art Director for* Longbow. *Let's start with your background with ORIGIN, and with other companies. How did you get where you are now?*

A: I was an art director in advertising for a number of years. I got out of advertising and was trying to build furniture out of my garage for awhile, but wasn't making any money. I got back into advertising, and took a freelance job doing some kids' music videos with a company here in town which I had worked with on some television commercials as the art director. They were going to buy a 3-D system — this was six years ago — so I stayed to learn that. It was a pretty new deal at the time. Unfortunately, the way technology changes, three years later the box they had was ancient history, so I started looking around for somebody that had something new. Talking to the SGI salesman I found out that ORIGIN had just bought a bunch of *Alias* software and Silicon Graphics equipment. So I came over here to see how things were going and dropped off a tape at noon, and at 4:00 had three messages on my answering machine at home. So I looked at all the cool toys here, and that's a big draw for an artist.

I got here right at the very beginning of *Longbow*, two years and two months ago. None of the artists really had any Alias experience. So my primary job was to teach the software to people and get them up to speed, and at the same time work on animations of screens and whatnot. And learn the game industry, because for the most part the artists had a minimal amount of game experience. But Carol Roberts and I did have a background in television production, television commercials and things like that, which was probably an advantage, because we weren't tainted by the limitations of game technology from years past. We were more interested in pushing the limits to try to get it up to ... not broadcast quality, but that's the kind of thing we were used to. So we were thinking more in terms of little television clicks and commercials, movie images, as opposed to little short Pac-Man sprites.

Q: *Someone comes to you and says, "I want you to be motivated and excited about this helicopter that isn't even on the market yet." What was that like? Did you like helicopters before you came here?*

A: Actually, I sort of wound up on the team by default. I got here just as the *Alias* software was making its initial impression. *Wing Commander* was hogging all the people up, and I think Andy shouted, "Hey, I need somebody to teach my people." And I was the next person through the door, so I ended up here. I didn't choose military things. But for the artists it's like playing with electronic clay. It's fun. Whether it's a spaceship or a helicopter, it's still fun to make things.

This is going to get me in trouble. If you're making a space game and you make an explosion and it winds up purple, you say, "Oh, that's cool. I can use that. That's the plasmotronic explosion." But in our game people know what an explosion looks like. They've seen the movies. In Hollywood we're used to seeing the big fire, gas-bomb explosion. So we Hollywood it a little bit. But for the most part they are real world explosions — when a tank blows up it goes bink! There's a little smoke and that's it. And the tanks have to roll on the ground. People know how wheels roll and how things bounce, and stuff like that. So those are some of the challenges.

The artists like that kind of stuff. Sometimes we say, "Oh, man, I wish I was doing a space game. That would be a lot easier." But that's one of the fun parts of being an artist — you have to make it look right. You know in your mind how it's supposed to look. And with the military stuff, people who play these games are hard-core sim types. They know what those vehicles look like. They know what those planes look like. So you have to be pretty accurate when you're building things. Again, as opposed to a non-real world game, where you say, "I'm going to put some spikes over here. That looks cool," you can't do that. This is like drawing. You have to make things look like they are supposed to.

Q: *How do you go about research? Obviously there's video footage. What kind of minute detail do you get into? Do you lie on the ground and watch a tank roll by?*

A: It was certainly harder early on, because there wasn't a lot of reference around here. Certainly the Jane's connection was a big push, because that's given us access to pictures of systems that are really neat. Also McDonnell Douglas footage has been a big help. It showed us exactly what rockets look like when they take off and what a machine gun looks like when it fires. We've accumulated a library of books and video footage that shows us what things are supposed to look like.

Q: *Some of the people on the team went to Fort Hood and met pilots. Any of your people?*

A: Brian Smith went to Ft. Hood and took lots of pictures of military vehicles that he used to build the 3-D objects in the game. Early on, we also took a couple of other field trips. The artists went to Camp Mabry and the Air Force Reserves. They don't have Apaches, but they do have Cobras and things like that around. And they were nice to let us come in and walk around and climb in them and sit in them — watch the chain gun move around, things like that. That gave us a pretty good idea of what the nuts and bolts looked like. We plan to continue doing that. We want to go to Ft. Hood and observe a live fire. That would be great.

Q: *What about future editions?*

A: I hope there will be more Easter eggs. We concentrated on realism, and all our Easter eggs went by the wayside. So they are lying around in the corners, waiting for us to gather them up and put them back in.

Q: *One final question — where do you go for reference on Panama City and other locations?*

A: We actually went to the library and got some books on that — what the architecture looked like, what the hill country looked like. Also, we pulled things down off the Internet to get an idea of Bridge of the Americas, one of the things that's there. It's a pretty distinctive landmark and it's near the base where you take off, so people who are down there would know that bridge is there. So we built that bridge and it's there. We got most of the information off of the Internet.

7. FARP Procedures:

a. Air: These are the primary steps for ingressing/egressing the FARP:

(1) Scouts/SCAT will recon the area ahead of the flight to ensure security.

(2) Scouts/SCAT establish contact with FARP and security around FARP, taking positions that will allow observation of the immediate area and provide early warning of incoming threat. One Scout/SCAT will then control all movement in and out of the FARP.

(3) Refuel points will be numbered from 1-5 starting from the left. Points 1-4 will always be AH-64 points. Point 5 will always be the OH-58/UH-60 point. refueling and Hellfire/Rocket loading will always take place on the refuel pads.

(4) Scouts/SCAT will rotate teams in and out of the FARP before refueling, the last team will relieve they refuel.

(5) Scouts will call FARP clear when they have departed the area.

(6) After refueling, troops reform as briefed and continue the mission.

(7) Radio usage will be minimum, always use brevity code.

b. Ground: The III/V platoon will normally deploy a main FARP (5 Points) and a Jump FARP (3 Points). Based on mission requirements, the platoon can operate (3) 3 point FARPs, 1 per troop. TO&E manning does not allow for 24 hour operations. The OPORD should contain the hours of operation of the FARP. The FARP will monitor the FARP 1 net and the Squadron Command Net. Call Sign will be As per the COMCARD utilizing the platoon leader suffix.

c. Lighting:
(1) Inverted "Y": White
(2) Hazards: Red
(3) Fuel Points: Blue
(4) 30mm Points: Orange

d. Signals: Strobes-Off, Clear to approach aircraft, Strobes-On, Ready to depart

Soviet Military Doctrine Implications of the Gulf War

IDR, 1 August, 1991, volume 24, issue 8, page 809

BY MARY FITZGERALD

According to the representatives of the Soviet General Staff Academy, the Gulf War was a clash between two concepts of warfare: the Iraqis lost because they were fighting in the past, while the Coalition forces won because they were fighting in the future. The Coalition's victory was quickly linked by the Soviet military to the achievement of surprise and air superiority. It confirmed the revolutionary vision of a future "air-space war" that had been developed by the Soviet military since the early 1980s.

Twenty-first century warfare, it was assumed, would rely heavily on so-called "reconnaissance-strike complexes": highly effective ground-, air- and space-based means of reconnaissance, surveillance and target acquisition, linked in realtime to powerful, global strike means. The wide-scale deployment of advanced conventional munitions (ACMs), of directed-energy weapons and of space-based systems would engender a military-technical revolution, the Soviet military argued, and change the nature of future war. Large groupings of ground troops would not be employed in it. Massed strikes would be delivered by remotely piloted precision-guided weapons and reconnaissance-strike systems capable of "automatically finding and destroying the target to any depth of the opponent's territory." The entire country being subjected to precision strikes would become the battlefield, and the war would proceed without borders or flanks. The terms "front" and "rear" will be replaced by the concepts of "subject to strikes" and "not subject to strikes." First-priority targets will be state and military command-and-control points, energy sources, and military targets, especially retaliatory strike means. These objectives can now be achieved without the capture and occupation of the opponent's territory — which was impossible in the past.

By airpower alone

While confirming assumptions about future warfare, the Gulf War also showed that some firmly rooted tenets of Soviet military art need to be revised. Heretofore, Soviet military thinking had focused on "stereo-types": war would start

with an offensive air operation lasting three to five days, followed by an invasion with ground troops. The invasion by ground troops was considered "the main content of war." Hence the need for a "strategic defensive operation" in the European theatres of military operations (TVDs). But today it is possible to escape this stereotype. With a vast arsenal of air-attack weapons, the probable opponent can initiate and subsequently conduct only an air war.

According to military experts, the Gulf War confirmed that ACMs can strike any target at any range. War can begin with surprise ACM strikes and be conducted by these strikes alone. The old principle was the massing of forces and weapons on an axis to achieve the quantitative superiority required to launch an offensive. The Gulf operations confirmed the success of a new principle: the concentration of firepower for pinpoint strikes to achieve air superiority. Initial Soviet comments stressed the role of radioelectronic warfare and of automated C^3I systems in facilitating the Coalition's immediate seizure of air superiority. As combat multipliers, these systems are said to have negated the Iraqi quantitative superiority in tanks, and to have radically shifted the correlation of forces in favour of the Coalition.

Authoritative Soviet analyses argue that the Gulf War dictates essential changes in the employment of ground forces. The war was not determined by a clash of a mass of ground troops and equipment. With use of novel elements such as ACMs — especially cruise missiles — it was a "technological operation" that was not massive, but sufficient to prove its effectiveness.

The Gulf War lesson, as it is interpreted by experts from the General Staff Academy, thus dictates significant changes in the draft military doctrine published in Military Thought in late 1990. Since the early 1980s, authoritative Soviet analyses have stressed the blurring of the boundary between offense and defense under the impact of emerging technologies. The "meeting engagement" — the type of military action in which both sides meet on the offensive — was emerging as the primary type of action as a result of this convergence. According to military experts, however, it would be a mistake to consider that the concepts of "offense" and "defense" as now understood have become obsolete. An offense or defense by ground forces is possible even in the future "air-space war." But they can occur in the course of the war — most probably in its concluding stage — and not at the outset as was previously believed. It is thus clear that the structure of the armed forces could change in the future. While their numbers will gradually decrease, their quality will improve as a result of saturation with new types of weapons.

According to Soviet military experts, the nature of future warfare thus dictates that the armed forces be allowed to conduct whatever forms of military action are necessary, the most effective, and correspond to the existing military situation. In compelling the Soviet military to conduct only defensive operations to repel aggression, the new defensive doctrine is thus "extremely dangerous" for both the armed forces and the Soviet Union. Instead, the Soviet armed forces must be fully prepared to conduct all types of combat actions: "The defensive doctrine does not mean a defensive strategy." Since the Gulf War, Soviet statements about "strictly defensive actions" at the outset of war have thus been replaced by another concept, that of "adequate response."

In late January, for example, General Major I.N. Vorob'yev published an article in Red Star that severely criticized the "one-sidedness" and "rigidity" of the 1990 draft military doctrine. Because the document states that the defense will be the main type of military action at the start of aggression, Vorob'yev charges that, "we are ordered to act passively under the circumstances. But in any war, especially a modern one, this is fraught with a loss of the strategic initiative and unpredictable consequences for the army and the nation. One has merely to recall the lessons of 1941."

Vorob'yev argues that military doctrine "cannot and should not" assign to military art a unilateral focus regarding the employment of any one type of military action. The theory and practice of military art should be considered instead on the basis of a strategy of "adequate response." The armed forces should select and employ, "those forms and methods of conducting an operation or battle which correspond to the existing situation and ensure the achievement of decisive superiority over the opponent.... The priorities in choosing the types of combat would not be defined ahead of time." Since the Gulf War, other military experts have reiterated these views.

Despite a noticeable degree of civil-military divergence regarding the future of the Soviet armed forces, the civilian leadership has not sought to impede the development of those technologies perceived to be at the heart of future Soviet military capabilities: ACMs, directed-energy weapons, and space-based systems. The Soviets predict that by the year 2000, these systems will be accumulated in sufficient numbers to conduct the "air-space war," and space-based systems will be capable of destroying 30-50 per cent of the opponent's retaliatory strike weapons. Warfare will then become a process in which complex, organizational technical "combat systems" mutually influence each other. As a result, the war's politico-military objectives can be accomplished for the first time without the capture and occupation of enemy territory. When the opponent's military capabilities and military-economic potential are destroyed by these "combat systems," his political system will not survive. During the ongoing transition period, warfare will resemble that conducted in the Persian Gulf, with a declining role for piloted aircraft and a growing role for air-, sea-, and space-based directed energy weapons.

The Gulf War demonstrated, in the view of Soviet military, that achieving surprise and air superiority at the outset of war was the "determining" factor, and that masses of ground troops and equipment in a defensive stance are "absolutely useless."

As a result, some of the most prominent Soviet military experts now demand that the defensive doctrine be replaced by a strategy of "adequate response." While the military's interpretation of the defensive doctrine had never converged with that of Gorbachev and the civilian experts, the current wave of divergence signifies an open offensive against one of the linchpins of Gorbachev's "new thinking."

AH-64 BLADE GETS MODIFICATIONS

IDR, 1 August, 1991, volume 24, issue 8, page 893

The joint Army/McDonnell Douglas Apache Readiness Improvement Program (formerly known as the Apache Action Team) has come up with a solution to the problem of main rotor blade debonding. The difficulties caused by short life of the original blades in US service were exacerbated by the severe storm damage suffered in 1989 at Fort Hood, Texas, when many blades were written off.

Currently, new blades fitted to three service helicopters seem set to pass the 1,500 flying-hour life called for by the US Army. Apaches are being fitted with the improved blades as they return to workshops for overhaul. The improvement program has also provided solutions to improve the life of the strap pack laminates and the tailrotor swashplate, although these are still being closely monitored "to assure complete user acceptance."

AH-64A APACHE

JDW, 12 October, 1991, volume 16, issue 15

Used operationally for the first time in Operation "Just Cause" in Panama in December 1989, the Apache was the first coalition aircraft to engage in operations against Iraq during the Gulf conflict.

The US Army plans continued production, but the Advanced Apache and MSIP Apache have been cancelled. Further development now rests with the AH-64C Longbow Apache, based on the Westinghouse mast-mounted radar and RF-seeker head Hellfire. Production deliveries are scheduled for 1996/97 and will comprise 227 airframes.

Apache a True Multi-Role Helicopter

IDR, 1 December, 1991, volume 24, issue 12, page 1356

BY MARK HEWISH

The US Army now plans to remanufacture 535 of its AH-64 Apache attack helicopters to advanced configurations, compared with 227 previously, following a series of critical design reviews held during the past summer and autumn. This program, together with export sales, will keep the production line open until at least 2002. McDonnell Douglas Helicopter Company (MDHC), which foresees an export market for up to 500 Apaches, is promoting the design as a multi-role combat helicopter rather than a dedicated anti-tank machine. The AH-64 was "the single biggest manoeuvre factor on the battlefield" during the Gulf War, according to Major General Barry McCaffery, commanding general of the US Army's 24th Infantry Division.

The US Army deployed 15 Apache battalions, totalling some 288 AH-64s, during the conflict. They destroyed in excess of 500 tanks, 120 armoured personnel carriers, 30 air-defense units, 120 artillery pieces, 325 miscellaneous vehicles, 10 radar installations, 50 bunkers/observation posts, 10 helicopters and the same number of fixed-wing aircraft. One battalion of Apaches destroyed more than 100 tanks and 40 armoured personnel carriers in an engagement lasting 3h, scoring 102 hits with Hellfire missiles out of 107 rounds launched.

The AH-64's payload of fuel and armament totals nearly 3,00kg — equal to the empty weight of an AH-1G, and 10 times the payload that the Huey Cobra can carry. This allowed Apaches to change missions during flight, without having to return to base to refuel or load different ordnance.

Task Force Normandy — comprising eight Apaches, each carrying eight Hellfires, 19 70mm rockets and 1,100 rounds of 30mm ammunition — opened the Coalition's offensive on 17 January 1991 when they attacked early-warning radar installations 80km inside Iraq. The helicopters fired 27 Hellfires, 100 rockets and 4,000 rounds, opening a 32km-wide corridor through which Coalition aircraft could pass. The mission lasted 15h, covered a total distance of nearly 1,300km.

Later in the war, as part of a 300-helicopter assault launched on 24 February, Apaches destroyed a bridge with six Hellfires after the US Air Force aborted an attack with smart bombs. For the following two days, bad weather grounded all Coalition combat aircraft apart from the US Army's a H-64s.

The helicopters also conducted other types of missions, including covert night reconnaissance deep inside enemy territory. This role — for which the US Army has no other suitable vehicles — was made possible by the Apache's comparative quietness, its long-range night-vision sensors and its ability to fly routine patrols of 360-720km. Rather than having to take notes, the Apache crews simply added their comments to the video recording in real time. On their return, the tape was fed into the intelligence network and distributed to a variety of users. A major advantage of this procedure was that the recordings, having been made at low level, showed terrain from almost the viewpoint of a ground observer rather than from overhead.

Overseas sales

MDHC will rely on export sales and remanufacturing programs once it has completed deliveries in late 1993 of the 807 Apaches ordered by the US Army. New potential customers for the Apache have emerged since the Gulf War, and MDHC says that several countries have accelerated their plans to acquire attack helicopters since the conflict.

The Israel Defense Force has received 18 helicopters diverted from US Army production, deliveries of which started in August 1990. A further 12 diverted aircraft will be supplied to Saudi Arabia from September 1992, with an additional 36 planned to follow from 1994/1995. Egypt has ordered 24 aircraft with the normal full lead time, deliveries of which start in January 1994.

The United Arab Emirates have requested 20 Apaches, with six being delivered early. Bahrain has asked for eight to be diverted in 1994, Kuwait has a requirement for at least 30, and Greece is seeking approval for the purchase of 12. Other sales could involve 37 to 55 Apaches for the Republic of Korea, and 85 to 90 for the Japanese Ground Self-Defense Force under a co-production program. Co-production or assembly are also possibilities in the UK, involving 80 to 125. The Netherlands and Spain are candidates to receive 52 and 32 AH-64s.

Gulf War spurs upgrade programs

Based on its experience during the Gulf War, the US Army has proposed a fleet-modernization plan that would increase the warfighting performance of its Apaches and improve the RAM (reliability, availability and maintainability) figures.

The proposed program involves remanufacturing 535 AH-64As to the AH-64C/D configuration by 2002, and modifying the remaining 254 to the AH-64B standard by means of field retrofit kits over two years from 1994. The AH-64C and -64D would be identical, apart from the use of more powerful General Electric T700-GE-701C turboshafts and the Longbow fire-control radar in the AH-64D, allowing them to be fielded in mixed units.

The AH-64C/D would receive all the improvements planned for the AH-64B (see below), together with a redesigned cockpit, additional cooling, enlarged forward avionics bays, more electrical power, upgraded dual redundant processors using VHSIC circuitry, and RF Hellfire missiles. The AH-64Ds would have the Longbow fire-control radar and -701C engines from the outset, with the AH-64Cs having provision for later incorporation of these changes. The Defense Acquisition Board approved plans in December 1990 for converting the first 227 AH-64As to the AH-64D Longbow Apache configuration, following an extended (70-month) development program.

A further 308 AH-64As would be remanufactured to the AH-64C standard for delivery from mid-1995, although this schedule could be accelerated if required.

Both the -64C and the -64D will have CRT-based cockpit displays, greatly enhancing situational awareness. They will also carry the Improved Data Modem (IDM) designed by the US Naval Research Laboratory, allowing them to exchange data with other platforms at much higher rates than is possible with the ATHS (Airborne Target Handover System), which is limited to the use of TACFIRE artillery fire control system protocols. The IDM will employ a universal protocol, allowing data to be exchanged with US Air Force, Navy and Marine Corps forces as well as with other Army assets. It will also, for example, permit an AH-64D to hand-off radar-acquired targets to AH-64Cs for engagement with their RF Hellfires.

Longbow integration

MDHC is working under a $194.6 million contract to integrate the Longbow fire-control radar and Hellfire missile on the helicopter, allowing it to engage targets from extended ranges in bad weather. The first of four AH-64As modified to become Longbow Apache prototypes is due to fly in April 1992, and deliveries of AH-64Ds are scheduled to begin in mid-1996.

The Longbow system consists of a Westinghouse millimetre-wave fire-control radar with a mast-mounted antenna, an IBM AN/APR-48 radio-frequency interferometer (RFI), and the Longbow Hellfire Modular Missile System (LHMMS). The radar is intended to automatically detect, locate and prioritize tanks, trucks, air-defense units and airborne targets, with the RFI detecting emitters. Targets are then automatically handed off to the LHMMS, which uses a Martin Marietta Hellfire missile carrying a new millimetre-wave active radar seeker for autonomous attack. Longbow Apache will retain its TADS (Target Acquisition and Designation System), which can be cued from the new radar to permit earlier visual detection of targets.

The Garrett Auxiliary Power Division of Allied-Signal Aerospace company is supplying its GTCP36-155 auxiliary power unit for flight trials in the Longbow prototypes. The APU provides more than 80shp to drive two electrical generators and two hydraulic pumps, in addition

(continued on page 198)

(continued from page 197)

to power for main-engine starting and the environmental control system.

The remaining 254 AH-64As would be converted to -64Bs between 1994 and 1996 at a unit cost of some $900,000. These will be allocated to front-line units until replaced by -64Cs, and then by -64Ds. New equipment may include "A-Kits," allowing the helicopters to carry air-to-air missiles, and additional avionics: SINCGARS radios, GPS receivers, an ATHS and other improvements resulting from Gulf War experience.

Following loss of contact with helicopters flying deep strike missions during the conflict, the US Army has drawn up a requirement for non-line-of-sight communications over distances of up to 300km: six times what is available today. MDHC and Rockwell's Collins Avionics & Communications Division have jointly funded development of such a system, based on the latter's ARC-217 HF radio with automatic link establishment (ALE), which completed trials on an Apache in March 1991. Reliable communications were achieved at ranges up to 300km, during the day and at night, with the helicopter flying only 10ft (3.05m) above the ground.

Continuous improvement

The Apache achieved an operational readiness rate of 92 per cent by the end of the Gulf War, dispelling the myth of unreliability that had surrounded it. MDHC and the US Army are jointly working on the Apache Readiness Improvement Program (ARIP) — formerly known as the Apache Action Team — to correct remaining deficiencies identified by the customer. The ARIP, which has already remedied 120 problems, is now addressing eight remaining top-priority issues. Of these, three are nearing completion:

The Apache's main-rotor blades have suffered from problems of delamination. Improved blades have completed more than 10,000 flight hours with no confirmed failures, and three sets in service at Fort Rucker are each approaching 1,500h with no indication of problems.

A new design of main-rotor strap pack has entered production and is being fielded. Adoption of the new pack obviates the need for special inspections at intervals of 2.5h and 10h.

All in-service Apaches have been fitted with an improved tail-rotor swashplate, which eliminates the need for a 10h inspection and for overhaul at 250h intervals. The time between overhauls of the new swashplate design is expected to at least meet the 1,500h requirement.

During recent trials, Apaches equipped to the latest standard demonstrated a mission mean time between failures (MTBF) of 24.2h (compared with the required 19.5h) and a system MTBF of 6.7h (compared with 2.8h specified). Further areas being addressed by the ARIP include changes to the hydraulic system, modifications to the shaft-driven compressor and enhancement of the gun system.

The US Army Aviation System Command's Applied Aviation Technology Directorate (AATD) is running the INTAAW (Integrated Air-to-Air Weapons) demonstration program in an effort to improve the accuracy of helicopter-mounted automatic cannon in the air-to-air mode. The aim is both to upgrade the M230 30mm Chain Gun in the AH-64 Apache, which was originally designed as an area weapon, and to assist in defining requirements for future systems.

INTAAW includes the evaluation of an all-digital adaptive turret control system and an active recoil-attenuation system, which are being developed by Integrated Systems Inc (ISI) and HR Textron respectively under the PAACE (Precision Aircraft Armament Control Experiment) program run by ARDEC (the US Army's Armament Research, Development and Engineering Center) at Picatinny Arsenal.

INTAAW also includes improvements to the Apache's sighting, target-acquisition and fire-control systems. These aspects, together with the two components of the PAACE program, were demonstrated in an AH-64 that flew 30 missions at Yuma Proving Ground during the summer of 1991. The aircraft shot down all 12 of the 3m-long drones that it engaged, some at greater ranges than originally planned. The Department of Defense has not yet allocated money to implement all these improvements in the Apache fleet, however, and alternatives are under consideration. These include an enhanced version of the M230, and the possible development of a new advanced-technology gun.

Apache Reliability in Gulf Questioned

JDW, 2 May, 1992, volume 17, issue 18, page 743

BY JOHN BOATMAN

AH-64 Apache attack helicopters experienced reliability problems with weapons and other systems during the Gulf conflict, says the US General Accounting Office (GAO).

During the air campaign, the Apache (right) was used mostly for armed night reconnaissance rather than its primary anti-armour role due to its night vision and videotape capabilities, reports the GAO.

It emphasizes, however, that overall the Apache was effective in combat and non-combat missions.

In its recent analysis of the Gulf conflict, the army said that the Apache was used for armed reconnaissance in poor weather, thick smoke or low visibility because other aircraft lacked its "survivability, range, mobility and versatility."

While not refuting all of GAO's specific reliability allegations, the army defended the Apache as a "solid performer" with mission capable rates of 93 per cent during the conflict.

Based on interviews with commanders of 11 of the 15 Apache units in the Gulf, the GAO says there were reliability problems with the Apache's Hellfire missile, 30 mm chain gun, night vision systems, targeting devices, and communications system.

In response, the army said the problems uncovered in the Gulf were already known and were being resolved. Specifically it mentioned continuing improvements in the chain gun and communications systems.

Brig Gen Charles McClain, Chief of Army Public Affairs, said the army continues to investigate several of the other shortcomings cited by the GAO, "some of which seem at variance with army data."

A total of 274 Apaches were deployed to the Gulf and 2876 Hellfire missiles were fired during the conflict.

The army has admitted that there were five accidental launches of Hellfire missiles, caused by one of two electrical circuit problems. Both problems are being corrected, it added.

Advanced INS for Longbow Apache

IDR, 1 July, 1992, volume 25, issue 7, page 709

Litton Guidance and Control Systems has delivered the first three LN-100 inertial navigation units to McDonnell Douglas for the AH-64D Longbow Apache program. The units will be installed for flight verification testing later this year and several hundred units are anticipated for production. The LN-100 system integrates INS data (using a solid-state "Zero-Lock" gyro) with GPS and Doppler inputs to arrive at a navigational solution.

The deliveries follow an eight-year research, design, and development program. In addition to Longbow Apache, the LN-100 will equip the Army's RAH-66 Comanche light helicopter as well as the USAF's F-22 Advanced Tactical Fighter.

THE INVISIBLE ART OF CAMOUFLAGE

IDR, 1 August, 1992, volume 25, issue 8, page 749

BY MURRAY HAMMICK

Battlefield camouflage, concealment, and deception (CCD) is an unlikely beneficiary of the recent widespread cuts in defense spending. It is not considered to be offensive in any way; it has not (to date) featured in any of the international arms limitation agreements, and has escaped the attention of political-pressure groups intent upon unilateral or multilateral disarmament. From a financial viewpoint (the other major inhibitor upon defense procurement), CCD hardly rates a mention, since a typical battlefield camouflage outfit rarely exceeds 0.25 per cent of the value of the equipment it is designed to protect. It is now acceptable to speak in terms of "protection" since it is possible to show that camouflage can increase the survival rates of equipment and troops as effectively as increasing firepower, protection, or mobility. On an individual basis, a well camouflaged tank might have a 50 per cent increase in survival rate in battle; this will have a direct armour-equivalent, and permits a valid comparison of costs of pursuing either option.

Increased individual survival rates will in turn improve the operational effectiveness of units and formations; the ability to survive a pre-emptive attack by virtue of a good camouflage and deception plan can be equated to having larger forces to begin with, or alternatively, investing in costly protective infrastructures and a comprehensive warning system. This last arguement will of course be familiar to many, since it is one of the cornerstones of the defensive strategies of all major nuclear powers. It is perhaps true, however, that the same principle has been applied less often to battlefield CCD, a state of affairs that many now believe will change as the concept of "force-multiplication" becomes more important as a means of offsetting some of the current defense cutbacks.

By and large, military capabilities respond to perceived threats; in the case of CCD it is the increasingly sophisticated array of battlefield surveillance systems used to detect and identify targets, as well as to control both direct and indirect fire weapons. However, the technology which forms the basis of infrared (IR), thermal, and radar sighting-systems also provides CCD technicians with the opportunity to make scientific assessments of an object's visibility; moreover, it gives them a headstart on how to make

men or equipment merge with their backgrounds in as wide a variety of environments as possible. In one of the first successful initiatives of its type, Creative Optics Incorporated, a US-based research company normally associated with automatic target-recognition systems, has been working on a Mobile Army Camouflage Evaluation (MACE) system which attempts to overcome the lengthy and subjective task of camouflage evaluation by using complex algorithms "to produce numerical measurements of the similarity of camouflage to backgrounds."

In the majority of armies, reconnaissance forces and surveillance assets are in fairly short supply, and hard-pressed to carry out all the tasks being bid for. This makes it necessary to adopt a graduated system, where a rapid check for any obvious signs of enemy activity is followed by increasingly detailed analysis of an area of responsibility. However, at every stage of this process, what is actually being looked for is any marked contrast between an object and its background; initially this would need to be little more than the visual or radar-equivalent of a thermal hot-spot, but it will provide justification for expending further effort needed to identify and locate the contacts — the basic requirements before any operational plan can be drawn up. The recognition process is as valid for an automatic surveillance system as it is for the human eye (operating in the visible bandwidth between 0.4 and 0.7μ), as indeed are the basic principles of camouflage. Most manuals of field-craft refer to four criteria when discussing camouflage, namely shape, shine, shadow and silhouette. They combine to create contrast, already described as a critical factor in the surveillance process. Effective modern camouflage systems have to consider these criteria in relation to each and all of the spectral bandwidths against which it is necessary to protect. As might be expected, full protection across the complete spectrum is not yet practical, and it is at this point that the scientist and manufacturer have to be advised by the military about threat priorities. For political and other reasons, this becomes a very sensitive issue, but it would be reasonable to assume that the majority of modern armies would consider it necessary to be protected against short wavelength, near-infrared, first-generation image intensifiers (II) operating in the 0.5-1.2μ waveband, and desirable to be protected against long wavelength, far IR thermal-imagers (TI) and forward-looking infrared (FLIR) systems operating in the 3-5μ and 8-14μ wavebands.

Beyond visual

The overlap between the wavelengths of first-generation II sights and human vision is significant, for it means that standard "visual" camouflage is partially effective against II sights. However, as one moves beyond the 0.7μ level, anomalies build up between traditional camouflage materials and typical backgrounds such as woods, hedges and grass. At this stage, the soldier can no longer rely simply upon a common-sense approach to camouflage, since he cannot use any of his innate senses to assess its effectiveness, and the picture becomes increasingly complex as one moves further from the visual bandwidth.

Ordinarily, the only natural material available for camouflage is foliage and turves. Once vegetation is cut, its yellow and red reflectance (of an external source of light, whether sunlight or artificial) in the near-IR spectrum (used by II sights) increases; the reflectance of chlorophyll is particularly high at wavelengths over 0.7μ, and it is between four and six times as reflective between 0.8 and 1.0μ as in the visible wavebands. Dying and dead foliage will therefore tend to contrast with surrounding living trees and bushes when viewed at IR-wavelengths, somewhat similar to the yellowing of greens as seen by the human eye. IR camouflage also has to allow for the fact that the green colour of foliage is transparent at wavelengths of 0.68μ and above, exposing the highly reflective, white-cellulose cell structure, and causing a significant increase in reflectance in near- and far-IR wavelengths.

Near-IR camouflage was one of the first non-visible wavelengths to be addressed, given the widespread use of IR sights and illumination by Warsaw Pact forces, and by 1957, Barracuda of Sweden had introduced the first visual/near-IR camouflage net. Using patches of IR-reflective

(continued on page 202)

(continued from page 201)

material rather than a solid screen, it is possible to create the depth and feel of a wide range of woodlands and vegetation. But, apart from applying different colour schemes to a reversible net, most visual/IR camouflage is tailored to fairly specific operational environments. Deciduous vegetation requires a net with about 65 per cent net cover (this is favoured by the British); it is also relatively cheap. Against a dense, coniferous background, over 90 per cent of the net is covered, and IR properties are adjusted to match the lower reflectance levels of this type of foliage. In contrast, the IR reflectance of tropical vegetation is much higher than European woodlands as a result of the higher level of chlorophyll present, which also makes for brighter greens. Nets for use in desert areas are almost invariably totally covered, matching the uniformity of the ground.

It is technically feasible to reduce the thermal signature of a vehicle or headquarters installation to a level at which it will cease to present a conspicuous hot-spot in a thermal viewer.

Snow presents another problem; whereas vegetation reflects about three per cent of ambient ultraviolet (UV) light (between 0.3 and 0.4μ), snow (particularly in extremely cold, dry conditions) reflects up to 80 per cent. When viewed through a UV filter, a covering of ordinary white material will appear black, in contrast to the white snow, since the common white pigment, titanium dioxide, absorbs heavily in UV wavelengths. This effect is partially visible to the human eye, where a net might appear slightly less "brilliant" than its background. Obvious alternatives to titanium dioxide (white lead, chalk, or zirconium dioxide) are usually heavier, more expensive, or impractical, and manufacturers are careful to guard their particular solutions to this problem. Coverage, as with desert camouflage, is normally total; reversible nets have therefore to provide partial-snow screening using painted patches rather than reducing scrim levels, a system used by the US company Sioux Manufacturing, North Dakota, in its arctic netting.

In practical terms, there is little need to combine temperate and arctic camouflage, and thus the issue of simultaneous matching of IR and UV signatures does not generally arise. However, multi-spectral screening in visible, near- and far-IR, and radar wavelengths is becoming a problem. Multi-spectral surveillance involves the near simultaneous use of different wavebands to either find a weakness in an enemy's camouflage, or to allow a comparison of views which might reveal a tell-tale anomaly. Typical combinations include super-imposing an II (image intensifier) picture on a thermal image, or a TI picture on a radar scan. In the former case, the camouflage has to deal with near and far-IR signatures; the latter with longer radar wavelengths (up to 3cm) and far-IR. Far-IR, or thermal camouflage, differs from camouflage against II sights since it involves controlling an active source of electro-magnetic radiation from relatively hot men and equipment.

Thermal screening

Although thermal imagers work in two fairly specific wavebands (3-5 and 8-14μ), it is not possible to match background signatures using the principle of reflectance for an active source. Instead, thermal camouflage is achieved by reducing the apparent temperature, size and emissivity of a heat source. In practical terms, it is almost impossible to eliminate the thermal signature of a vehicle or headquarters installation, for example, but it is technically feasible to reduce it to a level at which it will cease to present a conspicuous hot-spot in a thermal viewer, or act as a homing-source or trigger for a heat-seeking missile. For entirely unrelated reasons, most tank designs minimize the thermal signature of the major heat-source — the engine — by placing them at the rear, notable exceptions being the Israeli Merkava and almost every modern infantry fighting vehicle (IFV).

Exhausts present another problem, for these tend to be angled outwards or upwards to reduce the amount of dust thrown up, and can present a hot cloud above a vehicle. This can be countered to some extent by mixing-in air to cool the exhaust gases — a method already used on helicopters; it can also be remedied by filtering out hot fuel vapour and diesel smuts which actually create the problem-pure air has no measurable thermal signature. However, even clean exhaust will heat up nearby vegetation or buildings, and these will create useful clues for intelligence purposes, sometimes long after a location has been vacated. (Many readers will be familiar with IR line-scans of airfields which show heat silhouettes in the concrete surfaces of dispersal sites after aircraft have run-up their engines).

Emissivity, the rate at which heat is radiated from a surface, can be reduced by way of coatings, including paint. In theory, shiny, metallic surfaces emit less heat than matt or dark surfaces. Lighter paint-schemes are relevant in arctic or desert conditions; they reduce thermal signatures by reflecting solar radiation — US tanks in the Persian Gulf were sprayed with the new Tan 686A paint which reflects radiation by up to 85 per cent, reducing external surface temperatures by 15 degrees, as well as cooling the interior. However, these paint schemes are not always ideal in terms of visual (or radar) concealment, and surface coatings alone cannot achieve sufficient reductions for most tactical purposes. Moreover, most coatings tend to lose their effectiveness once covered in dust and mud — neither of which is in short supply on the battlefield.

An alternative solution is to use thermal screens to reflect heat away from surveillance sensors, and which can be placed far enough from the tank or weapon to avoid heating by conduction. A high degree of reflection is achieved by using plastic-coated metal-foil, such as the thin, polythene-coated screen (polythene is thermally "transparent") used in the British Thermal Camouflage Woodland (TCW) system. In some circumstances, better results may be achieved using a foil-strip "quilt." This is used, for example, by Flectalon Limited, of Wales, a company which has adapted its work on commercial insulation products to meet military requirements. Its quilted thermal insulation blanket significantly reduces a vehicle's thermal signature; it is light enough to be carried in addition to any netting, and is non-hygroscopic and flame-resistant. Its only specific drawbacks are that it is necessarily more bulky than some modern camouflage nets or single-thickness thermal blankets, and it is comparatively noisy when handled — a problem already being addressed. However, the effectiveness of any thermal camouflage varies greatly according to prevailing weather conditions, and it is particularly susceptible to warming by sunlight.

Thermal blankets can be covered by standard visual/IR camouflage, or alternatively, given a matt coating to meet visual and near-IR requirements. Barracuda's thermal camouflage system uses two separate layers to avoid producing a "solid" thermal block which might warrant closer inspection by reconnaissance forces. The inner screen is a single-layer thermal blanket consisting of a laminate of metal film coated in plastic and fibre. It is perforated by a patented system of "eyelid" holes which allow warmed air to escape, reducing the blanket's temperature; the layer of metal reflects the heat characteristics of its surroundings. The block-effect is broken up by placing a thermal camouflage net with varying emissivity-rates over the blanket, which also helps to create depth. From a user viewpoint, a double layer of camouflage might be considered too much trouble; however, it may be argued that at night the thermal blanket is more important than the net, and it would be a lot easier to put up in the dark.

The increased use of battlefield radar has forced camouflage manufacturers to examine the problem of screening against this relatively long-wavelength medium. The principles involved include absorption and scattering to reduce returns to levels similar to the surrounding vegetation. As with the thermal signature, radar signatures can be significantly reduced at the design stage for most vehicles and equipment. Companies such as Tracor GIE in the US, or UK-based GEC-Marconi or Dowty Signature Management (in association with Dowty Hoybond), are now consulted in the early stages

(continued on page 204)

(continued from page 203)

of design by vehicle prime-contractors, and a tank such as the Leclerc is in fact comparatively stealthy. Theoretically, it is possible to reduce a tank's radar cross-section from about 50 to $0.1m^2$ using careful design and radar-absorbent materials (RAM). However, field conditions can reduce the effectiveness of RAM technology; a covering of dust can create a good reflective surface in millimetric wavelengths, as will a wet surface (although rain will also reduce the effectiveness of a millimetric seeker, for example). In addition, RAM technology is still relatively expensive, and the majority of AFVs in service were designed with scant regard for considerations of stealth. In the majority of armies, the most cost-effective solution is to use separate radar-camouflage screening.

A double-net system will be viewed with misgivings by the troops who will have to put it up at night or in foul weather, and it is not very conducive to rapid movement.

The large bandwidth of radar frequencies presents a problem: battlefield radars tend to be millimetric (MM) to provide the definition needed for accurate location, whereas surveillance radars use longer wavelengths up to 3cm. Barracuda's radar camouflage net manages to incorporate radar scattering and absorption, as well as protecting in the visual and near-IR wavebands using a material only 0.2mm thick. The net is claimed to be effective against 1 — 10cm wavelengths (C to K bands) although its primary effects are aimed at 3cm (X band) systems; the frequencies cover the current range of synthetic aperture radars, sideways looking airborne radar and forward looking radars.

The degree of attenuation (reduction) in radar signatures required of high-performance camouflage is not clear. Barracuda's system is stated to provide a 12dB (90 per cent) reduction. IDR has been told that this might exceed normal operational requirements, in which case it could leave a radar "hole" which might be as detectable as a hot-spot. There is, however, continuing debate about the levels of attenuation required, since this is likely to vary with the target type and background clutter characteristics. For example, broadband radar camouflage might provide uneven attenuation at different wavelengths, peaking well below or above an average level. A UK initiative is about to invite industry to tender for a research study to determine the most suitable attenuation levels for specific scenarios and frequencies.

Within NATO, CCD research is carried out under the auspices of a special group of experts which has close liaison with military planners in the NAAG who generate operational requirements and standardization agreements. (The exchange of detailed research information is restricted to nations participating in the program, but commercial reality generally ensures that the technology is available to all NATO members, following the transition from research to the development phase). The question of standards in this and other camouflage-related matters has been a cause for concern to both manufacturers and users for some time: Dowty Signature Management prefers to offer equipment for evaluation, and not get involved in suggesting the level of the requirement.

To date, most modern multi-spectral camouflage has been aimed at a combination of visual, near-IR, and radar wavelengths. The missing bands cover far-IR or thermal wavelengths. This is of particular concern, given the development of light-weight thermal sights for individual weapons. Combined radar and thermal camouflage systems are difficult to achieve since low emissivity surfaces tend to provide good radar reflections as described above, although the Flectalon metal-foil blanket does provide a degree of attenuation through scatter. Currently, there is little alternative to using two layers of screening material, with a thermal layer screened by an outer radar net. However, as was the case in the earlier example, a double-net system will be viewed with misgivings by the troops who will have to put it up at night or in foul weather, and it is not very conducive to rapid movement.

The ease with which nets can be erected or taken down has always been a topic for discussion amongst users and makers alike. In some armies, the use of camouflage at night has been limited, with nets only being put up at first-light after a night-move into a new position. However, thermal camouflage is needed on a 24h basis, and if screens or nets cannot easily be taken down, it is probable that they will simply be discarded in a rapid move; this will be particularly likely in the case of a night move. It is possible, therefore, that losses of camouflage equipment will be significant in a protracted operation, and it might be difficult to make good any such deficiencies. Some now consider that it might be feasible to have thinner, lighter nets, which would have a shorter operational life than most current systems, but which could be carried in greater numbers by troops on the ground. Cheaper, less bulky nets might also address the problem of how to hold a comprehensive selection of camouflage for forces expected to operate in far more diverse environments than their more static predecessors. (This problem is already being considered by NATO planners.)

Decoys

Similarly, most current camouflage systems do not address the problem of concealment on the move, when thermal and radar signatures will be especially pronounced. Screens and nets are clearly impracticable in these circumstances, although most vehicle crews do not fully stow these, but instead drape them around turrets and hulls to provide some sort of cover (as well as to dry them out). Initially, any toning-down of silhouette and shine will be important, and products such as Camtex's Multispectral Texture Mats or Barracuda's Addcam become important. These can be fitted temporarily or permanently, and are claimed to be effective against the complete sensor bandwidth, from UV to radar. Last year's Gulf War demonstrated the vulnerability of columns of moving vehicles to surveillance by long-range radar. Within the medium term, it is considered unlikely that these sorts of signatures will be capable of being modified sufficiently to prevent detection at long ranges. One of the only means of reducing the accuracy of intelligence so gained is to use decoys. However, against a well informed enemy equipped with the latest intelligence analysis systems, it will be necessary to handle decoys very carefully, and only within the context of a well-organized, medium- to long-term deception plan. Vehicles and equipment appearing from nowhere, emitting little or no electromagnetic noise, and lacking any apparent logistic support are not going to appear on an intelligence officer's enemy listings for very long.

At unit-level or below, these considerations will be less important than speed of emplacement and visual reality. Typically, decoys have to be robust, cheap and effective at very close range before they attract investment from armed forces; the last point is particularly relevant, not from the point of view of fooling an enemy, but because the majority of potential users tend to inspect decoys from a few metres rather than from likely battlefield viewing distances. At this level, the intention would be either to draw attention — and fire — from real positions or weapons, in which case equal numbers of decoys and real equipment would be optimal, or alternatively to mislead an enemy into making a false tactical appreciation. It might be sensible for every tank to carry at least one or two "phantom friends," although as with camouflage nets, it is probable that these would soon be abandoned on the battlefield.

At unit-level or higher, systems such as the Motorola AN/PRT-10 Communications Deception System can complete the false electronics picture. This simulates two-way traffic between two or more units in the field, using pre-stored or managed scenarios to control the sequence of emissions so that the units appear to be communicating with each other. A computer allows the basic characteristics of the tactical scenario to be inserted, and any special requirements can be loaded in as and when the situation demands. Last-minute changes have been allowed for, since it is rare for full details of frequencies and so on to be available very far in advance. The system operates across the HF, VHF and UHF bands, and is fully independent (including a full built-in-test facility). It was used successfully in Desert Storm, an operation which provided ample evidence of the value of good deception.

Growth Prospects for Thermal Imaging Systems

IDR, 1 March, 1993, volume 60, issue 3S, page 17 (abridged)

BY CHARLES G. LEMESURIER

"History," as a distinguished manufacturer once said, "is bunk." Observers of the defense scene might not altogether agree with this view and it is interesting to reflect on the changes and improvements in doctrine, weapons and equipment which have occurred over the centuries and which have demanded, on occasion, some rapid re-thinking by the military. Our century has, of course, seen the pace of change accelerate dramatically. At sea the battleship has been replaced, as the capital ship, successively by the aircraft carrier and the nuclear submarine whilst on land the main battle tank has risen to dominate land warfare. The rise of air power has been the great 20th Century phenomenon and, though Air Marshals might disagree, it could be said that air power in war has proved most cost-effective (and of vital importance) when used in support of either land or sea forces.

Supporting these platform improvements, weapons and sensors have evolved at great pace — and especially during the two World Wars. As for weapons, missiles — delivered from a variety of platforms — have replaced the gun for many roles as, though costly, their range and high probability of hit make them essential for every nation's armoury. As for sensors, whilst 60 years ago the "Mark One Eyeball" together with a pair of binoculars or a telescope was the principal sensor, we now have a very wide variety of which radar is the best known and most widely used. Radar is also now relatively cheap, the low cost bringing the equipment within the price range of any self-respecting yachtsman.

Radar "won the Battle of Britain" and "won the Battle of the Atlantic" for the UK, it is sometimes claimed — and certainly it did make a vital contribution. The British had the good sense and the determination, having perceived radar's pos-

sibilities, to develop equipment which gave their Navy and Air Force significant advantages at critical moments in WWII. However, radar does not "see" and has to be interpreted — radar cannot, like the eyeball mentioned above, identify a target instantly.

Now, as we approach the 21st Century, advances in technology provide us with equipment which can do just that — and that is what this article is about — electro-optics and specifically thermal imaging — which provides vision in total darkness and, whilst there are some limitations, in extreme weather conditions of fog, mist and rain. Like the eminent manufacturer who opened this article, we will look forward, and not back into the past.

Thermal Imaging — What is it? An important point to clarify is a definition of thermal imaging (TI) and how it relates to other electro-optical military systems. Electro-optics, as the word implies, covers the whole field of systems that contain electronic and optical components. Optical components, however, have wider uses than just those associated with visible light and optical techniques can, in fact, be used with electromagnetic radiation across a range of wavelengths that extends from the micro-wave to the X-ray region.

In thermal imaging we are concerned with that range of wavelengths that are emitted by objects as a result of their temperature. These wavelengths are found in the so-called "infra-red" region — meaning waves that are longer in wavelength than visible red light. However, not all regions of the infra-red are associated with thermal imaging. Close to visible light, but still classified as infra-red, is a band of wavelengths that have been extensively used for low-light imaging and many laser applications. This so-called "near infra-red" band has many military applications that are correctly referred to as "night vision" and "infra-red systems," but these are not thermal imaging systems. Thermal imaging uses longer wavelengths, called the "mid infra-red" and "far infra-red," and the techniques are the subject of this article.

A further point on terminology concerns the use of the term "FLIR." This is an acronym for Forward Looking Infra-Red, and originated in the use of thermal imaging systems for ground attack aircraft. Because these systems were early in the field, the term FLIR has tended to become used for all manner of thermal imaging systems, many of which have no particular forward direction.

It was the deployment of night vision systems for the heavier weapons and attack aircraft that brought about the more wide-spread use of thermal imaging in the 1980s. As well as being almost impossible to detect, it provided them with important longer ranges and, furthermore, could provide images of targets in visually obscured conditions. In tanks and vehicle sights, however, image intensifiers still find a role as they are small and often easy to retrofit to a visual sight — and cheap, only costing 1/10th that of a thermal imager.

As new thermal imaging detectors increasingly enter military systems, there will, we believe, be a move away from image intensifiers (II). The uncooled focal plane array, working in the mid infra-red, competes directly with II devices for weapon sights, driving scopes and small field observation devices. It must be said, however, that because normal glass and plastic windows and windshields do not transmit wavelengths in the mid or far infra-red, applications that need the user to look through a window will generally exclude the use of thermal imagers. Estimates vary on the lead time for this technology, and only mass markets will produce truly low-priced devices, but a consensus seems to be that with support from commercial sales, many of these requirements will be filled by thermal imagers.

Visual and near infra-red imagers are, however, natural complements to thermal imagers in many surveillance applications. Thus in ships, reconnaissance aircraft and some land based installations, a suite of sensors can often be justified. Here the visual, near infra-red and thermal images are used either together or as alternatives depending on the time of day and "seeing" conditions.

This is the moment to give some indication of the cost of TI and, while a cost of any defence related equipment might be categorised as infinitely variable, it is useful to focus on the subject by providing some ball park figures:

(continued on page 208)

(continued from page 207)

ALTERNATIVE SENSING TECHNOLOGIES

Low-Light Imagers

Low Light Television or Image Intensifiers provide images that rely on natural or artificial illumination sources. Indeed, early systems when they first appeared in the 1950s utilised illuminators consisting of infra-red filters fitted to normal light sources.

Operators wore image intensification goggles, which being responsive to the near infra-red radiation, allowed them to see targets or the road ahead, as they were illuminated by the beams. However, these systems had very little tactical use, being easily detectable by the same image intensification goggles. A further disadvantage of these early systems was their large size, weight and power consumption.

Improvements in these older systems came with the introduction of newer Image intensification (II) devices in the 1960s. These provided both military and para-military users with a reasonably lightweight device that could be attached to a weapon sight. It provided amplification of ambient light during the hours of darkness. For the first time users were able to identify targets at night using an "easy to operate," reasonably lightweight device.

Compared to the thermal imager however, image intensification will always have weaknesses. It relies on some ambient light, and as such will always be limited in range for any reasonable image quality. However, this range (say up to 1,500m under good conditions) is adequate for most infantry, paramilitary or civilian night vision requirements. In conditions of total darkness or poor weather, thermal imaging dominates because, not only does it obviate the need for external light sources, but can better penetrate smoke, dust or fog. These gains are not however achieved without some penalties relative to image intensifiers. These are chiefly size, weight and cost, and in market terms, cost has probably been the most severe restraint on wider deployment of TI (up to 10 times that of II for a similar task).

Laser systems

A primary short-coming of an imaging system, when used for targeting, is that it provides no direct measure of range to the target. Thus, regardless of the imager type, some method of rangefinding is normally essential for a modern targeting system. Lasers are usually preferred, as their beam is sufficiently narrow to pick out a single point in the image for both ranging and target designation of a target. Because the weapon must carry a sensor for this illumination, near infra-red systems have predominated for this application. In spite of the better weather penetration of long-wave systems, today the relative costs of sensor technology in the disposable (weapon) part of the system usually leads to a near IR solution with any weakness in sensitivity being made up by adding laser power.

Radar

At first, mainly because of their size, early radars were confined to use in land installations, but within a very short time were fitted in ships and aircraft. Since the early days radars have been shrinking in size and have currently arrived at the stage where excellent battlefield radars, weighing 30kg with a range in excess of 20km, are available. Radar was a marvellous invention but performance varies — a succession of disasters to small fishing craft and yachts being run down by heavy ships in poor visibility testifies to this. As for military problems, "stealth" has become a whole industry.

Radars can be detected easily and except in casesof monopulse design are very easily decoyed. During the Gulf War use of radar by Iraqi forces proved to be almost suicidal and Allied aircraft with radar homing and warning sets and radar-seeking missiles wrought havoc amongst air defences. This would seem to suggest that radar can no longer be used for air defence, however if a long range detection capability is needed, there is no realistic substitute for radar and much effort has gone into restricting emissions to minimise the risk to the emitting source. In many cases an imaging sensor is increasingly being required to give the commander a visual confirmation of the target prior to engaging weapons. Thus in airborne interceptors and air defence systems on land and at sea, a thermal imaging system and a surveillance and tracking radar are commonly found together.

Millimetre-wave radar

Millimetre-wave (mmW) radars come closest to thermal systems in providing detailed information on a scene. This is because their short wavelength (0.3 to 3cm) can provide very precise range profiles of objects in a scene. Their wavelength is however several hundred times larger than thermal radiation, and therefore the angular resolution of a millimetre-wave radar is some hundreds of times worse that a thermal imager with the same collection aperture. Their real advantage however is in being able to rapidly pick up potential targets in a large scene. The radar characteristics of man-made objects tend to be quite different from natural objects; metals reflect strongly and with the ability to measure the extent and profile of an object, mmW radar provides a powerful cueing aid to a thermal targeting or guidance system. Their range capability is also well matched to thermal systems — 1km to 5km for solid state radars of 100mm to 500mm aperture. Common aperture systems with applications in missile guidance, as well as shared aperture surveillance and aircraft blind landing systems are currently in the research and development phase. These mmW radars are potentially quite cheap compared with radars that work at longer wavelengths, are of necessity small and can take advantage of modern micro-electronic manufacturing technology to increase reliability and reduce manufacturing costs. They do, however, usually contain precision mechanical assemblies for their gimbal or scanning mechanisms, and these are always likely to be somewhat costly and prone to shock and vibration. However, the improvement in target cueing performance that can be obtained may well lead to the use of these systems in high performance targeting systems.

There are at least 400 system applications of thermal imaging technology from about a hundred manufacturers world-wide.

Military applications and markets

Thermal imaging systems are used in a variety of applications in the land, sea and air sectors of military operations. On land this covers roles in missile systems, fighting vehicles, infantry weapons sights and observation systems whilst at sea we discuss fire control and surveillance systems. In the air we focus on seekers, search and track and reconnaissance and finally we look at commercial market opportunities.

To give some idea of the size of the market, we should note that there are, we believe, at least 400 system applications of thermal imaging technology from about a hundred manufacturers world-wide.

Land applications

Armies, particularly infantry forces, as well as relying on thermal systems have also made extensive use of image intensification technology for many years, primarily because II provides devices that are small, relatively cheap, and give useable performance for ranges out to one kilometre or so. However, as weapon ranges have lengthened and requirements for operation in poor weather and total darkness have become increasingly necessary, thermal systems have become more desirable. Thus thermal systems are now widely deployed throughout land forces, in anti-armour and air defence systems, in fighting vehicles and, as we will see below, systems for infantry weapons are now under development.

Anti-armour

Anti-armour weapons use thermal sights for target acquisition and tracking in both ground-launched and helicopter-launched versions. This provides a fully covert sensor with the necessary range (up to 4km for TOW) required for target acquisition at the stand-off range of the missile. Applications with shorter range missiles (Milan,

(continued on page 210)

(continued from page 209)

Typical detection ranges for aircraft and helicopters can be 10km, as the targets are comparatively hot relative to the background sky, but at these ranges identification is most unlikely.

Medium Range TRIGAT) are also reported, but in ground-to-ground armour engagements, longer ranges are rarely required, and therefore the current technology has a strong hold on these applications. However, as we will see below under air systems, anti-armour helicopters using the Hellfire missile need to be able to engage targets from over 8km, and for this requirement millimetre-wave radar offers a serious challenge. Nevertheless, there will often be a need to obtain visual identification of a target, and we believe that because of the practical limits on platform stability and image magnification, engagement of targets at 3km-4km will still be the first choice for most commanders.

There are now close to a dozen systems deployed and we believe there is a healthy future for thermal systems in anti-armour missile fire-control, the range and image quality requirements being well matched to the technology. For many users a thermal sensor will be the system of choice for this application.

Air defense

Regarding the prospects for thermal imaging technology in these applications, we find that for surface-to-air missile guidance radar has been the dominant technology, but in recent years, with the growing threat from anti-radar missiles, passive sensors have become increasingly important — a trend which, we believe, will continue. As with anti-armour systems, target identification may be required, and therefore large aperture optics may be necessary. Typical detection ranges for aircraft and helicopters can be 10km, as the targets are comparatively hot relative to the background sky, but at these ranges identification is most unlikely. As with anti-armour systems, a range of a few kilometres would seem to be more reasonable while achieving accurate target identification at the 7km to 20km range of the larger surface to air missiles, requiring much larger and costlier systems. We know of some 18 systems on the market.

Fighting vehicles

The main thrust of land forces lies in mobile armour, in which sector thermal imaging systems greatly increase the fighting potential of all classes of fighting vehicles — tanks, light tanks, recce vehicles and armoured personnel carriers. There are four types of system — tank fire control systems, gun sights, commander's sights and driver's sights.

Tank fire control

Tank fire control systems combine a thermal imager or II sensor with a laser range-finder, targeting computer and (in modern tanks) a gyro stabilisation system for the main armament. This latter equipment provides the ability to fire on the move. These thermal systems are very widely produced, with manufacturers in the USA, UK, Germany, Belgium, France, Israel, Italy, Japan and the Netherlands and, if image intensification systems are included, the list becomes even longer. As is generally the case with medium and longer range weapons, thermal imaging is preferred to II.

Engagement ranges closely match those of land based anti-armour missiles (approx 3km), and the imaging systems are therefore broadly similar. Because of the limited viewing points on a main battle tank, the sensor optics are usually integrated with the tank optical sight and a laser rangefinder, and certain systems are designed to replace optical sights on early tank models. Systems of this type have been available since the 1970s, and it is generally assumed that for modern armour a thermal sight is very much the system of choice. There are now some three dozen systems that are found amongst modern armoured vehicles and as upgrades of earlier systems.

Airborne applications

The military market for airborne thermal imaging systems has provided much of the cutting edge of this technology. Indeed, as discussed earlier, the term FLIR itself originates in the use of infra-red sensors as a forward looking night/foul-weather flying aid. Today, FLIR technology has been so widely developed that it is used in nearly all aspects of military air operations.

Airborne applications can be divided into four main areas for the application of thermal imaging technology:

- Missile seekers
- Search and Track
- Reconnaissance
- Flying aids

Missile seekers

Many missiles use infra-red detection for target tracking but in this article we are interested only in those missiles that use a TI sensor and we exclude, therefore, those that use infra-red sensors only for "hot-spot" tracking. This leaves missiles and glide bombs which are generally used against armour and fixed installations.

Imaging IR seekers operate in essentially the same way as TV seekers. In the case of Maverick, the guidance uses a "man in the loop," who observes the scene imaged by the missile and selects the missile aim point. In the Medium-Range-Trigat development, a fully autonomous imaging sensor is proposed. The benefits of thermal imaging technology are that, compared with television, it provides longer acquisition ranges, can detect targets visually obscured by fog or smoke and can, in certain cases, detect targets that are well camouflaged visually.

For medium range air-to-ground engagements, thermal imagers for fire control are well established as the method of guiding missiles although these sensors are expensive, requiring good target identification capability at 3km to 4km. To put such a sensor into the missile would be very costly, therefore the sensor is used to control the missile through a missile tracker and command link or via a designator system. This approach puts much less cost into the missile. The disadvantage is that the launch platform sensor must be locked onto the target during the engagement — and this increases the vulnerability of the aircraft. Some protection is afforded by laser designator systems because the laser can operate out to some 10km, with the additional benefit that the seeker is relatively cheap and simple to construct. But the requirement to obtain a visual confirmation of the target generally means that the aircraft still has to approach within 4km, a range at which much cheaper weapons can usually be employed.

Thus for air-launched weapons, the only incentive for an imaging seeker is that it should provide a fire-and-forget capability, with search and acquisition at about 4km but to do this at the required ranges may imply an imager that costs as much as current fire control sensors. Developments in imager technology indicate the potential for significant cost reduction in imagers that can be used in short range (say up to 1km) applications, but high sensitivity, long range systems will generally require the ultimate in optics, detectors, and signal processing technology.

Search and Track systems

In Search and Track systems we look at missile fire control, ground attack and navigation for helicopters and fixed-wing aircraft. These systems share a common requirement to give the pilot and navigator high quality thermal images (generally good enough to fly the aircraft), as well as being highly integrated with other avionics systems. In the case of attack helicopters and combat aircraft, these systems are often at the very centre of the platform's mission purpose and effectiveness, and as such can comprise a significant portion of its costs. This is a fertile area for future avionics research in that there are major challenges in the integration, processing and display of all the data and images needed to fly, navigate, search, acquire, kill and safely return from a mission. Thermal imagers have come to occupy a central role in many of these tasks.

(continued on page 212)

(continued from page 211)

Missile fire control

Thermal Imaging technology is used for missile fire control in a very similar manner to that discussed under missile seekers, above. The sensor is used to image the target and a "man-in-the-loop" selects the point of aim. Guidance may be autonomous to the missile or achieved through a link to the launch platform.

In the air-to-ground missile market, we believe that there is an increasingly important market for imagers for target detection and missile fire control from helicopters. The imaging system for these applications is not, in general, closely tied to the missile design and, particularly in helicopter-based systems, it is possible to consider a general purpose imager for these applications. Night and foul weather targeting capability provides, of course, significant advantages over day only systems.

Recent missile developments have moved away from thermal systems for guidance at longer ranges (greater than 4km), using instead laser designation (Hellfire and Trigat). The imager is still needed for target identification, although this may be performed at closer ranges by a forward observer. The sensor usually requires two fields of view, wide for target search and narrow for target identification and aiming. The tendency towards longer range weapons may be limited by the ability to meet the long range identification requirements. To obtain the necessary resolution (about 1m) a very high magnification lens is required.

Ground attack

All-weather attack systems currently represent the ultimate in performance of multi-sensor weapon control systems. Typically such a system will contain as well as the thermal sensor, a laser rangefinder, laser designator, target tracking system and gyrostabilised pointing system. A wide variety of bombs, missiles or guns may be used at all ranges from long stand-off (tens of km) to close air support (100s of metres in extreme cases). Furthermore, laser homing weapons may be launched not just from the targeting aircraft but also from other platforms. The cost of such systems is substantial as the performance will always tend to be at the cutting edge of what the technology can offer, and considerable costs are incurred in pod integration and development and test of weapon interfaces. Modern techniques were demonstrated on television to fascinated audiences during the Gulf conflict.

The full suite of Ground Attack Avionics can require just about every major system on the aircraft and it is interesting to note just how important accurate navigation and approach to the target are in completing an attack mission. Gulf conflict reports state that 40 per cent of coalition air-to-surface missions were aborted for reasons of weather and smoke, but that aircraft equipped with global positioning systems were always able to complete their mission to the point where ordnance was released. Thus, although not necessarily part of the ground attack system, global positioning or other accurate and reliable navigation techniques are essential for mission success. For this reason ground attack systems will generally consist of a navigation and a targeting system and the latter may be contained in an attack pod.

The attack pod consists of a thermal imager, processing unit and laser ranger/designator. Because of the operation on high speed aircraft, a thermal management unit is also required. Addition of other sensors is also common. TV sensors for daytime operation can be fitted along with systems for automatic hand-off to weapons. The targeting sensor generally offers a range of fields of view, wide (say 5 x 7 degrees) for search with narrow (1 x 2 degrees) for tracking. So that the aircraft can pull away immediately after weapons release, the sensors have a very wide field of regard. In the case of the UK TIALD system, this extends from +30 to -150 degrees from the aircraft centre line.

These systems require the very best in sensor technology for two main reasons. In the first case the image is moving very fast relative to the aircraft, and therefore integration times are low and scan rates are fast. Secondly, the requirement is to launch stand-off weapons, and therefore a targeting range of some 20 to 30km would be ideal. However, to recognise a target generally requires that it subtend some 10 per cent of the field of view. At 20km, a 10 metre target subtends an angle of 0.5 mrad (approx 0.1 degree) would be required to get good identification. Practical systems however, seem to be limited to about 1 degree field of view for targeting.

Reconnaissance

In conventional airborne reconnaissance, an aircraft flies a preplanned path over a designated area, to obtain detailed images of the ground for interpretation by intelligence staff. Many systems use optical or infra-red sensitive film to record the image of the ground, and it is usual for the camera film transport to be adjusted to the forward flight speed of the aircraft. This method however, does not provide real time imagery, and in the future we believe that there will be a strong trend towards using TV and thermal imagers so that the electronic data can be immediately transmitted back to the intelligence staff.

As was shown by the use of the French Mirage F1-CR aircraft in the Gulf conflict, real-time data links to ground receiving stations are an available option, and one that will be increasingly chosen to support attacks on mobile and relocatable targets. We believe that the importance of real-time tactical high resolution imagery for target location and battle damage assessment will continue to place these systems in the "must have" category. Both dedicated and multi-role recce aircraft are a vital asset in developing the mission plans of military forces, and the ability to operate these systems in real time, at night and in poor weather will come to be seen as an essential requirement.

Night flying aids

It hardly needs re-stating that the pilot of a high speed attack aircraft at night or in poor visibility has problems of an altogether different order of magnitude to the airline pilot whose requirements we discuss briefly below. Thermal Imaging is essential and a range of other systems are deployed to assist him, terrain following radars, radar or laser altimeters, imaging radars, global positioning systems, inertial navigation systems, and digital maps. TI has its short-comings and a thermal image obtaining its contrast from temperature variations in the scene will greatly depend on the time of day/night and weather. Hills, valleys, wooded areas and water courses may all look quite different from their visual images, and orientating a map to the terrain could therefore be very difficult.

However, in spite of these difficulties, it is clear that for high speed ground attack, both navigation and targeting capability are greatly enhanced by thermal systems and we expect that they will become a standard flying aid of these types of aircraft. For helicopters the situation is somewhat more complex, because the pilot, flying a contour or nap-of-the-earth route, needs a much wider field of view than can be provided with a head-up display. Accordingly the development of flying aids for these missions relies much more on the development of integrated helmet displays than on the thermal sensors. At present a mix of pilot's image-intensifier goggles (for flying) and thermal imaging (for navigation) seems to be the best available solution.

Longbow Links Up

JDW, 29 January, 1994, volume 21, issue 4, page 29

McDonnell Douglas Helicopter Systems has demonstrated transmission of targeting data from an AH-64D Longbow Apache attack helicopter to a mobile ground station via its Improved Data Modem. The IDM will be fitted to all AH-64Ds and allow digital secure transmission of targeting information to all IDM-equipped units.

Guided Longbow Hellfire trials

IDR, 1 March, 1994, volume 27, issue 3, page 15

A Martin Marietta/Westinghouse Longbow Hellfire anti-tank missile scored a direct hit on a stationary T72 at Eglin AFB, Florida, during its first guided test firing in December 1993. The round, fired from a ground-based rail, struck the base of the tank turret. Further extensive testing, from helicopters and ground-based launchers, is planned for this year. The weapon is scheduled to enter production in 1995, initially to arm US Army AH-64 Apaches and later to equip RAH-66 Comanches.

Sales Interest Grows in Longbow Apache

JDW, 7 May, 1994, volume 21, issue 18, page 8

BY JOHN BOATMAN

Export possibilities are growing for the AH-64D Longbow Apache now that all six prototypes are flying and tests and evaluations have begun.

Army Col Robert Atwell, Longbow Project Manager, said that besides the Dutch and UK interest in Longbow for their attack helicopter programmers, France, Germany, Japan and Israel have also made enquiries.

Japan is considering adding money to its next five-year plan to procure 90 to 126 attack helicopters toward the end of the decade, said Col Atwell. Tokyo has indicated that co-production would be an attractive option. The Israelis are looking to complement the AH-64A Apaches they acquired earlier, he added.

Col Atwell said the UK could end up buying a 50:50 mix of regular Apaches and Longbow Apaches. Despite the interest from other countries, US Government export clearance has been granted only for the UK and the Netherlands.

The army has designated all 750 remanufactured Apaches as AH-64Ds to simplify logistics. Previously, only the 227 that were to be equipped with the Longbow fire control system were to be D models and the non-Longbow remanufactured aircraft were to be AH-64Cs (JDW 15 May 1993).

Fire-and-forget Longbows have a mast-mounted millimetre wave radar and 16 radar-guided Hellfire missiles.

Prior to the D model remanufacturing, the army will open airframe work to industry competition. This includes structural upgrades and other changes to commonalize the fleet.

In October, three Longbow Apaches will take part in a force development test and experimentation exercise. Initial operational test and evaluation is due to run from January to March 1995.

A NEW VIEW ON THE WORLD

JDW, 25 June, 1994, volume 21, issue 25, page 19 (abridged)

Bernard Fitzsimons looks at the role of helmet-mounted display technology in combat aircraft and virtual reality training systems.

New combat aircraft have been designed with helmet-mounted displays (HMDs) as an integral part of their avionics systems. Helmet system developers are also promoting HMDs as a means of upgrading existing fighters, while the use of helmet-mounted visual display systems in mission simulators could be a pointer to future operational capabilities.

Systems under development for the next generation of combat aircraft and helicopters combine the facilities provided separately in the past by helmet-mounted sights, image-intensifying night vision goggles and visually coupled systems, such as the Honeywell integrated helmet and display sight system (IHADSS) used on the Apache, which projects imagery from slaved sensors on a monocular lens display.

Helmet-mounted sights, which operate with a position sensor to designate targets for aircraft sensors or weapon seekers, have been in service since Honeywell developed the VTAS visual target acquisition system for US Navy F-4s more than 20 years ago. They need only a 6-10° field of view to allow the projection of a target reticle generated by a light emitting diode onto a reflective patch on the visor.

Helmet displays need more light and a wider field of view. Cathode ray tubes (CRTs) project both HUD-like flight symbology and the imagery from sensors and helmet-mounted image intensifiers or low-light TV cameras onto separate monocular or binocular combining lenses or the surface of the integral visor. Head position can be tracked by infra-red, electro-magnetic or optical sensors.

Many in-service devices have been adopted despite drawbacks such as restrictions on the pilot's mobility or safety-driven limitations on the aircraft's flight envelope. Future systems, however, will need to incorporate standard protection features, with the addition of laser protection and possibly active noise reduction, while remaining light and comfortable and with a low enough centre of gravity to avoid impairing operational efficiency.

Ultimately, this could lead to helmet-mounted displays becoming virtual cockpits, combining computer-generated imagery with head-slaved sensor imagery and 3D sound cues. It dispenses with the need for any conventional displays except standby instruments. The demands of protection are already at odds with the conventional upright seated position. Studies have shown that reclining the pilot's seat has little impact on G tolerance until the angle is increased beyond 65 deg which is not compatible with an adequate view out of the cockpit. In that case synthetic displays could be a means to avoid the pilot's G tolerance imposing a limit on the agility of future fighters.

Enhanced synthetic viewing is not limited to aircraft. Armoured vehicle drivers could benefit from a panoramic helmet display view like that being developed by Vista Controls of the USA. In this helmet the crew can be "virtually" outside the vehicle with all the advantages of a clear view.

Commercial head-mounted displays developed for virtual reality entertainment applications have not demonstrated the features needed for military cockpit or simulator applications. The USN study concluded that HMDs able to meet its strike mission simulator requirements would be far too expensive for the commercial market.

However, the relatively rapid pace of consumer technology development suggests that there could be technological spin-offs applicable to military cockpit.

LONGBOW VARIANT PROCEEDS TOWARDS PRODUCTION

IDR, 1 July, 1994, volume 27, issue 7, page 13

The Longbow Apache has completed about 85% of its 70-month engineering and manufacturing development program and remains on schedule for a Defense Acquisition Board meeting in November 1995 to authorize production of 811 aircraft, including 227 equipped with the Westinghouse fire-control radar. All will now be designated AH-64Ds, for logistics and other reasons, whereas the non-radar model was previously known as the AH-64C.

The six prototypes—four with the radar and two without—had together accumulated about 1,000 flight hours by late April. All 10 development radars have been provided on schedule, and deliveries of the AN/APR-48 radio-frequency interferometer (RFI) will be completed in October.

Potential roles for the AH-64D include acting as a gap-filler for the E-8C Joint STARS surveillance aircraft and performing deep precision strike.

Combined technical testing, now beginning, involves both contractor and army trials simultaneously rather than sequentially as in previous programs. Force-development test and evaluation is planned for October, with a contract for long-lead production items due to follow in November. The six prototypes will participate in initial operational test and evaluation from January to March 1995, culminating in a force-on-force exercise.

Production AH-64Ds will incorporate a series of technology improvements, including some parts of composite materials, in order to enhance performance and reduce weight by 300-350lb (135-160kg); each pound saved adds 1ft/min to the climb rate. The twenty-fifth and successive aircraft will have colour liquid-crystal multifunctional displays, which are cheaper, lighter and consume less power than the monochrome units originally planned. The electronics power-management system will reduce from seven boxes to four, and 32-bit processors will replace 16-bit machines.

The adoption of an EGI (Embedded GPS/INU) installation in place of the MAGR (Miniaturized Airborne GPS Receiver) will provide range and range-rate information, and enhance targeting accuracy. Colonel Bob Atwell, Program Manager Longbow, says that he is working hard with his counterpart in the Comanche program office to adopt a common second-generation forward-looking infrared (FLIR) set for both helicopters, with Longbow Apache being the first application. Potential roles for the AH-64D include acting as a gap-filler for the E-8C Joint STARS surveillance aircraft and performing deep precision strike. In the latter case, for example, the helicopter could attack an anti-aircraft artillery battery next to a mosque rather than using a 2,000lb bomb delivered by an F-117A.

Possible additional domestic customers for the Longbow Apache include the US Special Operations Command, which is studying its use both for riverine operations and to escort the V-22 Osprey tilt-rotor.

New Helicopters for Old - Too Often an Afterthought?

JDSM, 1 July, 1994, volume7, issue 4, page 21

BY BRIAN WALTERS

As helicopters spend much of their time hovering or performing agile manoeuvres at very low heights, aerodynamics do not rate highly among the priorities in their design, although we have certainly progressed from the earliest days when an open framework was considered to be perfectly acceptable. Brian Walters takes a look at just what is being done to modernise helicopters today.

It is generally acknowledged that a helicopter can accept ugly accretions which would not be tolerated on a fixed-wing aircraft, while the airframes of rotary-winged craft are also less prone to metal fatigue than those of conventional combat aircraft.

The ability of a helicopter to accept whatever its payload will bear, has resulted in the development of some bizarre specialist models such as the French Army Puma fitted with the Thomson-CSF Horus battlefield radar and the AEW Sea King fitted with the Thorn EMI Electronics Searchwater radar.

The latter was a design developed by Westlands for the Royal Navy but kept in a filing cabinet until the 1982 Falklands conflict pointed to the vital need for this kind of protection for a fleet vulnerable to low-level air attack. The ten Royal Navy AEW Sea Kings are soon to be upgraded to facilitate operations with the forces of other nations. The first of the modernised helicopters should be in service by 1999.

The concept has been adopted by a few other countries including Spain, with Searchwater fitted to three SH-3D Sea Kings, and the CIS, which has developed an AEW variant of the Kamov Ka-29 (see JDSM, May/June 1994, p.38). Meanwhile, the Horus demonstrator (the lone example was pressed into service during the Gulf War where it proved the concept) has developed into the Horizon system with its Target X-band radar. The first of four modified helicopters was delivered to the French Army recently.

These examples of a new radar picket role for helicopters point to one of the problems that may be encountered when radically changing the function of a helicopter; while aerodynamics need not be a major consideration in such an update, the amount of power needed and the weight of the "add on" equipment can pose problems.

Certainly it is not uncommon for a helicopter to record a gradual deterioration in performance during its service life as, one after another, additional items of equipment are installed. Fortunately such problems can often be sorted out during a mid-life update when the opportunity is taken to re-design equipment installations so that they interface more readily, becoming less demanding in terms of space and power requirements.

To achieve such a tidy solution may well call for the services of a specialist company, such as Pennsylvania-based AEL, which has amassed considerable experience in the integration of new cockpit management systems, electronic warfare suites and weapons control systems. This company has carried out tasks as diverse as an avionics upgrade for the UH-1 Huey, an integrated cockpit management system for the UH-60A Black Hawk and the development of a launch control system for the AIM-9 Sidewinder missile mounted on the AH-1 Cobra. Cobras (both US Army and USMC) have also been fitted with EW systems by this company.

Specialist companies in several countries have established a niche for themselves by developing a particular capability. The UK's Alan Mann Helicopters, for example, has become skilled in modifying helicopter cockpits to make them compatible with night vision goggles (NVGs) and the company has also demonstrated a capability in extensively modifying the Agusta A109 for a Special Forces role.

(continued on page 218)

(continued from page 217)

An alternative path is being taken for the McDonnell Douglas AH-64 Apache modernisation programme. A team approach with the original manufacturer as the leader has been adopted for the conversion of helicopters to AH-64C/D standard. In the highly competitive environment in the United States, it cannot be taken for granted that the original manufacturer will, necessarily, win a modernisation contract. However, for McDonnell Douglas Helicopters, in a major upgrade designed to considerably extend the capability of the AH-64A, it is logical that the original manufacturer should be nominated as prime contractor—not least because it helps to keep a production line open which might otherwise have to close for want of new-build orders.

Apaches fitted with the Longbow fire-control radar above the rotor hub can easily be identified as having been modernised to AH-64D standard. The changes resulting in the C-model are hardly less radical, since much of the upgrade (involving the integration of advanced navigation, communication and weapons systems) is common to both. Indeed, JDSM understands that the C-designator has now been dropped. The AH-64D is claimed to offer a ten-fold improvement in the Apache's combat effectiveness.

AH-64A APACHE COMES TO EGYPT

JDC, 1 August, 1994, page 15

CAE-Link Corp, USA, has installed the first Foreign Military Sales (FMS) Apache simulator at Abu Hammad Air Base, Egypt.

The contract was awarded in March 1991 via the US Naval Air Warfare Center and was the first FMS AH-64A Apache Combat Mission Simulator (CMS).

The CMS features avionics unique for the Egyptians, and simulation of the Target Acquisition and Designation System/Pilot Night Vision System (TADS/PNVS), the Integrated Helmet and Display Sight System and all weapon systems.

LONGBOW APACHE MAKES ITS DIGITAL COMMS DEBUT

JDW, 29 October, 1994, volume 21, issue 17, page 6

A prototype AH-64D Longbow Apache helicopter has communicated digitally in flight for the first time with an E-8 Joint Surveillance Target Attack Radar System (Joint STARS) aircraft. A similar success was also achieved with a prototype Advanced Airborne Command and Control (A2C2) UH-60 Black Hawk helicopter.

An Improved Data Modem (IDM) built by Symetrics Industries of Florida was installed in each of the three aircraft.

Longbow, under development by McDonnell Douglas Helicopter Systems, was flying up to 240 km from the orbiting Northrop-Grumman Joint STARS aircraft during a demonstration last month when they successfully exchanged more than 30 TACFIRE fire support messages via secure UHF radio.

A separate September demonstration with the prototype A2C2 Black Hawk also involved an IDM-equipped Joint STARS Ground Station Module (GSM) built by Motorola.

The ability to communicate digitally will not only give the Longbow Apache a role in the future digital battlefield and in "Scud"-busting, but will also allow the army to gain efficiencies by fielding mixed IDM-equipped Apache aviation battalions.

In such units, the Longbow Apaches will be able to hand off digital targeting data to modernized AH-64Ds that do not have the Longbow fire control system.

Longbow Apache in Operational Testing

IDR, 1 March, 1995, volume 28, issue 3, page 45

BY CLIFFORD BEAL

The McDonnell Douglas/ Westinghouse AH-64D Longbow Apache is to complete its US Army operational testing in March, prior to entering production. Testing was conducted at China Lake and Hunter-Liggett Field, California. Six prototypes have been delivered to the army and some 3000h of evaluation had occurred in pre-production qualification through the end of 1994.

The Longbow successfully completed live firing of the new Martin Marietta/ Westinghouse RF Hellfire missile in which all 26 firings hit a target. Firings were conducted at Eglin AFB against a variety of moving and stationary, armoured, and unarmoured targets under varying weather conditions, as well as smoke and flame obscurants. RF Hellfire tracks targets while on the launch rail; however, it also has a lock-after-launch capability via its inertial guidance system and updates from the Longbow MMW radar. Moreover, the weapon utilizes Doppler beam sharpening techniques to hone the objective further, if necessary.

Testing has also validated hand-off of targeting information via the Apache's Improved Data Modem (IDM). With this, non-Longbow equipped Apaches can download targeting information directly to their RF Hellfire rounds and so engage targets that they cannot see, well in excess of 6km. The Longbow has also demonstrated IDM communications with the E-8 JSTARS aircraft. The IDM allows an Apache team to function more efficiently, allocating fire zones to each helo to prevent double-kills and establishing no-fire zones to protect friendly forces. Battle-damage assessment can also be performed: a "shot-at" file, maintained on up to 100 targets, can be radioed to an HQ, giving details of each engagement. The IDM has a range of some 277km.

Westinghouse has launched a study on using the Longbow radar as part of the Army's Battlefield Combat ID System, which is millimetre-wave-based, after the company recognized a number of IFF capabilities inherent in the Longbow system.

From the 10th production Longbow, all aircraft will have 6x8 flat-panel colour displays to make the most of the new targeting system. On the maintenance side, McDonnell Douglas sources say that the entire Longbow system, including antenna array, can be installed on an AH-64D Apache in 45min. This would allow an operator to exchange systems in the field. This is crucial, since the US Army will operate 12 Longbow and 12 non-Longbow Apaches in a 50:50 mix per battalion. The army has issued a long-lead procurement contract for more than 750 AH-64Ds.

Longbow Apache Sails Through Testing

IDR, 1 May, 1995, volume 28, issue 5, page 16

Initial operational test and evaluation (IOT&E) of the McDonnell Douglas AH-64D Longbow Apache attack helicopter was so successful that the US Army abandoned the last two of the planned 16 "vignettes" as being unnecessary. IOT&E involved all six prototypes, of which four were equipped with the Longbow fire-control radar. Phase I (gunnery), conducted on the China Lake range of the Naval Air Warfare Center's Weapons Division, involved the firing of 20 RF Hellfire missiles against moving and stationary targets that included T72s. Phase II (force-on-force), at Fort Hunter Liggett, compared the effectiveness of the AH-64Ds with that of in-service AH-64As. Longbow Apaches killed four times as many targets and suffered five simulated losses, compared with 30 for the earlier variant.

Each prototype is flying 25-30h a month, compared with 12h planned, and the total flight time exceeds 3700h. The first prototype to incorporate producibility enhancements—lightweight wiring, forward avionic bays constructed from composite materials, and other improvements—is due to rejoin the flight-test program this autumn. Remanufacturing of the AH-64A fleet to AH-64D standard is scheduled to begin in mid-1996, with deliveries starting in early 1997.

Aerial "Pit Bulls": Attack Helicopters Become a Battlefield Necessity

IDR, 1 March, 1995, volume 28, issue 3, page 44

BY JORIS JANSSEN LOK, BILL SWEETMAN, EDWARD TAIT

The post-Cold War era has brought enormous instability both in the Third World and on the edges of Europe itself. The current perceived need for a very high degree of flexibility (this partly to cover the eventuality of an enemy as yet not thought of) implies forces equipped with weapon systems capable of employment rapidly in a broad range of conflicts; this trend suits the attack helicopter very well, say its supporters in defiance of those who believe that its days are done with the apparent end to the likelihood of conflict on the European Central Front.

The attack helicopter boasts long reach, variety of weapons, ability to self deploy, protection, agility, day/night and poor-weather capability—some of these capabilities added in the dying days of the Cold War to enable it to survive role-changes, but they do lend this weapon system a high degree of flexibility unmatched at present by any other weapon concept.

The attack helicopter competitions of the 1990s all bring varying combinations of the same basic contenders on to the field against each other ....

.... Like many other nations, the UK conducts its procurement procedures mainly by competition among several types, and additionally within the framework of the issue to industry of a series of operational characteristics which contain a number of cardinal points. The weapon system which results is in each case an amalgam of these characteristics, and its effectiveness a result of the balance between them and their integration. The cardinal points for the British attack helicopter would apply for any similar procurement and are:

Lethality: the destruction of tanks remains predominant, but there is a requirement for defense against air and ground threats, and to destroy a range of other ground targets.

Survivability: the need here is to survive in high-intensity conflict, minimizing the risk of detection, employing defensive aids to reduce the risk of suffering a hit, and carrying sufficient protection to ensure the survivability of the machine or at least the crew.

Payload/range: the aim is to carry enough weapons to destroy at least four tanks, at a radius of action of 200km. Implicit in this is a high degree of probability of success, and the maintenance of a comprehensive self-defense capability.

Mission management: the need here is to integrate the flight information targeting and battle-management systems of the aircraft and the ground mission-planning stations.

Night/adverse weather: the requirement to fight the aircraft by night is extended to adverse weather and normal battlefield obscurants such as smoke and dust.

Supportability: a high level of availability is expected throughout the aircraft's planned 30-year span. The complete project has been subjected to the fully Integrated Logistic Support discipline which exposes for the first time the whole life cost of a major weapon system. While there is merit in this approach, it will fail to realize its potential until all new systems are similarly treated allowing accurate comparisons to be made.

The five major contenders, in alphabetical order are:

Longbow Apache: the model under development for the US Army and offered to the UK by McDonnell Douglas and Westland.

Cobra Venom: primed by GEC Avionics and Bell, this is likely to carry laser-designated Hellfire missile and would incorporate GEC's advanced glass-cockpit technology.

Comanche: under current plans, the Boeing Sikorsky Comanche will not enter US service until 2003-2004, some way beyond the preferred British ISD.

Rooivalk: Marshall and Atlas have combined to submit this development of the Puma , a relatively new arrival on the attack helicopter scene.

Tiger: The British Aerospace/Eurocopter Tiger is to be built in variants suitable for French and German procurement as well as for the British military if it wins this order.

Current British operation doctrine is based upon three core elements — find, fix, and strike. The ability to locate an enemy and to maintain contact is fundamental; to pin him down, denying his freedom to operate, follows — until a position is attained from which he can be dealt a decisive blow. The attack helicopter is well equipped to play a significant part in all three stages, its capability perhaps limited more by the imagination of the commanders than any other single factor.

These core elements can be applied equally to all types of conflict at the tactical level — defined as the level where troops are deployed in combat. It is in this arena that the attack helicopter displays its strength, its ability to manoeuvre rapidly unconstrained by ground, its use of heavy firepower applied at long range with pinpoint accuracy, and its inherent protection strengthened by its own active air-defense capability. Finally, there is that level of conflict now known as "operations other than war" — intervention at various levels, counterinsurgency, and peace-support operations. The last-named, specifically UN, task implies protective roles for the attack helicopter to undertake. The very high degree of weapon accuracy is well matched to such operations where the need to avoid collateral damage, or risk to civilian life, takes high priority ....

Article sources: Jane's All the World's Aircraft *and manufacturers' data.*

Attack Helicopters: A Comparison

Manufacturer, Type	Powerplant	Power (kW/SHP)	Max T/O Weight (kg)	Max Speed (kt)	Range (km)	HIGE* (m)	HOGE** (m)
Agusta A.129 Mangusta	2 x LHTEC T800-LHT-801	1343/1800	4100	159	462+	3140	1890
Bell AH-1W Supercobra	2 x General Electric T700-GE-401	1285/1723	6690	150	587	4495	915
OH-58D Kiowa Warrior	1 x Allison 250-C30R T703-AD-700	485/650	2041	128	463	3660	3415
Boeing/Sikorsky RAH-66 Comanche	2 x LHTEC T800-LHT-801	1002/1344	7790	177	N/A	N/A	N/A
Denel/Atlas Aviation Rooivalk	2 x Turbomeca Makila 1A2	1491/2000	8750	167	704	5545	5030
Eurocopter Tiger/Tigre	2 x MTU/Rolls-Royce/ Turbomeca MTR 390	873/1171	6000	151	670	N/A	2000
Kamov Ka-50 Hokum	2 x Klimov TV3-117VK	1633/2190	10800	189	500	N/A	4000
McDonnell Douglas AH-64D Apache	2 x General Electric T700-GE-701	1265/1696	9525	158	482	4570	3505
Mil Mi-28 Havoc	2 x Klimov TV3-117VM	1545/2070	11660	162	460	N/A	3600
Sokol W-3H Huzar	2 x WSJ-PZL Rzeszow PZL-10W	671/900	6400	240	761	3020	1900

* Hover, in-ground effect

** Hover, out-of-ground effect

N/A = Not available

TENTATIVE GO-AHEAD FOR APACHE AND HELLFIRE

JDW, 28 October, 1995, volume 24, issue 17

The US Army has been authorized to enter full-rate production for the AH-64D Longbow attack helicopter and low-rate initial production for the Longbow Hellfire missile.

The decision by US Under Secretary of Defense for Acquisition and Technology Paul Kaminski followed a 13 October Defense Acquisition Board readiness meeting of the army systems.

Dr Kaminski's approval is conditional on the army's ability to use FY97 offsets to fund fiscal 1999-2000 shortfalls in the missile unit cost reduction programme, according to the acquisition decision memorandum that Dr Kaminski signed on 17 October.

When the army submits its acquisition programme baseline to the Office of the Secretary of Defense, it must include cost and performance parameters relating to the entire system's life-cycle costs, the airframe's operational availability and the missile's probability of single shot kill, the memo said.

The army may also now award a single-year contract to McDonnell Douglas for a maximum of 18 Apaches. If Congress boosts FY96 funding, the army can offer a multi-year contract for at least 232 helicopters, the acquisition document said.

If Congressional budget approval or contract negotiations indicate that 232 aircraft will not be achievable, the Office of the Secretary of Defense will decide whether it can justify multi-year contracting at a lower quantity, Dr Kaminski said in the memo.

OSD has waived a 1,000 hour Test Analyze and Fix requirement as the Apache Longbow met its reliability objectives, and stipulated that the army outline, by February, a funding plan for high-priority pre-planned product improvements.

RUSSIAN FORCES ARE IN 'A STATE OF DEEP CRISIS'

JDW, 31 January, 1996, volume 25, issue 5, page 15

BY HEINZ SCHULTE—BONN

The Russian armed forces are no longer capable of power projection outside the country's "near-abroad" area due to a lack of carrier-borne aircraft and general deficiencies in its ground forces, according to a German Foreign Office report. The brief to the parliamentary defence committee entitled "The situation in Russia, especially the role of the armed forces" claims the Russian forces are in a state of deep crisis.

Last year around 35 per cent of war stocks, especially food and fuel, were used. Over half of all military personnel did not receive any payment for months and in 1993 and 1994 around 50,000 to 70,000 conscripts refused call up. The figure for the first quarter of last year alone is close to 20,000. Desertion is also a problem, with 3,000 service personnel absconding between January and June last year.

The real strength of the Russian armed forces at the beginning of last year has been estimated at less than 1.4 million, which is below the proposed 1995 level of 1.92 million and these figures are likely to drop further. The decline in the manufacture of major weapon systems continued with the exception of IFV export orders (especially BMP-2, BMP-3/BMD-3 and BTR-80) of which 380 were produced in 1994 (1993: 325). The two MBT production plants (Nizhniy Tagil and Omsk) virtually ceased production with an estimated 40 MBTs produced in 1994. The reports notes, however, that other estimates suggest a production figure of 160 to 170 MBTs in 1994.

The general staff in Moscow maintains operational control over all nuclear forces, while the physical control over nuclear warheads is the responsibility of the 12th main directorate.

By the end of this year Russia is expected to have returned all remaining nuclear warheads and carrier systems from the Ukraine, Belarus and Kazakhstan. Currently, operational systems remain in Belarus (under Russian operational control) and in the Ukraine (under Ukrainian administration without access to operational control).

GREAT HINT BOOKS FOR ELECTRONIC ARTS® GAMES!

Get the full inside scoop! Every book includes maps, hints, stats, strategy tips and a complete walkthrough of one of your favorite Electronic Arts games! Only official Electronic Arts books can tell you everything about our games — accept no imitations!

The Official Guide to Jane's Advanced Tactical Fighters (224 pages) (7699) **$19.95**
ORIGIN's Official Guide to Wing Commander IV (224 pages, 48 in full color) (10118) **$19.95**
ORIGIN's Official Guide to CyberMage (128 full-color pages) (10100) **$14.95**
ORIGIN's Official Guide to Crusader (192 pages, 96 in full color) (10101) **$19.95**
ORIGIN's Official Guide to BioForge (224 pages, 32 in full color) (10076) **$19.95**
ORIGIN's Official Guide to Wing Commander III (Includes *Behind the Screens CD*) (10094) **$24.95**
ORIGIN's Official Guide to Wings of Glory (Includes *Flight Recorder* disk) (10039) **$19.95**
Bullfrog's Official Guide to Magic Carpet (320 pages) (10119) **$19.95**
Bullfrog's Official Guide to Dungeon Keeper (224 pages) **$19.95**

MORE EXCITING HINT BOOKS, ONLY $14.95 EACH:

Fade to Black (7619)
System Shock (10062)
Wing Commander Armada (10075)
Pacific Strike (10018)
Privateer (6660)
Strike Commander (6659)
Noctropolis (7530)
Shadowcaster (6912)
Ultima VIII (10031)
Ultima VII, Part Two (6658)
Ultima Underworld II (6657)
Ultima Underworld (6662)
Martian Dreams (6691)

CAN'T GET ENOUGH OF WING COMMANDER? CHECK OUT THESE WC NOVELS FROM BAEN:

Freedom Flight (6708) $4.99
End Run (6709) $4.99
Fleet Action $4.99
Heart of the Tiger $5.99
The Price of Freedom $5.99

NEW BOOKS FROM EA SPORTS:

PGA TOUR 96 Player's Guide (7632) 19.95
FIFA Soccer 96 Player's Guide (7633) 19.95

HINT BOOKS FOR OUR CLASSIC TITLES:

Ultima VI (6689) $12.95
The Savage Empire (6690) $12.95
Ultima V (6688) $12.95
Ultima III (6686) $12.95
Wing Commander I & II (6710) $18.95
Ultima: The Avatar Adventures (6711) $18.95
Ultima VII and Underworld (6712) $18.95
Quest for Clues: The Manual of Swords (VI) (6706) $16.95
Quest for Clues: The Book of Orbs (V) (6705) $16.95
Quest for Clues III (6703) $24.99
Official Book of Ultima, 2nd Edition (6707) $12.95

Available at your favorite software or book retailer, or call 1-800-245-4525 *anytime* for MC/VISA/DISCOVER. (Prices subject to change.)

For more details about every book, plus exclusive screenshots and previews of all our games, surf the ORIGIN Home Page:

http://www.ea.com/origin.html

ORIGIN®
We create ***worlds***®

An Electronic Arts® Company
5918 W. Courtyard Dr. • Austin, TX 78730

FREE GAME! (maybe...)

AH-64D LONGBOW GUIDE BOOK AND DOCUMENTATION SURVEY

We're proud of our guide books, but everything can be improved. That's where you come in. We want to know what you like, and don't like, about this book. And while we have your attention, we'd appreciate some feedback on the game documentation itself. **What's in it for us?** We make our books better, we make more money, we retire at age 25 to a nudist camp in the Sangre de Christos. (Future survey forms will feature other staff fantasies ....) **What's in it for you?** You get books more like what you want ... and once a month, we'll send a free game to one person who responded that month (your choice from our line of products). And if someone gives us a really good idea, one we haven't thought of ourselves, we may send that person a game, as well.

Send responses to:

David Ladyman, Publications Manager
Incan Monkey God Productions
c/o ORIGIN Systems
5918 W. Courtyard Dr.
Austin, TX 78730

Your Name ______________________________

Address ______________________________

____

E-mail address ______________________________

Phone number ______________________________

Why did you buy this book?

(Please rate each reason: "0" means "it didn't influence me at all"; "5" means "I would have bought the book for this reason, even if I didn't like anything else about it.")

__ Great cover art.

__ I was stuck and couldn't continue the game.

__ Jane's material.

__ The mission maps.

__ The strategy and tactics tips.

__ Information about how the AI works.

__ The damage and scoring system information and stats.

__ Other reason ______________________________

What do you like/use most about this book? ______________________________

____

What do you dislike/use least about this book? ______________________________

____

What would you have added to this book? ______________________________

____

DOCUMENTATION QUESTIONNAIRE

Please rate each of these, and add a comment about what you liked, or didn't like:
("0" = "worthless", "5" = "so good it can't be improved.")

Install Guide Rating __ Comment ______________________________

____

Manual Rating __ Comment ______________________________

____

Reference Card Rating __ Comment ______________________________

____

Extra credit essay question: which type of game documentation do you prefer — online or printed? Why?